For Hilary
In memory of Ernest and Marjory

PROGRAMM
CLASSICS

PROGRAMMING CLASSICS

Implementing the world's best algorithms

Ian Oliver

PRENTICE HALL

New York London Toronto Sydney Tokyo Singapore

Acquisitions Editor: Andrew Binnie
Production Editor: Fiona Marcar
Typeset by James Young
Printed in Australia by Impact Printing, Brunswick, Victoria

3 4 5 97 96 95

ISBN 0 13 100413 1.

National Library of Australia
Cataloguing-in-Publication Data

Oliver, Ian.
Programming classics : implementing the world's best algorithms.

Bibliography.
Includes index.
ISBN 0 13 100413 1.

1. Computer algorithms. 2. Programming (Mathematics).
I. Title.

005.1

National Library of Congress
Cataloging-in-Publication Data

Oliver, Ian.
Programming classics : implementing the world's best algorithms / Ian Oliver.

p. cm.
Includes bibliographical references and index.
ISBN 0 13 100413 1.

1. Electronic digital computers – Programming. 2. Computer algorithms. I. Title.

QA76.6.042 1993 93–32080
005. 1—dc20 CIP

Prentice Hall, Inc., Englewood Cliffs, *New Jersey*
Prentice Hall Canada, Inc., *Toronto*
Prentice Hall Hispanoamericana, SA, *Mexico*
Prentice Hall of India Private Ltd, *New Delhi*
Prentice Hall International, Inc., *London*
Prentice Hall of Japan, Inc., *Tokyo*
Prentice Hall of Southeast Asia Pty Ltd, *Singapore*
Editora Prentice Hall do Brasil Ltda, *Rio de Janeiro*

PRENTICE HALL
A division of Simon & Schuster

Contents

Preface

Many of the problems that regularly face programmers have been solved by clever people all around the world, but the solutions are not well known. The algorithms are either hidden away in technical journals or discussed in mathematically oriented computer science textbooks. They are not readily available to the professional computer specialist and the hobby programmer. This book brings you the classic solutions for many such problems in a modern and easily understood form. All the algorithms have been rewritten to make them easy to use. In some instances efficiency has been improved and special cases eliminated.

The reader will find no higher mathematics in this book. There are no proofs. Instead, there is logical reasoning to give you an insight into the behavior of algorithms, and test programs to enable you to execute them. With a little experimentation on a personal computer you can find out a lot about the performance of algorithms. Mathematical analysis has produced deep insights into the nature of algorithms, but this is a practical book for practical people. Mathematical results are summarized in ordinary English wherever possible. If you want to delve into the mathematics, consult the references at the end of the book.

This book started one Tuesday, when I was sitting at a terminal attached to my client's mini computer, making some modifications to a payroll system. Thirteen years after I had designed and implemented the system, I was updating it to include a new superannuation scheme for staff. Staff were entitled to join the scheme 28 days after the start of their employment—not one month, or approximately four weeks, but exactly 28 days after being hired.

I had a problem on my hands. Dates in all the files were stored in the form DD/MM/YY. How was I to calculate whether two dates differed by 28 days or more? I had an algorithm at my office for comparing two dates, but the office was three-quarters of an hour away by car. Therefore, I made the decision to write a special-purpose subprogram, because it could not be all that difficult, or so I thought. As it turned out I spent hours trying to get the subprogram right. To make matters worse, I didn't get all the bugs out. My client was none too happy about the computer prematurely contributing to the superannuation fund for one particular staff member, because of a "≥" that should have been a ">".

Many programmers have told me about similar experiences. We think it's going to be quicker to rewrite a subprogram than to rummage through old programs to find a previously written version in the code. If we happen to locate the algorithm in a textbook, it is written in a language with which we are not familiar. Some of us are motivated by the challenge of finding a particularly elegant way to write it from scratch! I decided to eliminate this time-consuming problem once and for all by producing a book of classic algorithms for professional programmers.

This book is a reference tool to which you turn when you need to solve a particular programming problem. It will be used by most readers rather like a dictionary: you will look it up when you have a problem to solve. The book is not designed as a teaching text, although the descriptions of algorithms are educative. No specific knowledge is required. The book will enable you to learn and use classic algorithms in a professional manner, and to gain an understanding of their efficiency and any potential pitfalls. If several different approaches to solving a particular problem have been devised, such as with sorting and curve-fitting algorithms, the book provides comparative analyses to enable you to make an appropriate choice.

The book has been made accessible by careful choice of a specification mechanism. I wanted the algorithms to be readable without the reader having to learn a new programming language. There is little point in my giving you algorithms in Pascal if you are a C programmer. Similarly, a book of algorithms in C++, elegant as it might be, will be difficult for a Fortran programmer to use effectively. My problem was to find a method of presentation, or language, that was intuitive and readable.

The sources from which I have obtained algorithms use many different languages, the main ones apart from English being Algol, C, Cobol, Fortran, and Pascal. Such languages are not very suitable for communication of algorithms from one human to another. They are designed to represent algorithms in a technologically efficient manner, rather than to make them readable. You cannot simply pick up an algorithm written in one of these languages and casually peruse it. You need to use the language reference manual to interpret the abbreviations and special conventions.

There are quite a few computer terms and conventions that are so common, and used in so many languages, that they hardly need to be defined. They can be understood by anybody with a little experience in one of the major languages. For example, you might be a professional computer programmer who is familiar with Ada, C++, Cobol, or assembly language. You might be an engineer who uses Fortran, a hobby programmer who writes programs in Basic, or a student who uses a language such as Algol, Modula-2, Pascal, or Turing.

My objective was to tap into the features all these languages have in common. I believe I have achieved this objective, by using everyday programming concepts and simple unambiguous terms in describing algorithms. This should enable the reader to implement any particular algorithm in any given language without difficulty.

I am keen to keep this compendium up to date. I would welcome advice about bugs, errors of fact, or inefficiencies. In addition, I am particularly keen to receive information about widely useful algorithms that are not well known. All comments will be gratefully received and acknowledged.

Note: Unix is a trademark of AT&T Bell Laboratories. IBM is a trademark of IBM Corporation.

Acknowledgments

I have to thank many people, not least those whose brilliant minds have developed most of these algorithms. Donald Knuth's classic work *The Art of Computer Programming* contains many fine algorithms, although they are unstructured, difficult to read, and embedded in mathematics. I have structured and simplified a number of his contributions. Robert Sedgewick's book *Algorithms* is an important source, although it is oriented toward academic Pascal programmers. Gonnet's *Handbook of Algorithms and Data Structures* has provided valuable performance data on algorithms for sorting, searching, and data structures. The *Collected Algorithms from ACM* published by the Association for Computing Machinery is a key source of material. There are many other places from which algorithms have been culled.

Support has been provided by many people during this project. Jerry Weinberg was a strong motivating force, putting me in touch with publishers for the first time. I am particularly grateful to the thirty-one members of the Australian Computer Society who provided me with feedback at a seminar concerning the first draft. That seminar led to major simplifications of the presentation language, and to the removal of ambiguities. The reviewers selected by Prentice Hall Australia provided numerous suggestions, many of which have been incorporated. Adrian Mortimer pored over the first draft and suggested many improvements. Ron Cernich provided very helpful criticisms, particularly with respect to the design and structure of the presentation language, and the balance of content. Peter Jones conducted a thorough and detailed review of the second draft, helping me solve a number of problems. I received helpful support, encouragement, and ideas from Dick Kelly, Bruce McLaren, Pertti Malo, John Row, John Staples, and Mark Staples. It was a pleasure doing business with Andrew Binnie and Fiona Marcar of Prentice Hall Australia.

The prefaces of many books acknowledge the support provided by authors' families. At times, I had thought that certain acknowledgments seemed a little overgenerous. I am now sure that I was wrong. The endless hours I have spent at the computer have been taken from my family. I am extremely grateful to my wife, Hilary Langford, for continuing to support me during the four years of work. She has had to find other things to do on countless occasions when she would rather have spent time with me. I feel sad about the time lost from our relationship while I was in "book space". I thank my stepson Dominic, and apologize for the times when we did not do homework together, play pool, or engage in mind games. My other stepson, Chris, helped sustain the inner programmer with his culinary skills. My sister, Susan Gillieatt, assisted in the final preparation of the manuscript, and I very much appreciate her dedicated work.

1 Introduction

1.1 PURPOSE

This is a book of classic methods for solving problems. Each method is a recipe called an "algorithm", presented in a precise but readable style. The algorithms are "classic", because they are uniformly regarded by experts as the most efficient, practical, elegant, and simple ways to get particular jobs done. Just one of these algorithms could save you hours of programming or searching through textbooks and manuals.

Each algorithm is described in ordinary English, and is represented in typical computer code. This enables you to gain an understanding of an algorithm quickly, and then to implement the code in any programming language of your choice. The code will be understandable to any programmer, from C++ gurus, to Fortran buffs, to Basic novices.

1.2 FORMAT

Algorithms concerned with similar topics are grouped together into chapters. Within each chapter there may be from one to a dozen algorithms. Usually, each algorithm has a section to itself. For example, Chapter 2 has three sections concerned with arithmetic. Section 2.1 deals with arithmetic using decimal integers represented as text strings. Section 2.2 considers exact arithmetic in which numbers are represented as rational fractions. Section 2.3 looks at the problem of testing when two floating point numbers are approximately equal. In some cases, closely related algorithms are placed in one section, where they can be discussed as a group. Section 6.2, which is concerned with sorting algorithms, is a case in point.

You will find the term "subprogram" used frequently. A subprogram is the code that implements all or part of an algorithm. A subprogram is a group of instructions that has a defined and specific purpose related to the algorithm under discussion. The packaging of algorithms into subprograms helps you to understand rapidly the important parts of an algorithm. Depending on your background, a subprogram is a procedure, function, subroutine, or program. Simple algorithms may be implemented with a single subprogram, while more complex algorithms may require several subprograms.

Each section of the book, containing the subprograms for an algorithm, is organized as follows:

Purpose	The purpose of the algorithm is described in a few words below the section title. The aim is to capture the essence of the reason for the algorithm's existence.
Example	The example uses a specific case to show precisely how the algorithm is used as a black box. The example helps clarify the purpose, allowing you to decide quickly whether it does the job you expected it to do.
Subprograms	A one-line description of each subprogram is given.
Usage	The way in which the subprograms are used in practice is described. This provides an explanation of the interfaces the algorithm shares with the program using the algorithm, and with the user using the program.
Analysis	The technical basis for the algorithm is considered under this heading. Wherever possible, the analysis is carried out without the use of higher mathematics. Nevertheless, the discussion is technical and is meant to provide an understanding sufficient for the programmer (a) to know how the algorithm works, (b) to assess its efficiency, (c) to be aware of its limitations, and (d) to carry out enhancement or optimization relatively easily.
Implementation	A representation of the algorithm in typical computer code is given under this heading. At the beginning is a list of names used in the code, that is, a data dictionary. The code itself is documented with comments in a style that will be familiar to most programmers.
Test program	Every algorithm is accompanied by a test program. It has the dual purpose of clarifying the meaning of the algorithm and testing it thoroughly.

The implementation of a major subprogram is presented under three subheadings:

n.n.n name	The name of the subprogram preceded by a reference number is given here. The subprogram reference number n.n.n (where each n represents an integer) is used for cross-referencing with other parts of the book. Local subprograms, subsidiary to the main algorithm, are identified by the word "Local" instead of a reference number.

Pseudo code The subprogram is represented in a form that is a cross between computer code and English. The pseudo code gives an informal view of the main thrust of the subprogram, so that the programmer can get an overall understanding without having to pore over detailed code.

Code Precise code that embodies the algorithm, using the names defined in the data dictionary, is presented here.

You will notice a number of "notes" in various parts of the book. These are topics that do not have complete algorithms with test programs. The notes provide further useful material about a topic, give an outline of algorithms for which there is insufficient space in the book for a complete treatment, or provide a description of a problem-solving process that is not readily represented as an algorithm in the style of the others in the book.

1.3 TEST PROGRAMS

You are a practical programmer and you will find the test programs valuable in meeting your needs. The abstract concept of an algorithm can differ very widely from the reality of its implementation. That is why programmers usually have to "debug" the code they write. You need to be sure that an algorithm does what you think it does *in practice*. The test program enables you to execute the algorithm to prove to yourself that it:

- does the job that you thought it should do;
- has been correctly transcribed into your programming language;
- has no more bugs than were in it in this book (hopefully none).

The test programs are not throwaway extras. They are important elements of the algorithm implementation that should always be used when you are transcribing algorithms from this book. You will also find the test program helpful if you are having difficulty in making sense of an algorithm. Remember, however, computer guru Edsger Dijkstra's observation that testing proves the presence, and not the absence, of bugs. This book does not draw on the newly emerging field of mathematical verification methods, because such methods are not yet practical (Littlewood and Strigini 1992).

1.4 EFFICIENCY

You will frequently be interested in the efficiency of algorithms. This book uses the O notation as a shorthand method for talking about efficiency (Knuth 1968). The O notation describes the "order of" the speed of an algorithm as a function of the size of its data structure. Sorting algorithms (Chapter 6) provide a good example. The elementary sorting algorithms have a speed that is proportional to the square of N, the number of items to be sorted. This is represented as $O(N^2)$. The sorting method devised by D.L. Shell has a worst-case performance in which the speed is proportional to N multiplied by the square root of N. This is represented as $O(N^{1.5})$. Faster sorting algorithms have speed proportional to N times the logarithm of N. This is represented as O (N * *log* (N)), or more briefly as O (N *log* N). Any algorithm that runs at a constant speed, no matter how many items are involved, is said to have a speed "of the order of" 1, which is written as O (1). All algorithms in this book can be assumed to have O (1) efficiency unless otherwise stated.

Although the O notation is very useful, it has some drawbacks. It does not give the actual running times of algorithms, because there is an implied "constant of proportionality". If you do not take it into account the O notation will be positively misleading. For example, the O notation suggests that Shell's sort is faster than the elementary insertion sort algorithm. In practice, insertion sort will be faster than Shell's sort for moderate array sizes. In summary, the practical efficiency of algorithms as applied to small data structures is not described well by the O notation.

In early texts (e.g., Ralston and Wilf 1960) precise estimates of running time were given, based on the number of arithmetic operations in an algorithm. In those days arithmetic was very inefficient, and required much more execution time than control operations. It is not feasible for us to provide similar estimates today because of the reduction in relative execution times of arithmetic operations compared with those of control operations, the greater complexity of modern operating systems and programming languages, and the diversity of hardware on which programs may be run, including parallel architectures.

Some programmers will complain about apparent inefficiencies in certain algorithms. For example, consider the trivial *swap* subprogram used in many algorithms. It exchanges the values of its arguments. You can say that it is inefficient to call *swap* because there is some overhead involved in getting into and out of a subprogram. You are right. It would be more efficient to code the *swap* algorithm in-line if your compiler is not smart enough to do the necessary optimization on your behalf.

It is important to understand that the algorithms presented here are to be coded by you in your particular programming language. As presented here, the algorithms are *concepts*, albeit precisely specified and efficient concepts. Indeed, implementing most of the algorithms precisely as they are written will usually result in high efficiency. Nevertheless, there is always room for optimization with respect to a particular programming language.

A pertinent instance of the efficiency question involves the uniform random number generator. There are three versions—8.1.1a, 8.1.2, and 8.1.3—that produce identical results. The 8.1.3 version looks on the surface to be much less efficient than the other two. In fact, if 8.1.3 is coded in assembly language it will be the most efficient implementation of the algorithm. In other words, with careful programming you can make an algorithm more efficient by exploiting the characteristics of the particular language and computer you are using.

1.5 CODE

One fundamental design rule for this book was that you should not have to learn a new programming language. The other fundamental design rule was that all algorithms should be specified with absolute precision and freedom from ambiguity, but with minimal mathematics. To comply with both of these, the code for algorithms is presented in a "language" that is really a lowest common denominator to which any programmer should be able to relate. The next few pages will ensure that you fully understand and feel comfortable with this approach, even though you will have little trouble picking up the ideas.

The precise specification of the algorithms in computer code has enabled them to be tested thoroughly. The subprograms were translated by a crude cross-compiler into a little-known language (Holt 1990), for which an easy-to-use interpreter happened to be available. Minor adjustments were made manually in some algorithms to squeeze the representation past tight restrictions imposed by the language. The net result is that the algorithm code has been exercised in practice, and should therefore be reliable.

You will *not* be learning a new programming language. Perhaps some specialists such as Bentley (1986) would argue that this book has created a "little language". That is a rather academic point, which should not distract you. You will find the algorithm code quite simple to read, regardless of your background. The style of presentation captures the essence of the programming lingua franca, and there are no new concepts and constructs to learn.

To illustrate, suppose you were told that a certain language had a construct for carrying out tests using the word *if*. Could you identify the language? Certainly not! All languages have such a construct. Similarly, they all have constants, variables, arrays, loops, subprograms, assignment statements, and some way of communicating with the user. This book uses those constructs in a natural and straightforward way. There are no shorthand representations that must be "learned" before you can read the code. The meaning of a construct should be immediately apparent to you.

The code contains "key words" and "operators", as one would expect in a programming language, but as far as possible each key word means exactly what it means in English. This is the major difference from traditional languages. For example, Basic uses DIM to signify the declaration of array dimensions. In English one expects DIM to mean "not bright; obscure from lack of light; somewhat dark", as one dictionary defines the word. The use of DIM by Basic does indeed obscure rather than clarify, although it is convenient shorthand when you are familiar with the language.

There are many similar examples. Pascal uses *var*, which a dictionary defines as an abbreviation for "variant". In Pascal it seems to be short for "variable". C and Pascal use the semicolon inappropriately. In English it should simply "indicate a more distinct separation between parts of a sentence than that indicated by a comma". The impact of semicolons is far more significant, and a source of great heartache for many a programmer. Cobol requires careful use of the full stop. In English, the omission of a full stop is hardly a serious matter. In Cobol, its omission may cause quite different meanings from those intended by the programmer. Fortran has a special statement-numbering convention for the creation of counted loops. C uses *float*, a term that has nothing to do with "resting on the surface of a liquid". Further, C has operators such as ++, !=, &&, and +=. These are very convenient for programmers familiar with the language, but are useless for conveying the meaning of an algorithm to others.

Nevertheless, some words common to most programming languages are used in this book, even though their meanings are somewhat unusual in English. Examples include *procedure* and *text*. Our justification for using such words is that the book is written for people who are already able to write programs.

To summarize, this book uses key words and operators that most programmers will recognize instantly without reference to the definitions given below. Try skimming through a couple of algorithms to verify this point before reading on.

1.5.1 Names

All programming languages use symbols for referring to memory locations or constants. Such symbols are the names of those memory locations or constants. For example, to convert from Fahrenheit to Celsius, you might compute C from the formula (F – 32) * 5 / 9. C and F are the names of memory locations to contain the temperatures in Celsius and Fahrenheit respectively.

As another example, in a program involved with trigonometry you might define the symbol Pi at the beginning with the value 3.14159265358979. It is more convenient to refer to Pi each time you need it than to 3.14159265358979. Pi is the name of a constant in this circumstance.

Names are also given to subprograms. A subprogram may be used, or called, from several different places in a program. By giving it a name you can refer to it easily at each place where it is called. For example, in order to find the square root of a number you use a subprogram named SQR in Basic, *sqrt* in C and Pascal, and SQRT in Fortran.

In all languages, some names are defined by the language itself and some are defined by the programmer. The name of the square root subprogram, for example, is defined as an integral part of the four languages mentioned above. Cobol does not provide a square root subprogram, and so in that language it would have to be written by, and given a name by, the programmer.

Names and key words that are used throughout the book are shown in *lowercase italics*. All such words are defined in this chapter. For example, the square root subprogram is named *square~root*. You could compute the square root of Pi in Basic, C, Fortran, and Pascal by SQR (PI), sqrt (Pi), SQRT (PI), and sqrt (Pi) respectively. Any programmer will know immediately that *square~root* (Pi) has the same meaning, without feeling the need to dive for a manual.

Names that are defined for the purpose of a particular algorithm are shown in Roman type, and always start with a Capital Letter. Such names are defined in the chapters in which they are used.

1.5.2 Assignment

Putting a value in a memory location is usually called "assignment". For example, in temperature conversion you want to assign the value of the temperature in degrees Celsius to the variable named C. In the five major languages, here is how you might specify the assignment:

```
Basic:     LET C = (F – 32) * 5 / 9
C:         C = ((F – 32) * 5) / 9;
Cobol:     COMPUTE C = (F – 32) * 5 / 9.
Fortran:   C = ((F – 32) * 5) / 9
Pascal:    C := ((F – 32) * 5) / 9;
```

You will probably agree that the first approach is unambiguous and simple to read. The book uses extra parentheses to remove any ambiguity related to operator priorities. You will find assignments written in that style as follows:

let C = ((F – 32) * 5) / 9

1.5.3 Types

Languages typically enable programmers to declare the "types" of variables and constants. Almost all languages distinguish between strings of alphanumeric characters and numbers. Most languages distinguish between integral and floating point numbers. Some languages allow for variables and constants that can take only two possible values, *true* and *false*. This book has just four data types. The corresponding types in other languages are given in Table 1.1:

Table 1.1

	C	*Cobol*	*Fortran*	*Pascal*
integer	int	PIC 9(10)	INTEGER	integer
real	double	PIC 9(...)V9(...)	DOUBLE PRECISION	real
text	char [...]	PIC X(...)	CHARACTER * ...	string
true-false			LOGICAL	Boolean

You may think of *real* numbers as being implemented in extended precision using a 64-bit word. The algorithms are quite valid if the precision is restricted to 32-bit words.

The Basic language does not have type declarations. Names in this book that are defined as *integer* or *real* may be converted simply into numeric variables in Basic. Names defined as *text* equate with Basic variable names ending with a dollar sign ($). The *true-false* concept can be implemented in Basic as a numeric variable with two possible values, say 0 and 1. C does not have an exact correspondence with *true-false* variables. However, they may be easily implemented with bit fields, unsigned integers, or the enumerated type. Cobol does not provide floating point variables. This makes it difficult for Cobol programmers to implement algorithms that use *real* variables. Cobol allows only fixed point variables, where the numbers of digits before and after the decimal point are known. It may provide *true-false* variables indirectly, using the level 88 concept to define *true* and *false*.

The length of *text* strings is not specified in the declaration itself. Code that refers to text strings, however, always explicitly takes account of character positions (particularly the first and last) in *text* data. Therefore, programmers should not experience a great deal of difficulty in converting algorithms into languages that have relatively crude text-processing capabilities.

1.5.4 Literal Constants

Literal constants have a type determined by the appearance of the constant. A number such as 123, with no decimal point, has type *integer*. A number such as 123.0 has type *real*. A constant represented as a string of zero or more alphanumeric characters within double quotation marks has type *text*. Examples include "" (a null string of characters), "abc", and "123".

A character enclosed in single quotation marks, such as '0', 'A', or 'z', has type *integer* and a value equal to the binary value of the character within the quotation marks—for example, '0' = 48_{10} = 60_8. The two constants *true* and *false* have type *true-false* and obvious meanings.

1.5.5 Declarations

When the types of variables and constants are declared, any necessary storage is allocated at the same time. Here are some examples of declarations:

constant Pi = 3.14159265358979
constants One = 1, Two = 2, Three = 3
constant Alphabet = "abcdefghijklmnopqrstuvwxyz"
variables A, B, C *are real*
variables I, J, K *are integers*
variable T *is true-false*
variables String, StringPiece *are text*

Note the free and easy use made of the English words *is* and *are*, and the interchangeability of singular and plural.

1.5.6 Arrays and Matrices

An array is a set of locations with a name, each location accessed by a subscript. The subscript is written in brackets following the name. Square brackets [ ] are used for this purpose, a convention that will be familiar to C and Pascal programmers. Basic, Fortran, and Cobol use parentheses ( ) for subscripts. You will find the code easy to read (being less context-sensitive) because the characters used for subscripts differ from those used for grouping expressions. Programmers using languages such as Basic, Fortran, and Cobol simply need to replace square brackets by parentheses. For example, A[3] and Table[100] are locations in the arrays A and Table respectively. A matrix is an array with two subscripts, such as X[4, 5].

Arrays and matrices are declared in a similar way to variable names, with the addition of words that specify the lower and upper bounds on the size of each subscript. For example:

variables A, Table *are arrays* 1 *to* 100 *of integers*
variable X *is matrix* 1 *to* 4, 1 *to* 5 *of real*

These declare arrays A and Table with elements ranging from A[1] to A[100] and from Table[1] to Table[100] respectively, and a matrix X with four rows and five columns. The algorithms usually do not expect the lower bound to have any particular value. In fact, the code has been designed so that C programmers, for example, can use their customary 0 as the lower bound, and Fortran programmers their usual 1. The only exception is in some algorithms in which a lower bound of 1 is used by common convention.

1.5.7 Tests

You will find the ubiquitous *if* as the mechanism for carrying out tests. Here is a fragment of code that sets a flag equal to +1, 0, or –1 according to A > 0, A = 0, or A < 0 respectively:

```
if A > 0 then
    let Flag = 1
else-if A < 0 then
    let Flag = –1
else
    let Flag = 0
end if
```

Note the explicit *end if*. It eliminates ambiguity, and overcomes the tyranny of punctuation that dogs us in languages such as C, Pascal, and Cobol. The *else-if*, with a hyphen embedded in it, is not strictly necessary as a construct, but it improves readability and communication of meaning. By the way, the above fragment of code is implemented more simply by *let* Flag = *sign* (A).

1.5.8 Counted Loops

There is a variety of ways in which loops are set up in languages, using a variable to count the number of iterations, and a test to terminate the loop. For example, suppose you want to set the elements A[1] through A[10] of the array A to zero. Here is how it would be done in five languages:

```
Basic:      FOR I = 1 TO 10
                LET A(I) = 0
            NEXT I
C:          for (i = 1; i <= 10; i++) A[i] = 0;
Cobol:      PERFORM ZERO-A VARYING I FROM 1 BY 1 UNTIL I > 10.
        ZERO-A.
            MOVE ZERO TO A(I).
Fortran:    DO 1 I = 1, 10
          1   A(I) = 0
Pascal:     for I := 1 to 10 do A[I] := 0;
```

Again, Basic has a format that is easily understood. It makes quite clear where the loop ends, using a word instead of punctuation. This book standardizes on using the word *end* to terminate all structured constructs, and so you will find arrays initialized by code such as:

```
for i = 1 to 10
    let A[i] = 0
end for
```

The use of an explicit *end* for all structured constructs obviates the bracketing found in some languages, for example, the Pascal *begin* and *end*, and the C braces { and }. The strictly controlled use of indenting also serves to highlight the scope of structured constructs.

Note that the loop counter *i* is in lowercase italics. Loop counters are assumed to be defined by the word *for* rather than being declared outside the loop. This saves us explicitly defining loop counters in algorithms, and cluttering up the code and documentation with trivia. In converting algorithms into other languages you will probably need to declare variables used as loop counters.

The counter is always assumed to be incremented by 1 in each iteration. If a counter is to be decremented, *for decreasing* is used instead of *for*.

1.5.9 Pre-Tested Loops

Again, there are several ways in which to set up loops that are terminated by a test of some kind at the beginning. Suppose you want to divide S by 2 repeatedly until it is less than 1. Here are some variations:

```
Basic:     100 IF S < 1 THEN 130
           110 LET S = S / 2
           120 GO TO 100
           130 ...
C:             while (S >= 1) S = S / 2;
Cobol:         PERFORM HALF-S UNTIL S < 1.
           HALF-S.
               COMPUTE S = S / 2.
Fortran:     1 IF (S .LT. 1) GO TO 2
                  S = S / 2
               GO TO 1
             2 ...
Pascal:        while S >= 1 do S := S / 2;
```

The C and Pascal versions are the easiest to read and understand. The problem with these constructs is the flimsy delineation of the end of the loop. This book uses *end loop* in order to provide an unambiguous and visible loop boundary. The "sense" of the test follows Cobol rather than C and Pascal:

```
loop until S < 1
    let S = S / 2
end loop
```

1.5.10 Post-Tested Loops

Frequently in algorithms a loop has to be entered at least once. This is accomplished by a loop with a test at the end. C and Pascal have reasonably satisfactory constructs, which the other languages do not:

```
C:        do S = S / 2 while (S >= 1);
Pascal:   repeat S := S / 2 until S < 1;
```

Note the opposite sense of the tests in C and Pascal. You should have no difficulty understanding the variation of the Pascal approach used in this book:

loop
    let S = S / 2
end loop when S < 1

The conversion of such a post-tested loop into Basic, Cobol, or Fortran code requires the straightforward use of an IF and a GO TO at the end of the loop.

1.5.11 Termination

Test programs usually contain a conditional termination. A test program stops when it receives unexpected results from the algorithm. For example, suppose a test program expects to find N with the value 0. This is indicated as follows:

check N = 0

It is assumed that the program terminates immediately, with an appropriate error message if the check fails. Conditional termination also appears in some of the algorithms, which work correctly only when values supplied to them are within certain limits. For example, a square root algorithm might contain a check that the number supplied to it is non-negative.

The *check* construct is, in effect, an assertion. Computer science students will be familiar with assertions and invariants in demonstrating the correctness of programs. The *check* construct has a similar intent but is used less formally and more sparingly in these algorithms.

1.5.12 Text Processing

All the main languages allow access to characters in text strings. The precise method varies from language to language. Suppose, for example, you want to blank out characters of the 20-character string S. Here is how it could be accomplished:

Basic:	Define S as an array with DIM S%(20), and use a loop.
C:	Define S as a character array, and use a loop.
Cobol:	Define S with PIC X(20), and use MOVE SPACES TO S.
Fortran:	Define S with CHARACTER*20 and use S = ' '.
Pascal:	Define S as a packed character array and use a loop.

All these are quite straightforward, but every language has severe limitations that inhibit the range of operations you need to undertake on text strings. One or more of the following facilities is unavailable:

- Access to individual characters of strings not declared as arrays.
- Assignment of text strings as a whole.
- Easy growth and shrinkage of string size.

In order to accommodate the various limitations there is a small set of text operations that will be easy to implement in any language. These operations assume that a text string is a single entity along the lines of a Fortran or Basic character variable. This differs from the C and Pascal concept of text strings as arrays of characters.

Some algorithms assign entire *text* strings, and carry out comparisons of *text* strings. For example, putting "abc" into S is accomplished by:

let S = "abc"

To get at individual characters the algorithms use the *byte* function, which obtains one character as a binary integer. The format is *byte* (S, N), where S is the text string and N is the character position. The first character in a text string is at position *first*, which is a standard constant.

C programmers may assume that *first* = 0. Basic, Fortran, and Cobol programmers will want to believe that *first* = 1, and they may do so. Text-processing algorithms are presented so that the character position of the first character can be numbered in any way suitable to the programmer. For example, *byte* ("abc", *first* + 1) = 'b', regardless of whether the first byte is numbered 0 or 1.

There are two other functions that can be applied to a text string. The function *last* (S) returns the position of the last character in the string. This is interpreted to mean the last usable character previously inserted, not the last character potentially available. At times it is more convenient to use the function *length* (S), which gives the number of characters in the string. It is always true that *length* (S) = *last* (S) – *first* + 1, regardless of the value of *first*.

Apart from direct assignment, the algorithms modify text strings in only three ways. They may append one character to a string, shorten a string by one character, or reverse the order of the characters in a string. The last of these may seem surprising, but it makes easy the job of inserting characters at the beginning of a text string. The algorithm simply reverses the string, appends a character, and reverses it again. Here is an example, used in arithmetic on integers held as text strings, that inserts a zero at the front of a string S:

call reverse (S)
call append (S, '0')
call reverse (S)

An algorithm can use *shorten* for the inverse process, to remove the zero just inserted:

call reverse (S)
call shorten (S)
call reverse (S)

In one or two subprograms, it has been convenient to assume that there is a *substring* function available. This extracts a string from specified character positions of a given string. For example, if S contains "abcdefg", *substring* (S, *first* + 1, *last* (S) – 1) is equal to "bcdef".

Algorithms also need access to specific bits at times. This is achieved by, for example, *bit* (S, N), which obtains the N-th bit from S, where the leftmost bit is numbered zero (not *first*).

1.5.13 Arguments

In any programming language there is a need for some method of communicating between calling programs (or calling subprograms) and called subprograms. How do you describe (a) values passed to subprograms, and (b) variables to receive the results of subprogram calculations? For example, what term do you apply to Pi in the expression *square~root* (Pi)? The communication mechanism is termed different things in different languages. You supply "arguments" to the subprogram in Basic, C, and Fortran, a sequence of "USING operands" in Cobol, "actual parameters" in Pascal, and a "calling sequence" in assembly language. This book uses the term "actual argument", or just "argument". Thus, Pi in the above example is the argument to *square~root.*

1.5.14 Nicknames

When you define your own subprograms you need to be able to access the actual argument supplied by the calling program. You do this by means of a parameter list in Basic, a formal argument or parameter list in C, a linkage section in Cobol, dummy arguments in Fortran, and formal parameters in Pascal. Again, the lack of standardization of terms is a nuisance. Rather than use a term with a mathematical derivation, the term "nickname" is applied to formal or dummy arguments or parameters. This everyday term effectively defines the role of a nickname as being a convenient alias for something that has a different actual name.

To be precise, nicknames are assumed to be "called by reference", which is the way it works in Basic, Cobol, and Fortran. Programmers using these languages should have no difficulties in using nicknames, because no interpretation of foreign constructs is required.

In Pascal, formal *var* parameters are called by reference, but other formal parameters are called by value. In translating the code, a Pascal programmer must declare as *var* any parameters that receive values from computations within the subprogram. If this is not done properly, the conversion into Pascal will not produce a faithful translation of the algorithm.

The C programmer needs to appreciate that nicknames should be interpreted neither as copies of the actual arguments nor as pointers to the actual arguments. Nicknames must be seen as alternative names for the actual arguments. C passes the values of function arguments to subprograms, not the addresses. A straightforward translation to C requires the use of pointers. Actual arguments may be passed to subprograms as the addresses of the argument locations (using the operator &). The corresponding nickname may be treated as a pointer (using the indirection operator *).

1.5.15 Functions

Most languages allow a programmer to define functions. A *function* is a subprogram that is called implicitly (by referring to it in an expression) and that returns a value. For example, you obtained the square root of Pi by using *square~root* (Pi), which implicitly calls the *square~root* subprogram. The simplest form of a function can be written as a single statement in some languages. Here is a function called D, which converts temperatures from Fahrenheit degrees to Celsius degrees, written as briefly as possible in each language:

```
Basic:   DEF D (F) = (F – 32) * 5 / 9
C:       float D (float F);
             { return ((F – 32) * 5) / 9 }
```

```
Fortran:  REAL D,F
          D (F) = ((F – 32) * 5) / 9
Pascal:   function D (F : real) : real;
              D := ((F – 32) * 5) / 9
          end;
```

You will see a variation of the Pascal style throughout this book:

function D (F *is real*) *is real*
    result ((F – 32) * 5) / 9
end D

This way of representing the subprogram contains type definitions not found in Basic and handled differently in Fortran. The type of the nickname F is specified, as is the type of the function D itself. The result produced by the function is clearly indicated by the word *result.* The end of the function is delimited by the word *end,* which is followed by the name of the function for added clarity.

The algorithms defined as functions in this book are typically more complicated than temperature conversion. There may be many lines of code between the function header and the *end.* Such a function cannot be implemented easily in Minimal Basic. The rather limited GOSUB construct will have to be used, and arguments moved explicitly. More complicated functions may be implemented in Fortran using the FUNCTION subprogram rather than a statement function. In C and Pascal no particular difficulties are envisaged.

1.5.16 Procedures

In most languages it is possible to write subprograms that return without a result associated with the subprogram name. Such subprograms are called *procedures* in this book. In Minimal Basic, procedures must be implemented with GOSUB as for functions. In C, all subprograms are defined as functions, but it is permissible to have result-less functions equivalent to procedures. In Cobol, procedures may be implemented as separate programs, and accessed by the CALL verb. Fortran SUBROUTINES and Pascal procedures are just like the procedures in this book.

Procedures are called explicitly using *call.* C and Pascal programmers will see the *call* as redundant, but it is retained for clarity of expression. Examples of the use of *call* were given in the discussion of text string processing above. To illustrate how procedures are written, consider the temperature conversion function rewritten as a procedure taking two arguments. If you want to convert, say, 70°F to Celsius, you would use *call* D (70, Degrees), and expect to find the required result in the variable Degrees. Here is the procedure:

procedure D (F, C *are real*)
    let C = ((F – 32) * 5) / 9
end D

1.5.17 Subprogram Declarations

As the above examples have shown, the types of nicknames are defined in the header of the function or procedure. For the procedure D there was a list of two nicknames, F and C, both declared as *real.* Any number of nicknames may be declared by a natural extension of this idea. Here are some function and procedure headers from early chapters of the book:

function To~Integer (String *is text*) *is integer*
function Fractions~Numerate (Fraction *is array of integers*) *is real*
procedure Checker (Compute, Verify *are functions*, Testring *is text*)

Function and procedure names are frequently made up of two words, as a couple of these are. The words are joined, not by an underscore character as in C or extended Pascal, or a hyphen as in Cobol, but by a tilde. The tilde is not used for any purpose other than making up double-barreled subprogram names.

When a nickname is an array or a matrix, its dimensions are not explicitly declared. The handling of nickname dimensions in various languages is a vexed question, since quite different approaches are taken. Cobol is very restrictive, in that nickname properties must be identical with the properties of actual arguments. Minimal Basic is also restrictive, allowing only simple variables (not arrays or matrices) to be used as arguments and nicknames. Fortran allows more latitude, in that argument arrays or matrices with different dimensions may be referenced by a given nickname. Pascal is more restrictive than Fortran. C is a powerful language that provides a great deal of flexibility for specifying nicknames. This book steers a middle course, and leaves it to you to specify dimensions to conform to the idiosyncrasies of your particular language.

The Checker example above shows two function names being used as nicknames. Again, the capability for doing this, and the method of implementation vary widely among languages. Basic and Cobol simply do not permit it. Algorithms that use function names as nicknames will be difficult to implement in those languages. Sorry! In other languages you will need to take care to conform with the requirements of the language.

1.5.18 Subprogram Descriptions

A one-line description of each subprogram in a section is given at the beginning of each section. In addition, the one-line description for a particular subprogram is repeated at the start of the code for that subprogram. Such a description line is also given for "local" subprograms, which are subprograms incidental to the algorithm being presented.

Some nicknames will be used to supply data *to* a called subprogram. Others will receive results *from* a called subprogram. Some nicknames will be used to do both jobs, supplying data from an actual argument and then modifying the value of that argument. The heading line for each subprogram specifies how each nickname is to be used. For example, the three local subprograms in Section 2.1 have the following heading lines:

Local Zero~Suppress (updates String)
Local Group (receives String, Size; supplies Digits)
Local Ungroup (receives Digits, Size; *result text*)

These tell us that Zero~Suppress has one nickname that receives a value from the calling subprogram, and updates that value. The subprogram Group receives two values and supplies one value, while Ungroup receives two values. Ungroup is a *function*, which returns a value via the function name. To assist in easy recognition of this fact, the word *result* is put in the heading line, followed by the type of result produced by the function.

1.5.19 Serial Input-Output

Input-output does not appear frequently in this book. Some examples use input-output in order to communicate with the user. A few algorithms input data from disk and write results to disk. You may wish to skip Sections 1.5.19 and 1.5.20, returning to them only when necessary.

Input-output facilities are as limited as possible, in order to provide only the necessary capability for specifying algorithms. This book deliberately glosses over the issue of formatting and the insertion of new lines into output. C and Pascal require the programmer to insert new lines where needed. Basic, Cobol, and Fortran put new lines into output to terminate the processing of output statements. Broadly, the book follows the latter course, making the assumption that someone else looks after new lines.

The basic input-output facilities are provided by *input* and *output*. For example:

input A, B, C
output A, B, C

obtains three quantities from the keyboard and then displays them on the screen. The input quantities are separated by white space, and the output quantities are separated by single spaces. The types of the variables for *input* may be *integer*, *real*, or *text* in the algorithms. In the case of *text* a single word (separated by white space from other words) is *input*, unless the text is enclosed in quotation marks. Quotation marks are removed when the text is stored in a *text* variable.

Input-output to and from files is carried out with extensions to the *input* and *output* facilities. In keeping with Fortran and Pascal, a file is accessed by associating it with a file number or unit number. This is similar to the stream pointer in C. The association is managed by code such as:

create Data *file* "Data File"
close Data
open Data *file* "Data File"

The *create* statement is assumed to put a file number in the variable Data, and to associate this with a new file with the name in quotation marks. The *close* statement breaks the connection. The *open* statement makes the association with an existing file rather than creating a new file. All input-output statements that need to reference the file "Data File" must access the variable Data for its file number. For example:

input from Data *into* A, B, C
output into Results *from* A, B, C

does the same job as the earlier *input* and *output*, except that the input-output is to and from disk. Both files are assumed to be serial files: a record once *input* cannot be *input* again without reopening the file. The above two statements copy the three values A, B, and C from one file to another. Note the use of *from* and *into*, which indicate where the information is coming from and going to.

The function *end~of~file* supplies a *true-false* result, indicating whether or not the file is at its end. It is assumed that the end of file indication is not set until the program tries to read some nonexistent data. For example, suppose a file Data contains just a single integer. The first *input from* Data *into* N operation would obtain the value of N, with *end~of~file* (Data) = *false*. The second *input from* Data *into* N operation would result in *end~of~file* (Data) = *true*, the value of N being undefined. This is similar to the way it is done in Cobol and Fortran.

1.5.20 Random Input-Output

Only in Chapter 10 will you find random input-output. The file-updating algorithms need to access disk files so as to obtain information stored at particular positions in the file. This requires facilities for positioning the file and for determining how much disk storage is used when a given record is written. This book uses *read* and *write* rather than *input* and *output*. The interpretation is that *read* and *write* do input-output with internally formatted data. There is no conversion to human-readable form. Examples of the three facilities are:

read from F *into* T *size* 20
write into F *from* T *size* 20
seek F *position* P

Every open file is assumed to be positioned somewhere. A file is initially opened at its beginning, which is assumed to be byte zero. The position is updated with each *read* and *write*, and may be changed by a *seek*. The first line obtains 20 bytes of data from file F at its current position, incrementing the current file position by 20 bytes. The second line writes 20 bytes of data into file F at its current position, incrementing the current file position by 20 bytes. The third line changes the current position of the file to the byte position contained in the variable P.

The *seek* facility in particular may have to be implemented differently in your language. You may need to convert from specifying a byte position to specifying a record position, for example. Such a conversion should not be difficult to implement.

1.5.21 Operators

Following is a list of all operators used in the code. There should be few surprises in this list. Note the difference between the two forms of division, using the operators ÷ and /. You should not experience problems concerning operator precedence, because of the use of parentheses in the code. Just in case, however, the following table is in precedence sequence.

"	Open a literal that has the type *text*.
"	Close a literal that has the type *text*.
'	Open a character, evaluated as the *integer* value of the character. For example, 'a' = 141_8 or 97_{10}.
'	Close a character.

[...] Brackets. Enclose subscript(s) appended to an array or matrix name.

(...) Parentheses. Used in expressions for grouping terms, and for enclosing actual argument names and nicknames used by subprograms.

$*$ Multiply.

$/$ Divide, giving a result that is *real.*

$\div$ Divide, giving a result that is an *integer*, discarding any remainder. Used only for positive integers in these algorithms.

mod Divide, the result being the remainder that is an *integer*. Used only for positive integers in these algorithms.

$+$ Add, or plus.

$-$ Subtract, or minus.

$>$ Greater than.

$\geq$ Greater than or equal to.

$<$ Less than.

$\leq$ Less than or equal to.

$=$ Equal.

$\neq$ Not equal.

not Not. "*not* F" is *true* if and only if F is *false*.

and And. "F *and* G" is *true* if and only if F and G are both *true*.

or Or. "F *or* G" is *false* if and only if F and G are both *false*.

, Separator of array subscripts and constant definitions.

; Statement separator.

1.5.22 Standard Subprograms

Below are the subprograms that are used in many places in this book:

append (A, B) Lengthens *text* string A by one character and inserts the integer B as a character in the new position.

bit (A, N) Extracts the N-th bit from *text* string A, returning its value as an *integer*. If N specifies a bit position beyond the end of A, the value zero is returned. Bits are numbered from the left and start at zero.

byte (A, N) Extracts the N-th 8-bit byte from *text* string A, returning its value as an *integer*. If N specifies a nonexistent byte position of A, the value zero is returned. Bytes are numbered from *first* to *last* (A).

ceiling (X) Rounds *real* number X to the next larger whole number. Its value is the smallest *integer* greater than or equal to the *number* X. Used only for positive values of X in these algorithms.

divide (M, N, Q, R) Divides an *integer* M by an *integer* N, giving an *integer* quotient Q and a remainder R.

end~of~file (N) Tests whether a data file is at its end. Is *true* if file number N is at end of file, otherwise is *false*.

exp (X) Raises the number *e* to the power X.
Note: $log_e (exp (X)) = X$.

first	Position (usually considered as 0 or 1) of the first character in any *text* string.
last (A)	Position of the last character in the *text* string A, equal to *first* + *length* (A) – 1.
length (A)	The number of characters in the *text* string A. If A is a null string, *length* (A) = 0.
log_e (X)	The natural logarithm of X, i.e., the logarithm to base *e*.
log_{10} (X)	The logarithm of X to base 10, equal to log_e (X) / log_e (10).
log_2 (X)	The logarithm of X to base 2, equal to log_e (X) / log_e (2).
magnitude (P)	The value of the number P, ignoring its sign. Equivalent to *if* P ≥ 0 *then result* +P *else result* –P *end if*.
maximum (P, Q)	The larger of the specified arguments. Equivalent to *if* P ≥ Q *then result* P *else result* Q *end if*.
minimum (P, Q)	The smaller of the specified arguments. Equivalent to *if* P ≤ Q *then result* P *else result* Q *end if*.
power (P, Q)	Raises P to the power Q. Equivalent to *exp* (log_e (P) * Q).
reverse (A)	Reverses the sequence of the characters in the *text* string A. For example, "abcde" is replaced by "edcba".
round (X)	Rounds *real* number X to the nearest *integer*. Used only for positive values of X in these algorithms.
shift (I, J)	Multiplies *integer* I by 2^J, giving an *integer* result.
shorten (A)	Shortens the *text* string A by one character, removing the last character, and thereby reducing *length* (A) by one.
sign (P)	Obtains the sign of a number. Equivalent to *if* P > 0 *then result* +1 *else-if* P < 0 *then result* –1 *else result* 0 *end if*.
square~root (X)	Calculates the square root of the number X.
substring (A, I, J)	Extracts from the *text* string A the *text* string located in character positions I through J.
swap (A, B)	Interchanges the values of A and B.
truncate (X)	Rounds *real* number X to the next smaller whole number. Its value is the largest *integer* less than or equal to the *number* X. It is used only for positive values of X in these algorithms.

1.5.23 Constants

Here are all the constants used in the algorithms that are not otherwise defined in the algorithm code. These constants are therefore "global" in their scope.

e	Base of natural logarithms. Its value accurate to 128 bits is 2.7182818284590452353602874713526624977572.
maxbits	Maximum number of bits in the fraction part of a *real* number. A typical value is *maxbits* = 53.
maxexponent	Largest exponent that a number may have. A typical value is *maxexponent* = 1023.
maxinteger	Largest integer that the computer can store. A 32-bit machine typically has *maxinteger* = 2147483647.

maxreal Largest number that the computer can store. A typical value is approximately 2.0 raised to the power *maxexponent*.

pi Ratio of a circle's circumference to its diameter. Its value accurate to 128 bits is 3.14159265358979323846264338327950288 41972.

1.5.24 Data Dictionary

At the start of each implementation description, all the names used in the code are listed. The names are grouped under the following headings:

Exported names Names that are defined within the subprogram but available for use elsewhere are listed. Typically, there will be just one exported name per subprogram, and that will be the name of the subprogram itself.

Imported names Names that are defined elsewhere in the book but used by the current algorithm are listed here.

Local subprograms Names of subsidiary subprograms used locally in representing the algorithm, but not of sufficient interest or generality to be exported, are listed here.

Nicknames Nicknames that communicate between a calling subprogram and a called subprogram are listed here, with a brief description of the data.

Global names Names defined outside subprograms and used within those subprograms are listed here, with a brief description of the purpose.

Local names Names defined and used solely within subprograms in this section are listed here, with a brief description of the purpose.

1.6 STORAGE ALLOCATION

There are a couple of fine points about storage allocation you may wish to skip at the first reading. You rarely need to consider the difference between "compile time" and "run time". The meanings of the algorithms are unchanged whether you regard, for example, the definitions of variables and constants as executable code on the one hand or compile-time definitions on the other hand.

Very frequently, variables and constants are defined at the beginning of a subprogram. These names are assumed to come into existence at the point, and the time, the definitions are executed in the code. The names cease to exist when the subprogram exits. This approach is usually called "automatic" allocation and is typical of most programming languages.

If there is a need to use "static" variables, which persist beyond a single execution of a subprogram, such variables are defined as automatic variables outside and prior to the subprogram code. This means that there is only one method of defining variables, which is simple and intuitive. Names defined outside subprograms are automatically allocated for the single execution of the program as a whole. Names defined inside a subprogram are automatically allocated for each execution of the subprogram.

Occasionally, "dynamic" arrays are used—for example, in the network algorithms in Chapter 13. Dynamic arrays are those whose dimensions are determined at run time. Most programming languages do not permit the use of dynamic arrays, and it will be necessary for you to convert them to automatic or static arrays. Rather than merely allocate a fixed amount of storage in this book, the dynamic specifications are provided so that you can understand how the storage requirements need to be determined.

That completes our discussion of the style of presentation. Now that you've reached this point you are ready to start delving into the world's best algorithms.

2 Arithmetic

In this chapter you will find algorithms for doing arithmetic with integers represented in forms other than simple binary *integers* or *real* numbers. There are algorithms for doing arithmetic with integers in text form and with rational fractions. There is also an algorithm for dealing with problems caused by having to truncate real numbers to finite approximations for storage in normal computer words.

A typical credit card number is sixteen digits long. Product codes have twelve or more digits. Checking accounts have codes for state, bank, branch, and account number that may total fifteen to twenty digits. International telephone numbers have around fifteen or sixteen digits. Certain check digit algorithms described in Chapter 3 require you to do arithmetic with long numbers.

Most programming languages, with the notable exception of Cobol, restrict arithmetic on integers to about nine decimal digits. Extended precision floating point arithmetic can typically accommodate about fifteen digits, but there are potential problems. Fifteen digits of accuracy is not enough for some purposes, and rounding errors can creep in and produce incorrect results. For these reasons, Section 2.1 provides you with algorithms for carrying out integer arithmetic on the text representation of integers of any length.

The algorithms may be generalized very easily to carry out arithmetic using bases other than 10. For example, you could generate results in hexadecimal, with base 16. This requires little more than replacing every occurrence of "10" by the base in which you want to work, and telling the subprograms the external representation of digits outside the range 0–9. The requirement to use other bases is relatively infrequent. In order to keep the subprograms simple you will see only the decimal versions here.

In certain kinds of computational work you need to do arithmetic with fractions in such a way that exact results are produced. The typical way of computing with floating point arithmetic is not exact. For example, something as simple as dividing 1 by 3 in floating point arithmetic gives a result that is almost right, but that has a very small rounding error in it. In some applications, such small errors can accumulate and produce significant errors in the results. These errors can be avoided by doing exact arithmetic, with numbers represented as rational fractions. Every number is represented as a pair of integers throughout such calculations, being the numerator and denominator of the number expressed as an improper fraction. The relevant algorithms are found in Section 2.2.

There are many applications in which programmers do not carry out computations with rational fractions, and therefore need to test whether two numerical quantities are "approximately" equal. For example, suppose you are writing a computer-based training tool for elementary mathematics. One of the questions you build in is to ask students to enter an approximation to the value of π (the ratio of the circumference of a circle to its diameter), correct to four significant digits. How can a computer program easily measure whether a given answer such as 3.14 or 3.142 is correct to four significant digits? The number similarity algorithm in Section 2.3 does the job for you.

2.1 DECIMAL ARITHMETIC

Doing arithmetic with numbers represented as text strings

Example

To find the quotient and remainder when 314159265358 is divided by 27182818:

> *variables* Quotient, Remainder *are text*
> *call* Decimal~Divide ("314159265358", "27182818", Quotient, Remainder)
> *output* Quotient, Remainder

Subprograms

All nicknames are *text* strings, unless otherwise stated.

2.1.1 To~Integer (receives String; *result integer*)
2.1.2 To~Text (receives *integer* Numeric; *result text*)
2.1.3 Decimal~Compare (receives Number1, Number2; *result integer*)
2.1.4 Decimal~Add (receives Augend, Addend; *result text*)
2.1.5 Decimal~Subtract (receives Minuend, Subtrahend; *result text*)
2.1.6 Decimal~Multiply (receives Multiplicand, Multiplier; *result text*)
2.1.7 Decimal~Divide (receives Dividend, Divisor; supplies Quotient, Remainder)
2.1.8 Fast~Multiply (receives Multiplicand, Multiplier; *result text*)

Usage

The first two subprograms—To~Integer and To~Text—carry out the basic task of converting integers between text and binary form. The function To~Integer is supplied with a text string consisting of digits, and it produces a binary integer as its result. The function To~Text is supplied with a binary integer, and it produces a text string consisting of digits as its result. For any binary integer I, To~Integer (To~Text (I)) = I.

The remaining subprograms are used for arithmetic on text strings of decimal digits. A likely use is in applications where microsecond efficiency is not required. For example, a point-of-sale terminal needs to read a long number. A check-digited string of digits is entered, and it is required to verify the check digit. Under these circumstances the amount of arithmetic is minimal and these simple algorithms will do an adequate job. The algorithms are not efficient enough for number theoretical work where high-performance extended precision arithmetic is required. However, the algorithms are historically important, being the "classical" arithmetic algorithms (Knuth 1969).

Decimal~Compare is used by Decimal~Divide, but may also be used independently to find the larger of two integers that are in text form. The result returned by Decimal~Compare is similar to that returned by *sign*. Decimal~Add, Decimal~Subtract, Decimal~Multiply, and Decimal~Divide not surprisingly carry out the basic arithmetic operations on text strings, returning their results as text strings. Decimal~Divide is a procedure rather than a function, because it returns a quotient and a remainder. Fast~Multiply is a more efficient version of Decimal~Multiply. The code is more complicated, but this version should be used when efficiency is important. There is no corresponding Fast~Divide subprogram. If a more efficient division process is required, it will be necessary to use specialist multiple precision integer arithmetic algorithms, which are beyond the scope of this book.

Analysis

These subprograms use the "naive" method, akin to the way in which arithmetic operations are taught in schools. Addition and subtraction are quite efficient, running in time proportional to the sizes of the numbers. For multiplication and division the running times are proportional to the product of the sizes of the numbers. This quadratic run-time performance may be quite acceptable in many applications, and be inexpensive in programmer time. Theoretically faster, but much more complex, algorithms may be useful for very large numbers or programs that consume a great deal of computer time (Sedgewick 1988).

All subprograms except Fast~Multiply work digit by digit. These algorithms are described adequately by the pseudo code and will not be considered further. The key idea behind Fast~Multiply is to operate on groups of digits instead of single digits. Groups of three decimal digits are converted to binary. The resulting "digits" with base 1,000 are held in elements of *integer* arrays. The multiplication algorithm computes all possible cross-products of these base-1,000 digits, and forms intermediate sums for each possible base-1,000 digit position. In diagrammatic form the process of multiplying 123456789 by 987654321 is shown in Figure 2.1.

The product of the two integers is held in successive elements of an array, each element corresponding to a power of 1,000. In this example the first product, 123 * 987, is to be considered as multiplied by 1,000 raised to the power 4, or 10^{12}. The second sum of products, (123 * 654) + (987 * 456), is multiplied by 10^9, and so on.

The intermediate sums may easily be greater than 1,000,000, but a standard 32-bit binary word can hold integers that exceed nine decimal digits. The algorithms as written are therefore suitable for integers in *text* form that may contain hundreds of digits. It is important that these intermediate products not result in integer overflow. For this rea-

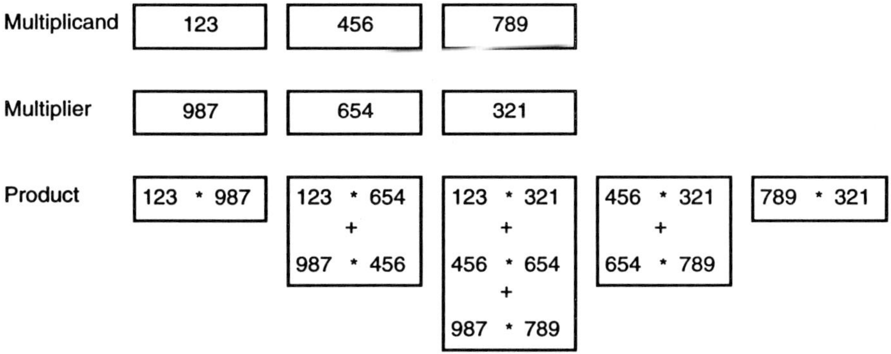

Figure 2.1

son, the group size of three digits represents a suitable compromise between speed and length of numbers that can be multiplied.

The final task of Fast~Multiply is to convert the array representation back to a *text* string. This is done by starting at the end of the product. In the example, 789 * 321 is taken *mod* 1,000, giving the last three digits for the product equal to 269. The quotient (789 * 321) ÷ 1,000 is 253. This is the base-1,000 "carry", which is added to the sum of products (456 * 321) + (654 * 789) in the second-last product array element. The same process is then successively applied to the array elements until the most significant element has been processed. Any carry from the first element of the array is then converted to decimal digits, thus completing the multiplication process.

The binary arrays used by Fast~Multiply are defined "dynamically" in the code. This means that the subprogram sees how long the text strings are and then allocates sufficient storage for the corresponding binary arrays. Most programming languages do not allow dynamic allocation. However, this form has been retained so that you can see precisely how the storage requirements need to be calculated.

IMPLEMENTATION

<u>Exported Names</u>

Decimal~Add	Adds two positive integers in *text* form (2.1.4)
Decimal~Compare	Compares two positive integers in *text* form (2.1.3)
Decimal~Divide	Divides two positive integers in *text* form (2.1.7)
Decimal~Multiply	Multiplies two positive integers in *text* form (2.1.6)
Decimal~Subtract	Subtracts two positive integers in *text* form (2.1.5)
Fast~Multiply	Quickly multiplies two positive integers in *text* form (2.1.8)
To~Integer	Converts an integer in *text* form to an *integer* (2.1.1)
To~Text	Converts an *integer* number to *text* form (2.1.2)

<u>Local Subprograms</u>

Group	Convert *text* digits to base-1,000 binary
Ungroup	Convert base-1,000 binary to *text* form
Zero~Suppress	Remove leading zeros from *text* string

Nicknames

Augend	Integer to which Addend is added
Addend	Integer to be added to Augend
Character	The character to be converted
Digit	The integer value to be converted
Digits	Array of base-1,000 "digits" of an *integer*
Dividend	Integer into which Divisor is divided
Divisor	Integer that divides into Dividend
Minuend	Integer from which Subtrahend is subtracted
Multiplicand	Integer that is multiplied by Multiplier
Multiplier	Integer that multiplies Multiplicand
Number1	The *text* form of an integer
Number2	The *text* form of an integer
Numeric	The *integer* form of an integer
Quotient	Integer result of the division
Remainder	Integer remainder
Size	Maximum subscript for array Digits
String	The *text* form of an integer
Subtrahend	Integer subtracted from Minuend
Width	Number of characters required in left-filled number

Local Names

Carry	The "carry" when doing arithmetic
Comparison	The result of the function
Difference	Accumulated *text* value of the difference
Digit, Digit2	Temporary locations for a single digit
I, J, K	Loop counters and indexes
N	Larger of the numbers of characters in Number1 and Number2
Offset	An increasingly long *text* string of zeros
Plicand	Array of base-1,000 "digits" for Multiplicand
Plier	Array of base-1,000 "digits" for Multiplier
Product	The product of Multiplicand and Multiplier
Remainder	The remaining part of the integer still to be converted
SizePlicand	Maximum subscript for array Plicand
SizePlier	Maximum subscript for array Plier
SizeProduct	Maximum subscript for array Product
String	The *text* form of the integer
Sum	Accumulated binary value of the number

2.1.1 To~Integer (receives String; *result integer*)

Pseudo Code

let Sum = 0
for i = first character of String *to* last character of String
multiply previous Sum by 10 and add value of current character String [*i*] to it
end for

Code

```
function To~Integer (String is text) is integer
    variables Digit, Sum are integers
    let Sum = 0
    for i = 1 to length (String)
        let Digit = byte (String, first + i – 1)
        check Digit ≥ '0' and Digit ≤ '9'
        let Sum = (Sum * 10) + Digit – '0'
    end for
    result Sum
end To~Integer
```

2.1.2 To~Text (receives *integer* Numeric; *result text*)

Pseudo Code

```
initialize text string String to the null string
loop
    insert the last decimal digit of Numeric into the front of String
    divide Numeric by 10, removing the last decimal digit
end loop when Numeric is zero
```

Code

```
function To~Text (Numeric is integer) is text
    variable Remainder is integer
    variable String is text
    check Numeric ≥ 0
    let Remainder = Numeric
    let String = ""
    loop
        call append (String, (Remainder mod 10) + '0')
        let Remainder = Remainder ÷ 10
    end loop when Remainder = 0
    call reverse (String)
    result String
end To~Text
```

2.1.3 Decimal~Compare (receives Number1, Number2; *result integer*)

Pseudo Code

```
initialize Comparison to 0
initialize I to prior to the first character of Number1 and Number2
loop until I ≥ last character of Number1 and Number2 or Comparison ≠ 0
    let I = I + 1
    if I-th digit of Number1 > I-th digit of Number2 then
        let Comparison = +1
    else-if I-th digit of Number1 < I-th digit of Number2 then
        let Comparison = –1
    end if
end loop
```

Code

```
function Decimal~Compare (Number1, Number2 are text) is integer
    variables Comparison, I, J, K, N are integers
    let Comparison = 0
    let N = maximum (length (Number1), length (Number2))
    let I = 0
    loop until I ≥ N or Comparison ≠ 0
        let I = I + 1
        let J = last (Number1) – N + I
        let K = last (Number2) – N + I
        let Comparison = sign (byte (Number1, J) – byte (Number2, K))
    end loop
    result Comparison
end Decimal~Compare
```

2.1.4 Decimal~Add (receives Augend, Addend; *result text*)

Pseudo Code

```
initialize String to the null string
initialize Carry to zero
for i = 0 to maximum of the lengths of Augend and Addend
    calculate the sum of the digits at position i from the end of each number
    add the previous Carry to this sum
    append the last decimal digit of the sum to the front of String
    let Carry = the quotient when the sum is divided by 10
end for
```

Code

```
function Decimal~Add (Augend, Addend are text) is text
    variable String is text
    variable Carry is integer
    let String = “”
    let Carry = 0
    for i = 0 to maximum (length (Augend), length (Addend))
        if i < length (Augend) then
            let Carry = Carry + byte (Augend, last (Augend) – i) – ‘0’
        end if
        if i < length (Addend) then
            let Carry = Carry + byte (Addend, last (Addend) – i) – ‘0’
        end if
        call append (String, (Carry mod 10) + ‘0’)
        let Carry = Carry ÷ 10
    end for
    call reverse (String)
    call Zero~Suppress (String)
    result String
end Decimal~Add
```

2.1.5 Decimal~Subtract (receives Minuend, Subtrahend; *result text*)

Pseudo Code

```
initialize Difference to the null string
initialize Carry to zero
for i = 0 to maximum of the lengths of Minuend and Subtrahend
    calculate the signed difference of the digits at position i from the end of each
            number
    add the previous Carry to this difference
    append the last decimal digit of the difference to the front of Difference
    let Carry = the signed quotient when the difference is divided by 10
end for
```

Code

```
function Decimal~Subtract (Minuend, Subtrahend are text) is text
    variable Difference is text
    variable Carry is integer
    check Decimal~Compare (Minuend, Subtrahend) ≥ 0
    let Difference = ""
    let Carry = 0
    for i = 0 to maximum (length (Minuend), length (Subtrahend)) – 1
        if length (Minuend) > i then
            let Carry = Carry + (byte (Minuend, last (Minuend) – i) – '0')
        end if
        if length (Subtrahend) > i then
            let Carry = Carry – (byte (Subtrahend, last (Subtrahend) – i) – '0')
        end if
        let Carry = Carry + 10
        call append (Difference, (Carry mod 10) + '0')
        let Carry = (Carry ÷ 10) – 1
    end for
    call reverse (Difference)
    call Zero~Suppress (Difference)
    result Difference
end Decimal~Subtract
```

2.1.6 Decimal~Multiply (receives Multiplicand, Multiplier; *result text*)

Pseudo Code

```
initialize String to the null string
for j = last digit of Multiplier to first digit of Multiplier
    initialize Carry to zero
    initialize Product to a string of (last (Multiplier) – j) zeros
    select j-th Digit of Multiplier
    for i = last digit of Multiplicand to first digit of Multiplicand
        multiply Digit by i-th digit of Multiplicand and add Carry
        append last digit of the sum to front of Product
        let Carry = the quotient when the sum is divided by 10
    end for
```

```
        append last digit of Carry to front of Product
        add Product to String using Decimal~Add
    end for
```

Code

```
function Decimal~Multiply (Multiplicand, Multiplier are text) is text
    variables Offset, Product, String are text
    variables Carry, Digit are integers
    let String = ""
    let Offset = ""
    for decreasing j = last (Multiplier) to first
        let Carry = 0
        let Product = Offset
        let Digit = byte (Multiplier, j) – '0'
        for decreasing i = last (Multiplicand) to first
            let Carry = Carry + (Digit * (byte (Multiplicand, i) – '0'))
            call append (Product, (Carry mod 10) + '0')
            let Carry = Carry ÷ 10
        end for
        call append (Product, (Carry mod 10) + '0')
        call reverse (Product)
        let String = Decimal~Add (String, Product)
        call append (Offset, '0')
    end for
    result String
end Decimal~Multiply
```

2.1.7 Decimal~Divide (receives Dividend, Divisor; supplies Quotient, Remainder)

Pseudo Code

```
initialize Quotient and Remainder to null strings
initialize I to prior to first character of Dividend
loop until I ≥ last character of Dividend
    append digits from front of Dividend to end of Remainder until Remainder ≥
            Divisor
    let I = I + number of digits extracted from Dividend
    append "0" to Quotient for each digit extracted from Dividend after the first
    subtract Divisor repeatedly from Remainder while Remainder ≥ Divisor
    let next digit of Quotient = number of times Divisor was subtracted from
            Remainder
end loop
```

Code

```
procedure Decimal~Divide (Dividend, Divisor, Quotient, Remainder are text)
    variables I, J are integers
    check Decimal~Compare (Divisor, "0") > 0
    let Quotient = ""
    let Remainder = ""
    let I = first – 1
```

```
    loop until I ≥ last (Dividend)
        loop
            let I = I + 1
            call append (Quotient, '0')
            call append (Remainder, byte (Dividend, I))
        end loop when Decimal~Compare (Remainder, Divisor) ≥ 0 or
                I ≥ last (Dividend)
        call shorten (Quotient)
        let J = 0
        loop until Decimal~Compare (Remainder, Divisor) < 0
            let Remainder = Decimal~Subtract (Remainder, Divisor)
            let J = J + 1
        end loop
        call append (Quotient, J + '0')
    end loop
    call Zero~Suppress (Quotient)
    call Zero~Suppress (Remainder)
end Decimal~Divide
```

2.1.8 Fast~Multiply (receives Multiplicand, Multiplier; *result text*)

Pseudo Code

convert Multiplicand and Multiplier to base-1,000 form in integer arrays
initialize the Product to zero
accumulate all possible cross-products of Multiplicand and Multiplier base-1,000 "digits"
convert integer array of product components to a *text* string

Code

```
function Fast~Multiply (Multiplicand, Multiplier are text) is text
    constant SizePlicand = (length (Multiplicand) + 2) ÷ 3
    constant SizePlier = (length (Multiplier) + 2) ÷ 3
    constant SizeProduct = SizePlicand + SizePlier – 1
    variable Plicand is array 1 to SizePlicand of integers
    variable Plier is array 1 to SizePlier of integers
    variable Product is array 1 to SizeProduct of integers
    call Group (Multiplicand, Plicand, SizePlicand)
    call Group (Multiplier, Plier, SizePlier)
    for i = 1 to SizeProduct
        let Product[i] = 0
    end for
    for i = 1 to SizePlicand
        for j = 1 to SizePlier
            let Product[i+j–1] = Product[i+j–1] + (Plicand[i] * Plier[j])
        end for
    end for
```

```
    result Ungroup (Product, SizeProduct)
  end Fast~Multiply
```

Local **Zero~Suppress** (updates String)

Removes leading zeros unless string is just one zero

```
  procedure Zero~Suppress (String is text)
    call reverse (String)
    loop until length (String) ≤ 1 or byte (String,
          last (String)) ≠ '0'
      call shorten (String)
    end loop
    call reverse (String)
  end Zero~Suppress
```

Local **Group** (receives String, Size; supplies Digits)

Converts trios of decimal digits into binary integers in elements of an *integer* array

```
  procedure Group (String is text, Digits is array
        of integers, Size is integer)
    variable K is integer
    let K = last (String) – (Size * 3)
    for i = 1 to Size
      let K = K + 3
      let Digits[i] = 0
      for j = maximum (first, K – 2) to K
        let Digits[i] = (Digits[i] * 10) + byte (String, j) – '0'
      end for
    end for
  end Group
```

Local **Ungroup** (receives Digits, Size; *result text*)

Converts *integer* array representation of a number to a *text* string

```
  function Ungroup (Digits is array of integers,
        Size is integer) is text
    variable String is text
    variable Carry is integer
    let String = ""
    let Carry = 0
    for decreasing i = Size to 1
      let Carry = Carry + Digits[i]
      for j = 1 to 3
        call append (String, (Carry mod 10) + '0')
        let Carry = Carry ÷ 10
      end for
    end for
    loop until Carry = 0
      call append (String, (Carry mod 10) + '0')
      let Carry = Carry ÷ 10
    end loop
    call reverse (String)
    result String
  end Ungroup
```

TEST PROGRAM

<u>Subprograms Tested</u>

Decimal~Add	Adds two positive integers in *text* form (2.1.4)
Decimal~Compare	Compares two positive integers in *text* form (2.1.3)
Decimal~Divide	Divides two positive integers in *text* form (2.1.7)
Decimal~Multiply	Multiplies two positive integers in *text* form (2.1.6)
Decimal~Subtract	Subtracts two positive integers in *text* form (2.1.5)
Fast~Multiply	Quickly multiplies two positive integers in *text* form (2.1.8)
To~Integer	Converts an integer in *text* form to an *integer* (2.1.1)
To~Text	Converts an *integer* number to *text* form (2.1.2)

<u>Local Names</u>

A	Dividend
B	Divisor
Q	Quotient
R	Remainder

Pseudo Code

```
for i = 0 to 12
    initialize A to (increasingly large) integer with known factors
    for j = 0 to i
        initialize B to (increasingly large) integer with known factors
        divide B into A, calculating Q and R
        check Q and R have correct values
    end for
end for
```

Code

```
variables A, B, Q, R are text
for i = 0 to 12
    let A = To~Text (power (2, i))
    check To~Text (To~Integer (A)) = A
    for j = 0 to i
        let B = To~Text (power (2, j))
        call Decimal~Divide (A, B, Q, R)
        check Decimal~Multiply (Q, B) = A and R = "0"
        check Fast~Multiply (Q, B) = A
    end for
end for
```

2.2 FRACTIONAL ARITHMETIC

Doing arithmetic with numbers represented as ratios of two integers

Example

To compute (inefficiently) ten successive rational approximations to the value of π, using the identity $\pi = 4 * (1 - 1/3 + 1/5 - 1/7 + \dots)$:

```
constants Num = 1, Den = 2
variables R, S are arrays Num to Den of integers
call Fractions~Fractionate (4, 1, R)
call Fractions~Fractionate (4, 1, S)
for i = 1 to 10
    let R[Num] = –R[Num]
    let R[Den] = R[Den] + 2
    call Fractions~Add (S, R, S)
    output S[Num], "/", S[Den]
end for
```

Subprograms

All nicknames are two-element *integer* arrays, unless otherwise stated.

2.2.1 Fractions~Numerate (receives Fraction; *result real*)
2.2.2 Fractions~Fractionate (receives *integers* I, J; supplies Fraction)
2.2.3 Fractions~GCD (receives *integers* I, J; *result integer*)
2.2.4 Fractions~Simplify (updates Fraction)
2.2.5 Fractions~Add (receives Augend, Addend; supplies Sum)
2.2.6 Fractions~Subtract (receives Minuend, Subtrahend; supplies Difference)
2.2.7 Fractions~Multiply (receives Multiplicand, Multiplier; supplies Product)
2.2.8 Fractions~Divide (receives Dividend, Divisor; supplies Quotient)

Usage

Fractions are represented by two binary integers. The integer pair is held in adjacent locations of a two-element array. To take an example, Fractions~Add receives two such pairs in the arrays with nicknames Augend and Addend. The sum is reduced to its lowest terms and supplied via the nickname Sum. Subtraction, multiplication, and division are carried out in a similar manner. For convenience, Fractions~Numerate is a function that does the simple job of converting a fraction to its *real* approximation. Fractions~Fractionate also carries out an elementary task—putting two integers into a two-element array. Fractions~Simplify may be used independently to reduce a fraction to its lowest terms.

Fractions~GCD provides a moderately useful application for Euclid's famous algorithm for computing the greatest common divisor, abbreviated to GCD, of two numbers (Claussen 1960). Every schoolchild has been taught at some time or another how to operate Euclid's algorithm. No doubt those same children have also wondered why on earth anyone would want to do such a thing. Computer science textbooks contain lengthy analyses of the algorithm, perhaps because it is one of the shortest nontrivial algorithms known. Professor Edsger Dijkstra (1976) at least had the decency to apologize: "At the risk of boring my readers I shall now devote yet another chapter to Euclid's algorithm". In this book we will carry out no analysis at all, demonstrating the differences in our priorities.

The algorithms for carrying out arithmetic with fractions are not at all difficult to understand. They quite straightforwardly carry out arithmetic using the same methods we all learned in school. Naturally, the methods will fail when integer overflow occurs. For certain practical applications it will be necessary to implement the algorithms in multiple precision arithmetic. The algorithms for multiple precision calculations are beyond the scope of this book.

IMPLEMENTATION

Exported Names

Fractions~Add	Adds two fractions (2.2.5)
Fractions~Divide	Divides two fractions (2.2.8)
Fractions~Fractionate	Converts two integers to a fraction (2.2.2)
Fractions~GCD	Computes greatest common divisor of two integers (2.2.3)
Fractions~Multiply	Multiplies two fractions (2.2.7)
Fractions~Numerate	Converts a fraction to a *real* (2.2.1)
Fractions~Simplify	Reduces a fraction to its lowest terms (2.2.4)
Fractions~Subtract	Subtracts two fractions (2.2.6)

Nicknames

Augend	Fraction to which Addend is to be added
Addend	Fraction to be added to Augend
Difference	Difference between Minuend and Subtrahend
Dividend	Fraction to be divided by Divisor
Divisor	Fraction to divide Dividend by
Fraction	Two-element array containing numerator and denominator of fraction
I	Integer, the numerator of a fraction
J	Integer, the denominator of a fraction
Minuend	Fraction from which Subtrahend is subtracted
Multiplicand	Fraction to be multiplied by Multiplier
Multiplier	Fraction to multiply Multiplicand by
Product	Product of Multiplicand and Multiplier
Quotient	Quotient of Dividend and Divisor
Subtrahend	Fraction to be subtracted from Minuend
Sum	Sum of Augend and Addend

Global Names

Num	Position in two-element array of numerator for fraction
Den	Position in two-element array of denominator for fraction

Local Names

A	Temporary location for an integer, initially equal to I
B	Temporary location for an integer, initially equal to J
GCDivisor	Greatest common divisor of numerator and denominator
P	Two-element array for developing product
Q	Two-element array for developing quotient
R	Remainder when A is divided by B

Code

constant Num = 1
constant Den = 2

2.2.1 Fractions~Numerate (receives Fraction; *result real*)

Pseudo Code

result is (numerator / denominator) expressed as a *real* number

Code

```
function Fractions~Numerate (Fraction is array of integers) is real
    result Fraction[Num] / Fraction[Den]
end Fractions~Numerate
```

2.2.2 Fractions~Fractionate (receives I, J; supplies Fraction)

Pseudo Code

result is I inserted in Fraction[Num] and J inserted in Fraction[Den]

Code

```
procedure Fractions~Fractionate (I, J are integers, Fraction is array of integers)
    let Fraction[Num] = I
    let Fraction[Den] = J
end Fractions~Fractionate
```

2.2.3 Fractions~GCD (receives I, J; *result integer*)

Pseudo Code

```
initialize A to I and B to J
loop until B is zero
    let B = A and let A = remainder when A is divided by B
end loop
result is A
```

Code

```
function Fractions~GCD (I, J are integers) is integer
    variables A, B, R are integers
    let A = magnitude (I)
    let B = magnitude (J)
    loop until B = 0
        let R = A mod B
        let A = B
        let B = R
    end loop
    result A
end Fractions~GCD
```

2.2.4 Fractions~Simplify (updates Fraction)

Pseudo Code

divide numerator and denominator by their greatest common divisor

Code

```
procedure Fractions~Simplify (Fraction is array of integers)
    variable GCDivisor is integer
    let GCDivisor = Fractions~GCD (Fraction[Num], Fraction[Den])
    let Fraction[Num] = Fraction[Num] ÷ GCDivisor
    let Fraction[Den] = Fraction[Den] ÷ GCDivisor
end Fractions~Simplify
```

2.2.5 Fractions~Add (receives Augend, Addend; supplies Sum)

Pseudo Code

let numerator = the sum of the cross-products of the numerators and denominators
let denominator = the product of the denominators
result is (numerator / denominator) simplified to its lowest terms

Code

```
procedure Fractions~Add (Augend, Addend, Sum are arrays of integers)
    let Sum[Num] = (Augend[Num] * Addend[Den]) +
            (Augend[Den] * Addend[Num])
    let Sum[Den] = Augend[Den] * Addend[Den]
    call Fractions~Simplify (Sum)
end Fractions~Add
```

2.2.6 Fractions~Subtract (receives Minuend, Subtrahend; supplies Difference)

Pseudo Code

let numerator = the difference of the cross-products of the numerators and denominators
let denominator = the product of the denominators
result is the fraction simplified to its lowest terms

Code

```
procedure Fractions~Subtract (Minuend, Subtrahend, Difference are arrays of
        integers)
    let Difference[Num] = (Minuend[Num] * Subtrahend[Den]) – (Minuend[Den] *
            Subtrahend[Num])
    let Difference[Den] = Minuend[Den] * Subtrahend[Den]
    call Fractions~Simplify (Difference)
end Fractions~Subtract
```

2.2.7 Fractions~Multiply (receives Multiplicand, Multiplier; supplies Product)

Pseudo Code

divide out common factors in numerator of Multiplicand and denominator of Multiplier, and vice versa

result numerator is product of reduced numerators
result denominator is product of reduced denominators

Code

procedure Fractions~Multiply (Multiplicand, Multiplier, Product *are arrays of integers*)
variable GCDivisor *is integer*
variable P *is array* Num *to* Den *of integers*
let GCDivisor = Fractions~GCD (Multiplicand[Num], Multiplier[Den])
let P[Num] = Multiplicand[Num] ÷ GCDivisor
let P[Den] = Multiplier[Den] ÷ GCDivisor
let GCDivisor = Fractions~GCD (Multiplier[Num], Multiplicand[Den])
let Product[Num] = P[Num] * (Multiplier[Num] ÷ GCDivisor)
let Product[Den] = P[Den] * (Multiplicand[Den] ÷ GCDivisor)
end Fractions~Multiply

2.2.8 Fractions~Divide (receives Dividend, Divisor; supplies Quotient)

Pseudo Code

divide out common factors in numerators and denominators of Dividend and Divisor
result numerator is product of reduced Dividend numerator and Divisor denominator
result denominator is product of reduced Dividend denominator and Divisor numerator
sign of result is sign of Dividend numerator times sign of Divisor numerator

Code

procedure Fractions~Divide (Dividend, Divisor, Quotient *are arrays of integers*)
variable GCDivisor *is integer*
variable Q *is array* Num *to* Den *of integers*
let GCDivisor = Fractions~GCD (Dividend[Num], Divisor[Num])
let Q[Num] = Dividend[Num] ÷ GCDivisor
let Q[Den] = Divisor[Num] ÷ GCDivisor
let GCDivisor = Fractions~GCD (Dividend[Den], Divisor[Den])
let Q[Num] = Q[Num] * (Divisor[Den] ÷ GCDivisor)
let Q[Den] = Q[Den] * (Dividend[Den] ÷ GCDivisor)
let Quotient[Num] = Q[Num] * *sign* (Q[Den])
let Quotient[Den] = Q[Den] * *sign* (Q[Den])
end Fractions~Divide

TEST PROGRAM

Imported Names

Num	Position in two-element array of numerator for fraction
Den	Position in two-element array of denominator for fraction

Local Names

D	Difference
IJ	i divided by j

JI   j divided by i
S, T   Intermediate values

Pseudo Code

```
for i = 1 to 10
    for j = 1 to 10
        let S = (i/j) + (j/i)
        let D = (i/j) – (j/i)
        let T = ((D / S) / D) * S, when D ≠ 0
        check T = 1
    end for
end for
```

Code

```
variables D, IJ, JI, S, T are arrays Num to Den of integers
for i = 1 to 10
    for j = 1 to 10
        if i ≠ j then
            call Fractions~Fractionate (i, j, IJ)
            call Fractions~Fractionate (j, i, JI)
            call Fractions~Add (IJ, JI, S)
            call Fractions~Subtract (IJ, JI, D)
            check Fractions~GCD (D[Num], D[Den]) = 1
            check sign (D[Den]) = 1
            call Fractions~Divide (D, S, T)
            call Fractions~Divide (T, D, T)
            call Fractions~Multiply (T, S, T)
            check Fractions~Numerate (T) = 1
        end if
    end for
end for
```

2.3 NUMBER SIMILARITY

Testing whether floating point numbers are "nearly" equal

Example

The two approximations to pi, 3.141592653 and 3.141592654, are very nearly equal. The number of binary digits (bits) they have in common (30) is calculated and displayed by:

output Similarity~Bits (3.141592653, 3.141592654, 1)

Subprograms

Both functions have nicknames that are *real*:

2.3.1 Similarity~Bits (receives A, B, Scale; *result integer*)
2.3.2 Similarity~Test (receives A, B, Scale; *result true-false*)

Usage

The usage of these functions is best explained by an example. Suppose you have written a function to compute the cube root of a number. During testing, you want a *check* statement that terminates the program if the computed result is incorrect. To calculate a cube root you need to take the logarithm of the number, divide it by three, and then exponentiate it. Of course, any negative sign needs to be handled appropriately. You would like to write:

```
function Cube~Root (X is real) is real
    variable T is real
    let T = exp (log_e (magnitude (X)) / 3) * sign (X)
    check T * T * T = X
    result T
end Cube~Root
```

Testing revealed that the function works properly when X = 2, but terminates when X = 3, even though the result is almost exactly correct. You need a test that halts if the computation fails to be *almost* exactly correct. To achieve the desired result you need to replace:

```
check T * T * T = X
```

by:

```
check Similarity~Test (T * T * T, X, X) = true
```

The Similarity~Test function gives a *true* result if the two numbers supplied to it are very similar but not necessarily exactly equal.

Similarity~Test calls on Similarity~Bits to compute the number of leading bits that the two numbers have in common. If the number of bits in common is greater than one half the maximum number of significant digits in the numbers, the numbers are judged to be "similar". This implies that the result must be accurate to nearly eight significant decimal digits for a typical extended precision number (a floating point number using 64 bits in the standard IEEE format).

You need to tell the algorithm the scale you have in mind, that is, the typical size of numbers of the kind being compared. To see why the scale is important, consider trying to decide whether two given measurements that differ by unity are almost equal or not. If you were measuring the number of atoms of air in a room, the two measurements would be considered identical to all intents and purposes. If you were measuring the numbers of drawers in two desks you were considering buying, the numbers would most certainly not be nearly equal in your eyes. This implies that two numbers A and B can be compared for approximate equality only if the scale of measurement is known. If the scale is specified as zero, the algorithm chooses the larger of the two numbers to use as the scale; otherwise, it uses your specified scale as described below.

Analysis

The meaning of "similarity" is closely related to the meaning of "relative error" (Goldberg 1991). In fact, the algorithm computes the logarithm of the inverse of the relative error. If 3.14 is given as an approximation for π, the relative error is $|\pi - 3.14|/\pi$, or about 0.0005. Similarity~Bits (3.14, π, π) gives the result *truncate* (log_2 (π/|π – 3.14|)), or 10. You can see that log_2 (1/0.0005) is approximately equal to 10. The book uses "similarity" rather than "relative error" for several reasons. Almost all calculations are done in practice without knowing the accuracy of the original data. You do not often have the luxury of knowing the right answers, such as π. Therefore, "relative error" has a connotation that may be misleading. More important for its use in practice, the similarity measure is a simple statement of the number of bits that two numbers have in common. This will be found useful in a number of algorithms.

In some languages, Similarity~Bits can be implemented very efficiently without using logarithms. The idea is to obtain the exponent of the floating point representation of (Assumed / Difference). In the π example, the floating point representation of π/|π – 3.14| is approximately 1.926×2^{10}. You can see the similarity of 10 bits in the power to which 2 is raised. Similarity~Bits as written is slower, calculating logarithms to base 2.

IMPLEMENTATION

<u>Exported Names</u>

Similarity~Bits	Finds the number of bits in common in two numbers (2.3.1)
Similarity~Test	Tests the similarity of two numbers (2.3.2)

<u>Nicknames</u>

A, B	Numbers to be compared
Scale	Representative number demonstrating the size of A and B

<u>Local Names</u>

Assumed	If specified scale is zero, assume maximum of A and B
Difference	Absolute difference between A and B

2.3.1 Similarity~Bits (receives A, B, Scale; *result integer*)

Pseudo Code

```
if the A and B are equal then
    the similarity is equal to the maximum number of bits in a word
else
    if Scale has been specified then
        use the specified Scale
    else
        use the larger of A and B as Scale
    end if
    calculate similarity as base 2 logarithm of Scale / magnitude (A – B)
end if
```

Code

```
function Similarity~Bits (A, B, Scale are real) is integer
    variables Assumed, Difference are real
    let Difference = magnitude (A – B)
    if Difference = 0 then
        result maxbits
    else
```

```
        if Scale > 0 then
            let Assumed = Scale
        else
            let Assumed = maximum (magnitude (A), magnitude (B))
        end if
        result truncate (maximum (0, log2 (Assumed / Difference)))
    end if
end Similarity~Bits
```

2.3.2 Similarity~Test (receives A, B, Scale; *result true-false*)

Pseudo Code

```
if number of bits of similarity > half the maximum number of bits in a number then
    result is true
else
    result is false
end if
```

Code

```
function Similarity~Test (A, B, Scale are real) is true-false
    if Similarity~Bits (A, B, Scale) > maxbits / 2 then
        result true
    else
        result false
    end if
end Similarity~Test
```

TEST PROGRAM

Pseudo Code

the similarity of a number with itself is the maximum number of bits in a number
the similarity of 1 with 2 is zero, there being no bits in common between the two numbers
the similarity of 1 with 1.125 is 3 bits
the similarity of 1 with 1.25 is 2 bits, and this is not "nearly" equal to 3

Code

```
check Similarity~Bits (1, 1, 1) = maxbits
check Similarity~Bits (2, 1, 1) = 0
check Similarity~Bits (1, 1.125, 1) = 3
check Similarity~Test (Similarity~Bits (1, 1.125, 1), 3, 1) = true
check Similarity~Test (Similarity~Bits (1, 1.25, 1), 3, 1) = false
```

3 Numeration

In this chapter you will find algorithms for creating numbers that are self-checking, for numbering the days of our lives, and for handling Roman numerals.

Self-checking numbers are widely used for providing security for code numbers. Examples include credit card numbers, account numbers, product codes, international standard book numbers, tax file numbers, social security numbers, and many others. Numbers are made self-checking by adding one or more additional "check" digits computed mathematically from the basic number. These digits are appended to the basic number and are treated as an inseparable part of it. Check-digited numbers are more difficult to forge, and enable equipment reading them to detect most instances of reading errors. Section 3.1 deals with check digits.

Dates have three numeric components: the year, the month, and the day. This in itself makes dates more complicated to process than ordinary numbers. There is the additional complication that there are varying numbers of days per month, and years that have an additional day (leap years). The processing of dates can be simplified by keeping them in the computer in a more straightforward numeric form. The internal representation of a date is an integer, which denotes the number of days from some agreed but arbitrary date in the past. Arithmetic on dates is facilitated by such a representation. For example, it is easy to find the number of days between any two dates, merely by calculating the difference of their internal representations. It is necessary to convert to and from this internal representation so that dates manipulated by programs are understandable to humans. The date algorithms in Section 3.2 enable you to do that.

In addition, there are two different algorithms for calculating the date of Easter Sunday, the date of which changes from year to year, based on a complicated formula.

Roman numerals are hardly essential to the survival of the planet. They are interesting anachronisms that survive in a few places. They are used, for example, in film copyright dates. Certain numbers in cataloging data or within books, such as "added entry" heading numbers and page numbers in the preface, are traditionally specified in Roman numerals. Conversion between Arabic and Roman numerals is not totally straightforward. The problem arises from the strange rule that a digit of lower value placed before a digit of higher value implies subtraction. For example, "vi" represents six ("v" = five and "i" = one), but "iv" is equal to four. The Roman numerals algorithms in Section 3.3 carry out the conversions in either direction.

3.1 CHECK DIGITS

Protecting a number with self-checking "check" digits

Example

The check digit (5) for the number 12345 using the "IBM" method is calculated by:

output IBM~Compute ("12345")

Subprograms

For each algorithm, say A, there are two subprograms: A~Compute to calculate the check digit(s) for a number, and A~Verify to assess the correctness of a check-digited number. In addition, there is an initialization subprogram Dihedral~Initialize for the dihedral algorithm. If n represents a digit, the general format is:

3.1.na A~Compute (receives Basic; *result text*)
3.1.nb A~Verify (receives Checked; *result true-false*)
3.1.nc A~Initialize

The subprogram groups are:

3.1.1 Mod 10
3.1.2 ISBN
3.1.3 IBM
3.1.4 Bank
3.1.5 Dihedral
3.1.6 Mod97
3.1.7 Mod997
3.1.8 Mod9973

Usage

Check digits are used to minimize errors when numbers are entered into a computer. They make use of the concept of *redundancy*. Anything in everyday life that is redundant is considered of no value and to be eliminated. In computer applications redundancy is useful. It provides additional data that enable the checking of primary data for accuracy.

Without some form of redundancy a computer may make an error that cannot be detected. For example, if your 16-digit credit card number did not have some redundancy built into it, an error in reading the card could result in someone else being charged for your purchases. Although that might seem beneficial for you, the downside is that you may be incorrectly charged for expenses incurred by others. One reason that code numbers such as credit card numbers are so long is that they are to a large extent self-checking, with considerable built-in redundancy.

Check digits are digits appended to the basic number. The basic number is never used on its own externally to the computer. The new combined number can be checked by the computer to assess its accuracy. For example, the book by Knuth (1968) has the International Standard Book Number 0-201-03809-9, the last digit of which is a check digit.

There are several types of errors that commonly occur when numbers are transcribed by hand. These are:

Single errors	An error is made in a single digit—for example, writing 8 instead of 5.
Format errors	The number has one fewer or one more digit than it should have.
Transpositions	Two adjacent digits are interchanged.

Other types have been classified, such as jump transpositions, phonetic errors, twin errors, and random errors, but these are rarer, accounting for less than 5% of all errors (Wagner and Putter 1989). All methods presented in this book detect 100% of single errors. Effectiveness varies widely with format errors and transpositions, as discussed below.

Check digit methods may be classified into two types: (a) single-digit methods and (b) multiple-digit methods. Single-digit methods have the advantage of requiring fewer check digits than multiple-digit methods. Multiple-digit methods have the advantage of superior error-checking capability.

The single-digit methods provided for you are the Mod 10, ISBN (used for International Standard Book Numbers), IBM™ (attributed to IBM Corporation), Bank (used by banks in the United States for so-called processing numbers on checks), and Dihedral methods. The Compute subprogram in each case generates a single-character *text* result, which is the check digit. The Verify subprogram for each gives a *true-false* result, *true* if the check-digited number is correct, and *false* otherwise.

The multiple-digit methods discussed here are the Mod 97, Mod 997, and Mod 9973 methods. The Compute subprograms for each of these generate two, three, and four check digits respectively as *text* strings. The Verify subprograms operate as for the single-digit methods.

Analysis

The Mod 10, ISBN, and Bank methods all have a similar approach, calculating a weighted sum of the digits in the check-digited number. The key idea is that the weighted sum should have a remainder of zero when divided by 10 (Mod 10 and Bank methods) or 11 (ISBN method). In the Mod 10 method the weights are all 1. The ISBN method weights each successive digit (starting from the rightmost end of the number) by successively larger integers starting from 1. The weights for a typical 10-digit ISBN are therefore 10, 9, 8, ..., 1. Some organizations are known to use a modified version of the ISBN method, in which the weights are powers of 2 rather than successive integers. Provided that the modulus is 11 and not 10, the modified method is shown by exhaustive computer simulation to be as effective as the ISBN method itself. The Bank method weights the digits (starting from the first digit) by 3, 7, 1, 3, 7, 1, 3, 7, 1. The method was designed for 9-digit codes, but will work similarly on check-digited numbers that have a multiple of three digits.

The IBM method does not use weighting as such. It generates a sum of the digits, with the first and every alternate digit modified by the following formula. If any given alternate digit is D, it is replaced in the sum by $((2 * D) \div 10) + ((2 * D) \mathit{mod}\ 10)$.

The Dihedral method is quite different in approach. Suppose the array P contains a certain permutation of the digits 0, ..., 9 in P[0] to P[9]. Call the digits of the checked number D_n, ..., D_1, D_0, with D_0 being the check digit. Replace each digit by new digits, say E_n, ..., E_1, E_0, using the following scheme: $E_0 = D_0$, $E_1 = P[D_1]$, $E_2 = P[P[D_2]]$, $E_3 = P[P[P[D_3]]]$, and so on. For ease of computation, multiple permutations are kept in a two-dimensional array F, so that $E_0 = F[0, D_0]$, $E_1 = F[1, D_1]$, $E_2 = F[2, D_2]$, $E_3 = F[3, D_3]$, and so on. The new digits are then combined successively by being looked up in the "multiplication" table for the dihedral group. This is just a two-dimensional array G of digits with a particular pattern. Accumulate a "product" S as follows: $S = G[0, E_n]$, $S = G[S, E_{n-1}]$, ..., $S = G[S, E_0]$. The check digit D_0 is valid if the "product" S is equal to zero.

In order to compute the check digit for a basic number a similar process is applied, except of course for digit D_0, which has to be computed from E_0. At the final step there will be a "product" S computed from E_1. An "inversion" step is required to convert S to the check digit D_0. Fortunately, the fifth permutation, in row 5 of the array F, happens to contain the required inverse for each digit.

If you think for a minute about random numbers, you are likely to come to the conclusion that a single check digit will be fortuitously correct about 10% of the time. This conclusion is about right, a single check digit catching about 90% of all "random" errors. Similarly, two, three, and four check digits will catch about 99%, 99.9%, and 99.99% of random errors respectively. The various single-digit methods have been devised to catch a higher percentage of specific types of errors (while still doing no better with "random" errors).

All single-digit methods are about equally effective with single errors and format errors. The methods detect 100% of single errors and about 90% of format errors. The ISBN and Dihedral methods detect 100% of adjacent transpositions. In fact, the ISBN method detects transpositions of any two digits, whether adjacent or not (Wagner and Putter 1989). The ISBN method performs well because it uses the modulus 11, which gives rise to the unsatisfactory need for a check "digit" with a value of 10, represented by the Roman numeral X. The Dihedral method is a truly decimal method that is clearly superior to all other single-digit methods. The mathematical properties of the dihedral group ensure that all the most common errors are caught.

The ability of the various methods to detect transpositions is shown in Table 3.1. Note that the IBM method is almost as good as the Dihedral method. In fact, it detects all transpositions except 90/09. Wagner and Putter (1989) claim that the Dihedral method is superior to all other methods for the rarer errors mentioned above, detecting around 95% of them, although our simulations have failed to confirm this point. The specific permutation (values for the array P above) used by Wagner and Putter did not detect 100% of adjacent transpositions in our tests, and should be avoided.

Table 3.1

Method	*Transpositions*
Mod 10	Detects none
ISBN	Detects all
IBM	Detects 98%
Bank	Detects 90%
Dihedral	Detects all

Although devised by Verhoeff in the late 1960s, the Dihedral method did not surface until the mid-1980s. Verhoeff's work is relatively inaccessible, and the theory was independently expounded and published by Gumm (1985). Because it emerged only recently, many applications continue to use inferior methods. You may have to stick with such methods if item codes were assigned some years ago. For specialized applications the other methods might be suitable even now. For example, when transposition errors cannot occur, as in optical scanning, the Mod 10 method could be used fairly safely with the aim of detecting errors in single digits.

The multiple-digit methods are much simpler in concept, in that they merely use the remainder when the entire number is divided by a prime number such as 97, 997, or 9973. A review of the literature by Gumm (1985) suggests that multiple check digits may be inadvisable because "the number of errors that occur roughly doubles when the number of digits increases by two". Nevertheless, multiple check digits are much more effective in detecting errors than single check digits.

Sometimes it is required not only to detect an error in a number but also to determine what the correct number is. If there is sufficient redundancy in a check-digited number, the error may be correctable automatically. Error correction is beyond the scope of this book, and you should consult Hamming (1986) for further information.

IMPLEMENTATION

Exported Names

Bank~Compute	Computes a Bank check digit for a number (3.1.4)
Bank~Verify	Verifies a Bank check-digited number (3.1.4)
Dihedral~Compute	Computes a dihedral check digit for a number (3.1.5)
Dihedral~Initialize	Initializes permutation and "multiplication" table (3.1.5)
Dihedral~Verify	Verifies a dihedral check-digited number (3.1.5)
IBM~Compute	Computes an IBM check digit for a number (3.1.3)
IBM~Verify	Verifies an IBM check-digited number (3.1.3)
ISBN~Compute	Computes check digit for an ISBN (3.1.2)
ISBN~Verify	Verifies an ISBN (3.1.2)
Mod10~Compute	Computes a mod 10 check digit for a number (3.1.1)

Mod10~Verify	Verifies a mod 10 check-digited number (3.1.1)
Mod97~Compute	Computes two mod 97 check digits for a number (3.1.6)
Mod97~Verify	Verifies a mod 97 check-digited number (3.1.6)
Mod997~Compute	Computes three mod 997 check digits for a number (3.1.7)
Mod997~Verify	Verifies a mod 997 check-digited number (3.1.7)
Mod9973~Compute	Computes four mod 9973 check digits for a number (3.1.8)
Mod9973~Verify	Verifies a mod 9973 check-digited number (3.1.8)
Imported Names	
Decimal~Divide	Divides two positive integers in *text* form (2.1.7)
Decimal~Subtract	Subtracts two positive integers in *text* form (2.1.5)
To~Integer	Converts an integer in *text* form to an *integer* (2.1.1)
To~Text	Converts an *integer* number to *text* form (2.1.2)
Local Subprograms	
Bank~Sum	Computes the weighted sum of the digits in a number
IBM~Sum	Computes the weighted sum of the digits in a number
ISBN~Sum	Computes the weighted sum of the digits in a number
Mod10~Sum	Computes the sum of the digits in a number
Nicknames	
Basic	Basic number to be check-digited
Checked	Number with check digit appended
String	Basic or checked number to be summed
Global Names	
F	Array of rows of permutations of digits 0 to 9 for dihedral algorithm
G	"Multiplication" table for digits 0 to 9 using the dihedral group
Local Names	
Check	Check digit in text form, or basic number to be checked
Digit	Check digit in integer form
K1, K2	Intermediate digits
Sum	Sum of the digits, weighted where necessary

3.1.1a Mod 10~Compute (receives Basic; *result text*)

Pseudo Code

```
let Sum = 0
for i = first character of Checked to last character of Checked
    let Sum = Sum + Checked[i]
end for
check Sum mod 10 = 0
```

Code

```
function Mod10~Compute (Basic is text) is text
    result To~Text (9 – ((Mod10~Sum (Basic) – 1) mod 10))
end Mod10~Compute
```

3.1.1b Mod 10~Verify (receives Checked; *result true-false*)

```
function Mod10~Verify (Checked is text) is true-false
    if Mod10~Sum (Checked) mod 10 = 0 then
        result true
    else
        result false
    end if
end Mod10~Verify
```

Local **Mod10~Sum** (receives String; *result integer*)

```
function Mod10~Sum (String is text) is integer
    variable Sum is integer
    let Sum = 0
    for i = first to last (String)
        let Sum = Sum + byte (String, i) – '0'
    end for
    result Sum
end Mod10~Sum
```

3.1.2a ISBN~Compute (receives Basic; *result text*)

Pseudo Code

```
let Sum = 0
for i = 1 to length of Checked
    let Sum = Sum + Checked[first character position + i – 1] *
            (length [Checked] – i + 1)
end for
check Sum mod 11 = 0
```

Code

```
function ISBN~Compute (Basic is text) is text
    variable Digit is integer
    let Digit = 10 – ((ISBN~Sum (Basic) – 1) mod 11)
    if Digit = 10 then
        result "X"
    else
        result To~Text (Digit)
    end if
end ISBN~Compute
```

3.1.2b ISBN~Verify (receives Checked; *result true-false*)

```
function ISBN~Verify (Checked is text) is true-false
    variables Digit, Sum are integers
    variable Check is text
```

```
        let Check = Checked
        call shorten (Check)
        let Sum = ISBN~Sum (Check)
        let Digit = byte (Checked, last (Checked))
        if Digit = 'X' then
            let Sum = Sum + 10
        else
            let Sum = Sum + Digit – '0'
        end if
        if Sum mod 11 = 0 then
            result true
        else
            result false
        end if
    end ISBN~Verify
```

Local **ISBN~Sum** (receives String; *result integer*)

```
    function ISBN~Sum (String is text) is integer
        variables Digit, Sum are integers
        let Sum = 0
        for i = 1 to length (String)
            let Digit = byte (String, first + i – 1) – '0'
            let Sum = Sum + Digit * (length (String) – i + 2)
        end for
        result Sum
    end ISBN~Sum
```

3.1.3a IBM~Compute (receives Basic; *result text*)

Pseudo Code

```
    let Sum = 0
    for i = first digit of Checked to last digit of Checked
        if i mod 2 = first then
            let Sum = Sum + ((i-th digit * 2) mod 10) + ((i-th digit * 2) ÷ 10)
        else
            let Sum = Sum + i-th digit
        end if
    end for
    check Sum mod 10 = 0
```

Code

```
    function IBM~Compute (Basic is text) is text
        variable Digit is integer
        let Digit = 9 – ((IBM~Sum (Basic) – 1) mod 10)
        if length (Basic) mod 2 = 0 then
            let Digit = (Digit ÷ 2) + ((Digit mod 2) * 5)
        end if
```

```
    result To~Text (Digit)
end IBM~Compute
```

3.1.3b IBM~Verify (receives Checked; *result true-false*)

```
function IBM~Verify (Checked is text) is true-false
    if IBM~Sum (Checked) mod 10 = 0 then
        result true
    else
        result false
    end if
end IBM~Verify
```

Local **IBM~Sum** (receives String; *result integer*)

```
function IBM~Sum (String is text) is integer
    variables Digit, Sum are integers
    let Sum = 0
    for i = first to last (String)
        let Digit = byte (String, i) – '0'
        if i mod = first then
            let Sum = Sum + ((Digit * 2) mod 10) + ((Digit * 2) ÷ 10)
        else
            let Sum = Sum + Digit
        end if
    end for
    result Sum
end IBM~Sum
```

3.1.4a Bank~Compute (receives Basic; *result text*)

Pseudo Code

```
let Sum = 0
for i = 1 to length of Checked
    if i mod 3 = 1 then
        let Sum = Sum + (3 * i-th character of Checked)
    else-if i mod 3 = 2
        let Sum = Sum + (7 * i-th character of Checked)
    else
        let Sum = Sum + i-th character of Checked
    end if
end for
check Sum mod 10 = 0
```

Code

```
function Bank~Compute (Basic is text) is text
    variable Digit is integer
    check (length (Basic) + 1) mod 3 = 0
    let Digit = 9 – ((Bank~Sum (Basic) – 1) mod 10)
    result To~Text (Digit)
end Bank~Compute
```

3.1.4b Bank~Verify (receives Checked; *result true-false*)

```
function Bank~Verify (Checked is text) is true-false
    check length (Checked) mod 3 = 0
    if Bank~Sum (Checked) mod 10 = 0 then
        result true
    else
        result false
    end if
end Bank~Verify
```

Local **Bank~Sum** (receives String; *result integer*)

```
function Bank~Sum (String is text) is integer
    variable Sum is integer
    let Sum = 0
    for i = 1 to length (String)
        if i mod 3 = 1 then
            let Sum = Sum + ((byte (String, first + i – 1) – '0') * 3)
        else-if i mod 3 = 2 then
            let Sum = Sum + ((byte (String, first + i – 1) – '0') * 7)
        else
            let Sum = Sum + byte (String, first + i – 1) – '0'
        end if
    end for
    result Sum
end Bank~Sum
```

3.1.5a Dihedral~Compute (receives Basic; *result text*)

Pseudo Code

```
let Digit = last character of Checked
for i = first character of Checked to last character of Checked – 1
    let Digit = Digit "multiplied" by Checked[i]-th digit from i-th permutation
end for
check Digit = 0
```

Code

```
function Dihedral~Compute (Basic is text) is text
    variables Digit, K1, K2 are integers
    let Digit = 0
    for i = 0 to length (Basic) – 1
        let K1 = (length (Basic) – i) mod 10
        let K2 = byte (Basic, first + i) – '0'
        let Digit = G[Digit, F[K1, K2]]
    end for
    result To~Text (F[5, Digit])
end Dihedral~Compute
```

3.1.5b Dihedral~Verify (receives Checked; *result true-false)*

```
function Dihedral~Verify (Checked is text) is true-false
    variables Digit, K1, K2 are integers
    let Digit = 0
    for i = 0 to length (Checked) – 1
        let K1 = (length (Checked) – i – 1) mod 10
        let K2 = byte (Checked, first + i ) – '0'
        let Digit = G[Digit, F[K1, K2]]
    end for
    if Digit = 0 then
        result true
    else
        result false
    end if
end Dihedral~Verify
```

3.1.5c Dihedral~Initialize

Pseudo Code

initialize rows of F as successive permutations of integers 0 to 9
initialize G to contain "multiplication" table for the dihedral group

Code

```
variables F, G are arrays 0 to 9, 0 to 9 of integers
procedure Dihedral~Initialize
    for j = 0 to 9
        let F[0, j] = j
        if j < 5 then                          Set up first two rows of
            let F[1, j] = (5 – j) mod 5        permutations of digits 0 to 9
        else
            let F[1, j] = ((j – 2) mod 5) + 5
        end if
        for i = 0 to 4                         Set up "multiplication" table
            let G[i, j] = ((i + j) mod 5) + ((j ÷ 5) * 5)   for the dihedral group
            let G[i+5, j] = ((i – j + 10) mod 5) –
                    ((j ÷ 5) * 5) + 5
        end for
    end for
    for i = 2 to 9                             Set up last eight rows of
        for j = 0 to 9                         permutations of digits 0 to 9
            let F[i, j] = F[i–1, F[1, j]]
        end for
    end for
end Dihedral~Initialize
```

3.1.6a Mod97~Compute (receives Basic; *result text*)

Pseudo Code

```
let Remainder = Checked mod 97
check Remainder = 0
```

Code

```
function Mod97~Compute (Basic is text) is text
    variables Check, Quotient, Remainder are text
    let Check = Basic
    call append (Check, '0')
    call append (Check, '0')
    call Decimal~Divide (Check, "97", Quotient, Remainder)
    let Check = Decimal~Subtract ("97", Remainder)
    if length (Check) = 1 then
        call append (Check, '0')
        call reverse (Check)
    end if
    result Check
end Mod97~Compute
```

3.1.6b Mod97~Verify (receives Checked; *result true-false*)

```
function Mod97~Verify (Checked is text) is true-false
    variables Quotient, Remainder are text
    call Decimal~Divide (Checked, "97", Quotient, Remainder)
    if Remainder = "0" then
        result true
    else
        result false
    end if
end Mod97~Verify
```

3.1.7a Mod997~Compute (receives Basic; *result text*)

Pseudo Code

```
let Remainder = Checked mod 997
check Remainder = 0
```

Code

```
function Mod997~Compute (Basic is text) is text
    variables Check, Quotient, Remainder are text
    let Check = Basic
    for i = 1 to 3
        call append (Check, '0')
    end for
```

```
        call Decimal~Divide (Check, "997", Quotient, Remainder)
        let Check = Decimal~Subtract ("997", Remainder)
        call reverse (Check)
        loop until length (Check) = 3
            call append (Check, '0')
        end loop
        call reverse (Check)
        result Check
    end Mod997~Compute
```

3.1.7b Mod997~Verify (receives Checked; *result true-false*)

```
    function Mod997~Verify (Checked is text) is true-false
        variables Quotient, Remainder are text
        call Decimal~Divide (Checked, "997", Quotient, Remainder)
        if Remainder = "0" then
            result true
        else
            result false
        end if
    end Mod997~Verify
```

3.1.8a Mod9973~Compute (receives Basic; *result text*)

Pseudo Code

```
    let Remainder = Checked mod 9973
    check Remainder = 0
```

Code

```
    function Mod9973~Compute (Basic is text) is text
        variables Check, Quotient, Remainder are text
        let Check = Basic
        for i = 1 to 4
            call append (Check, '0')
        end for
        call Decimal~Divide (Check, "9973", Quotient, Remainder)
        let Check = Decimal~Subtract ("9973", Remainder)
        call reverse (Check)
        loop until length (Check) = 4
            call append (Check, '0')
        end loop
        call reverse (Check)
        result Check
    end Mod9973~Compute
```

3.1.8b Mod9973~Verify (receives Checked; *result true-false*)

```
function Mod9973~Verify (Checked is text) is true-false
    variables Quotient, Remainder are text
    call Decimal~Divide (Checked, "9973", Quotient, Remainder)
    if Remainder = "0" then
        result true
    else
        result false
    end if
end Mod9973~Verify
```

TEST PROGRAM

Local Names

C Check digit(s)

T Basic number without check digit(s)

Pseudo Code

```
initialize arrays for use by dihedral algorithm
initialize Testring to null string
for i = 1 to 9
    append i to Testring to create a number with i digits
    for each check digit method
        compute check digit(s)
        append check digit(s) to Testring
        check Testring to ensure check is correct
        remove check digit(s) from Testring
    end for
end for
```

Code

```
variable Testring is text
let Testring = ""
call Dihedral~Initialize
for i = 1 to 9
    call append (Testring, i + '0')
    call Checker (Mod10~Compute, Mod10~Verify, Testring)
    call Checker (ISBN~Compute, ISBN~Verify, Testring)
    call Checker (IBM~Compute, IBM~Verify, Testring)
    if (i+1) mod 3 = 0 then
        call Checker (Bank~Compute, Bank~Verify, Testring)
    end if
    call Checker (Dihedral~Compute, Dihedral~Verify, Testring)
    call Checker (Mod97~Compute, Mod97~Verify, Testring)
    call Checker (Mod997~Compute, Mod997~Verify, Testring)
    call Checker (Mod9973~Compute, Mod9973~Verify, Testring)
end for
```

```
Local Checker (receives Compute, Verify; updates Testring)
   procedure Checker (Compute, Verify are functions, Testring is text)
      variable C is text
      let C = Compute (Testring)
      for j = 1 to length (C)
         call append (Testring, byte (C, first + j – 1))
      end for
      check Verify (Testring) = true
      for j = 1 to length (C)
         call shorten (Testring)
      end for
   end Checker
```

3.2 DATE CONVERSION AND EASTER DATE

Converting dates into sequential integers, and vice versa

Examples

Easter Sunday in the year AD 2000 is calculated by:

```
variables Month, Day are integers
call Easter~Sunday (20, 00, Month, Day)
output Month, Day
```

The number of days between September 1, 1990, and March 1, 1991, is calculated by:

```
output Serial~To (19, 91, 3, 1) – Serial~To (19, 90, 9, 1)
```

Subprograms

Two algorithms deal with dates expressed as a number of days from some fixed date in the past. A pair of subprograms for each algorithm, called From and To in each pair, convert year, month, and day from or to a number of days from a given date. In addition, there are algorithms for checking dates, calculating leap years, and finding the date of Easter. The subprograms are:

3.2.1 Leap~Days (receives Century, Year; *result integer*)
3.2.2 Date~Integrity (receives Century, Year, Month, Day; *result true-false*)
3.2.3 Easter~Sunday (receives Century, Year; supplies Month, Day), alternative 1
3.2.4 Easter~Sunday (receives Century, Year; supplies Month, Day), alternative 2
3.2.5 Annual~To (receives Century, Year, Month, Day; *result integer*)
3.2.6 Annual~From (receives Century, Year, DayNumber; supplies Month, Day)
3.2.7 Serial~To (receives Century, Year, Month, Day; *result integer*)
3.2.8 Serial~From (receives Century, Year, DayNumber; supplies Month, Day)

Usage

Astronomers keep their dates in a form called Julian day numbers. A Julian day number is the number of days between the given date and the first day in January 4713 BC. (Julian days as used by astronomers begin at midday instead of midnight.) This idea is used in "serial" day numbers, which consist of the number of days from some agreed date in the past, typically AD 0 or some recent date this century. A great deal of software makes use of serial day numbers, including the ubiquitous spreadsheet programs for personal computers.

You never need to know what a serial day number "means". All programs can be written with dates in the usual form for communicating with the outside world, that is, with year, month, and day. But any internal computations on dates are made much simpler if they are done on serial day numbers rather than on the dates themselves.

It is easy to determine the day of the week for any given date. Just take the value of the serial day number *mod* 7, and you have a weekday number in the range 0 to 6. To accord with ISO Standard 2711 the days of the week should be numbered from 1 to 7 for Monday to Sunday respectively. To achieve this, just add a correction in the range 0–6 to the serial day number, and add one to the result *mod* 7. The correction needs to be chosen so that day 1 falls on a Monday.

The serial day number subprograms Serial~To and Serial~From use a starting date of AD 0. This means that serial day numbers require 6 digits, or about 20 bits of storage. To squeeze a serial day number into a 16-bit word you should start from a different date, for example, the beginning of 1990. Dates occupying just 15 bits are good for a range of nearly ninety years.

For some purposes you will require a date to be expressed as the number of days since the beginning of the current year. For example, the day of the year for January 1 is 1. In a leap year the day of the year for December 31 is 366, and in nonleap years it is 365. The two algorithms provided to manipulate days of the year are Annual~To and Annual~From. These are simpler than Serial~From and Serial~To, although the latter would do the job. The annual algorithms need to know the number of leap days in the year. This is calculated by Leap~Days.

Serial date numbers can be used for many useful purposes. For example, to produce a calendar for any given year: (1) use Serial~To to find the serial day number of January 1 in that year; (2) in a loop, increment the serial day number and convert it to year, month, and day using Serial~From; (3) take the serial day number *mod* 7 to find the day of the week. Another example finds the date for the n-th occurrence of Friday in a given month: (1) convert the first of the month to a serial day number; (2) convert it to the day of the week; (3) find the first occurrence of the day you are seeking; (4) find the n-th occurrence of that day in the month; (5) convert the date back into year, month, and day format, and check that the requested day actually exists. Our final example finds the number of weekdays between now and Christmas: (1) find the total number of days between today and Christmas; (2) divide by seven and multiply by five; (3) find how many of the days in the remainder from the division are weekdays.

Many applications allow dates to be entered by a user. The validity of such dates can be checked by Date~Integrity. Errors such as an incorrect month number (e.g., 13) or an invalid day number (such as 31 in April or 29 in February 1991) are detected.

The first week in any year is defined, by ISO standard 2015, as the week in which the first Thursday of the year falls. Because a week starts with a Monday, by ISO convention the first week of the year has at least four days in it.

The date of Easter Sunday, which occurs on the first full moon on or after March 21, is calculated by a quite complicated formula. There are two procedures for Easter~Sunday, which are used by giving them the year. They return the month and day on which Easter Sunday falls. One of the subprograms (Hill 1965) makes extensive use of the subprogram *divide*, which obtains both the quotient and remainder resulting from a division. You may prefer this version if you are programming in assembly language, or are using a programming language that provides access to both the quotient and remainder. Otherwise, the quotation and remainder must be obtained by two separate division and *mod* operations.

Analysis

We will not analyze in any detail the algorithms for calculating the date of Easter. You should consult Knuth (1968) and O'Beirne (1961) for more information. The other date algorithms are worthy of further consideration because of their importance in practice.

The algorithms should not be used for dates prior to 1583. A major change was made to the calendar system in the year 1582. The Gregorian calendar (named after Pope Gregory) refined the leap year system, which had been gradually making the seasons occur later and later over the centuries. The method of dealing with leap years is different before and after 1582.

Much earlier, Julius Caesar had dealt with a similar problem. In the year AD 46 a total of 80 days were added to the calendar because the number of days in preceding years had been inexact. For several hundred years the absence of leap years had made calendar years too short. In order to prevent further problems Julius Caesar brought in the leap year idea (and standardized on 12 months per year), it being thought that this would keep the calendar in step with the seasons.

In fact, a shade too many years are made leap years by this method. Over the period of nearly sixteen centuries to the time of Pope Gregory the seasons and the calendar became badly out of step again. In 1582 ten days were deleted from the calendar in October. From then on the century years such as 1700, 1800, and 1900 were declared as nonleap years to prevent a recurrence of the problem. Years divisible by 400, such as 1600 and 2000, were retained as leap years so that the astronomically correct length of a year was observed by the calendar. Unfortunately for simplicity of communication in the world at that time, not everyone adopted the Gregorian calendar simultaneously. England, for example, did not fall into line until 1752!

The date algorithms, which are drawn from Tantzen (1963), rely on the Gregorian calendar. To see how they work, think of the length of a year, which is 365.2422 days (Duffet-Smith 1990). The usual assumption is that a year has 365.2425 days, an approximation that is correct to one day in 3,000 years. In practice, you cannot operate with fractional days, and that is the reason for the use of leap days in certain years. The correct number of leap days is determined as follows. A century has 36524.25 days. A quatercentenary (period of 400 years) has 4 times 36524.25, or 146097 days. Now you have an integral number of days to work with. That is why the Gregorian calendar is based on a 400-year cycle.

To achieve a 146097-day quatercentenary in practice, there are three successive centuries with 36524 days, followed by a fourth century with 36525 days. The fourth century has a leap day that the other centuries do not have. The constant 146097 will be seen in the date algorithms.

A century consisting of 36525 days is easy to work with. Each year has, on average, 365.25 days. This is implemented by three successive years of 365 days, and 366 days in the fourth year. A period of four years has 3 × 365 plus 366, or 1461 days. The constant 1461 is also used in the date algorithms. What about the centuries that have only 36524 days? These are catered for by dropping the leap day in the century years themselves.

Unfortunately, there is the nasty complication that leap days are traditionally added at the end of February rather than at the end of a calendar year. In order to accommodate this requirement it is convenient for the bulk of the algorithms to assume that years start on March 1 rather than January 1. Leap days are then added at the end of these modified "years". Adjustments are made at the beginning or end of the calculations to ensure that the correct traditional month numberings are used in interaction with the user.

The number of days in each month form an awkward sequence. Starting from March, the numbers of days in the first eleven months are 31, 30, 31, 30, 31, 31, 30, 31, 30, 31, 31. The cumulative number of days preceding each month is 0, 31, 61, 92, 122, 153, 184, 214, 245, 275, 306, 337. There is a pattern that repeats itself every five months. The total number of days in the five-month sequence is 153 and so the average is 153/5 or 30.6. The cumulative number of days in the year up to a given month number can be calculated using this fact. The expression (Month * 153 + 2) ÷ 5 does the job, generating the increasing sequence of day numbers. (The +2 is needed to ensure that the integer division truncates to the correct number of days.) A modification of this relation was used by Stone (1970) in his algorithms for serial date numbers within a given year, upon which Annual~From and Annual~To are based. He used the closer approximation 30.55, instead of 30.6, as the average number of days per month, but the results are similar.

IMPLEMENTATION

Exported Names

Annual~From	Converts a day number to month and day within the year (3.2.6)
Annual~To	Converts a date to a day number within the year (3.2.5)
Date~Integrity	Checks validity of a date (3.2.2)
Easter~Sunday	Calculates the date of Easter Sunday in a given year (3.2.3, 3.2.4)
Leap~Days	Computes number of leap days in a year (3.2.1)
Serial~From	Converts a serial day number to a date (3.2.8)
Serial~To	Converts a date to a serial day number (3.2.7)

Nicknames

Century	Integer century number ≥ AD 0
Day	Integer day number within a month
DayNumber	Sequential day number
Month	Integer month number within a year
Year	Integer year number > AD 0

Local Names

C	Century
D	Day
Epact	Date on which full moon occurs
Fours	Number of quatercentenaries or quadrennia
Golden	Golden number of the year in the 19-year Metonic cycle
M	Month

NonLeap	Number of nonleap centuries in this quatercentenary
Q, R	Quotient and remainder of integer division
Sunday	March date ((–Sunday) *mod* 7) is a Sunday
Synch	Correction to synchronize Easter with moon's orbit
Y	Year

3.2.1 Leap~Days (receives Century, Year; *result integer*)

Pseudo Code

result is 0 if Century/Year is not divisible by 400 or Year is not divisible by 4
otherwise result is 1

Code

```
function Leap~Days (Century, Year are integers) is integer
    if (Year = 0) and (Century mod 4 ≠ 0) then
        result 0
    else-if (Year mod 4 = 0) then
        result 1
    else
        result 0
    end if
end Leap~Days
```

3.2.2 Date~Integrity (receives Century, Year, Month, Day; *result true-false*)

Pseudo Code

result is *true* if Day and Month are permissible for given Century and Year,
otherwise *false*

Code

```
function Date~Integrity (Century, Year, Month, Day are integers) is true-false
    constant Days is array 1 to 12 of integers = 31, 29, 31, 30, 31, 30, 31, 31, 30,
            31, 30, 31
    if Month < 1 or Month > 12 then
        result false
    else-if Day > Days[Month] then
        result false
    else-if Month = 2 and Day > (28 + Leap~Days (Century, Year)) then
        result false
    else
        result true
    end if
end Date~Integrity
```

3.2.3 Easter~Sunday (receives Century, Year; supplies Month, Day)

Pseudo Code (Alternative 1)

let Golden = golden number for Century and Year
let NonLeap = number of nonleap centuries
let Synch = correction to synchronize Easter with moon's orbit

```
let Epact = result of formula applied to Golden, Century, NonLeap, and Synch
let Epact = result of formula that finds first appropriate full moon
let Sunday = correction to ensure Easter is on a Sunday
let Month, Day = first Sunday following full moon that occurs on or after March 21
```

Code (Alternative 1)

```
procedure Easter~Sunday (Century, Year, Month, Day are integers)
    variables Golden, NonLeap, Synch, Sunday, Epact, Y are integers
    let Y = (Century * 100) + Year
    let Golden = (Y mod 19) + 1
    let NonLeap = ((Century * 3 + 3) ÷ 4) – 12
    let Synch = (((Century * 8) + 13) ÷ 25) – 5
    let Epact = ((Golden * 11) + (Century * 30) + Synch – NonLeap + 20) mod 30
    if (Epact = 25 and Golden > 11) or Epact = 24 then
        let Epact = Epact + 1
    end if
    let Epact = 44 – Epact
    if Epact < 21 then
        let Epact = Epact + 30
    end if
    let Sunday = ((Y * 5) ÷ 4) – NonLeap – 10
    let Day = Epact – ((Sunday + Epact) mod 7) + 7
    let Month = 3
    if Day > 31 then
        let Day = Day – 31
        let Month = 4
    end if
end Easter~Sunday
```

3.2.4 **Easter~Sunday** (receives Century, Year; supplies Month, Day)

Pseudo Code (Alternative 2)

```
let Golden = golden number for Century and Year
let Fours = number of quatercentenaries since AD 0
let NonLeap = number of nonleap centuries in current quatercentenary
let Synch = correction to synchronize Easter with moon's orbit
let Epact = result of formula applied to Golden, Century, Fours, and Synch
let Fours = number of quadrennia to date in current century
let Day = Epact + result of formula to align Epact and Sunday
let Month, Day = first Sunday following full moon that occurs on or after March 21
```

Code (Alternative 2)

```
procedure Easter~Sunday (Century, Year, Month, Day are integers)
    variables C, Fours, Golden, M, NonLeap, Synch, Epact, Y are integers
    let Y = (Century * 100) + Year
    call divide (Y, 19, C, Golden)
    call divide (Century, 4, Fours, NonLeap)
    let Synch = ((8 * Century) + 13) ÷ 25
```

```
        let Day = (19 * Golden) + Century – Fours + 15 – Synch
        call divide (Day, 30, Month, Epact)
        call divide (Year, 4, Fours, Y)
        let Month = (2 * (NonLeap + Fours)) – Epact – Y + 32
        call divide (Month, 7, Month, Day)
        let Day = Epact + Day – (7 * ((Golden + (11 * Epact) + (19 * Day)) ÷ 433))
        let Month = (Day + 90) ÷ 25
        let Day = Day + (33 * Month) + 19
        call divide (Day, 32, M, Day)
    end Easter~Sunday
```

3.2.5 Annual~To (receives Century, Year, Month, Day; *result integer*)

Pseudo Code

```
    let D = number of days preceding current day, assuming February has 30 days
    if Month is in the range March to December then
        let D = D minus the number of days between the last day in February and
                March 1
    end if
    result is D
```

Code

```
    function Annual~To (Century, Year, Month, Day are integers) is integer
        variable D is integer
        let D = Day + ((3055 * (Month + 2)) ÷ 100) – 91
        if Month > 2 then
            let D = D + Leap~Days (Century, Year) – 2
        end if
        result D
    end Annual~To
```

3.2.6 Annual~From (receives Century, Year, DayNumber; supplies Month, Day)

Pseudo Code

```
    let Day = DayNumber
    if Day puts the date in the range March to December then
        let Day = Day plus the number of days between the last day in February and
                March 1
    end if
    let Month = number in the range 3 to 14, determined by a linear equation
    let Day = number of days following the end of Month
    let Month = Month – 2
```

Code

```
    procedure Annual~From (Century, Year, Month, Day, DayNumber are integers)
        let Day = DayNumber
```

```
        if Day > (59 + Leap~Days (Century, Year)) then
            let Day = Day – Leap~Days (Century, Year) + 2
        end if
        let Month = ((Day + 91) * 100) ÷ 3055
        let Day = Day – ((Month * 3055) ÷ 100) + 91
        let Month = Month – 2
    end Annual~From
```

3.2.7 Serial~To (receives Century, Year, Month, Day; *result integer*)

Pseudo Code

adjust Year and Month to start years at March 1 instead of January 1
let D = number of days in complete centuries from AD 0 to Year
let D = D + number of days in complete years in current Century
let D = D + number of days in complete months in current Year
result is D + number of days in current Month up to Day

Code

```
function Serial~To (Century, Year, Month, Day are integers) is integer
    variables C, D, M, Y are integers
    call divide (Month + 9, 12, Y, M)
    let Y = Y + (Century * 100) + Year – 1
    call divide (Y, 100, C, Y)
    let D = (C * 146097) ÷ 4
    let D = D + ((Y * 1461) ÷ 4)
    let D = D + (((M * 153) + 2) ÷ 5)
    result D + Day
end Serial~To
```

3.2.8 Serial~From (receives Century, Year, DayNumber; supplies Month, Day)

Pseudo Code

let Century = number of complete centuries of 146097/4 days up to DayNumber
let Day = number of days in current incomplete Century up to DayNumber
let Year = number of complete years of 1461/4 days in Day days
let Day = number of days in current incomplete Year up to DayNumber
let Month = number of complete months of 153/5 days up to DayNumber
adjust Year and Month to start years at January 1 instead of March 1

Code

```
procedure Serial~From (Century, Year, Month, Day, DayNumber are integers)
    variable Y is integer
    let Day = (DayNumber * 4) – 1
    call divide (Day, 146097, Century, Day)
    let Day = ((Day ÷ 4) * 4) + 3
    call divide (Day, 1461, Year, Day)
```

```
        let Day = (Day ÷ 4) * 5 + 2
        call divide (Day, 153, Month, Day)
        let Day = (Day ÷ 5) + 1
        let Month = Month + 2
        call divide (Month, 12, Y, Month)
        let Year = Year + Y
        let Century = Century + (Year ÷ 100)
        let Year = Year mod 10
        let Month = Month + 1
    end Serial~From
```

TEST PROGRAM

Local Names

CC	Century
DD	Day
ED	Days of months in which Easter falls, 1976–1990
EM	Months in which Easter falls, 1976–1990
MM	Month
YY	Year

Pseudo Code

```
    initialize starting date CCYYMMDD to January 1, 1800
    for i = 1 to 10
        for j = 1 to number of days in year CCYY
            convert day j to a day number within the year
            convert day number within the year back to a date
            check the calculated date is correctly represented in the form CCYYMMDD
            convert day j to a serial day number
            convert serial day number plus 1 back to a date
        end for
        check date has advanced to January 1 in the year CCYY + 1
        advance CCYY to next multiple of 50 years
    end for
    for i = 1 to 15
        calculate and check date of Easter Sunday for year 1975 + i
    end for
```

Code

```
    variables CC, YY, MM, DD are integers
    constant ED is array 1 to 15 of integers = 18, 10, 26, 15, 6, 19, 11, 3, 22, 7, 30, 19,
            3, 26, 15
    constant EM is array 1 to 15 of integers = 4, 4, 3, 4, 4, 4, 4, 4, 4, 4, 3, 4, 4, 3, 4
    let CC = 18                                      Check date conversion algorithms
    let YY = 0
    let MM = 1
    let DD = 1
```

```
for i = 1 to 10
    for j = 1 to (365 + Leap~Days (CC, YY))
        call Annual~From (CC, YY, MM, DD, Annual~To (CC, YY, MM, DD))
        check Date~Integrity (CC, YY, MM, DD) = true
        call Serial~From (CC, YY, MM, DD, Serial~To (CC, YY, MM, DD) + 1)
    end for
    check (YY mod 50) = 1 and MM = 1 and DD = 1
    let YY = (CC * 100) + YY + 49
    call divide (YY, 100, CC, YY)
end for
for i = 1 to 15                              Check several known dates of
    call Easter~Sunday (19, 75 + i, MM, DD)  Easter
    check MM = EM[i] and DD = ED[i]
end for
```

3.3 ROMAN NUMERALS

Converting between Roman and Arabic numerals

Example

The conversion of 1991 to Roman numerals, mcmxci, is carried out by:

output Roman~To (1991)

Subprograms

3.3.1 Roman~From (receives *text* RomanNumerals; *result integer*)
3.3.2 Roman~To (receives *integer* NumericInteger; *result text*)

Usage

Both subprograms are implemented as functions. One form of an integer is supplied and the other form is returned as the result. Note that Roman~From accepts valid variants such as iiii, although Roman~To converts 4 to iv. The convention has been used that Roman numbers less than 5,000 are specified in lowercase. Uppercase is used for numbers in the thousands or millions. (Strictly speaking, the former should be specified in capital letters and the latter in capital letters with a bar over the top.) So, for example, 1991 is represented here by mcmxci and 1991000 by MCMXCm.

The test program checks several ranges of numbers automatically. It converts an Arabic number into Roman form, and then converts it back to Arabic. The program checks that the original number is reproduced.

Analysis

The trickiest part of the Roman numerals algorithms involves the subtractive convention. Normally, numerals are additive. When one reads a Roman number from left to right, the numerals are usually in sequence of descending values. The value of the number is obtained by summing the values of the numerals in this descending sequence.

However, the strictly descending sequence is modified for some numbers. A numeral of lower value placed before a numeral of higher value subtracts rather than adds. For example, "vi" represents 5 + 1, but "iv" represents –1 + 5. The programming logic has a look-ahead feature because, for example, the value of "x" in a number such as "mxc" cannot be determined until the "c" has been recognized.

The Roman numerals in ascending sequence "ivxlcdmVXLCDM" have values that are alternately powers of ten and five times a power of ten. The logic of the algorithms relies on this alternating sequence, processing in one way for powers of ten and in another way for five times a power of ten.

Implementation

<u>Exported Names</u>

Roman~From	Converts Roman numerals to Arabic integers (3.3.1)
Roman~To	Converts Arabic integers to Roman numerals (3.3.2)

<u>Nicknames</u>

NumericInteger	Arabic integer to be converted to Roman numerals
RomanNumerals	Roman numerals to be converted to Arabic integer

<u>Local Names</u>

Character	One letter from Roman numerals
Letters	Roman numerals, supplied or to be computed
Number	Arabic number, supplied or to be computed
Numeral	Array of values of Roman letters corresponding to Symbol array
PreviousType	Type for preceding character in Roman numerals
PreviousValue	Value for preceding character in Roman numerals
Symbol	Array of symbols used in Roman numerals (leading space)
Type	Integer = 0 if value is a power of 10, otherwise = 1
Value	Integer value of current symbol in Character
Which	Integer to select values from arrays Numeral and Symbol

Code

constant Numeral *is array* 1 *to* 14 *of integers* = 0, 1, 5, 10, 50, 100, 500, 1000, 5000, 10000, 50000, 100000, 500000, 1000000
constant Symbol *is text* = " ivxlcdmVXLCDM"
variables Character, Number, PreviousType, PreviousValue, Type, Value, Which *are integers*
variable Letters *is text*

3.3.1 Roman~From (receives integer RomanNumerals; *result integer*)

Pseudo Code

initialize Roman numerals with a blank space at the end
let Number = 0
loop until last character of Roman numerals has been processed
  let Character = next character from Roman numerals
  let Value = numeric value of Character
  let Type = 0 or 1, for Value being one or five times a power of ten respectively

```
        if Type of preceding character = 0 and Value > value of preceding character
            let Number = Number – value of preceding character
        else
            let Number = Number + value of preceding character
        end if
        save Value and Type for next iteration of loop
    end loop
    result is Number
```

Code

```
function Roman~From (RomanNumerals is text) is integer
    let Letters = RomanNumerals
    call append (Letters, ' ')                     Add a space at the end to simplify
    let Number = 0                                 algorithm
    let PreviousValue = 0
    let PreviousType = –1
    for i = first to last (Letters)
        let Character = byte (Letters, i)          Get next letter from Roman
        let Value = 0                              numerals text string
        for j = 1 to 14
            if Character = byte (Symbol, j) then   Convert Roman letter to an
                let Type = j mod 2                 integer value and get its
                let Value = Numeral[j]             "type" (0 or 1)
            end if
        end for
        if PreviousType = 0 and Value >            Accumulate numeric value of
                PreviousValue then                 entire string in Number, and
            check Value ≤ 10 * PreviousValue       check syntax
            let Number = Number –
                    PreviousValue
        else
            check PreviousType < 0 or Value ≤ PreviousValue
            let Number = Number + PreviousValue
        end if
        let PreviousValue = Value                  Save type and value of
        let PreviousType = Type                    current letter
    end for
    result Number
end Roman~From
```

3.3.2 Roman~To (receives NumericInteger; *result text*)

Pseudo Code

```
let Number = Arabic integer to be converted to Roman numerals
initialize Letters to null string
```

```
for decreasing i = 7 to 1
    let Which = i * 2, selecting one of the seven possible powers of ten in decreasing
            magnitude
    let Value = number of times current power of ten has to be output
    let Number = remainder of Number after current power of ten has been
            processed
    if Value = 4 or 9 then
        append current subtractive symbol to Letters
    end if
    if Value = 9 then
        append the symbol for the next higher power of ten to Letters
    else
        if Value = 4, 5, 6, 7, or 8 then
            append symbol for five times the current power of ten to Letters
            let Value = Value – 5
        end if
        append Value copies of the symbol for the current power of ten to Letters
    end if
end for
result is Letters
```

Code

```
function Roman~To (NumericInteger is integer) is text
    let Number = NumericInteger
    let Letters = ""
    for decreasing i = 7 to 1                     There are seven different
        let Which = i * 2                         Roman letters, ivxlcdm
        let Value = Number ÷ Numeral[Which]
        let Number = Number mod Numeral[Which]
        if Value = 4 or Value = 9 then            Subtractive method if digit is
            call append (Letters, byte (Symbol,   4 or 9
                    first + Which – 1))
        end if
        if Value = 9 then
            check i < 7                           Can't represent numbers
            call append (Letters, byte (Symbol,   larger than 3,999,999
                    first + Which + 1))
        else
            if Value > 3 then
                check i < 7                       Can't represent numbers
                call append (Letters, byte        larger than 3,999,999
                        (Symbol, first + Which))
                let Value = Value – 5
            end if
            for j = 1 to Value                    Concatenate digits of number
                call append (Letters, byte
                        (Symbol, first + Which – 1))
            end for
```

```
        end if
    end for
    result Letters
end Roman~To
```

TEST PROGRAM

Pseudo Code

```
for i = 1 to 100
    convert i to Roman numerals and back again, checking that the result is i
    convert i * 111 to Roman numerals and back again, checking that the result is
            i * 111
    convert i * 11111 to Roman numerals and back again, checking that the result is
            i * 11111
end for
```

Code

```
for i = 1 to 100
    check Roman~From (Roman~To (i)) = i
    check Roman~From (Roman~To (i * 111)) = i * 111
    check Roman~From (Roman~To (i * 11111)) = i * 11111
end for
```

4 Permutations and Combinations

If there is one thing that computers are really good at, it is repetitive computation. They are well suited to doing the same job over and over, with only slight changes in the data. Many problems need a brute force approach to solve them. A typical requirement is to try all possible combinations of some factors, to see which combination comes up with the right answer. The algorithms in this chapter deal with various forms of combinatorial processing.

Section 4.1 provides some simple formulas for determining the number of permutations and combinations applicable to certain kinds of problems. Section 4.2 shows how to program a nest of loops within loops, the depth of which is determined at run time. A key application is in the processing of multidimensional tables. Section 4.3 shows how to summarize a table of figures by means of a grand total, subtotals, sub-subtotals, and so on to any depth of subtotaling. Section 4.4 provides subprograms for generating all possible permutations of a set of "tokens". Section 4.5 deals with generating all possible combinations of a subset of tokens drawn from a set.

Many puzzles are good examples of problems involving permutations and combinations. For example, in how many different ways can triplet sisters in one family be married to triplet brothers in another? The answer is calculated by a formula given in Section 4.1, Products~Factorial (3). How many possible doubles pairings are there in a five-person tennis squad? The answer is Products~Combinations (5, 2).

A two-dimensional table can have row and column totals, and a grand total. A three-dimensional table has row, column, and layer totals, and a grand total. It also has three other one-dimensional arrays of subtotals. For example, the two-dimensional tables for each layer have a grand total, as do the two-dimensional tables for each row and for each column. There is an array of subtotals corresponding to the grand totals of all possible combinations of two-dimensional tables that can be formed. When there are more dimensions, there are more complex sets of totals. The notes provided in Section 4.2 describe a simple method of calculating all possible totals for tables that have any number of dimensions. This requires a systematic approach for generating all possible subscripts for a multidimensional array in a set of nested loops.

An alternative problem arises frequently in accounting and stock control applications, where transactions are identified with stock codes or account codes. A common requirement is to process a sorted file of data, developing sub-subtotals for codes that have a close relationship with each other, then producing subtotals of the sub-subtotals to group the codes under some major headings, and finally obtaining a grand total. In large applications there may be more levels of nesting of the totals and subtotals. The difference between this requirement and the development of multidimensional tables is as follows. Section 4.2 deals with multidimensional tables that have one entry per cell. The nested totals algorithm in Section 4.3 processes data with any number of entries for a given code, and with many possible codes never used at all. Because of this key difference, the latter operates on files of data rather than on tables.

One important algorithm for finding an optimum among competing alternatives is the method of linear programming, which is discussed in Section 11.3. The method starts with any feasible solution and then systematically improves it where any improvement is possible. This avoids having to consider all possible combinations of options. In many kinds of scheduling and allocation problems, such systematic improvement cannot be done because the problem cannot be expressed in a form to which linear programming, or related algorithms, can be applied. In such circumstances the only way in which to determine the optimum result is to examine all possible options. Methods for systematically generating permutations and combinations of options are given in Sections 4.4 and 4.5.

With the exception of the nested totals algorithm, the combinatorial methods in this section arc useful for small problems only. As the number of factors increases the computer time required grows at an exponential rate. Nevertheless, the methods have been used on some very practical problems, and every programmer needs to understand how to deal with permutations and combinations in a systematic way.

NOTES—BACKTRACKING

Making brute force combinatorial searching more efficient

A method called "backtracking" may be used for solving combinatorial problems. The backtracking method does not lend itself to providing an algorithm, because the details of backtracking are usually problem-dependent. The key idea in backtracking is to skip permutations if it becomes clear that the partial solution developed so far cannot possibly be the basis for an optimum solution. It will be convenient to illustrate the concept with a specific example.

Suppose you are trying to solve a particular puzzle using backtracking. You are asked whether it is possible to find N digits in the range 0 to 9 that total N^2 and whose squares total N^3. You observe that any sequence of N digits, each of which is N, has this property, for example, 22, 333, 4444. Are there any others? A recursive backtracking solution to the problem is as follows:

```
variables D, T, S are arrays 0 to 9 of integers
procedure Backtrack (N, M are integers)
    if N = M then
        if T[N] = M * M and S[N] = M * M * M then
            call Found (D, M)
        end if
    else-if T[N] < M * M and S[N] < M * M * M then
        for i = 0 to 9
            let D[N+1] = i
            let T[N+1] = T[N] + i
            let S[N+1] = S[N] + i * i
            call Backtrack (N+1, M)
        end for
    end if
end Backtrack
for i = 0 to 9
    let T[0] = 0
    let S[0] = 0
    call Backtrack (0, i)
end for
```

The first part of the Backtrack procedure checks to see whether a solution has been found, and if so, calls the procedure Found with the array of digits D. If not, the *else-if* checks whether the cumulative totals of the digits and their squares already exceed their target. If either does so, there is no point in adding further digits to the sequence, and the procedure backtracks by exiting. If neither target has been exceeded, the loop tries every digit from 1 to 9 appended to the current digit string. For this particular problem backtracking is more efficient than trying every possible combination, but there is still a very large number of combinations that must be investigated.

4.1 PRODUCTS

Computing the values of formulas related to the factorial

Example

The number of possible combinations of eight things taken three at time can be computed and displayed by:

output Products~Combinations (8, 3)

Subprograms

4.1.1 Products~Factorial (receives N; *result real*)
4.1.2 Products~Log~Factorial (receives N; *result real*)
4.1.3 Products~Permutations (receives N, K; *result real*)
4.1.4 Products~Combinations (receives N, K; *result real*)

Usage

The number of possible permutations of N objects is given by N * (N – 1) * ... * 2 * 1. This product of all integers less than or equal to a given integer N is called the factorial of the number, usually written as N!. The factorial of a given number is computed by the subprogram Products~Factorial. Caution is required in computing with factorials, because the value of N! increases exponentially as N increases in size. The value of 70! is greater than Googol (10^{100}).

If you need to do computations with factorials, it may be safer to use logarithms to avoid numerical overflow errors. The natural logarithm of N!, obtained by Products~Log~Factorial, is approximated by a formula developed by the English mathematician James Stirling (Knuth 1968).

The number of ways in which combinations of K things can be selected from N is given by Products~Combinations. If one wishes to consider the permutations of every combination as distinct, their number can be computed by Products~Permutations. These two functions won't list out all the possible permutations or combinations. They just tell you how many are possible. Use the procedures in Sections 4.4 and 4.5 to get all the variations listed in sequence.

Analysis

The approximation used by Products~Log~Factorial is reasonably accurate even for small values of N, although its accuracy is greater with larger values of N. This is easy to check using Similarity~Bits, as the test program demonstrates. It checks that the accuracy of the computed value of $\log_e$ (N!) has at least (N * 2) + 6 bits of accuracy. This linear relationship is a rough one that applies for small values of N. Thus, even the logarithm of a factorial as small as 1! is computed to three decimal digits of accuracy.

Only the simplest of product formulas have been given here, the ones most widely used in practice. There are hundreds of others for calculating numbers that are useful to a select few people. For example, engineers use a whole range of Bessel numbers, statisticians use gamma, beta, and hypergeometric numbers, mathematicians studying algorithms use harmonic numbers and Stirling numbers, to name just a few. There are Chebychev numbers, Hermite numbers, Laguerre numbers, Legendre numbers, Riccati–Bessel numbers, Neumann numbers, and Hankel numbers, to name some more.

Most professional and hobby programmers will never need to calculate these numbers, and so we have exercised a writer's privilege to leave them out of this book. If there is a demand for some of them, they will be included in the next edition.

IMPLEMENTATION

Exported Names

Products~Combinations	Computes number of combinations of K things out of N (4.1.4)
Products~Factorial	Calculates factorial of an integer N (4.1.1)
Products~Log~Factorial	Calculates an approximation to $\log_e$ (N!) (4.1.2)
Products~Permutations	Computes number of permutations of K things out of N (4.1.3)

<u>Nicknames</u>

N	Size of the set under consideration
K	Size of the set selected from the set of N

<u>Local Names</u>

Product	Progressive intermediate value of product being calculated

4.1.1 Products~Factorial (receives N; *result real*)

Pseudo Code

```
initialize Product to 1
for i = 2 to N
    let Product = previous value of Product multiplied by current value of i
end for
result is Product
```

Code

```
function Products~Factorial (N is integer) is real
    variable Product is real
    check N ≥ 0
    let Product = 1
    for i = 2 to N
        let Product = Product * i
    end for
    result Product
end Products~Factorial
```

4.1.2 Products~Log~Factorial (receives N; *result real*)

Code

```
function Products~Log~Factorial (N is integer) is real
    variable Product is real
    check N > 0
    let Product = 139 + (571 / (48 * N))
    let Product = 1 – (Product / (180 * N))
    let Product = 1 + (Product / (24 * N))
    let Product = 1 + (Product / (12 * N))
    result ((N + 0.5) * log_e (N)) – N + (0.5 * log_e (2 * pi)) + log_e (Product)
end Products~Log~Factorial
```

4.1.3 Products~Permutations (receives N, K; *result real*)

Pseudo Code

```
initialize Product to 1
for i = 0 to (K – 1)
    let Product = previous value of Product multiplied by current value of N – i
end for
result is Product
```

Code

```
function Products~Permutations (N, K are integers) is real
    variable Product is real
    check N ≥ 0 and K ≥ 0 and N ≥ K
    let Product = 1
    for i = 0 to (K – 1)
        let Product = Product * (N – i)
    end for
    result Product
end Products~Permutations
```

4.1.4 Products~Combinations (receives N, K; *result real*)

Pseudo Code

```
initialize Product to 1
for i = 0 to (K – 1)
    let Product = previous value of Product multiplied by value of (N – i) divided by
            (K – i)
end for
result is Product
```

Code

```
function Products~Combinations (N, K are integers) is real
    variable Product is real
    check N ≥ 0 and K ≥ 0 and N ≥ K
    let Product = 1
    for i = 0 to (K – 1)
        let Product = Product * (N – i) / (K – i)
    end for
    result Product
end Products~Combinations
```

TEST PROGRAM

Imported Names	
Similarity~Bits	Number of digits in common in two numbers (2.1.1)
Similarity~Test	Test of the similarity of two numbers (2.1.2)
Local Names	
C	Number of combinations
P	Number of permutations
R	Ratio, or logarithm of the ratio, of quantities to be compared

Pseudo Code

```
for n = 1 to 10
    for k = 1 to n
        let R = ratio of two different ways of calculating combinations of k things
                from n
```

```
        check ratio R is approximately equal to 1
        let R = difference of logarithms of two calculations of combinations of k
                things from n
        check difference R is approximately equal to 0
    end for
end for
```

Code

```
variables P, C, R are numbers
for n = 1 to 10
    for k = 1 to n
        let P = Products~Permutations (n, k)
        let C = Products~Combinations (n, k)
        let R = Products~Factorial (k) * C / P
        check Similarity~Test (R, 1, 1) = true
        let R = Products~Log~Factorial (k) + log_e (C) – log_e (P)
        check Similarity~Bits (R, 0, 1) > (k * 2) + 6
    end for
end for
```

NOTES—RECURSION

Knowing when to avoid recursive programming

The procedure Products~Factorial computes a basic function frequently discussed in computer science courses to illustrate simple recursion. We discuss it further to introduce some cautions about recursion. For those who have not heard of the term, a recursive function is one that calls itself within the code describing the function. This mind-bending concept might need a little more explanation. It's easy to write Factorial mathematically in a form that defines N! in terms of (N – 1)!:

$$0! = 1$$
$$N! = (N - 1)! * N, \text{ for } N > 0$$

There are two parts to this recursive definition: what to do when N is zero, and what to do when N is greater than zero. Programming languages that permit recursion typically don't allow you to write it in this form. Both parts of the definition have to be in one block of code as follows:

```
function Factorial (N is integer) is real
    check N ≥ 0
    if N = 0 then
        result 1
    else
        result N * Factorial (N – 1)
    end if
end Factorial
```

Note that within the Factorial subprogram, Factorial itself is used to find the factorial of (N – 1). This step is performed repeatedly on successively smaller values until 0 is reached. Recursive functions like this one call themselves in the middle, before each computation is complete. It is important that the programmer understand what goes on behind the scenes in recursive algorithms. In order to implement recursion, the computer has to build up a sequence of partly complete results and then put them all together at the end, in this case when the factorial of 0 has been computed. The housekeeping for this takes time and space.

Recursion is often used to simplify the presentation of algorithms (e.g., Gonnet and Baeza-Yates 1991). Implementors of algorithms generally try to remove recursion and to replace it by iteration. Recursion is usually inefficient, and there is always the danger of the implicit stack of intermediate results overflowing in the depths of the computation. From the point of view of style, the iterative version loses some of the mathematical elegance of recursion. In addition, storage for intermediate results may have to be provided explicitly, for example, by means of a stack or an array. However, iterative representations of algorithms are not always more complicated. The iterative version of Factorial needs a temporary storage location, but is otherwise straightforward:

```
function Factorial (constant N is integer) is real
    variable Product is real
    check N ≥ 0
    let Product = 1
    for i = 2 to N
        let Product = Product * i
    end for
    result Product
end Factorial
```

Languages such as Basic, Fortran, and Cobol don't permit recursive programming, and require that iterative algorithms be employed exclusively. The conversion of recursive algorithms to an iterative form is not always easy. For those interested in the topic Sedgewick (1988) provides some guidelines on how to perform the conversion. We avoid expressing algorithms recursively in this book, partly to accommodate programmers familiar only with nonrecursive languages, and partly to obtain efficient and safe implementations.

Nevertheless, we use recursion in some examples, where it would be complicated and artificial not to do so. For example, backtracking is explained at the beginning of this chapter using recursion. A simple recursive explanation of the permutations algorithms is given in Section 4.4.

Regarding efficiency, our tests reveal that the iterative version of Factorial runs about 30% more quickly than the recursive subprogram using a Turing interpreter, and 10% more quickly using an extended Fortran compiler. These figures lend support to the argument that iteration should be used for efficiency instead of recursion.

4.2 NESTED LOOPS

Simulating a variable number of loops inside each other

Example

Assume that a number of loops with the following structure is required:

```
for Index[1] = Lower[1] to Upper[1]
    for Index[2] = Lower[2] to Upper[2]
        for Index[3] = Lower[3] to Upper[3]
            ...
                for Index[N] = Lower[N] to Upper[N]
                    call Work
                end for
            ...
        end for
    end for
end for
```

It is implemented as follows:

```
call Loops~Initialize (N, Lower, Upper, Index)
loop until Index[0] = 0
    call Work
    call Loops~Increment (N, Lower, Upper, Index)
end loop
```

Subprograms

The algorithms use three arrays: Index, Lower, and Upper. The roles of the arrays are illustrated in the above example.

4.2.1 Loops~Initialize (receives N, Lower, Upper; supplies Index)
4.2.2 Loops~Increment (receives N, Lower, Upper; updates Index)
4.2.3 Loops~Subscript (receives N, Lower, Upper, Index; *result integer*)

Usage

None of the common programming languages makes it easy to set up nonrecursively a variable number of loops nested within each other. The need is filled by the subprograms in this section. In the notes below is an example that shows how such a facility might be used in practice.

You must initialize N and the Lower and Upper arrays before calling Loops~Initialize. All possible permutations of the values in the ranges specified by the Lower and Upper arrays are generated in Index, and delivered in lexicographic (sorted) sequence by successive calls to Loops~Increment. Note that the arrays Lower and Upper have one as the first subscript, while Index has zero as the first subscript. This is to allow Index[0] to contain a counter used by the algorithm. The user may test for the end of all loops by checking for Index[0] = 0.

Many applications that make use of nested loops also require access to multidimensional arrays. For example, with normal indexing in *for* loops nested three deep, one would access arrays using subscripted array references such as Array[i, j, k]. When the depth of the nest is variable, programming languages do not allow for variable numbers of subscripts. We would like to write, perhaps, Array[N, Index], where Index is the array of subscripts. Given that this is not legal, we provide an equivalent facility with the function Loops~Subscript, which develops a single subscript from the multiple subscripts in Index. The single subscript can then be used to access a one-dimensional array. Thus, Array[Loops~Subscript (N, Lower, Upper, Index)] achieves the required result.

Analysis

Loops~Increment uses the straightforward approach of incrementing the innermost loop first. This is achieved by the *for* loop using a decreasing rather than an increasing counter. At every entry the value of Index[0] will be N, and so the subprogram always attempts to increment the innermost subscript first.

The subscript calculated by Loops~Subscript echoes this arrangement, assuming that the last subscript varies the most quickly. Fortran programmers may wish to change Loops~Subscript so that the first subscript varies the most quickly. This is achieved simply by changing the *for* loop to increment in increasing instead of decreasing sequence, and initializing Subscript to Lower[1].

Loops~Subscript contains one inefficiency that you should remove. The value of Offset is computed every time the subprogram is called, although there are only N possible values of Offset. The N values should be calculated once by Loops~Initialize and saved in an array to be accessed by Loops~Subscript. We have left Offset to be calculated by Loops~Subscript to highlight the intimate connection between the formulas for calculating Offset and Subscript.

To understand how Loops~Subscript works, imagine a three-dimensional array with subscripts i, j, and k that take any of M_i, M_j, and M_k possible values respectively. For simplicity, assume that i ranges from 0 to M_i–1, j from 0 to M_j–1, and k from 0 to M_k–1. The value of the single subscript is given by Subscript = $i*M_j*M_k + j*M_k + k$. Note that Subscript *mod* $M_k = k$ and Subscript $\div M_k = i*M_j + j$. The second relation has the same structure for two subscripts as the three-subscript formula. These relations can be used to recover the individual subscripts from the value of Subscript if necessary. Adjustments are required to take account of the fact that subscripts range, for example, from Lower[i] to Upper[i] rather than from 0 to M_i.

The method for simulating multidimensional arrays in one dimension has been rediscovered many times, by researchers involved in survey work and the statistical analysis of factorial experiments. We have generally followed the approach taken by the first writer Gower (1962, 1968), which is consistent with similar work by Oliver (1967), Gentleman (1975), Burr (1980), and O'Flaherty and MacKenzie (1982). A related recursive method was proposed by Hill (1971), although it offers no gains in efficiency or simplicity.

IMPLEMENTATION

<u>Exported Names</u>

Loops~Increment	Increments Index element by unity (4.2.2)
Loops~Initialize	Sets all Index elements to the values in Lower (4.2.1)
Loops~Subscript	Evaluates simulated multidimensional array subscripts (4.2.3)

<u>Nicknames</u>

Index	Simulated loop counters
Lower	Lower limits for loop counters
N	Number of dimensions, depth of nested loops
Upper	Upper limits for loop counters

<u>Local Names</u>

Mark	Counter marking current depth of simulated nest of loops
Offset	Base position for simulated subscript at current level of nest
Subscript	Position in one-dimensional array of simulated multiple subscripts

4.2.1 Loops~Initialize (receives N, Lower, Upper; supplies Index)

Pseudo Code

```
initialize each element of Index to corresponding element of Lower
initialize Mark, saved in 0-th element of Index, to N
```

Code

```
procedure Loops~Initialize (N is integer, Lower, Upper, Index are arrays of
        integers)
    for i = 1 to N
        let Index[i] = Lower[i]
    end for
    let Index[0] = N
end Loops~Initialize
```

4.2.2 Loops~Increment (receives N, Lower, Upper; updates Index)

Pseudo Code

```
initialize Mark to its saved value, the 0-th element of Index
loop
    if Index[Mark] has reached Upper[Mark] then
        reset Index[Mark] to Lower[Mark]
        decrement Mark by 1
    else
        increment Index[Mark] by 1
        reset Mark to N, to start at innermost loop
    end if
end loop when Mark = 0 or N
save Mark in 0-th element of Index
```

Code

procedure Loops~Increment (N *is integer*, Lower, Upper, Index *are arrays of integers*)
    variable Mark *is integer*
    let Mark = Index[0]
    loop
        if Index[Mark] = Upper[Mark] *then*
            let Index[Mark] = Lower[Mark]
            let Mark = Mark – 1
        else
            let Index[Mark] = Index[Mark] + 1
            let Mark = N
        end if
    end loop when Mark ≤ 0 *or* Mark = N
    let Index[0] = Mark
end Loops~Increment

4.2.3 Loops~Subscript (receives N, Lower, Upper, Index; *result integer*)

Pseudo Code

initialize Offset to 1
initialize Subscript to last lower limit Lower[N]
for decreasing i = N *to* 1
    increment Subscript by product of Offset and difference between Index[*i*] and Lower[*i*]
    recalculate Offset for next Index position
end for
result is subscript

Code

function Loops~Subscript (N *is integer*, Lower, Upper, Index *are arrays of integers*) *is integer*
    variables Offset, Subscript *are integers*
    let Offset = 1
    let Subscript = Lower[N]
    for decreasing i = N *to* 1
        let Subscript = Subscript + ((Index[*i*] – Lower[*i*]) * Offset)
        let Offset = Offset * (Upper[*i*] – Lower[*i*] + 1)
    end for
    result Subscript
end Loops~Subscript

TEST PROGRAM

Local Names

Count	Counter that should always equal the value of Loops~Subscript
Depth	Depth of simulated nest of loops

I	Array of indexes for nest of loops
L, U	Arrays of lower and upper limits for indexes

Pseudo Code

```
for j = 1 to Depth
    initialize index limits L[j] and U[j] to successively larger integers
    initialize Count to the first multidimensional subscript equivalent to be
            computed
    loop until end of nested loops
        compute multidimensional subscript equivalent, and check its value against
                Count
    end loop
end for
```

Code

```
constant Depth = 5
variables L, U are arrays 1 to Depth of integers
variables I is array 0 to Depth of integers
variable Count is integer
for j = 1 to Depth
    let L[j] = j
    let U[j] = j * 2
    let Count = L[j]
    call Loops~Initialize (j, L, U, I)
    loop until I[0] = 0
        check Count = Loops~Subscript (j, L, U, I)
        let Count = Count + 1
        call Loops~Increment (j, L, U, I)
    end loop
end for
```

NOTES—PASSWORD INSECURITY

Understanding why passwords are less effective than expected

How is it that hackers often find it easy to break into supposedly secure computer systems? Designers of sensitive military or banking applications spend much time and effort in creating multilevel password protection, only to find skilled hackers getting into the system with comparative ease. Why is a password system not very effective?

Ever since time-shared computers became available in the 1960s people have been advised to change their passwords regularly, presumably to make it more difficult for hackers to steal computer time. People tend not to take this advice because it is inconvenient to have to remember new passwords, and inadvisable to write them down. If you change passwords regularly, you can get totally confused about which is the current one.

For those reasons people tend to choose a *meaningful* password, one that can be easily remembered. This makes it much easier for a hacker, because he or she can make guesses about what is meaningful to you. It is also more difficult for you to change your password easily if you have a meaning very clearly in mind.

In order to make a password meaningful we tend to choose words that are important to us in some way, such as our own names or addresses, names of our family members, birthdays, telephone numbers, and various permutations of these. These are all poor choices because they are so easy for a hacker to guess at. We are creatures of meaning, and tend to resist using totally random strings of characters as passwords, despite their greater security. To be secure, a password should look like a random number or random word, such as N0Qz3Lmf, in the sense that it does not appear to relate to anything meaningful. But how can you remember it if it's not meaningful?

There is not a really satisfactory answer to that question. You might try to derive the password from some meaningful information you have that a hacker could not possibly know. This can be difficult, because most of us give away clues. For example, if you choose your favorite color as a password, do you frequently wear clothes of that color? Anyway, the names of colors are meaningful words in themselves, and do not look like random strings of characters.

The better the password, the more work a hacker has to do to get through your security. You want to force a hacker to have no other method available than to try every possible password. Suppose your system uses passwords of up to eight characters, with each character an upper- or lowercase letter or a digit. Allowing for the space character and a full stop or a hyphen, there are 64 or 2^6 possible characters in each position. There are 64^8 or 2^{48} possible passwords altogether, a huge number approaching one quadrillion. Theoretically, a hacker should have to sift through all 2^{48} possible passwords. If the password is truly *meaningless* in itself, the system is fairly secure because no hacker could invest this amount of computational effort. Hackers succeed far more easily than the theory suggests because user passwords rarely appear meaningless.

Just how long does it actually take to test all possible combinations of passwords? You can experiment with passwords of different lengths, with different numbers of allowable characters in any given password, using the example given at the beginning of this section. The program can be written to allow N, the number of characters in the password, to be entered from the keyboard. Each of the first N elements of Lower and Upper should be set to 'A' and 'Z' respectively. Then it's just a matter of turning the loop loose and measuring the time required to complete all iterations.

NOTES—MULTIDIMENSIONAL TABLES

Extracting simple tables from multidimensional arrays

Census information is used widely in industry, commerce, and academia. One very convenient way in which to summarize census data is in the form of a multidimensional table. For example, suppose you are interested in population distributions in various districts, and want to examine differences with respect to age, sex, income, and marital status.

An appropriate data structure might be a five-dimensional array, with each dimension used as follows: (1) age coded into 10 age categories by decade of life; (2) sex coded into 2 categories, for male and female; (3) income coded into 10 categories; (4) marital status coded into 2 categories, for married and single; and (5) district coded into 15 geographic areas by postal or zip code. Each cell of the array contains the number of people having the attributes specified by the particular values of the subscripts for each of the five dimensions. The array requires a total of 10 * 2 * 10 * 2 * 15, or 6,000 storage locations. The census data can be relatively easily converted into the form required for storage in this array.

There are too many individual cells in the array to allow an easy search for patterns. By developing subtotals we can make the data more manageable and easier to understand. There are two problems to consider: how to calculate all possible subtotals and how to display the results. In this example we consider the former problem but not the latter. That is, we will examine the process of computing all the subtotals for the five-dimensional array of census data.

In Figure 4.1 we show how the subtotals for marital status and sex might be represented in a two-dimensional array. The two categories for each dimension have been extended by a third category to contain the totals at the margins of the table. The lightly shaded areas contain the subtotals over just one dimension, with marital status at the end of each row and sex at the bottom of each column. The heavily shaded cell contains the total of the subtotals, which is computed as the sum of the row subtotals or the sum of the column subtotals.

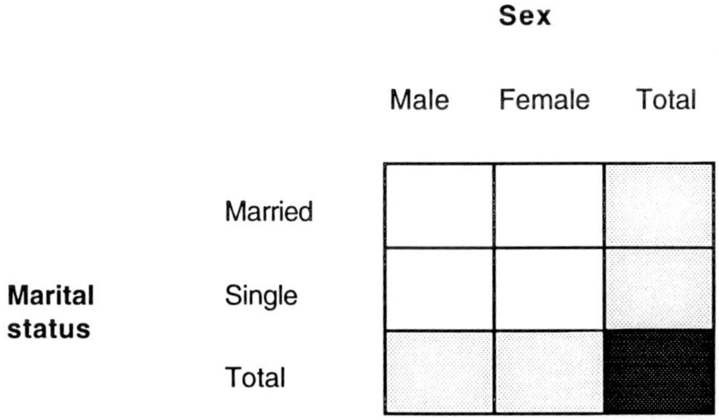

Figure 4.1

To provide the necessary locations for marginal subtotals in the census data array, the data structure is extended by adding an additional level to each of the five dimensions. The array now requires 11 * 3 * 11 * 3 * 16, or 17,424 storage locations. (Note how this apparently minor addition to storage requirements has actually tripled the array size. This is an example of the exponential growth characteristics of combinatorial problems.)

Let us set up three arrays—Lower, Upper, and Margin—that give us the ranges of the five dimensions. We assume that sex has two coded values, 0 and 1, and that the marginal totals for sex will be represented by the third coded value, 2. Marital status will be treated in the same way. Age and income will be coded from 0 to 9, and the marginal totals will have a code of 10. District will be coded from 0 to 14, with 15 used for marginal totals. To make the code easier to understand, let us define five constants—Age, Sex, Income, Status, and District—as 1, 2, 3, 4, and 5 respectively, for referring to the five dimensions. Now we set up the three arrays:

```
constants Age = 1, Sex = 2, Income = 3, Status = 4, District = 5
let Lower[Age] = 0; let Upper[Age] = 9; let Margin[Age] = 10
let Lower[Sex] = 0; let Upper[Sex] = 1; let Margin[Sex] = 2
let Lower[Income] = 0; let Upper[Income] = 9; let Margin[Income] = 10
let Lower[Status] = 0; let Upper[Status] = 1; let Margin[Status] = 2
let Lower[District] = 0; let Upper[District] = 14; let Margin[District] = 15
```

The first thing we must do is to clear the totals to zero. This is done most simply by setting all 17,424 locations in the Data array to zero. Now we insert the data from the census into the multidimensional array, which is really the one-dimensional array Data. Suppose we have a function Census that gives us the number of people having a specified age, sex, income, and marital status, and living in a particular district. We supply Census with the Index array, and it returns the number of people for the combination of index values contained in it. The subscripts in the loop vary from Lower[*i*] to Upper[*i*] but are calculated to allow space for the margins with the range Lower[*i*] to Margin[*i*]. The single subscript is computed in the *integer* variable Subscript.

```
call Loops~Initialize (N, Lower, Margins, Index)
loop until Index[0] = 0
    let Subscript = Loops~Subscript (N, Lower, Margins, Index)
    let Data[Subscript] = Census (Index)
    call Loops~Increment (N, Lower, Upper, Index)
end loop
```

The following section of code generates all possible marginal totals, using the method given by Oliver (1967). In this loop one value in the array Upper is changed at each iteration to be equal to the corresponding value in the array Margin. Naturally, if the original values of Upper are required in later stages of processing, they will have to be restored. A few additional temporary *integer* storage locations—J, K, and Save—are required.

```
for i = Age to District
    call Loops~Initialize (N, Lower, Upper, Index)
    loop until Index[0] = 0
        let J = Loops~Subscript (N, Lower, Margin, Index)
        let Save = Index[i]
        let Index[i] = Margin[i]
        let K = Loops~Subscript (N, Lower, Margin, Index)
        let Index[i] = Save
        let Data[K] = Data[K] + Data[J]
        call Loops~Increment (N, Lower, Upper, Index)
    end loop
    let Upper [i] = Margin [i]
end for
```

All possible marginal totals have now been computed. To illustrate how the totals are accessed, the following code calculates the values for the two-dimensional array

Table, which is the marital status by sex table, with its marginal totals. This table has been aggregated over the other three dimensions—age, income, and district.

```
call Loops~Initialize (N, Lower, Margin, Index)
let Index[Age] = Margin[Age]
let Index[Income] = Margin[Income]
let Index[District] = Margin[District]
for i = 0 to 2
    let Index[Status] = i
    for j = 0 to 2
        let Index[Sex] = j
        let K = Loops~Subscript (N, Lower, Margin, Index)
        let Table[i, j] = Data[K]
    end for
end for
```

4.3 NESTED TOTALS

Computing sub-subtotals within subtotals within totals to any depth

Example

The two files "Test Data" and "Output" show what the algorithm achieves for totals nested three deep, using three-digit keys. For example, the line "Total 111 6" contains the total for all lines with the key "111". The line "Total 11 21" contains the total for all lines with "11" as the first two digits in the key. The line "Total 1 45" contains the total for all lines with "1" as the first digit in the key. The grand total is given in the line "Grand total 60".

Subprograms

4.3.1 Totals~Calculate (receives Data, Print; disk file input-output)

Usage

The subprogram inputs lines of text, each of which contains a sort key and a number. The input file (Data) must be in sorted order before calling the subprogram. The data file is copied to the output file (Print) with the required totals interspersed in the correct places at key breaks. Key breaks are points in the data file where there is a difference in at least one of the characters in two successive keys.

For a file with N key elements there are N + 1 possible levels of total. The subprogram assumes that each key element is a single character. In the test file the keys are assumed to have three elements, each of which is a single digit, and four levels of totals are generated. For this reason the array of totals has a subscript ranging from 0 to N, while the elements of the key are thought of as being numbered from 1 to N.

The *text* string "end" is used as a dummy key that represents the end of the file. The value of the string may be changed by the user, provided only that the key value it contains must differ from all real keys that can occur in the data file. There is no requirement that its value have any particular position in the collating sequence of the computer's character set.

Analysis

Assuming that there are N characters in the key, the data value is added to the innermost total Total[N] at every iteration. When there is a key break, the value of Total[N] is output. At the same time, Total[N] is added to the next level of total Total[N–1] and Total[N] is cleared. The algorithm then checks whether there is a break in the first N–1 characters of the key (ignoring the last character of the key). If so, Total[N–1] is output, added to Total[N–2], and then cleared.

The algorithm always has two of the data records available to it. The simplicity of the algorithm is ensured by having the next record available while the current record is being processed. That is, the algorithm contains a look-ahead feature that permits easy detection of the key breaks.

IMPLEMENTATION

<u>Exported Names</u>	
Totals~Calculate	Calculates nested totals for a sorted data file (4.3.1)
<u>Nicknames</u>	
Data	Integer file number for data file
Print	Integer file number for output results
<u>Local Names</u>	
K	Character position in key
Key	Value of key obtained from current data record
N	Number of characters in key, each assumed to be a key element
NextKey	Value of key obtained from next data record
Position	Position in key of key break
Total	Array of totals
Value	Value of data item obtained from current record

4.3.1 Totals~Calculate (receives Data, Print; disk file input-output)

Pseudo Code

```
read first record into Key and Value, determining the length N of the key
clear the totals Total[i]
loop until Key = "end"
    output the current record
    add Value to Total[N]
    if end of file then
        let Key = "end"
    else
        read next data record into NextKey and Value
    end if
    calculate character number Position at which key break occurs, or N + 1 if none
```

```
    for decreasing i = N to Position
        output first i characters of key and Total[i]
        add Total[i] to Total[i–1], and clear Total[i]
    end for
    let Key = NextKey
end loop
output grand total Total[0]
```

Code

```
procedure Totals~Calculate (Data, Print are integers)
    variables Key, NextKey are text
    variables K, N, Position, Value are integers
    input from Data into Key, Value                    Get first data record and initial-
    let N = length (Key)                               ize totals
    variable Total is array 0 to N of integer
    for i = 0 to N
        let Total[i] = 0
    end for
    loop until Key = "end"                             Loop to process each input
        output into Print from "Item", Key, Value      record and accumulate totals
        let Total[N] = Total[N] + Value
        if end~of~file (Data) = true then              Get next input record, checking
            let NextKey = "end"                        for end of file
        else
            input from Data into NextKey, Value
        end if
        let Position = N + 1                           Calculate position of key break,
        for i = 1 to N                                 if any has occurred
            let K = first + i – 1
            if byte (Key, K) ≠ byte (NextKey, K) and Position > N then
                let Position = i
            end if
        end for
        for decreasing i = N to Position                     Output totals for all
            output into Print from "Total", Key, Total[i]    levels of key break
            let Total[i–1] = Total[i–1] + Total[i]
            let Total[i] = 0
            call shorten (Key)
        end for
        let Key = NextKey
    end loop
    output into Print from "Grand total", Total[0]     Output grand total separately
end Totals~Calculate
```

TEST PROGRAM

<u>Local Names</u>

In   Data input file number
Out   Output results file number

Pseudo Code

open input and output files
call Totals~Calculate

Code

variables In, Out *are integers*
open In *file* "Test Data"
open Out *file* "Results"
call Totals~Calculate (In, Out)

Test Data

```
111   1
111   2
111   3
112   4
112   5
113   6
121   7
122   8
122   9
211   1
212   2
212   3
221   4
221   5
```

Results

```
Item    111    1
Item    111    2
Item    111    3
Total   111    6
Item    112    4
Item    112    5
Total   112    9
Item    113    6
Total   113    6
Total   11    21
Item    121    7
Total   121    7
Item    122    8
Item    122    9
Total   122   17
Total   12    24
Total   1     45
Item    211    1
Total   211    1
Item    212    2
```

Item	212	3
Total	212	5
Total	21	6
Item	221	4
Item	221	5
Total	221	9
Total	22	9
Total	2	15
Grand total		60

4.4 PERMUTATIONS

Generating every possible permutation of given items

Example

The following code prints in sorted sequence all possible permutations of the four integers in the array locations Item[1] ... Item[4]:

```
variable Item is array 1 to 4 of integers
call Permutations~Initialize (4, Item)
for i = 1 to Products~Factorial (4)
    output Item[1], Item[2], Item[3], Item[4]
    call Permutations~Sorted (4, Item)
end for
```

Subprograms

4.4.1 Permutations~Initialize (receives N; supplies Item)
4.4.2 Permutations~Fast (receives N; updates Item)
4.4.3 Permutations~Sorted (receives N; updates Item)

Usage

The algorithms require distinct tokens of some kind to be set up in the Item array. For ease of presentation, the test program assumes that the tokens consist of a sequence of integers. Permutations~Initialize must be called before any permuting is done. You must choose whether to use the fast or sorted method, and then use that method consistently in generating all required permutations. The algorithm generates one permutation of the integer tokens with each call of Permutations~Fast or Permutations~Sorted. The total number of distinct permutations that will be generated, the factorial of the number of tokens, may be computed by Products~Factorial. Permutations~Sorted restores the original sequence of the tokens at the end.

The computer time for permutation generation grows exponentially with the number of tokens.

Analysis

Permutation generation has been a popular topic with computer scientists for many years, and a large number of algorithms have been proposed. A survey by Sedgewick (1977) provides an analysis of the best methods known at that time. Surprisingly, later work on algorithms for generating lexicographically sorted permutations, for example, by Rohl (1978), Irving (1984), and Er (1987), has produced algorithms that are inferior to the best of those presented by Sedgewick. They are less easy to use, require more temporary storage when converted from recursive to iterative, and are considerably slower than the algorithms presented here.

The subprogram Permutations~Fast is based on algorithms by Heap (1963) and Ives (1976), while the subprogram Permutations~Sorted relies on the work of Ord-Smith (1968). Both subprograms are implemented broadly as suggested by Sedgewick (1977). They are further revised and simplified here to increase their efficiency, to highlight the similarities between the algorithms, and to replace reverse lexicographic by natural lexicographic order.

If the code near the calls to *swap* is eliminated, it will be observed that the remainder of the code in the two algorithms is actually identical. The code for keeping track of interchanges, using the array Count, has precisely the same structure in both algorithms. The structure implements "factorial counting". Think of a mixed-radix number, the last digit having a base of one, the second last having a base of two, and in general the n-th last digit having a base of n. The structure effectively cycles through successively larger integers expressed in this mixed-radix system, with the "digits" of the number in locations Count[1] to Count[N]. The N's complement of all digits is used in practice to simplify the code.

The factorial counting system can be easily implemented using modulus arithmetic on a single integer, rather than simulated counting with the array Count. Our tests show that no gain in speed is achieved by this device and the code is a little more complex.

An informal description of the method is best presented bottom-up, by consideration of progressively larger problems. The algorithm for permuting two tokens, say T_1 and T_2, is obvious, merely requiring an interchange to produce the permutation T_2, T_1. Call this process Permute~2. Now consider a third token, T_3. There are three pairs: (1) T_1, T_2, (2) T_1, T_3, and (3) T_2, T_3. Pair (1) does not contain T_3. Pairs (2) and (3) both contain T_3 and have either T_2 or T_1 removed respectively. Now generate the six possible permutations in three stages: T_3 with both permutations of T_1 and T_2, T_2 with both permutations of T_1 and T_3, and T_1 with both permutations of T_2 and T_3. Call this process Permute~3. Permute~4 is defined by applying Permute~3 four times with T_4 either out of the permutation of three, or replacing one of T_1, T_2, or T_3. The extension of this process to produce Permute~n is obvious. Expressed recursively, the thrust of the algorithm is illustrated by the following subprogram, which will produce all permutations of, say, four tokens by *call* Permute (4):

```
procedure Permute (N is integer)
    for i = 1 to N
        call Permute (N – 1)
```

```
        if i < N then
            call swap (T[Choose (N, i)], T[N])
            call Use~Permutation
        end if
    end for
end Permute
```

There are many ways of choosing a suitable sequence in which to substitute T_n for each of T_1, T_2, ... T_{n-1}. Much of the discussion in the literature involves optimizing this sequence. The function Choose shown above has two parameters, illustrating that the choice depends on both N and the position of the token in the sequence. Sedgewick (1977) describes many alternative versions of Choose. We have selected versions that produce simple and efficient code.

The difference between the algorithms Permutations~Fast and Permutations~Sorted lies in the way Choose is implemented. Permutations~Fast carries out only one exchange per iteration of the loop. Permutations~Sorted also carries out one exchange every time, but it has to use a loop to reverse the positions of the last few tokens on occasion. Permutations~Fast will therefore be rather faster than Permutations~Sorted. It should be remembered that your own processing required for each permutation may take far longer than the permutation generation itself. It may make little practical difference to execution time which algorithm is implemented, and there may be advantages in having sorted permutations. If speed is important, the nicknames should be removed so that the subprograms refer to the actual arrays in the calling programs.

IMPLEMENTATION

Exported Names

Permutations~Fast	Generates permutations (4.4.2)
Permutations~Initialize	Initializes counters for the permutation algorithm (4.4.1)
Permutations~Sorted	Generates sorted permutations (4.4.3)

Nicknames

Item	Array containing tokens to be permuted
MaxItem	Maximum number of items that can be permuted
N	Number of tokens

Local Names

Count	Array of counters for factorial counting
Position	Position in Count currently under consideration

4.4.1 Permutations~Initialize (receives N; supplies Item)

Pseudo Code

initialize N counters in array Count to count down from N
initialize storage for Count position marker to –1

Code

variable Count *is array* 1 *to* MaxItem *of integers*

```
procedure Permutations~Initialize (N is integer, Item is array of integers)
    for j = 1 to N
        let Count[j] = N
    end for
    let Item[0] = –1
end Permutations~Initialize
```

4.4.2 Permutations~Fast (receives N; updates Item)

Pseudo Code

```
for decreasing i = (N – 1) to 1
    if Count_i > i then
        if i is odd or even as N is odd or even respectively then
            swap Item_i with Item_N
        else
            swap Item_i with Item_J, where J = Count_i
        end if
        decrement Count_i by 1
        exit from loop
    else
        restore Count_i its starting value N
    end if
end for
```

Code

```
procedure Permutations~Fast (N is integer, Item is array of integers)
    variable Position is integer
    let Position = N – 1
    loop until Position ≤ 0
        if Count[Position] > Position then
            if Position mod 2 = N mod 2 then
                call swap (Item[Position], Item[N])
            else
                call swap (Item[Position], Item[Count[Position]])
            end if
            let Count[Position] = Count[Position] – 1
            let Position = 0
        else
            let Count[Position] = N
        end if
        let Position = Position – 1
    end loop
    let Item[0] = Position
end Permutations~Fast
```

4.4.3 Permutations~Sorted (receives N; updates Item)

Pseudo Code

```
for decreasing i = (N – 1) to 1
    if Count_i > i then
        swap Item_i with Item_J, where J = Count_i
        reverse the sequence of the array elements Count_i+1 to Count_N
        decrement Count_i by 1
        exit from loop
    else
        restore Count_i its starting value N
    end if
end for
```

Code

```
procedure Permutations~Sorted (N is integer, Item is array of integers)
    variable Position is integer
    let Position = N – 1
    loop until Position ≤ 0
        if Count[Position] > Position then
            call swap (Item[Position], Item[Count[Position]])
            for j = 1 to ((N – Position + 1) ÷ 2)
                call swap (Item[Position+j], Item[N–j+1])
            end for
            let Count[Position] = Count[Position] – 1
            let Position = 0
        else
            let Count[Position] = N
        end if
        let Position = Position – 1
    end loop
    let Item[0] = Position
end Permutations~Sorted
```

TEST PROGRAM

<u>Imported Names</u>

Products~Factorial	Calculates factorial of an integer N (4.1.1)

<u>Local Names</u>

Factorial	Number of permutations to be generated
MaxItem	Maximum number of items that can be permuted
Item	Array containing tokens to be permuted

Pseudo Code

```
initialize elements of Item to sequence of MaxItem integers
initialize permutations counters
```

```
for i = 1 to (MaxItem)!
    calculate next permutation in lexicographic order
end for
check that current counter position has been zeroized to indicate the end of the
        sequence
check that the tokens are in the reverse order of the original sequence
initialize permutations counters
for i = 1 to (MaxItem)!
    calculate next permutation using the fast method
end for
check that current counter position has been zeroized to indicate the end of the
        sequence
```

Code

```
constant MaxItem = 7
constant Factorial = Products~Factorial (MaxItem)
variable Item is array 0 to MaxItem of integer
for i = 1 to MaxItem
    let Item[i] = i
end for
call Permutations~Initialize (MaxItem, Item)
for i = 1 to Factorial
    call Permutations~Sorted (MaxItem, Item)
end for
check Item[0] = 0
for i = 1 to MaxItem
    check Item[i] = MaxItem – i + 1
end for
call Permutations~Initialize (MaxItem, Item)
for i = 1 to Factorial
    call Permutations~Fast (MaxItem, Item)
end for
check Item[0] = 0
```

NOTES—TRAVELING SALESPERSON

Finding the shortest route through several cities

Generating all possible permutations of anything is a brute force technique for solving a problem. While it may be the only possible way to crack some tough problems, the method requires exponential computing time. That is, each increase in size of the problem by one multiplies the required computing time by the current size of the problem. If it takes one microsecond to generate all possible permutations of two numbers, it will take two seconds for 10 items, seven and half days for 15 items, and an unbelievable 40,000 years for 20 items. Thus, it is practical to generate all possible permutations only for small problems.

There is a classical puzzle called the "traveling salesperson" problem. A salesperson has to visit a number of cities. What is the cheapest way to do it? There has been a lot of interest in solving this problem for the 48 state capital cities in the contiguous United States, but the problem is far too large for brute force algorithms. Even solving the problem for the major capital cities in Europe is too big a task for a personal computer. In Australia, however, the problem is just the right size for applying the permutation algorithm. A certain transport company based in the national capital, Canberra, has two jet aircraft, one of which flies to every one of the seven capital cities in Australia every day. What is the shortest round trip it can make, returning to Canberra each day?

The problem can be solved by generating all possible combinations of the capital cities other than Canberra, and calculating the length of each route. First, we construct Table 4.1, showing the distances between the cities (in kilometers):

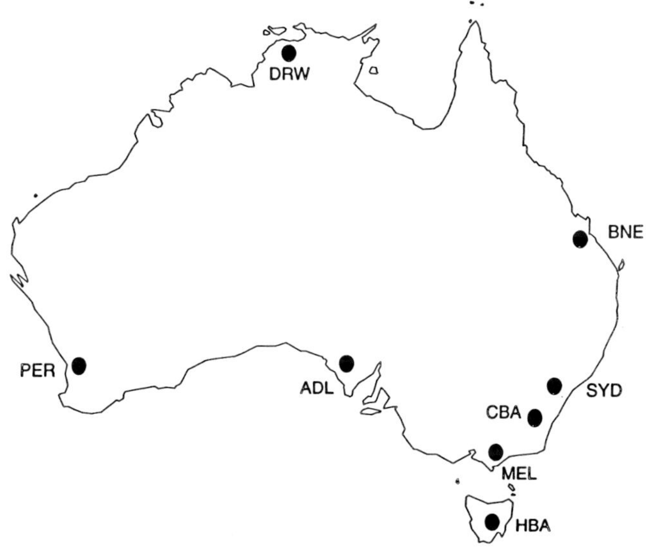

Table 4.1

	ADL	*BNE*	*DRW*	*HBA*	*MEL*	*PER*	*SYD*	*CBA*
Adelaide		1600	2600	1150	650	2100	1150	950
Brisbane	1600		2850	1800	1400	3600	750	1000
Darwin	2600	2850		3700	3150	2600	3150	3100
Hobart	1150	1800	3700		600	3050	1050	850
Melbourne	650	1400	3150	600		2700	700	450
Perth	2100	3600	2600	3050	2700		3300	3050
Sydney	1150	750	3150	1050	700	3300		250
Canberra	950	1000	3100	850	450	3050	250	

Assuming this table of distances is stored in the array Distance, the code for calculating the shortest round trip into and out of Canberra is:

```
constant N = 7
variable Item is array 1 to N of integers
constant Cities = N + 1
variable Distance is array 1 to Cities, 1 to Cities of integers
variables Shortest, Trip are integers
let Shortest = maxinteger                          Initialize Shortest to a large
call Permutations~Initialize (N, Item)             number
for j = 1 to Products~Factorial (N)
    let Trip = Distance[Cities, Item[1]] + Distance[Item[N], Cities]
    for i = 1 to (N – 1)                                Accumulate trip distance
        let Trip = Trip + Distance[Item[i], Item[i+1]]
    end for
    if Trip < Shortest then                        If trip is shortest so far, save its
        let Shortest = Trip                        length and output it
        for i = 1 to N
            output Item[i]
        end for
        output Shortest
    end if
    call Permutations~Fast (N, Item)
end for
```

The shortest possible route has some legs that might surprise even experienced pilots. With typical high-volume passenger aircraft travel in mind, one might expect the route in southeastern Australia to pass through Sydney, Canberra, and Melbourne in that order. However, there is a shorter path involving travel to other cities between these ones.

4.5 COMBINATIONS

Generating every possible combination of items selected from a set of items

Example

The following code prints all possible combinations of four ones and three zeros stored in the elements of the array Item:

```
variable Item is array 1 to 7 of integers
call Combinations~Initialize (7, 4, Item)
for i = 1 to Products~Combinations (7, 4)
    for j = 1 to 7
        output Item[j]
    end for
    call Combinations~Enumerate (7, 4, Item)
end for
```

Subprograms

4.5.1 Combinations~Initialize (receives N, K; supplies Item)
4.5.2 Combinations~Enumerate (receives N, K; updates Item)

Usage

The subprogram Combinations~Initialize puts K ones and N – K zeros into an array Item. The array elements are permuted by Combinations~Enumerate. For the above example the seven elements of the array, Item[1] to Item[7], are set to the values 1, 1, 1, 1, 0, 0, 0 respectively. After each call to Combinations~Enumerate a permutation of these digits is returned. The ones represent the selected items in each particular combination of four chosen from the seven, and the zeros represent the nonselected items.

Each successive combination differs from the previous one by the exchange of a one with a zero. For example, 1110100 is the next combination after 1111000, interchanging Item[4] and Item[5].

Table 4.2, reading down the columns, shows the output from the algorithm, selecting combinations of 3 things from 6:

Table 4.2

111000	100110	001011	010110
101001	100011	011001	010011
101010	000111	011010	110001
101100	001101	011100	110010
100101	001110	010101	110100

Analysis

Algorithms for generating combinations were surveyed in a paper by Ehrlich (1973). Liu and Tang (1973) published a new algorithm at around the same time. This algorithm is the most efficient we have been able to find, being about 30% faster than Ehrlich's best in our tests. Unlike the Erlich algorithms, it requires no additional storage for marks or counters to be retained between calls.

It is interesting to speculate why the survey by Sedgewick (1977) of the permutations literature did not refer to the work of Liu and Tang. The reason is quite likely that the Liu–Tang algorithm appears full of special cases and is very difficult to read. Although hampered somewhat by the inadequacies of unstructured Fortran, the published subprogram contains no fewer than 21 *go to* statements packed into fewer than 50 lines of executable code! Two of these are backward branches, although they do not create loops! With considerable effort we were able to convert the algorithm into a well-structured form, and to eliminate many of the special cases.

Examination of the code reveals little about how the algorithm works. However, inspection of the sequence of combinations produced by the algorithm gives some insight into its properties. Its operation can be fully understood by examining only four bit positions. These are the positions of (1) the rightmost zero, (2) the rightmost one, (3) the rightmost zero in the rightmost-but-one string of zeros (if any), and (4) the rightmost one in the rightmost-but-one string of ones (if any).

The algorithm exchanges zeros and ones at two of these positions, or at positions on either side of those positions. The selection of the two particular positions on each entry depends largely on whether there are zeros or ones currently at the end of the combination, and whether the number of ones to the left of the rightmost zero is even or odd. A precise statement of the selections that are made is given in the pseudo code and the code itself. The mathematical justification for the Liu–Tang algorithm may be found in the literature.

The array Item is initialized to contain a certain pattern of ones and zeros. However, the algorithm is cyclic, and any pattern of ones and zeros may be used as the starting point.

It is not difficult to write a general subprogram for computing the positions of the n-th rightmost zeros or ones in an array of ones and zeros, although a special version is used in the algorithm. Suppose the two-dimensional array P is to contain the results, where P[0, N] and P[1, N] are the positions of the N-th rightmost zeros and ones respectively. The following code does the job, where B represents the value of a particular bit. The value of J indicates how many digit positions are recorded. Don't forget to initialize appropriate elements of the array P to zero before calling the algorithm.

```
let B = –1
let I = N
let J = 0
loop until I = 0
    if Item[I] ≠ B then
        let B = Item[I]
        let P[B, J÷2] = I
        let J = J + 1
    end if
    let I = I – 1
end loop
```

IMPLEMENTATION

Exported Names

Combinations~Enumerate	Generates permutations of the indicators (4.5.2)
Combinations~Initialize	Initializes indicators to be permuted (4.5.1)

Nicknames

B1, B2	Positions of indicators selected for exchanging in array
Item	
Item	Array containing indicators to be permuted
K	Number of items to be selected from the set of N
N	Number of items

Local Names

Change	Position in Item array at which bit differing from next
bit is found	
LastBit	Value of Item[N]
NextOne	Position of rightmost one, or rightmost-but-one one
RightZero	Position of rightmost zero

4.5.1 Combinations~Initialize (receives N, K; supplies Item)

Pseudo Code

```
initialize the first K of the N indicators in Item to 1
initialize the last N – K of the N indicators in Item to 0
```

Code

```
procedure Combinations~Initialize (N, K are integers, Item is array of integers)
    check N > K and K > 0
    for j = 1 to K
        let Item[j] = 1
    end for
    for j = (K + 1) to N
        let Item[j] = 0
    end for
end Combinations~Initialize
```

4.5.2 Combinations~Enumerate (receives N, K; updates Item)

Pseudo Code

```
let Change = last position in Item array where Item[Change] ≠ Item[Change+1]
let RightZero = position in Item of the rightmost zero
let NextOne = last position in Item of a one at or preceding Item[Change]
if number of ones preceding rightmost zero in Item is even then
    swap items at positions Change and Change + 1 + Item[N]
else
    if NextOne is at position 1 then
        swap items at positions 1 and RightZero
    else
        if item preceding NextOne is a zero then
            swap it with the item at position Change + Item[N]
        else
            swap it with the item at position RightZero
        end if
    end if
end if
```

Code

```
procedure Combinations~Enumerate (N, K are integers, Item is array of integers)
    variables B1, B2, LastBit, Change, NextOne, RightZero are integers
    check N > K and K > 0
    let LastBit = Item[N]
    let Change = N                              Determine from the last bit where
    loop                                        a change of bit occurs
        let Change = Change – 1
    end loop when Item[Change] ≠ LastBit
```

```
    if LastBit = 0 then                          Determine the position of the
        let RightZero = N                        rightmost zero
    else
        let RightZero = Change
    end if
    let NextOne = Change                         Find the position of the next one
    loop until NextOne = 0 or Item[NextOne] =    at or preceding the change
            1
        let NextOne = NextOne – 1
    end loop
    if (K – (N – RightZero)) mod 2 = 0 then      Determine which items to
        let B1 = Change                          exchange
        let B2 = minimum (Change + 1 +
                LastBit, N)
    else
        if NextOne = 1 then
            let B1 = 1
            let B2 = RightZero
        else
            let B1 = NextOne – 1
            if Item[B1] = 0 then
                let B2 = Change + LastBit
            else
                let B2 = RightZero
            end if
        end if
    end if
    call swap (Item[B1], Item[B2])               Exchange a one and a zero
end Combinations~Enumerate
```

TEST PROGRAM

Imported Names

Products~Combinations	Number of combinations of K things selected from N (4.1.4)

Local Names

Item	Array containing tokens to be permuted
MaxItem	Maximum number of items that can be permuted

Pseudo Code

```
for k = 1 to (MaxItem – 1)
    for n = (k + 1) to MaxItem
        initialize the pattern to a sequence of k ones followed by n – k zeros
        generate all possible distinct permutations of the pattern
        check the starting pattern has been reproduced as the last pattern
    end for
end for
```

Code

```
constant MaxItem = 10
variable Item is array 1 to MaxItem of integers
variables In, Out are integers
for k = 1 to (MaxItem – 1)
    for n = (k + 1) to MaxItem
        call Combinations~Initialize (n, k, Item)
        for j = 1 to Products~Combinations (n, k)
            call Combinations~Enumerate (n, k, Item)
        end for
        for j = 1 to k
            check Item[j] = 1
        end for
    end for
end for
```

NOTES—ORGANIZATIONAL COMMUNICATION PATTERNS

Finding cliques within a group of people

We used this algorithm for assessing the communication patterns of a work team in a branch of a public sector organization in the mid-1980s. Each staff member was given a staff list and was asked to indicate those staff members with whom he or she communicated regularly about work. All these perceptions were fed into a program that looked at the amount of communication in various subgroups. We needed to assess whether the formal structure of the organization matched the communication patterns. Table 4.3 shows the array of communication scores we obtained.

There were 18 middle- to senior-level people in the branch, but one was on sick leave when the data were collected. Each person is identified by the initials of his or her first and last names. The ratings of SJ had to be ignored because of his absence. The scores are in the range 0 to 5, where 0 represents no contact and 5 means a great deal of communication. The data were stored in the array Talk, where Talk[I, J] indicates person I's view of how much communication took place with person J in the group.

We wanted to find the most cohesive subgroups for each possible size from 2 to 16 people. For each subgroup size we generated all possible combinations of people and calculated the total amount of communication for each combination. The variable Group contains this total at any stage. If Group is greater than the maximum value obtained so far, the current value is saved in Best. The overall flow of the program is:

```
constant N = 17
variables In, Out, Group, Best are integers
variable Item is array 1 to N of integers
variable Talk is array 1 to N, 1 to N of integers
for i = 2 to (N – 1)
    let Best = 0
    let Group = 0
    call Combinations~Initialize (N, i, Item)
```

```
    for j = 1 to Products~Combinations (N, i)
        call Measure (i)
        call Combinations~Enumerate (N, i, Item)
    end for
end for
```

Table 4.3

	MP	*FR*	*SD*	*HR*	*WD*	*GK*	*SJ*	*CD*	*JR*	*KH*	*GS*	*AD*	*ND*	*DA*	*QP*	*MJ*	*FJ*	*CB*
MP		4	5	5	4	4	3	4	4	4	4	4	4	4	4	3	3	5
FR	3		3	3	3	3	3	3	3	3	2	2	3	3	0	3	3	3
SD	5	3		5	4	4	2	2	2	3	4	3	3	3	3	4	3	5
HR	5	4	5		4	4	4	3	4	4	4	4	4	4	4	4	4	5
WD	2	2	2	3		0	0	0	0	0	0	0	2	0	0	0	0	2
GK	4	2	3	4	4		4	3	4	4	4	4	3	4	3	0	4	5
SJ																		
CD	4	3	2	3	3	2	0		1	4	2	3	5	0	0	3	0	5
JR	4	4	4	5	4	4	4	4		4	0	4	4	4	4	4	4	4
KH	3	3	3	3	0	1	1	3	3		1	1	3	3	4	4	2	4
GS	4	0	3	5	2	2	0	2	2	1		2	2	0	2	2	4	4
AD	4	1	1	2	1	1	1	2	4	3	2		4	4	4	4	4	4
ND	4	3	3	3	3	3	3	3	4	3	2	4		4	3	4	4	4
DA	2	4	4	4	0	2	0	0	4	4	3	4	3		4	4	4	4
QP	3	3	4	4	0	2	0	3	4	4	4	5	4	4		5	4	4
MJ	4	2	3	3	2	2	0	2	3	3	3	3	3	5	5		5	4
FJ	4	4	3	4	4	4	0	3	3	3	3	3	3	5	3	5		5
CB	5	4	4	4	3	4	4	0	3	4	3	4	4	3	4	3	4	

The total amount of communication is computed by tracking the *changes* as one person is dropped and one included in each new combination. We added a little extra code to the subprogram in order to obtain the item numbers of the two items changed in each iteration. This was achieved by adding two new nicknames, In and Out, for the positions of the zero changed to a one and the one changed to a zero. Care is needed to take account of the fact that any current combination includes In but does not include Out. The following code calculates the amount of communication and outputs the group member numbers for the largest total so far. The last output will obviously reflect the most cohesive subgroup.

```
procedure Measure (N is integer)
    for i = 1 to N
        if Item[i] = 1 then
            let Group = Group + Talk[In, i] – Talk[Out, i]
            let Group = Group + Talk[i, In] – Talk[i, Out]
        end if
    end for
    let Group = Group + Talk[In, Out] + Talk[Out, In]
```

```
    if Group ≥ Best then
        let Best = Group
        for i = 1 to N
            if Item[i] = 1 then
                output i
            end if
        end for
        output Group
    end if
end Measure
```

The output from the program is very interesting. The results show that MP, the branch manager, was involved in the most cohesive group, no matter what group size was examined. A lot of communication was taking place between staff members and the manager. This points to the manager being too involved in day-to-day matters. A better-functioning section would have shown some of the most cohesive subgroups as omitting the manager.

Person FR does not appear in any of the most cohesive groups until the group size examined by the program reaches 14. FR had a sad history, being in charge of the branch at one time but then being demoted, supposedly to second in charge. The results suggest that he was second in charge in name only, because he did not figure in the most cohesive groups of any size. One would expect communication between the second in charge and staff to be much higher than between the top manager and the rest of the team.

After this survey SD was transferred out of the section, MP resigned, and HR became acting manager. It is interesting to note that SD and HR were consistently in the most cohesive groups. One can see why HR was appointed manager, given the amount of communication that took place between him and the rest of the team. He was quite possibly keeping his visibility high and building strong support from the group.

CD had been delegated by MP to manage a major organizational change using a project team of selected staff. MP considered later that he had chosen the wrong person for the job. Subjectively, the credibility of CD seemed to be low. CD does not appear in any of the most cohesive groups until the group size reaches 15, thus providing evidence to support the subjective impression.

WD was a disillusioned employee. He had no interest in his work or his colleagues. He is the last person to be included by the program in cohesive groups of any size. In fact, he is not included until the size becomes 17, the total number of people involved. Again, the data support the common wisdom.

This analysis shows how enumerating combinations can be used to assess the strengths and weaknesses of team performance in a small organizational unit.

5 Data Structures

Universities devote whole courses to data structures, the topic being fundamental to computing. This chapter does not attempt to be comprehensive in providing a description of all known algorithms for all data structures. Instead, it introduces one practical and efficient algorithm for each major type of structure. It assumes that you are familiar with the simple array structure. The only common structure not dealt with is the "set", which is provided as a construct in languages such as Pascal. The set has to be implemented using lower-level concepts, such as sorted lists accessed by binary search or hashing. Sorting, binary search, and hashing are examined in other chapters of this book, but the set is not.

Table 5.1

Structure	*Access By*	*First Key*	*Next Key*	*Prev Key*	*Insert*	*Remove*
Unsorted array	Key sequence	O (N)	O (N)	O (N)	O (1)	O (N)
Sorted array	Key sequence	O (*log* (N))	O (1)	O (1)	O (N)	O (N)
Stack	LIFO	O (1)	O (1)	Unavail.	O (1)	O (1)
Queue	FIFO	O (1)	O (1)	Unavail.	O (1)	O (1)
Heap	Key sequence	O (1)	Unavail.	O (1)	O (*log* (N))	O (*log* (N))
List	Key sequence	O (N)	O (1)	O (N)	O (1)	O (1)
Doubly linked	Key sequence	O (N)	O (1)	O (1)	O (1)	O (1)
Balanced tree	Key sequence	O (*log* (N))	O (1)	O (1)	O (1)	O (1)

You can think of data structures as places in which to put things until they are needed later. They differ in their capacity to provide access by position or key, and by differing sequences in which the keys may be made available. Table 5.1 compares the efficiencies of the structures presented in this chapter. It shows that no one data structure is better than another for all applications. The unsorted array is fast for insertion, because new items are merely appended to the end of the array. Deletion is slow because items must be squeezed out by relocating by one location all items beyond the deleted item. Finding keys is slow because about half of the array on average has to be searched in order to find a given key.

Insertion and deletion for unsorted arrays are elementary tasks, but it is easy to get the code wrong the first time you try programming it. Suppose you want to remove the item A[K] from the array A, where the array has items up to location A[N]. The following loop does the job:

```
let N = N – 1
for i = K to N
    let A[i] = A[i+1]
end for
```

If you want to insert Value into array position A[K], you need to move the items into higher array positions in reverse sequence as follows:

```
for decreasing i = N to K
    let A[i+1] = A[i]
end for
let A[K] = Value
let N = N + 1
```

A sorted array has the advantage that specified items can be found in O (*log* N) time by binary search. The required key having been found, the next or previous key in sequence can be found in the next or previous array location respectively. Unfortunately, insertion of new items in the correct place requires moving by one location all items between the point of insertion and the end of the array. Deletion is just as slow as with unsorted arrays.

A stack does not permit access to any key except the one most recently inserted and not yet removed. Once a key has been removed, it is lost from the structure and cannot be accessed again, except by being reinserted. For applications that require such last-in first-out (LIFO) storage, insertion and deletion are very fast. Stacks are useful, for example, for decoding bracketed expressions of arbitrary depth, for servicing hardware interrupts, and for solving combinatorial problems using "backtracking".

A queue does not permit access to any key except the one least recently inserted and not yet removed. Once a key has been removed, it is lost from the structure and cannot be accessed again, except by being reinserted. For applications that require such first-in first-out (FIFO) storage, insertion and deletion are very fast.

A heap does not permit access to any key except the largest one inserted and not yet removed. Once a key has been removed, it is lost from the structure and cannot be accessed again. Heaps are used for priority queues, in which items of higher priority are processed before those of lower priority. Insertion and deletion of items of random size are carried out in O (*log* N) time.

A list is a structure in which each item "points" to (contains the address of) the next one. It is not possible to access any given item directly. A specific item is accessed by following the chain of pointers down the list, the process therefore being slow. It is easy to obtain the previous item in a singly linked list only if a temporary location is used to save the address of the current location when the next location is obtained. However, applying this process recursively requires an array of previous locations, effectively substituting an array structure for the list. For this reason, you will observe that, using only a list structure, the previous location is in general obtainable only by scanning the list from the beginning. Insertion and deletion are fast when the required item has been found, because all that is required is the updating of a few pointers, regardless of where the insertion or deletion point is in the list. The efficiency of updating list structures makes it the data structure of choice for a variety of applications.

A doubly linked list is similar to a list, but each item points to the previous one as well as to the next one. Access to the item previous to a given item is very fast with doubly linked lists, but slow with ordinary singly linked lists. Updating of doubly linked lists is very efficient, although there are obviously more pointers to deal with than for a singly linked list.

The tree is a very versatile structure, in which items are kept in sorted sequence. All operations on trees except searching can be made to operate in O (1) time. Searching is slower, requiring O (*log* N) time. Any item in a tree is readily accessible, and items may be retrieved in random sequence or sorted sequence. It is just as easy to obtain items in reverse sorted sequence as in forward sorted sequence. Efficiency questions for trees are quite complex, and are considered more fully in Section 5.8.

The first three algorithms presented here—Stack Array, Queue Array, and Heap—implement the stack, queue, and heap using arrays. The disadvantage of arrays is that you must know ahead of time the maximum number of storage locations required for the structures, so that the array dimensions can be given to your compiler. This is not always convenient. The remaining algorithms use linked lists instead of arrays.

List algorithms are particularly easy to implement using languages such as Pascal, which allocate storage dynamically. In such languages a request is made via a function call for a block of "free" storage. The address of that block is returned to the calling program. When the program has finished using the block, the program may return it to the "free list" maintained by the operating system or run-time system. This facility permits programs to request a potentially large number of blocks of storage, without having to know in advance how many blocks will be required. The linked-list structure permits blocks to be made available and returned in arbitrary sequence with minimal processing overhead.

The Free List algorithm in Section 5.4 implements the free list facility using an array to simulate available memory. You may choose to implement the algorithm precisely as it is presented here, although you will have to allocate a specific number of locations for the memory array. In older languages such as Basic, Cobol, and Fortran there is no other feasible option, because dynamic storage allocation is not supported in most versions. Languages that support dynamic storage allocation obviate the necessity to implement the Free List algorithm. You merely call a function such as *free*, which returns a pointer to a free block of memory.

The remaining algorithms make use of the Free List algorithm. There are list versions of the stack and queue algorithms, called Stack List and Queue List respectively.

The heap structure cannot be efficiently implemented using linked lists, and a list implementation of that algorithm is not presented. The Double List algorithm implements the doubly linked list, and the Balanced Tree algorithm implements the tree data structure.

Pascal and C programmers may wonder how list and tree structures can be presented without the *pointer* construct. Sedgewick (1988) has made the observation that there is very little difference between the subscripted array and pointer constructs. A pointer is a memory address, which can be thought of as a subscript for a generic Memory array that represents the whole of computer memory. The list-processing algorithms make use of this correspondence by storing all records in a global Memory array. You can replace any array reference such as Memory[*i*] by a pointer if this method of access is better suited to the task at hand.

Data structures are discussed very fully in most computer science textbooks, including the classics of Knuth (1969) and Sedgewick (1988). Mathematical formulas for the performances of a wide range of data structures are provided by Gonnet and Baeza-Yates (1991).

5.1 STACK ARRAY

Maintaining items in last-in first-out sequence, using an array structure

Example

To output the positive integer N as a sequence of separate digits, you push the digits onto a stack least significant digit first, and pop them from the stack most significant digit first:

```
call Stack~Initialize
loop
    call Stack~Push (N mod 10)
    let N = N ÷ 10
end loop when N = 0
loop
    call Stack~Pop (N)
    output N
end loop when Stack~Size ( ) = 0
```

Subprograms

5.1.1	Stack~Push (receives Data)
5.1.2	Stack~Pop (supplies Data)
5.1.3	Stack~Initialize
5.1.4	Stack~Size (*result integer*)

Usage

The essential characteristic of a stack, which contrasts it with a queue, is that the items are removed from it in the reverse order of their insertion. This type of data structure is useful particularly to writers of programming language compilers and interpreters. It helps in decoding parenthesized expressions, for example, where each right parenthesis must be matched with the most recent left parenthesis. It is also useful in operating systems, where device interrupts can themselves be interrupted. Restoration of execution must be to the most recently interrupted code.

The stack must be initialized before use. This is done by a call to Stack~Initialize. The stack is assumed to be stored in a global array named Stack, which has subscripts ranging from Lower to Upper. The constants Lower and Upper may have any desired values.

An item is inserted into the stack by a call to Stack~Push, and is removed from the stack by a call to Stack~Pop. By common convention the terms "push" and "pop" are used for "insert" and "remove" respectively. The function Stack~Size returns the number of items currently in the stack.

Analysis

Stack[Lower] contains the number of items currently in the stack, and is referred to as the stack pointer. Items are pushed into locations Stack[Lower+1] to Stack[Upper]. A maximum of (Upper – Lower) items may therefore be stored in the stack.

IMPLEMENTATION

<u>Exported Names</u>

Stack~Initialize	Initializes the stack (5.1.3)
Stack~Pop	Removes an item from the stack (5.1.2)
Stack~Push	Inserts an item into the stack (5.1.1)
Stack~Size	Calculates the number of items in the stack (5.1.4)

<u>Nicknames</u>

Data	Item to be pushed onto the stack or popped from the stack

<u>Global Names</u>

Lower	Lower Limit of the array Stack
Stack	Array in which the stack is stored
Upper	Upper limit of the array Stack

Code

constant Lower = 0
constant Upper = 100
variable Stack *is array* Lower *to* Upper *of integers*

5.1.1 Stack~Push (receives Data)

Pseudo Code

increment stack pointer by one
insert item at position in Stack given by stack pointer

Code

```
procedure Stack~Push (Data is integer)
    check Stack[Lower] < Upper
    let Stack[Lower] = Stack[Lower] + 1
    let Stack[Stack[Lower]] = Data
end Stack~Push
```

5.1.2 Stack~Pop (supplies Data)

Pseudo Code

get item at position in Stack given by stack pointer
decrement stack pointer by one

Code

```
procedure Stack~Pop (Data is integer)
    check Stack[Lower] > Lower
    let Data = Stack[Stack[Lower]]
    let Stack[Lower] = Stack[Lower] – 1
end Stack~Pop
```

5.1.3 Stack~Initialize

Pseudo Code

let stack pointer = lower limit of the array holding the stack

Code

```
procedure Stack~Initialize
    let Stack[Lower] = Lower
end Stack~Initialize
```

5.1.4 Stack~Size (*result integer*)

Pseudo Code

result is stack pointer minus lower limit of the array holding the stack

Code

```
function Stack~Size ( ) is integer
    result Stack[Lower] – Lower
end Stack~Size
```

TEST PROGRAM

Imported Names

Lower	Lower Limit of the array Stack (5.1)
Upper	Upper limit of the array Stack (5.1)

Local Names

Item	Item popped from stack

Pseudo Code

initialize stack pointer to zero
push (Upper – Lower) consecutive integers onto the stack in reverse sequence
pop (Upper – Lower) consecutive integers from the stack, checking the correctness of each
check stack size = 0

Code

```
variable Item is integer
call Stack~Initialize
for decreasing i = Upper to (Lower + 1)
    call Stack~Push (i)
end for
for i = (Lower + 1) to Upper
    call Stack~Pop (Item)
    check Item = i
end for
check Stack~Size ( ) = 0
```

5.2 QUEUE ARRAY

Maintaining items in first-in first-out sequence, using an array structure

Example

The following code obtains the values J = 1 and K = 2, and leaves the queue empty:

```
call Queue~Initialize
call Queue~Insert (1)
call Queue~Insert (2)
call Queue~Remove (J)
call Queue~Remove (K)
check Queue~Size ( ) = 0
```

Subprograms

5.2.1 Queue~Insert (receives Data)
5.2.2 Queue~Remove (supplies Data)
5.2.3 Queue~Initialize
5.2.4 Queue~Size (*result integer*)

Usage

The essential characteristic of a queue, which contrasts it with a stack, is that the items are removed from it in the same order as that in which they were inserted. For many purposes this order is the most logical, and relates easily to examples from everyday life, such as supermarket checkouts, telephone calls, and motor vehicle traffic.

The queue must be initialized before use. This is done by a call to Queue~Initialize. The queue is assumed to be stored in a global array named Queue, which has subscripts ranging from Lower to Upper. The constants Lower and Upper may have any desired values.

An item is inserted into the queue by a call to Queue~Insert, and is removed from the queue by a call to Queue~Remove. The function Queue~Size returns the number of items currently in the queue.

Analysis

Queue[Lower] contains a pointer to the front of the queue. Queue[Lower+1] contains a pointer to the rear of the queue. Items are queued in locations Queue[Lower+2] to Queue[Upper]. This leaves (Upper – Lower – 1) locations for the queue itself. Because of the way in which the algorithm keeps track of its pointers, one queue location is wasted. The maximum number of items that can be held in the queue is therefore (Upper – Lower – 2).

The algorithm operates by using Queue as circular storage, in which the location in the queue following Queue[Upper] is taken to be Queue[Lower+2]. The *mod* function is used for the purpose of "wrapping" the queue around from the end of the array to the beginning.

IMPLEMENTATION

Exported Names

Queue~Initialize	Initializes the queue (5.2.3)
Queue~Insert	Inserts an item into the queue (5.2.1)
Queue~Remove	Removes an item from the queue (5.2.2)
Queue~Size	Calculates the number of items in the queue (5.2.4)

Nicknames

Data	Item to be inserted into the queue or removed from the queue

Global Names

Front	Position in the Queue array of the pointer to the front of the queue
Lower	Lower limit of the array Queue
Queue	Array in which the queue is stored
Rear	Position in the Queue array of the pointer to the rear of the queue
Size	Number of locations in the Queue array used for the queue itself
Upper	Upper limit of the array Queue

Code

```
constant Lower = 0
constant Upper = 100
variable Queue is array Lower to Upper of integers
```

```
constant Front = Lower
constant Rear = Lower + 1
constant Size = Upper – Rear
```

5.2.1 Queue~Insert (receives Data)

Pseudo Code

increment pointer to rear of queue by one, with wraparound if necessary
insert item at position in Queue given by rear pointer
abort if pointer to rear of queue has overlapped pointer to front of queue

Code

```
procedure Queue~Insert (Data is integer)
    let Queue[Rear] = (Queue[Rear] mod Size) + 1
    let Queue[Queue[Rear] + Rear] = Data
    check Queue[Rear] ≠ Queue[Front]
end Queue~Insert
```

5.2.2 Queue~Remove (supplies Data)

Pseudo Code

abort if pointer to front of queue has overlapped pointer to rear of queue
increment pointer to front of queue by one, with wraparound if necessary
get item at position in Queue given by pointer to front of queue

Code

```
procedure Queue~Remove (Data is integer)
    check Queue[Front] ≠ Queue[Rear]
    let Queue[Front] = (Queue[Front] mod Size) + 1
    let Data = Queue[Queue[Front] + Rear]
end Queue~Remove
```

5.2.3 Queue~Initialize

Pseudo Code

initialize position of front of queue
initialize position of rear of queue

Code

```
procedure Queue~Initialize
    let Queue[Front] = 0
    let Queue[Rear] = 0
end Queue~Initialize
```

5.2.4 Queue~Size (*result integer*)

Pseudo Code

initialize position of front of queue
initialize position of rear of queue

Code

```
function Queue~Size ( ) is integer
    result (Queue[Rear] – Queue[Front] + Size) mod Size
end Queue~Size
```

TEST PROGRAM

<u>Imported Names</u>

Lower	Lower limit of the array Queue (5.2)
Upper	Upper limit of the array Queue (5.2)

<u>Local Names</u>

Item	Item removed from queue

Pseudo Code

```
initialize queue
for i = (Lower + 3) to Upper
    insert i successive integers into the queue
end for
for j = 1 to 3
    for i = (Lower + 3) to Upper
        remove an item from the front of the queue and insert it at the end
        check the item is equal to i
    end for
end for
```

Code

```
variable Item is integer
call Queue~Initialize
for i = (Lower + 3) to Upper               Put integers in all available queue
    call Queue~Insert (i)                  locations
end for
for j = 1 to 3                             Remove and insert three times as
    for i = (Lower + 3) to Upper           many integers as in queue
        call Queue~Remove (Item)
        check Item = i
        call Queue~Insert (Item)
    end for
end for
for i = (Lower + 3) to Upper               Check that integers in queue are
    call Queue~Remove (Item)               in correct sequence
    check Item = i
end for
check Queue~Size ( ) = 0
```

5.3 HEAP

Maintaining items in random-in largest-out sequence

Example

The following code obtains the values J = 3, K = 2, and L = 1, and leaves the heap empty:

call Heap~Initialize
call Heap~Insert (2)
call Heap~Insert (1)
call Heap~Insert (3)
call Heap~Remove (J)
call Heap~Remove (K)
call Heap~Remove (L)
check Heap~Size ( ) = 0

Subprograms

5.3.1 Heap~Insert (receives Data)
5.3.2 Heap~Remove (supplies Data)
5.3.3 Heap~Initialize
5.3.4 Heap~Size (*result integer*)

Usage

A heap is a convenient way of keeping an array of items in sorted sequence. It is useful when items are continually being inserted and removed, as happens in many real-time applications. Items may be inserted into the heap in any sequence by Heap~Insert. Heap~Remove always retrieves the largest item currently in the heap.

The heap must be initialized before use. This is done by a call to Heap~Initialize. The heap is assumed to be stored in an array named Heap, which has subscripts ranging from Lower to Upper. The constants Lower and Upper may have any desired values.

An item is inserted into the heap by a call to Heap~Insert, and is removed from the heap by a call to Heap~Remove. The function Heap~Size returns the number of items currently in the heap.

Analysis

Heap[Lower] contains the number of items currently in the heap. Items are inserted into locations Heap[Lower+1] to Heap[Upper]. A maximum of (Upper – Lower) items may be stored in the heap.

Bentley (1985) provides a useful introduction to heaps, which is helpful if you are unfamiliar with the structure. Even though the items in a heap are stored in an array, they are actually placed so that they may be accessed using the properties of binary trees. Consider the heap in Figure 5.1 of thirteen integers represented in the form of a binary tree.

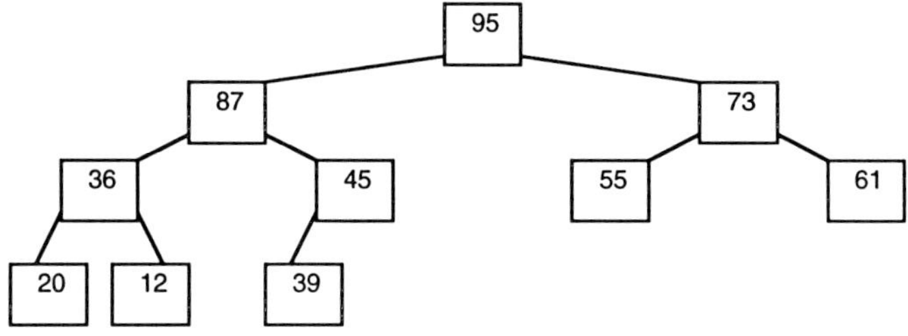

Figure 5.1

Each node has two "children". The value of the node is always greater than the value of its children. The children may be in either of the two possible orders. The tree is as balanced as it can be. To be "perfectly" balanced, the number of items must be exactly one less than a power of two.

The number of nodes in each level of the tree is always a power of two, except for the lowest level. The heap is stored level by level in successive locations of Heap. Suppose, for the sake of discussion, that Lower = 0. The first level, with one item, is stored in Heap[1]. The second level is stored in Heap[2] and Heap[3]. The third level is stored in Heap[4] … Heap[7], and so on. The last subscript for every level is a power of two minus one.

The insert and remove operations ensure that the heap property (that the parent is larger than both children) is preserved. Insertion puts the new item in location Heap[N+1], where N is the number of items currently in the heap. N is then incremented by 1. Suppose the new item is 74. It becomes the second child of 45. However, the heap property is now violated. To deal with this problem the new item is exchanged with its parent. This operation restores the heap property at that level. The process is repeated at higher levels until the heap property is not violated or the top of the heap is reached.

The remove operation always takes the top item from the heap, that is, Heap[1]. The spare location is filled by Heap[N]. N is then decremented by one. Of course, this replacement of Heap[1] by Heap[N] may result in the heap property being violated. If Heap[1] is less than either of its children, it is exchanged with the largest child. The process is repeated at each lower level at which the heap property is violated.

The number of items at any level of the heap is twice the number at its parent level. Because of this geometric increase, only about log_2 (N) iterations of the insertion or deletion loops are required to move from the bottom of the heap to the top, or vice versa. Insertions and deletions will therefore require in the worst case log_2 (N), and on average half that number of iterations of the loops.

IMPLEMENTATION

<u>Exported Names</u>

Heap~Initialize	Initializes the Heap (5.3.3)
Heap~Insert	Inserts an item into the heap (5.3.1)
Heap~Remove	Removes an item from the heap (5.3.2)
Heap~Size	Calculates the number of items in the heap (5.3.4)

Nicknames

Data Item to be inserted into the heap or removed from the heap

Global Names

Heap Array in which the heap is stored

Lower Lower limit of the array Heap

Upper Upper limit of the array Heap

Local Names

Child Position of a child item in the heap

End Position of the last item in the heap

Parent Position of a parent item in the heap

Code

```
constant Lower = 0
constant Upper = 100
variable Heap is array Lower to Upper of integers
```

5.3.1 Heap~Insert (receives Data)

Pseudo Code

```
increment heap size by one
insert item at the end of heap, to become the child
find position of the parent of the child
loop until parent ≥ child
    interchange parent and child
    let child = parent
    let parent = parent of child
end loop
```

Code

```
procedure Heap~Insert (Data is integer)
    variables Child, End, Parent are integers
    check Heap[Lower] < Upper
    let End = Heap[Lower] + 1
    let Heap[Lower] = maxinteger          Dummy parent on top of heap to
    let Child = End                       terminate loop when encountered
    let Heap[Child] = Data
    let Parent = (Child + Lower) ÷ 2
    loop until Heap[Parent] ≥ Heap[Child]
        call swap (Heap[Parent], Heap[Child])
        let Child = Parent
        let Parent = (Parent + Lower) ÷ 2
    end loop
    let Heap[Lower] = End
end Heap~Insert
```

5.3.2 Heap~Remove (supplies Data)

Pseudo Code

```
return item at top of heap to calling program
replace item at top of heap by item at bottom
decrement heap size by one
select as the first parent the top of the heap, the parent of all parents
select as the child the first child of the top of the heap
loop until child is beyond the end of the heap
    if child is less than second child then
        select the second child as the child
    end if
    exit loop when parent ≥ child
    interchange parent and child
    select position of first child of parent in its new position
end loop
```

Code

```
procedure Heap~Remove (Data is integer)
    variables Child, End, Parent are integers
    let End = Heap[Lower]
    check End > Lower
    let Data = Heap[Lower+1]
    let Heap[Lower+1] = Heap[End]
    let Heap[End] = –maxinteger                    Dummy child to terminate loop
    let End = End – 1                              when encountered
    let Parent = Lower + 1
    let Child = Lower + 2
    loop until Child > End
        if Heap[Child] < Heap[Child+1] then
            let Child = Child + 1
        end if
        if Heap[Parent] ≥ Heap[Child] then
            let Child = End
        else
            call swap (Heap[Parent], Heap[Child])
        end if
        let Parent = Child
        let Child = (Child + Lower) * 2
    end loop
    let Heap[Lower] = End
end Heap~Remove
```

5.3.3 Heap~Initialize

Pseudo Code

let heap pointer = lower limit of the array holding the heap

Code

```
procedure Heap~Initialize
    let Heap[Lower] = Lower
end Heap~Initialize
```

5.3.4 Heap~Size *(result integer)*

Pseudo Code

result is pointer to bottom of heap minus lower limit of the array holding the heap

Code

```
function Heap~Size ( ) is integer
    result Heap[Lower] – Lower
end Heap~Size
```

TEST PROGRAM

Imported Names

Lower Lower Limit of the array Heap (5.3)

Upper Upper limit of the array Heap (5.3)

Local Names

Item Item removed from heap

Pseudo Code

initialize heap
insert (Upper – Lower) integers into the heap
remove (Upper – Lower) successive integers from the heap
check removed integers are in reverse numerical order

Code

```
variable Item is integer
call Heap~Initialize
for i = Lower to (Upper – 1)
    call Heap~Insert (i)
end for
for decreasing i = (Upper – 1) to Lower
    call Heap~Remove (Item)
    check Item = i
end for
check Heap~Size ( ) = 0
```

5.4 FREE LIST

Maintaining a "free-list" of free memory locations

Example

The following code initializes the "free list", and obtains a "record" containing eight free memory locations of the global array Memory, from Memory[Location] to Memory[Location+7]:

call Free~Initialize (8)
call Free~Get (Location)

Subprograms

5.4.1	Free~Get (supplies Location)
5.4.2	Free~Give (receives Location)
5.4.3	Free~Initialize (receives Size)
5.4.4	Free~Size (*result integer*)

Usage

This algorithm is coded to supply "records" (sets of contiguous locations) of a given size to the calling program. Only one size of record may be used in any one program, using the algorithm as it is currently coded.

The free list must be initialized before it is used. This is done by a call to Free~Initialize, specifying the size of record required. Free~Initialize constructs the free list out of all available free memory.

The procedure Free~Get supplies the location of a free record, that is, the first location in the set of contiguous locations comprising the record. A call to Free~Give returns to the free list a record no longer required by the calling program. The size of the free list may be obtained at any point in a program by a call to Free~Size. This operation requires O (N) processing time.

Analysis

The code simulates the use of actual computer memory by using the evocative name Memory for the array in which the free list is constructed. Assembly language, C, and Pascal programmers, and others who can obtain access to actual memory locations via language constructs called *pointers*, can make the required adjustments to the algorithm. As noted in the introduction to this chapter, there is very little difference in concept between pointers for accessing memory locations and subscripts for accessing array locations.

Using the above example, Free~Initialize sets up the free list in the form shown in Figure 5.2, where the integers at the left are "addresses", or subscripts of the array Memory. The array Memory is currently dimensioned with limits Lower = 0 and Upper = 100, allowing for twelve records.

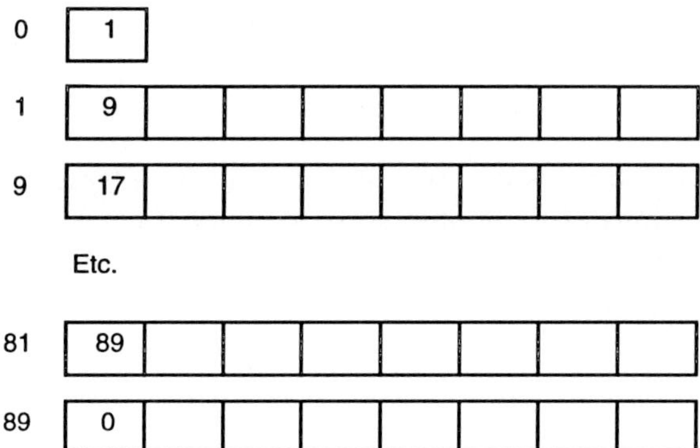

Figure 5.2

The first location in each record in the free list contains the address of the next record in the list. Location Lower in the memory array, that is, Memory[Lower], contains the address of the first location in the list. The last item in the list contains a zero as the address of the nonexistent next record.

After execution of the call to Free~Give in the above example, the memory array takes the form shown in Figure 5.3. Note that Memory[Lower] has been altered to "point" to the second record. The value of Memory[1] is now irrelevant to the free list algorithm, the record with address 1 having been given to the calling program. The address of the record must not be lost by the calling program, of course.

A call to Free~Give at this point, specifying location 1 as the address of the record to be returned to the free list, will restore the memory array to its original state.

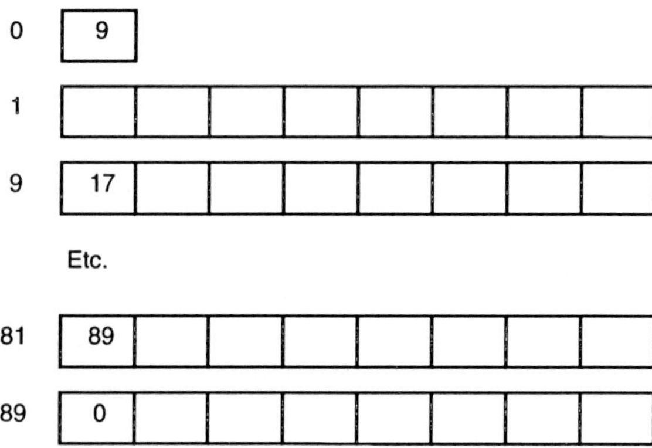

Figure 5.3

IMPLEMENTATION

<u>Exported Names</u>

Free~Get	Obtains the address of a free record (5.4.1)
Free~Give	Returns a record to the free list (5.4.2)
Free~Initialize	Constructs a free list of records of a given size (5.4.3)
Free~Size	Calculates the number of records in the free list (5.4.4)

<u>Nicknames</u>

Location	Pointer to (index of) first user location in a Memory record
Size	Number of integer locations required for each record

<u>Global Names</u>

Lower	Lower limit of the array Memory
Memory	Array of memory for records of a given size
Upper	Upper limit of the array Memory

<u>Local Names</u>

Count	Counter of number of locations in the free list
Location	Pointer to (index of) pointer location in a Memory record
Next	Pointer to next record in Memory
This	Pointer to current record in Memory

Code

```
constant Lower = 0
constant Upper = 100
variable Memory is array Lower to Upper of integers
```

5.4.1 Free~Get (supplies Location)

Pseudo Code

let Location = pointer to next free record
make pointer to first free record point to location pointed to by Location

Code

```
procedure Free~Get (Location is integer)
    check Memory[Lower] ≠ 0
    let Location = Memory[Lower]
    let Memory[Lower] = Memory[Location]
end Free~Get
```

5.4.2 Free~Give (receives Location)

Pseudo Code

make pointer in current record point to first free record
make pointer to first free record point to current record

Code

```
procedure Free~Give (Location is integer)
    let Memory[Location] = Memory[Lower]
    let Memory[Lower] = Location
end Free~Give
```

5.4.3 Free~Initialize (receives Size)

Pseudo Code

```
for i = 1 to maximum number of records minus 1
    let pointer for record = pointer to next record
end for
let pointer for last record = 0
let pointer to first free record = address of first record
```

Code

```
procedure Free~Initialize (Size is integer)
    variables This, Next are integers
    let This = Lower + 1
    for i = 2 to ((Upper – Lower) ÷ Size)
        let Next = This + Size
        let Memory[This] = Next
        let This = Next
    end for
    let Memory[This] = 0
    let Memory[Lower] = Lower + 1
end Free~Initialize
```

5.4.4 Free~Size (*result integer*)

Pseudo Code

```
let Location = pointer to first free record
loop until Location = 0
    let Count = Count + 1
    let Location = pointer to next free record in Memory
end loop
```

Code

```
function Free~Size ( ) is integer
    variable Count, Location is integer
    let Location = Memory[Lower]
    let Count = 0
    loop until Location = 0
        let Location = Memory[Location]
        let Count = Count + 1
    end loop
    result Count
end Free~Size
```

TEST PROGRAM

Local Names

Item	Various quantities obtained from procedures being called
M	Maximum size of memory array
N	Number of records that will fit into memory
R	Record size

Pseudo Code

```
set up memory for N records of size R each
for i = 1 to N
    get next free record and check its address
end for
check the free list is empty
for i = 1 to N
    return each record to the free list
end for
check the free list is the same size as it was initially
```

Code

```
variable Item is integer
constant R = 4
constant N = (Upper – Lower) ÷ R
call Free~Initialize (R)
check Free~Size ( ) = N
for i = 1 to N
    call Free~Get (Item)
    check Item = ((i – 1) * R) + 1
end for
check Free~Size ( ) = 0
for i = 1 to N
    call Free~Give (((i – 1) * R) + 1)
end for
check Free~Size ( ) = N
```

5.5 STACK LIST

Maintaining items in last-in first-out sequence, using a free-list structure

Example

This example illustrates a stack using storage supplied by the free list algorithm discussed in Section 5.4. The following code initializes the stack (and incidentally obtains the total number of available free list records Limit), using the location S to contain the location of (pointer to) the top of the stack. It then delivers J = 2 and K = 1 and leaves the stack empty:

```
variables Limit, S are integers
call Stack~Initialize (S, Limit)
call Stack~Push (S, 1)
call Stack~Push (S, 2)
call Stack~Pop (S, J)
call Stack~Pop (S, K)
check Stack~Size (S) = 0
```

Subprograms

5.5.1 Stack~Push (receives Stack, Data)
5.5.2 Stack~Pop (receives Stack; supplies Data)
5.5.3 Stack~Initialize (receives Stack; supplies MaxStack)
5.5.4 Stack~Size (receives Stack; *result integer*)

Usage

This algorithm has overall properties similar to those of the array version given in Section 5.1, which you should consult before continuing with this section. There are four subprograms with the same names, but they have different nicknames to accommodate the different data structure. The stack is stored in "records" supplied by the free list algorithm discussed in Section 5.4. You should also be familiar with that section, and in particular should understand how linked lists operate.

The subprograms communicate via two nicknames each (except Stack~Size, which has one), the first nickname in each case being an integer location containing a pointer to the first item in the list. Naturally, this pointer is updated upon each call to any of the subprograms.

The free list is set up by a call to Stack~Initialize to generate records containing two locations, one for a pointer and one for a data item. Stack~Push inserts records into the stack and Stack~Pop removes them. The size of the stack is computed by Stack~Size.

This implementation of the stack algorithm offers more flexibility than the array version, in that multiple stacks may be used in the same program. All that is required is to use a different integer location to point to the list corresponding to each stack.

Analysis

The list version of the stack algorithm is considerably less efficient than the array version, because more work has to be done in transferring records from the free list and in adjusting the pointers. Worse, this version uses two locations for each record instead of one. The reason is that pointers need to be kept as well as data items. With arrays no pointers are required and there is one location per stack item.

The key advantage of this version is that a virtually unlimited number of records may be used in the list, without the number having to be known in advance. The other advantage, mentioned earlier, is that multiple stacks may be used without wastage of memory. Using the stack array algorithm one would have to allocate storage for many arrays, much of which could be unused. The stack list algorithm uses a minimum amount of storage.

This algorithm admits the possibility of segmenting the list so that not all of it resides in memory. If necessary, more sophisticated code than is provided in Section 5.4 can be written to segment the list into blocks, thus saving blocks on disk storage media.

IMPLEMENTATION

<u>Exported Names</u>

Stack~Initialize	Initializes free list for the stack (5.5.3)
Stack~Pop	Removes an item from the stack (5.5.2)
Stack~Push	Inserts an item into the stack (5.5.1)
Stack~Size	Calculates the number of items in the stack (5.5.4)

<u>Imported Names</u>

Free~Get	Supplies address of next free record in Memory (5.4.1)
Free~Give	Returns address of a record in Memory to free list (5.4.2)
Free~Initialize	Makes all of Memory available (5.4.3)
Free~Size	Calculates number of records in free list (5.4.4)
Memory	Array containing records for stack (5.4)

<u>Nicknames</u>

Data	Item to be pushed onto the stack or popped from the stack
MaxStack	Maximum number of locations available for stack
Stack	Pointer to current stack location in Memory

<u>Local Names</u>

Count	Counter of number of records in the stack
Location	Pointer to (index of) a Memory location

5.5.1 Stack~Push (receives Stack, Data)

Pseudo Code

get a free record from the free list (the "current" record)
let first location of current record = pointer to previous top of stack
let second location of current record = data item Data
let pointer to top of stack = location of current record

Code

```
procedure Stack~Push (Stack, Data are integers)
    variable Location is integer
    call Free~Get (Location)
    let Memory[Location] = Stack
    let Memory[Location+1] = Data
    let Stack = Location
end Stack~Push
```

5.5.2 Stack~Pop (receives Stack; supplies Data)

Pseudo Code

let pointer to top of stack = pointer from first location of current record
let Data = data item from second location in current record at top of stack
give back record no longer needed to the free list

Code

```
procedure Stack~Pop (Stack, Data are integers)
    variable Location is integer
    let Location = Stack
    let Stack = Memory[Location]
    let Data = Memory[Location+1]
    call Free~Give (Location)
end Stack~Pop
```

5.5.3 Stack~Initialize (receives Stack; supplies MaxStack)

Pseudo Code

```
let pointer to top of stack = 0
set stack memory to free records with two locations each (pointer and data item)
calculate MaxStack as maximum size of stack
```

Code

```
procedure Stack~Initialize (Stack, MaxStack are integers)
    let Stack = 0
    call Free~Initialize (2)
    let MaxStack = Free~Size ( )
end Stack~Initialize
```

5.5.4 Stack~Size (receives Stack; *result integer*)

Pseudo Code

```
initialize counter to zero
initialize Location to record at top of stack
loop until Location is record at bottom of stack
    let Location = record pointed to by current record
    let Count = Count + 1
end loop
result is Count
```

Code

```
function Stack~Size (Stack is integer) is integer
    variable Count, Location are integers
    let Count = 0
    let Location = Stack
    loop until Location = 0
        let Location = Memory[Location]
        let Count = Count + 1
    end loop
    result Count
end Stack~Size
```

TEST PROGRAM

Local Names

M Maximum number of records available for the stack
S Pointer to linked list of Memory locations for the stack
T Temporary location to hold item popped from stack

Pseudo Code

initialize stack, calculating the maximum number of records M
push M consecutive integers onto the stack in reverse sequence
pop M consecutive integers from the stack
check popped integers are in ascending sequence
check the stack is empty

Code

```
variables M, S, T are integers
call Stack~Initialize (S, M)
for decreasing i = M to 1
    call Stack~Push (S, i)
end for
check Stack~Size (S) = M
for i = 1 to M
    call Stack~Pop (S, T)
    check T = i
end for
check Stack~Size (S) = 0
```

5.6 QUEUE LIST

Maintaining items in first-in first-out sequence, using a free-list structure

Example

This example illustrates a queue using storage supplied by the free list algorithm discussed in Section 5.4. The following code initializes the queue (and incidentally obtains the total number of available free list records Limit), using the locations F and R to contain the locations of (pointers to) the front and rear of the queue. It then delivers J = 1 and K = 2 and leaves the queue empty:

```
variables Limit, F, R are integers
call Queue~Initialize (F, R, Limit)
call Queue~Insert (F, R, 1)
call Queue~Insert (F, R, 2)
call Queue~Remove (F, R, J)
call Queue~Remove (F, R, K)
check Queue~Size (F, R) = 0
```

Subprograms

5.6.1 Queue~Insert (updates Front, Rear; receives Data)
5.6.2 Queue~Remove (updates Front, Rear; supplies Data)
5.6.3 Queue~Initialize (supplies Front, Rear, MaxQueue)
5.6.4 Queue~Size (receives Front, Rear; *result integer*)

Usage

This algorithm has overall properties similar to those of the array version in Section 5.2, which you should consult before continuing with this section. There are four subprograms with the same names, but they have different nicknames to accommodate the different data structure. The queue is stored in "records" supplied by the free list algorithm discussed in Section 5.4. You should also be familar with that section, and in particular should understand how linked lists operate.

The subprograms communicate via three nicknames each (except Queue~Size, which has two), the first two nicknames in each case being integer locations containing a pointer to the front and rear of the queue respectively. These pointers are updated by the subprograms.

The free list is set up by a call to Queue~Initialize to generate records containing two locations, one for a pointer and one for a data item. Queue~Insert inserts records into the rear of the queue and Queue~Remove removes them from the front. The size of the queue is computed by Queue~Size.

This implementation of the queue algorithm offers more flexibility than the array version, in that multiple queues may be used in the same program. All that is required is to use a different integer location to point to the list corresponding to each queue. The analysis of the stack algorithm in Section 5.5 is relevant also to the queue algorithm and will not be repeated here.

IMPLEMENTATION

<u>Exported Names</u>

Queue~Initialize	Initializes free list for the queue (5.6.3)
Queue~Insert	Inserts an item at the rear of the queue (5.6.1)
Queue~Remove	Removes an item from the front of the queue (5.6.2)
Queue~Size	Calculates the number of items in the queue (5.6.4)

<u>Imported Names</u>

Free~Get	Supplies address of next free record in Memory (5.4.1)
Free~Give	Returns address of a record in Memory to free list (5.4.2)
Free~Initialize	Makes all of Memory available (5.4.3)
Free~Size	Calculates number of records in free list (5.4.4)
Memory	Array containing records for queue (5.4)

<u>Nicknames</u>

Data	Item to be inserted or removed
MaxQueue	Maximum number of locations available for queue
Queue	Pointer to current queue location in Memory

Local Names

Count	Counter of number of records in the queue
Location	Pointer to (index of) a Memory location

5.6.1 Queue~Insert (updates Front, Rear; receives Data)

Pseudo Code

```
get the location of a free record (the "current" record)
if queue is empty then
    let pointer to front of queue = location of the current record
else
    let pointer in record at rear of queue = location of the current record
end if
let first location of current record = null pointer to signify end of queue
let second location of current record = data item Data
let pointer to rear of queue = location of current record
```

Code

```
procedure Queue~Insert (Front, Rear, Data are integers)
    variable Location is integer
    call Free~Get (Location)
    if Rear = 0 then
        let Front = Location
    else
        let Memory[Rear] = Location
    end if
    let Memory[Location] = 0
    let Memory[Location+1] = Data
    let Rear = Location
end Queue~Insert
```

5.6.2 Queue~Remove (updates Front, Rear; supplies Data)

Pseudo Code

```
define current record as record pointed to by pointer to front of queue
let pointer to front of queue = pointer in first location of current record
let data item Data = second location of current record
give back the location of current record to the free list
if queue is empty then
    let pointer to rear of queue = null pointer
end if
```

Code

```
procedure Queue~Remove (Front, Rear, Data are integers)
    variable Location is integer
    check Front > 0
```

```
        let Location = Front
        let Front = Memory[Location]
        let Data = Memory[Location+1]
        call Free~Give (Location)
        if Front = 0 then
            let Rear = 0
        end if
    end Queue~Remove
```

5.6.3 Queue~Initialize (supplies Front, Rear, MaxQueue)

Pseudo Code

```
    let pointer to front of queue = null pointer
    let pointer to rear of queue = null pointer
    set queue memory to free records with two locations each (pointer and data item)
    calculate MaxQueue as maximum size of queue
```

Code

```
    procedure Queue~Initialize (Front, Rear, MaxQueue are integers)
        let Front = 0
        let Rear = 0
        call Free~Initialize (2)
        let MaxQueue = Free~Size ( )
    end Queue~Initialize
```

5.6.4 Queue~Size (receives Front, Rear; result integer)

Pseudo Code

```
    initialize counter to zero if queue is empty, otherwise to one
    initialize Location to record at front of queue
    loop until Location is record at rear of queue
        let Location = record pointed to by current record
        let Count = Count + 1
    end loop
    result is Count
```

Code

```
    function Queue~Size (Front, Rear are integers) is integer
        variable Count, Location are integers
        if Front = 0 then
            let Count = 0
        else
            let Count = 1
        end if
        let Location = Front
```

```
        loop until Location = Rear
            let Location = Memory[Location]
            let Count = Count + 1
        end loop
        result Count
    end Queue~Size
```

TEST PROGRAM

Local Names

- F Pointer to (index of) a Memory location, the front of the queue
- M Maximum number of records available for the queue
- R Pointer to (index of) a Memory location, the rear of the queue
- T Temporary location to hold item removed from the queue

Pseudo Code

```
initialize queue, calculating the maximum number of records M
insert M consecutive integers in the queue
remove M consecutive integers from the queue
check removed integers are in ascending sequence
check the queue is empty
```

Code

```
variables F, M, R, T are integers
call Queue~Initialize (F, R, M)
for i = 1 to M
    call Queue~Insert (F, R, i)
end for
check Queue~Size (F, R) = M
for i = 1 to M
    call Queue~Remove (F, R, T)
    check T = i
end for
check Queue~Size (F, R) = 0
```

5.7 DOUBLY LINKED LIST

Maintaining items in a linear list linked in both directions

Example

The test program creates a doubly linked list containing integer keys in reverse numerical sequence. The list is sorted, and a check is made that the sorting has been carried out successfully. Moving forward and backward in a doubly linked list is very simple. Suppose C points to the current record. The following two lines move C forward to the next record and then move C backward to return it to the current record:

let C = Get (Forward, C)
let C = Get (Backward, C)

Subprograms

There are five procedures for manipulating a doubly linked list. All except the fifth begin with the word "Double", and they comprise parts of the doubly linked list manipulation algorithm. The last procedure presents an entirely separate algorithm for sorting, which uses the merge sort process. It is presented here as well as in Chapter 6 because merge sort is particularly suited to sorting linked lists.

5.7.1 Double~Search (receives Header, KeyValue)
5.7.2 Double~Insert (updates Current; receives KeyValue, DataValue)
5.7.3 Double~Remove (updates Current)
5.7.4 Double~Initialize (supplies Header)
5.7.5 Merge~Sort (receives Header)

Usage

For some purposes the use of a doubly linked list will constitute overkill. A singly linked list, like that maintained by the free list algorithm in Section 5.4, is adequate provided that you want to search the list only in one direction. A doubly linked list allows you to search either forward or backward. More significantly in some applications, a doubly linked list allows you to delete records randomly. To remove a record, just connect up the two records to which the record to be deleted points.

The doubly linked list is stored in "records" supplied by the free list algorithm discussed in Section 5.4. You should be familar with that section, and in particular should understand how linked lists operate. It will also aid in understanding the more complex doubly linked list algorithm if you are familiar with list processing using the stack and queue algorithms in Sections 5.5 and 5.6.

A doubly linked list has the distinguishing characteristic that every record points in two directions—to the record following it and to the record preceding it. In this section of the book, records may contain both "keys" and other data. The term "key" is widely used in computing but not often defined. A key is a field (or a group of fields) in a record, the contents of which comprise an identifier for the record. For simplicity of presentation, assume that records have one integer field that acts as a key, and one integer field to contain an item of data.

The programming for doubly linked lists is greatly simplified by sandwiching the list between a header record and a trailer record. The procedure Double~Initialize sets up the header and trailer records. The null list created by this initialization has the form shown in Figure 5.4.

The header and trailer records have been allocated locations 1–4 and 5–8 respectively. The header record points forward to the trailer record and the trailer record points backward to the header record. In addition, for programming convenience the header record points backward to the trailer record, and the trailer record points to itself. These are somewhat arbitrary conventions that help to minimize the complexity of the code. The key and data fields are not initialized, but the key field of the trailer record is set and used by Double~Search and Double~Sort.

	Backward	Forward	Key	Data	
1	5	5			Header
5	1	5			Trailer

Figure 5.4

Double~Insert inserts a record into the list immediately before the "current" record. The inserted record then becomes the current record. For some purposes it makes more sense to insert the new record *after* the current record. If you want to search the list before insertion to ensure that the new key is not already in the list, it will be more convenient to insert before the current record, because Double~Search stops with the trailer record as the current record if a key is not found. On the other hand, if you want to create a sorted list by inserting keys that are already in sorted sequence, it is more convenient for the algorithm to insert the new record after the current record. We have implemented the former method here, so that we easily obtain a list with keys in reverse sequence for exercising Merge~Sort. Double~Insert can be modified to insert after by getting the *next* record instead of the *previous* record on entry, and then replacing references to "previous" by "current" and "current" by "next". Figure 5.5 shows how the list looks after a record with key and data fields equal to 2 has been inserted.

	Backward	Forward	Key	Data	
1	5	10			Header
10	1	5	2	2	
5	10	5			Trailer

Figure 5.5

Double~Remove removes the "current" record. Removal of the above record 10, for example, would restore the list to its original initialized state. If the address of the record is not known, but the key is known, it is necessary to use Double~Search to find the address. Double~Search is a function that searches the list for a given key, and returns either the address of the record in which the key was found, or the address of the trailer if the key was not found.

Merge~Sort sorts the entire list by the key fields. The Merge~Sort algorithm does not make use of the doubly linked property. The same algorithm can be applied to singly linked lists merely by deleting references to backward pointers.

No specific subprogram is provided for finding the size of the list. It is left to you to implement a subprogram along the lines of Stack~Size in Section 5.5 if such a facility is needed.

Analysis

Double~Initialize, Double~Insert, and Double~Remove operate in O (1) time. Double~Search requires O (N) time, where N is the size of the list. These are all relatively simple subprograms and will not be considered further.

Merge~Sort is implemented largely along the lines suggested by Sedgewick (1988). This is the "bottom-up" version, which is nonrecursive. It is an efficient and clean implementation, which eliminates a little of the overhead in Sedgewick's version (chasing down merged sublists merely to update pointers). Nevertheless it still contains a minor inefficiency that is hard to remove without complicating the code. We will refer to that in a moment.

In the first pass through the list the method processes pairs of adjacent records. Each pair is sorted, the record with the lower key preceding the record with the higher key. In the second pass pairs of sorted sublists of two items are merged to produce sorted sublists of four records. The process is applied iteratively until the entire list is in sorted sequence. The sublists are merged in place, without creating new records, merely by changing the values of pointers. The code determines when to stop by checking when just one pair of sublists has been merged in the major loop (i.e., when M = 1). The trailer is set up initially to contain a key greater than any of the keys in the list. This allows the merging process to take place without special tests being made for the trailer record.

Because of the doubling of the length of the sublists in each iteration, the process is very efficient, requiring about log_2 (N) iterations. The execution time for the algorithm is therefore O (N *log* N).

The code works most efficiently if N is a power of two. In general, this will not be the case, and the two *for* loops may do nothing useful for a greater or lesser part of the time while the algorithm is processing the last pair of sublists in each iteration of the major loop. When the *for* loop reaches the trailer, it finds that the forward pointer of the trailer points to the trailer again. The *for* loop merely cycles from the trailer to the trailer until the loop counter reaches N. At the expense of complicating the code, the *for* loops could be replaced by loops that both count and test whether the trailer has been reached. These complications introduce additional instructions into the loops, and might actually make the code run slower than the current implementation.

IMPLEMENTATION

<u>Exported Names</u>

Double~Initialize	Initializes free list for the doubly linked list (5.7.4)
Double~Insert	Inserts an item at the rear of the doubly linked list (5.7.2)
Double~Remove	Removes an item from the front of the doubly linked list (5.7.3)

Double~Search	Searches for a given key in the doubly linked list (5.7.1)
Merge~Sort	Sorts doubly linked list on key fields (5.7.5)
Imported Names	
Free~Get	Supplies address of next free record in Memory (5.4.1)
Free~Give	Returns address of a record in Memory to free list (5.4.2)
Free~Initialize	Makes all of Memory available (5.4.3)
Free~Size	Calculates number of records in free list (5.4.4)
Memory	Array containing records for doubly linked list (5.4)
Local Subprograms	
Get	Retrieves a field from a specified position in a specified record
Put	Stores a field in a specified position in a specified record
Nicknames	
Current	Pointer to current doubly linked list record in Memory
DataValue	Data item to be inserted in doubly linked list record
Header	Pointer to header record of doubly linked list in Memory
KeyValue	Value of key to be inserted in record or to be searched for
Global Names	
Backward	Offset in record for backward pointer
Data	Offset in record for data item
Forward	Offset in record for forward pointer
Key	Offset in record for record key
Local Names	
Location	Pointer to a Memory location
End	Pointer to next record following end of second sublist
First	Pointer to first sublist selected for merging
M	Counter of number of merges (pairs of sublists)
N	Length of sublist
Next	Pointer to record following current record in list
Previous	Pointer to record preceding current record in list
Second	Pointer to second sublist selected for merging
Trailer	Pointer to trailer record of list

Code

constant Backward = 0
constant Forward = 1
constant Key = 2
constant Data = 3

5.7.1 Double~Search (receives Header, KeyValue)

Pseudo Code

initialize current record to first record in list
loop until end of list or required record is found
  let current record = record following current record
end loop
result is current record

Code

```
function Double~Search (Header, KeyValue are integers) is integer
    variable Next, Trailer is integer
    let Trailer = Get (Backward, Header)
    call Put (Key, Trailer, KeyValue)
    let Next = Get (Forward, Header)
    loop until Get (Key, Next) = KeyValue
        let Next = Get (Forward, Next)
    end loop
    result Next
end Double~Search
```

5.7.2 Double~Insert (updates Current; receives KeyValue, DataValue)

Pseudo Code

```
get a free record from the free list
set backward pointer in free record to point to record preceding current record
set forward pointer in free record to point to current record
put key and data item into free record
set backward pointer in current record to point to free record
set forward pointer in record preceding current record to point to free record
let current record = free record
```

Code

```
procedure Double~Insert (Current, KeyValue, DataValue are integers)
    variables Previous, Location are integers
    let Previous = Get (Backward, Current)
    call Free~Get (Location)
    call Put (Backward, Location, Previous)
    call Put (Forward, Location, Current)
    call Put (Key, Location, KeyValue)
    call Put (Data, Location, DataValue)
    call Put (Backward, Current, Location)
    call Put (Forward, Previous, Location)
    let Current = Location
end Double~Insert
```

5.7.3 Double~Remove (updates Current)

Pseudo Code

```
set backward pointer in record following current record to point to record preceding
        current record
set forward pointer in record preceding current record to point to record following
        current record
give current record back to the free list
let current record = record following current record
```

Code

```
procedure Double~Remove (Current is integer)
    variables Previous, Next are integers
    let Next = Get (Forward, Current)
    let Previous = Get (Backward, Current)
    call Put (Backward, Next, Previous)
    call Put (Forward, Previous, Next)
    call Free~Give (Current)
    let Current = Next
end Double~Remove
```

5.7.4 Double~Initialize (supplies Header)

Pseudo Code

```
set memory to free records with four locations each (for 2 pointers, key, and data)
get record from the free list to contain the header
get record from the free list to contain the trailer
set backward and forward pointers in header to point to the trailer
set backward pointer in trailer to point to header
set forward pointer in trailer to point to the trailer itself
```

Code

```
procedure Double~Initialize (Header is integer)
    variable Trailer is integer
    call Free~Initialize (4)
    call Free~Get (Header)
    call Free~Get (Trailer)
    call Put (Backward, Header, Trailer)
    call Put (Forward, Header, Trailer)
    call Put (Backward, Trailer, Header)
    call Put (Forward, Trailer, Trailer)
end Double~Initialize
```

5.7.5 Merge~Sort (receives Header)

Pseudo Code

```
initialize size of sublists, N, to 1
loop
    initialize current record position to header position
    loop
        let First = pointer to record following previous end of two sublists (or header
                if none)
        skip N records down the list (or to the trailer, whichever comes first)
        let Second = pointer to record following end of first sublist
        skip N records down the list (or to the trailer, whichever comes first)
        loop until First = Second
```

```
            if key in First record ≤ key in Second record
                link First record to current record and advance First to next record
            else
                link Second record to current record and advance Second to next
                        record
            end if
        end loop
    end loop when end of second sublist is at the trailer
    let N = N * 2
end loop when only the merge loop was executed only once
```

Code

```
procedure Merge~Sort (Header is integer)
    variables Current, End, First, M, N, Previous, Second, Trailer are integers
    let N = 1
    let Trailer = Get (Backward, Header)
    call Put (Key, Trailer, maxinteger)          Key higher than any real key
    loop
        let Current = Header
        let End = Get (Forward, Header)
        let M = 0
        loop
            let First = End                      Establish extent of first sublist,
            let Second = First                   marking its beginning and end
            for i = 1 to N
                let Second = Get (Forward, Second)
            end for
            let Previous = Get (Backward, Second)
            call Put (Forward, Previous, Trailer)
            let End = Second                     Establish extent of second sublist,
            for i = 1 to N                       marking its beginning and end
                let End = Get (Forward, End)
            end for
            let Previous = Get (Backward, End)
            call Put (Forward, Previous, Trailer)
            loop until First = Second                     Merge the sublists
                if Get (Key, First) ≤ Get (Key, Second) then
                    call Put (Forward, Current, First)
                    call Put (Backward, First, Current)
                    let Current = First
                    let First = Get (Forward, First)
                else
                    call Put (Forward, Current, Second)
                    call Put (Backward, Second, Current)
                    let Current = Second
                    let Second = Get (Forward, Second)
                end if
            end loop
```

```
            let M = M + 1
        end loop when End = Trailer
        call Put (Backward, End, Current)
        let N = N * 2
    end loop when M = 1
end Merge~Sort
```

Local **Get** (receives Field, Pointer; *result integer*)

```
function Get (Field, Pointer is integer) is integer
    result Memory[Pointer+Field]
end Get
```

Local **Put** (receives Field, Pointer; supplies Value)

```
procedure Put (Field, Pointer, Value are integers)
    let Memory[Pointer+Field] = Value
end Put
```

TEST PROGRAM

Local Names

C Pointer to current record in the doubly linked list
H Pointer to the front of the doubly linked list
M Maximum number of records available for the doubly linked list

Pseudo Code

initialize doubly linked list, calculating the maximum number of useful records M
insert M records, with keys in the range 1 to M
attempt to find the last inserted key and check that it follows the header
attempt to find a missing key and check that current record is the trailer
sort the records
find and remove records, checking the key of the removed record
check the list is empty

Code

```
variables C, H, M are integers
call Double~Initialize (H)
let M = Free~Size
let C = Get (Forward, H)
for i = 1 to M                              Insert integers in reverse
    call Double~Insert (C, i, i)            numerical sequence
end for
check Double~Search (H, M) = Get (Forward, H)
check Double~Search (H, 0) = Get (Backward, H)
call Merge~Sort (H)
let C = Get (Forward, H)
```

```
for i = 1 to M                          Check that integers are now in
    check Get (Key, C) = i              forward sequence
    call Double~Remove (C)
end for
check Get (Backward, H) = Get (Forward, H)
```

5.8 BALANCED TREE

Maintaining items efficiently in sorted sequence

Example

The test program creates a tree with keys consisting of random integers. The records are then deleted in the sequence of their memory addresses (not the sequence of the keys), this being a pseudorandom sequence. Any particular key is found in the tree by calling Tree~Search. For example, if the header record for the tree is H, the record C containing a given key K is found by:

call Tree~Search (H, C, K)

The key "next" to any key is the key preceding or following the given key in the sequence in which the keys in the tree are maintained. The next key is found in the record pointed to by C, where C is the record pointer obtained by a call to Tree~Next, as below. The value of Direction must be +1 or –1 to select the following or preceding key respectively.

call Tree~Next (Direction, H, C)

Subprograms

5.8.1 Tree~Search (receives Header; supplies Current; receives KeyValue)
5.8.2 Tree~Next (receives Field, Header; supplies Current)
5.8.3 Tree~Insert (receives Header, NewRecord, KeyValue, DataValue)
5.8.4 Tree~Remove (receives Header, OldRecord)
5.8.5 Tree~Initialize (supplies Header)

Usage

A "tree" enables you to keep records in sorted sequence. The "records" are supplied by the free list algorithm discussed in Section 5.4. You should be familiar with that section, and in particular should understand how linked lists operate. Your understanding the balanced tree algorithm will be helped if you are familiar with the heap algorithm in Section 5.3 and the doubly linked list algorithm in Section 5.7.

You saw a binary tree structure for the first time with the heap algorithm in Section 5.3. In that case the tree was implicit, elements of the tree being located according to the value of subscripts in an array. In the current algorithm each key is in a record, and each record contains three pointers. The "left" and "right" pointers are the addresses of the left subtree and right subtree respectively of the current record. The "up" pointer contains the address of the parent record of the current record.

For example, look at the small binary tree represented diagrammatically as shown in Figure 5.6. The tree is "balanced", a point we will return to in a moment. First, look at the properties of the tree. Every record is at the top of a subtree. The lowest records have null subtrees. For each record, all keys in its left subtree are less than the key in the record itself, which is in turn less than all keys in the right subtree.

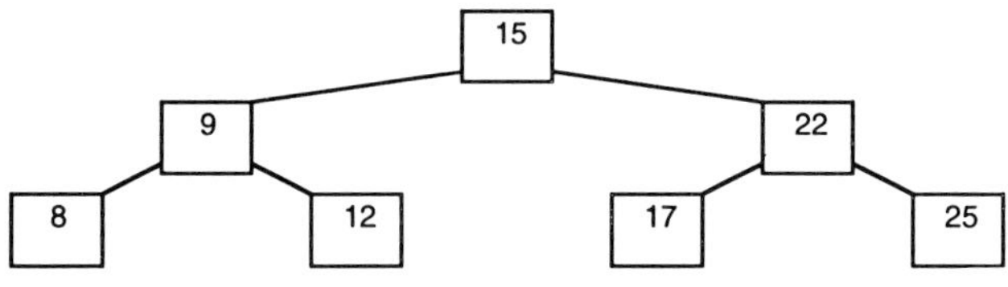

Figure 5.6

As with the doubly linked list, the tree is sandwiched between a header record and a trailer record. The procedure Tree~Initialize sets up the header and trailer records. The null tree created by this initialization has the form shown in Figure 5.7.

	Left	Up	Right	Key	Data	
1	6	6	6			Header
6	6	1	6			Trailer

Figure 5.7

The header and trailer records have been allocated locations 1–5 and 6–10 respectively. For programming convenience there are a number of special arrangements. The header record points to the trailer record as both its left and right subtrees. The header record points "up" circularly to the trailer record. The trailer record points to itself as its left and right subtrees and points up to the header record. The key and data fields are not initialized. The up pointer and key fields of the trailer record are set and used by Tree~Search.

The complete binary tree might be allocated storage as illustrated in Figure 5.8. Pointers to null subtrees are represented as pointers to the trailer record. The up pointer in the trailer record may have one of a number of values, and is shown as blank. Similarly, the data fields are shown as blank.

It is a simple matter to find any particular key. Start at the header record and find the record it points to, calling this the "current" record. If the desired key is less than the key in the current record, change the current record to the left subtree of the current record. If the desired key is greater than the key in the current record, change the current record to the right subtree of the current record. This process is applied iteratively until either the desired key is found or the bottom of the tree (trailer record) is reached. If the desired key is not found, the search process will stop at the place where the nonexistent key should be inserted. This method is used by the Tree~Search subprogram.

	Left	Up	Right	Key	Data	
1	11	6	11			Header
6	6		6			Trailer
11	16	1	21	15		
16	26	11	31	9		
21	36	11	41	22		
26	6	16	6	8		
31	6	16	6	12		
36	6	21	6	17		
41	6	21	6	25		

Figure 5.8

At this point you will need to understand the differences between binary trees and balanced trees. If you create a binary tree with keys 15, 9, 22, 8, 12, 17, 25 inserted in that sequence, you will produce the tree in Figure 5.8. If you insert the keys in the sorted sequence 8, 9, 12, 15, 17, 22, 25, you will end up with the tree shown in Figure 5.9.

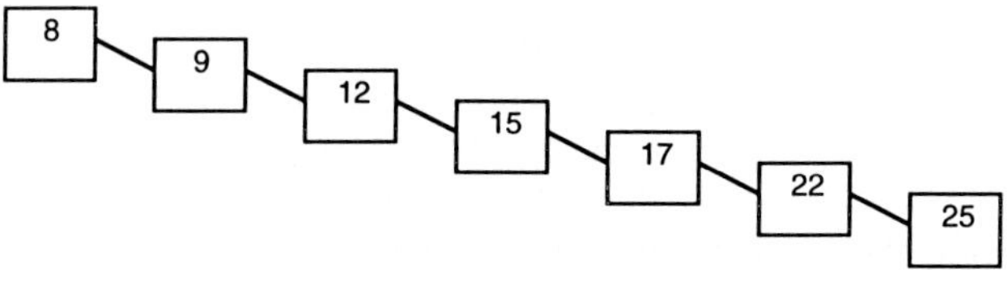

Figure 5.9

This "tree" is no more than a doubly linked list, the left pointers providing no useful information. For most practical purposes you cannot allow a program the possibility of creating such a degenerate tree, in which the efficiency of searching drops from O (log N) to O (N). Various methods of ensuring that trees are balanced have been proposed, and our balanced tree algorithm uses a structure called a B-tree. In earlier writings the structure was called a 2-3 tree or a 3-2 tree. The clever part of this algorithm is that the structure is used as if it were a binary tree when it suits us, and as a B-tree when it suits us. You can have your cake and eat it too!

For the moment, consider the tree as a B-tree. To avoid ambiguous terminology we will use the term "block" to refer to B-tree records. A B-tree has all its terminal blocks (often called "leaf" nodes) on the same level. This is accomplished by allowing blocks to have either one or two keys, as needed, implemented as either one or two records. Inserting the seven keys 8, 9, 12, 15, 17, 22, 25 into a B-tree in that sorted sequence produces the balanced tree at the top of this section rather than the horribly unbalanced doubly linked list. Figure 5.10 shows the sequence of trees generated during the insertion process.

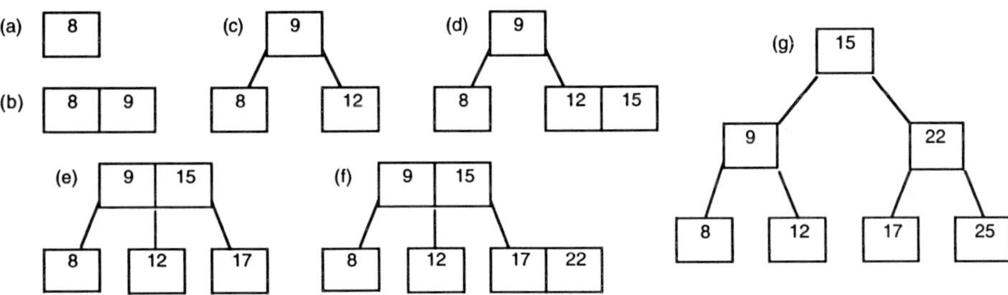

Figure 5.10

The subprogram Tree~Insert inserts a record into the tree. Before Tree~Insert is called, a call to Tree~Search must be carried out. The search will, of course, be unsuccessful, but it locates the position at the bottom of the tree at which the insertion should take place. Tree~Insert is given the address determined by the unsuccessful search and the key and associated data value. The subprogram creates a new record linked into the tree, and adjusts the tree to ensure that the tree remains balanced.

The subprogram Tree~Remove removes a record from the tree, given the address (rather than the key) of the record to be removed. Tree~Remove makes use of the subprogram Tree~Next, which finds the key immediately following the key to be moved, in sorted sequence. This is discussed more fully in the analysis below. In summary, if the record to be removed is not at the bottom of the tree, then its successor will be at the bottom. The actual removal always takes place from the bottom of the tree, and so a record to be removed that is not at the bottom is, in effect, replaced by its successor so that the successor can be removed. The method relies on removal from the bottom, in order to balance the tree properly.

Notwithstanding this replacement of records, the code is arranged so that the net effect is that the record specified for removal ends up being the record actually removed. In other words, once a key has been assigned to a particular record, it remains in that record for its lifetime.

You can use the Tree~Next subprogram to retrieve the records in sequential order of the keys. Tree~Next can be called with any particular record in the tree specified as the actual argument. The subprogram returns the predecessor or successor of that record, or the header record if the current record contains the lowest or highest key in the tree.

Analysis

A tree is "balanced" when the length of the path from the header record to the trailer record is constant (or as nearly so as possible), no matter which route downward through the subtrees is followed. Various methods for balancing trees have been proposed. Knuth (1973) and Sedgewick (1988) discuss a variety of methods, which are interesting theoretically. Some of them require much more programming than others. From a practical point of view it is desirable to have the shortest possible algorithm to achieve a given level of efficiency. For this reason we have selected the B-tree as superior to AVL trees, 2-3-4 trees, and red-black trees. The B-tree used here is a simplified case of the generalized B-tree. Our B-tree blocks can have either one or two keys. More general B-trees may have blocks with larger numbers of keys.

To be able to assess efficiency, you need to understand a little more about how the algorithm works. First, consider insertion. Take as an example the creation of the B-tree by inserting keys in sorted sequence, discussed above. When 8 was the only key in the tree, key 9 was inserted simply by adding it to the block in which key 8 resided. To insert key 12 we have our first complication. The block in which key 12 should be inserted is full, containing the maximum of two keys 8 and 9. The algorithm splits the full block into two separate blocks, puts key 8 into one and key 12 into another, and passes the middle key 9 up to the next level. At this higher level, key 9 and the header record are considered. The height of the tree is increased by one, and the tree is "rotated" so that the header record points to the record containing key 9 rather than the record containing key 8.

Key 15 is added easily by putting it in the same block as key 12. Key 17 is processed just like key 12 initially. Keys 12 and 17 are put in separate blocks and key 15 is passed up to the next level. At the higher level, key 15 is added into the block containing key 9. Key 22 is easily handled. Key 25 causes further block splitting at two levels, and also causes an increase in tree height. This informal description has covered the main operations involved in inserting new records into the tree, while maintaining its balance.

In practice, there is a simple method of representing blocks that leads to efficient programming. The idea is to link two records within a block by "horizontal" pointers, using precisely the same record structure discussed above for pure binary trees. For example, when key 8 and key 9 are put into the same block to create a tree with two records, the tree will be represented as shown in Figure 5.11. The "horizontal" link, to represent the fact that keys 8 and 9 are pictured as being side by side in the same block, is indicated by the negative up pointer in record 16, containing the second of the two keys. The negative pointer is ignored when you are searching the tree; the tree is treated just as if it were an ordinary binary tree in this circumstance. That's the good news. The bad news is that the tree is not in fact perfectly balanced now. The paths from the header to keys 8 and 9 should have identical lengths. In fact, the path to key 9 is one link longer than the path to key 8.

	Left	Up	Right	Key	Data	
1	11	6	11			Header
6	6		6			Trailer
11	6	1	16	8		
16	6	−11	6	9		

Figure 5.11

Fortunately, the bad news is not too bad. The path lengths can range by at most a factor of two. This makes the implementation no worse than the implementations of the other kinds of balanced trees, which also have effective path lengths that may vary by a factor of two or more. For example, AVL trees have the property that the heights of the left and right subtrees of any node differ by at most one. It is not difficult to construct AVL trees in which the longest path is twice the length of the shortest path. Similar comments apply to 2-3-4 trees and red-black trees.

Now look at removal. Consider removing the keys in the reverse sequence of their insertion. We encounter the most complicated case first in the above example. To delete key 25, the algorithm deals with its parent key 22 and the key of its sibling 17. It retrieves key 22 from the parent record, putting keys 17 and 22 into the one block. A null key is passed up to the next level of the tree. At that higher level a null key is on the same level as key 9, both being siblings of the parent with key 15. The algorithm brings keys 9 and 15 into the one block and passes the null key up to the top level. At the top level the null key and the header record are processed together, resulting in rotation of the tree so that the header points to the record with key 9 rather than the record with key 15.

Key 22 is easily deleted, simply by removing it from the block that also contains key 17. To remove key 17, the sibling key 12 and the parent key 15 are coalesced into one block and a null key is passed up to the next level. At the higher level the null key is handled by putting key 9 into a block by itself. It is not difficult to trace through the remaining deletions until the tree is empty. This discussion has somewhat oversimplified the deletion process. There are several other special cases that are considered more fully in the pseudo code. However, the general approach is along the lines we have described so far.

Now we will be analytical instead of descriptive. Note that some insertion and deletion operations require passing keys (null or non-null) up to the next level and some do not. On occasion (such as deleting key 25) there is a need to pass keys through two or even more levels. Thus, the insertion and deletion operations in the code are embedded loops that may be executed 1, 2, 3, or more times, up to a maximum number of times given by the number of levels in the tree.

Inserting keys into a block that contains only one record does not require passing a key up to the next level. Similarly, removing a key from a block that has two records does not require passing a null key up to the next level. This simple fact enables us to estimate the efficiency of the loops in both the insertion and deletion algorithms. In a random tree there will be approximately equal numbers of one-record and two-record blocks. Therefore, the loops will be executed once about half of the time. As each level of the tree has the same structure, the argument can be applied repeatedly at each level. The loops will be executed twice about one quarter of the time, three times about one eighth of the time, and so on. The sum of the series (1 * 0.5) + (2 * 0.25) + (3 * 0.125) + ... carried to infinity is 2. Thus there is an upper bound of 2 for the average number of times the loop is executed. In other words, the code in the loops is executed in an average time that is independent of the number of the records in the tree, or O (1).

This implies that removal of records from the tree is very efficient, being carried out in constant time. Unfortunately, the same is not true for insertion, except in special cases. The insertion algorithm requires not only the loop itself, but also a prior search for the key being inserted, so that the correct place for insertion can be found. Remember that the tree is in effect a binary tree for searching purposes, and that the time required for searching is O (*log* N), N being the number of records in the tree. The execution time for insertion in random sequence is effectively the execution time for searching, or O (*log* N). Insertion is an O (1) operation when keys are inserted in sorted key sequence, because no search has to be carried out.

Finding the predecessor or successor to a given key is usually expressed as a simple recursive procedure in the literature. Strangely, the nonrecursive version has been thought to be far more complex than is really necessary (Hatter 1984). The Tree~Next subprogram shows that finding the successor need not be a complicated process when expressed without recursion. The simplicity is achieved by noting that it is easy to determine whether any given node is in the left or right subtree of its parent. The algorithm merely checks whether the left or right pointer in the parent node is pointing to the current record.

There are several subprograms used by the main components of the algorithm. The Get and Put subprograms manipulate particular fields in a record. The subprogram Rotate changes the structure of the tree by moving one pointer of a parent node so that it points to a different record. The subprogram Connect joins parent and child nodes together by setting the relevant up pointer in the child and left or right pointer in the parent. The subprogram Squeeze requires a little more explaining. Suppose we have a record X that we wish to link to a parent record P and its *right* child record C. Squeeze inserts the current record X between P and C, so that the P points *right* to X, which in turn points *left* to C. Squeeze also operates in the other orientation, with left and right interchanged. This subprogram is used extensively for moving pointers while changing the structure of the tree.

Tree~Insert deals with six special cases, and Tree~Remove with nine. Although this produces quite a large amount of code, the subprograms are very efficient. For any given iteration of the loop in each subprogram the required special case is quickly isolated by several *if* tests, and a few Connect or Squeeze operations effect the required changes to the tree. The special cases are identified clearly in the pseudo code.

IMPLEMENTATION

<u>Exported Names</u>

Tree~Initialize	Initializes free list for the tree (5.8.5)
Tree~Insert	Inserts an item in the tree (5.8.3)

Tree~Next	Obtains key preceding or following current key in the tree (5.8.2)
Tree~Remove	Removes an item from the tree (5.8.4)
Tree~Search	Searches for a given key in the tree (5.8.1)
<u>Imported Names</u>	
Free~Get	Supplies address of next free record in Memory (5.4.1)
Free~Give	Returns address of a record in Memory to free list (5.4.2)
Free~Initialize	Makes all of Memory available (5.4.3)
Free~Size	Calculates number of records in free list (5.4.4)
Memory	Array containing records for doubly linked list (5.4)
<u>Local Subprograms</u>	
Compose	Initializes all five values (left, up, right, key, and data) in a node
Get	Retrieves the value in a specified position in a specified record
Connect	Links a parent node to a child node with pointers each way
Put	Inserts a value into a specified position in a specified record
Rotate	Changes a parent node to point to a different node
Squeeze	Inserts a node between a parent node and one of its down pointers
<u>Nicknames</u>	
Current	Address of current tree record in Memory
DataValue	Data item to be inserted in tree record
Header	Address of header record of tree in Memory
KeyValue	Value of key to be inserted in record or to be searched for
LeftPointer	Pointer to left subtree
Neighbor	Address of a record in the vicinity of Current and Parent
NewRecord	Address of record determined by search or insertion
OldRecord	Address of record to be removed from tree
RightPointer	Pointer to right subtree
<u>Global Names</u>	
Data	Offset position of data item in a record
Left	Offset position of left downward pointer in a record
Key	Offset position of record key in a record
Right	Offset position of right downward pointer in a record
Up	Offset position of upward pointer in a record
<u>Local Names</u>	
Field	Offset position in a record, to select left, up, right, key, or data
Neighbor	Address of a record in the vicinity of Current and Parent
New	Address of new record to be inserted
Old	Address of old record to be removed
Parent	Address of parent of current record
Save	Address of old record to be removed
Sibling	Address of record at same level in tree as target record
Trailer	Address of trailer record of tree
Value	Value being inserted in one of the fields of a record

Code

```
constant Left = –1                    Left = –Right, in order to make
constant Up = 0                       algorithms symmetrical
constant Right = +1
constant Key = 2
constant Data = 3
```

5.8.1 **Tree~Search** (receives Header; supplies Current; receives KeyValue)

Pseudo Code

```
insert the required key in the trailer in case the search is unsuccessful
initialize current record to header record of tree
loop
    let upward pointer of trailer point to current record, to provide complete upward
            path
    if required key < key in current record then
        set current record to left subtree of current record
    else
        set current record to right subtree of current record
    end if
end loop when required key is equal to the key in the current record
```

Code

```
procedure Tree~Search (Header, Current, KeyValue are integers)
    call Put (Key, Get (Up, Header), KeyValue)
    let Current = Header
    loop
        call Put (Up, Get (Up, Header), Current)
        if KeyValue < Get (Key, Current) then
            let Current = Get (Left, Current)
        else
            let Current = Get (Right, Current)
        end if
    end loop when KeyValue = Get (Key, Current)
end Tree~Search
```

5.8.2 **Tree~Next** (receives Field, Header; supplies Current)

Pseudo Code

```
if right (left) pointer of current record points to trailer then
    loop until current record is in left (right) subtree of its parent
        let current record = parent of current record
    end loop
    let current record = parent of current record
else
    let current record = right (left) subtree of current record
    loop until left (right) subtree of current record is empty
        let current record = left (right) subtree of current record
    end loop
end if
```

Code

```
procedure Tree~Next (Field, Header, Current are integers)
    if Get (Field, Current) = Get (Up, Header) then
```

```
        loop until Current = Get (–Field, Get (Up, Current))
            let Current = magnitude (Get (Up, Current))
        end loop
        let Current = magnitude (Get (Up, Current))
    else
        let Current = Get (Field, Current)
        loop until Get (–Field, Current) = Get (Up, Header)
            let Current = Get (–Field, Current)
        end loop
    end if
end Tree~Next
```

5.8.3 Tree~Insert (receives Header, NewRecord, KeyValue, DataValue)

Pseudo Code

```
initialize Sibling to record at bottom of tree with closest key to new key
compose the new record in the location New
loop
    let Parent = parent of Sibling
    if Sibling is header record then
        join header record to New
        exit loop
    else-if Sibling is second record in block containing two records then
        if key in New < key in Sibling then
            set up New to point downward to Parent and Sibling as two separate
                    blocks
            pass New up to next level in tree
        else
            set up Sibling to point downward to Parent and New as two separate
                    blocks
            pass Sibling up to next level in the tree
        end if
        let Sibling = parent of Parent
    else-if Sibling is first record in block containing two records then
        set Sibling to point to New and right of Sibling as two separate blocks
        pass Sibling up to next level in the tree
    else-if key in New < key in Sibling then
        insert New ahead of Sibling in one block
        exit loop
    else
        insert New after Sibling in the one block
        exit loop
    end if
end loop
```

Code

```
procedure Tree~Insert (Header, NewRecord, KeyValue, DataValue are integers)
    variables New, Parent, Sibling are integers
    check NewRecord = Get (Up, Header)                  Must start from bottom of
    let Sibling = Get (Up, NewRecord)                   tree
    call Free~Get (NewRecord)
    call Compose (NewRecord, Get (Up, Header), 0, Get (Up, Header), KeyValue,
            DataValue)
    let New = NewRecord
    loop until New = 0
        let Parent = magnitude (Get (Up, Sibling))
        if Sibling = Header then                        Insert at header
            call Connect (Left, Sibling, New)
            call Connect (Right, Sibling, New)
            let New = 0
        else-if Get (Up, Sibling) < 0 then              Insert at second record in
            if Get (Key, New) < Get (Key, Sibling) then block
                call Squeeze (Right, New, Sibling)
            else
                call Connect (Right, Sibling, New)
                let New = Sibling
            end if
            let Sibling = Get (Up, Parent)
            call Squeeze (Left, New, Parent)
        else-if Get (Up, Get (Right, Sibling)) < 0 then Insert at first record in
            call Connect (Left, Sibling, New)           block containing two
            call Connect (Right, Sibling,               records
                    Get (Right, Sibling))
            let New = Sibling
            le  t Sibling = Parent
        else-if Get (Key, New) < Get (Key, Sibling) then Insert at block
            call Rotate (Parent, Sibling, New)          containing one record
            call Squeeze (Right, –New, Sibling)
            let New = 0
        else                                            Insert at block containing
            call Connect (Right, –Sibling, New)         one record
            let New = 0
        end if
    end loop
end Tree~Insert
```

5.8.4 Tree~Remove (receives Header, OldRecord)

Pseudo Code

```
if record to be deleted is not leaf node then
    find node that contains next key higher than key to be removed
    move successor key to record containing key to be removed (for removing
            successor)
```

```
end if
let Old = record to be removed
loop
    let Parent = parent of Old record
    if Parent is header record then
        join header to record on right of Old
        exit loop
    else-if one block contains both Parent and Old then
        remove Old from block
        join Parent to record on right of Old
        exit loop
    else-if Old is pointed to by left pointer of Parent then
        if Parent is only record in its block then
            let Sibling = address of sibling of Old pointed to by Parent
            if Sibling is only record in its block then
                insert Parent ahead of Sibling in its block
                join Old to Parent
                pass null Old key up to next level
            else
                rotate subtree to set Sibling to head of subtree
                join Sibling to Parent and sibling of Sibling as two separate blocks
                pass null Old key up to next level
                exit loop
            end if
        else
            let Sibling = address of second record in block containing Parent
            if left child of Sibling is only record in its block then
                rotate subtree to set Sibling to head of subtree
                join Sibling to Parent
                insert Parent and left child of Sibling into same block
                exit loop
            else
                rotate subtree to set left child of Sibling to head of subtree
                shift left Old, Parent, left child of Sibling, sibling of left child of
                        Sibling
                exit loop
            end if
        end if
    else
        let Sibling = address of other record pointed to by Parent
        if Sibling is only record in its block then
            rotate subtree to set Old to head of subtree
            set Old to point down to Sibling and Parent brought into same block
            pass null Old key up to next level
```

```
        else
            rotate subtree to set right child of Sibling to head of subtree
            set right child of Sibling to point down to Sibling and Parent in different
                    blocks
            exit loop
        end if
    end if
end loop
```

Code

```
procedure Tree~Remove (Header, OldRecord are integers)
variables Neighbor, Old, Parent, Save, Sibling are integers
let Save = OldRecord
if Get (Right, Save) ≠ Get (Up, Header) then       If record for removal is not
    call Tree~Next (Header, Save)                  at bottom of tree, find its
    call Put (Key, OldRecord, Get (Key, Save))     successor
    call Put (Data, OldRecord, Get (Data, Save))
end if
let Old = Save
loop until Old = 0
    let Parent = magnitude (Get (Up, Old))
    if Parent = Header then                        Remove at header
        call Connect (Left, Parent, Get (Right, Old))
        call Connect (Right, Parent, Get (Right, Old))
        let Old = 0
    else-if Get (Up, Old) < 0 then                 Remove second record in
        call Connect (Right, Parent, Get (Right, Old))   block
        let Old = 0
    else-if Get (Up, Get (Right, Old)) < 0 then    Remove first record in
        call Rotate (Parent, Old, Get (Right, Old))    block containing two
        let Old = 0                                records
    else-if Old = Get (Left, Parent) then
        let Sibling = Get (Right, Parent)
        if Get (Up, Sibling) > 0 then              Remove left child of par-
            if Get (Up, Get (Right, Sibling)) > 0 then   ent whose right child is in
                call Rotate (Get (Up, Parent),     block containing one
                        Parent, Old)               record
                call Squeeze (Right, Old, Parent)
                call Put (Up, Sibling, –Parent)
            else                                   Remove left child
                call Rotate (Get (Up, Parent), Parent,   of parent whose right child
                        Sibling)                   is in block containing two
                call Squeeze (Right, Old, Parent)  records
                call Squeeze (Left, Sibling, Parent)
                call Put (Up, Get (Right, Sibling), Sibling)
                let Old = 0
            end if
```

```
        else
            let Neighbor = Get (Left, Sibling)
            if Get (Up, Get (Right, Neighbor)) > 0 then
                call Rotate (Get (Up, Parent), Parent,
                        Sibling)
                call Squeeze (Right, Old, Parent)
                call Squeeze (Left, Sibling, –Parent)
            else
                call Rotate (Get (Up, Parent), Parent,
                        Neighbor)
                call Squeeze (Right, –Neighbor,
                        Sibling)
                call Squeeze (Right, Old, Parent)
                call Squeeze (Left, Neighbor, Parent)
            end if
            let Old = 0
        end if
    else
        let Sibling = Get (Left, Parent)
        if Get (Up, Get (Right, Sibling)) > 0 then
            call Rotate (Get (Up, Parent), Parent, Old)
            call Squeeze (Right, –Sibling, Parent)
            call Connect (Right, Parent, Get (Right,
                    Old))
            call Connect (Right, Old, Sibling)
        else
            let Neighbor = Get (Right, Sibling)
            call Rotate (Get (Up, Parent),
                    Parent, Neighbor)
            call Squeeze (Left, Neighbor, Sibling)
            call Squeeze (Right, Neighbor, Parent)
            call Connect (Right, Parent, Get (Right, Old))
            let Old = 0
        end if
    end if
end loop
if Save ≠ OldRecord then
    call Rotate (Get (Up, OldRecord), OldRecord,
            Save)
    call Connect (Left, Save, Get (Left, OldRecord))
    call Connect (Right, Save, Get (Right, Old
            Record))
    call Put (Key, Save, Get (Key, OldRecord))
    call Put (Data, Save, Get (Data, OldRecord))
end if
call Free~Give (OldRecord)
end Tree~Remove
```

Remove left child of parent whose sibling has left child in block containing one record

Remove left child of parent whose sibling has left child in block containing two records

Remove right child of parent whose left child is in block containing one record

Remove right child of parent whose left child is in block containing two records

If record to be removed was not at bottom of tree, restore successor to correct record

5.8.5 Tree~Initialize (supplies Header)

Pseudo Code

```
set memory to free records with five locations each (for left, up, and right pointers,
        key, and data)
get record from the free list to contain the header
get record from the free list to contain the trailer
compose the header and trailer records
```

Code

```
procedure Tree~Initialize (Header is integer)
    variable Trailer is integer
    call Free~Initialize (5)
    call Free~Get (Header)
    call Free~Get (Trailer)
    call Compose (Header, Trailer, Trailer, Trailer, 0, 0)
    call Compose (Trailer, Trailer, Header, Trailer, 0, 0)
end Tree~Initialize
```

Local **Get** (receives Field, Current; *result integer*)

```
function Get (Field, Current are integers) is integer
    result Memory[magnitude (Current)+Field+1]
end Get
```

Local **Put** (receives Field, Current, Value)

```
procedure Put (Field, Current, Value are integers)
    let Memory[magnitude (Current)+Field+1] = Value
end Put
```

Local **Rotate** (receives Parent, Current, Neighbor)

```
procedure Rotate (Parent, Current, Neighbor are integers)
    if Get (Left, Parent) = Current then
        call Put (Left, Parent, Neighbor)
    end if
    if Get (Right, Parent) = Current then
        call Put (Right, Parent, Neighbor)
    end if
    call Put (Up, Neighbor, Get (Up, Current))
end Rotate
```

Local **Connect** (receives Field, Parent, Current)

```
procedure Connect (Field, Parent, Current are integers)
    call Put (Field, Parent, Current)
    call Put (Up, Current, Parent)
end Connect
```

Local **Squeeze** (receives Field, Parent, Current)
procedure Squeeze (Field, Parent, Current *are integers*)
call Connect (–Field, Current, Get (Field, Parent))
call Connect (Field, Parent, *magnitude* (Current))
end Squeeze

Local **Compose** (receives Current, LeftPointer, Parent, RightPointer, KeyValue, DataValue)
procedure Compose (Current, LeftPointer, Parent, RightPointer, KeyValue, DataValue *are integers*)
call Put (Left, Current, LeftPointer)
call Put (Up, Current, Parent)
call Put (Right, Current, RightPointer)
call Put (Key, Current, KeyValue)
call Put (Data, Current, DataValue)
end Compose

TEST PROGRAM

Imported Names

Get	Retrieves the value in a specified position in a specified record (5.8)
Integer~Initialize	Initializes random integer generator (8.1.4b)
Left	Offset position of left downward pointer in a record (5.8)
Random~Integer	Generates random integer in a specified range (8.1.4a)
Up	Offset position of upward pointer in a record (5.8)

Local Names

C	Pointer to current record in the tree
H	Pointer to the header record of the tree
M	Maximum number of records available for the tree

Pseudo Code

initialize tree, calculating the maximum number of useful records M
insert M records, with random keys
let C = address of trailer record in memory
loop until C refers to nonexistent record
remove record at address C
end loop
check the tree is empty

Code

variables C, H, K, M *are integer*
call Tree~Initialize (H)
call Integer~Initialize (1, *maxinteger*)
let M = Free~Size ( )

```
for i = 1 to M
    call Random~Integer (K)
    call Tree~Search (H, C, K)
    call Tree~Insert (H, C, K, 0)
end for
let C = Get (Up, H)
for i = 1 to M
    let C = C + 5
    call Tree~Remove (H, C)
end for
check Get (Left, H) = Get (Up, H)
```

6 Sorting and Merging

Don't start writing your own sort routine until you have checked whether one is available. Sorting is a commonly required function, and the chances are that you will be able to save time and effort by using a sort routine that has been programmed already. Check your program library.

It is quite likely that more attention has been devoted to sorting than to any other topic in computer science. Sorting is a fascinating process, and dozens of algorithms have been devised. There is not a "best" algorithm for all purposes. Some algorithms are good for sorting a few items, while others work more efficiently on a large number of items. Some are suited to items that are almost in sequence and some work best on items that are in random order. Some are to be preferred when the sorting keys are long. Some require more memory than others.

The algorithms presented here assume that you want to sort integers into ascending sequence. If you need to sort text into descending sequence, you will need to make the necessary modifications to data types and key comparisons. This should be a simple process.

You should also consider using a dynamic data structure of some kind. For example, it may be more efficient overall to use the balanced tree algorithm described in Section 5.8. The decision depends largely on whether the set of items to be maintained in sorted sequence is static or not. If there are to be insertions and deletions, a dynamic data structure may be preferable, despite the increased costs of memory usage. Such an algorithm maintains the data in sorted sequence, obviating the necessity to carry out sorting as such.

Sometimes one thinks about sorting an array when all that is required is to obtain, say, the median value. More generally, it might appear necessary to sort an array to obtain the K-th largest value. In fact, selection of the K-th largest element of an array can be carried out more efficiently than doing a full sort. Perhaps the easiest approach is a simplification of Quick~Sort, described in Section 6.2. Use the partitioning process, but apply it repeatedly only to the segment of the array that contains the required element.

What is the most efficient way in which to sort a few items into ascending sequence? If you don't think about it too hard, you are likely to say that either the selection or insertion method is the most efficient. Yes, these methods are good for sorting small arrays, but there is a more efficient method when the number of items is known in advance. These methods are called "sequencing" algorithms to distinguish them from the better-known array sorting algorithms. Sequencing algorithms are derived from sorting networks, a topic that is discussed by Knuth (1973). To give a specific example, a sequencing algorithm will sort four items using five exchanges. The selection method requires six exchanges. The sequencing algorithms have the further advantage that they contain no loops, and therefore have minimal overhead.

You will find here only the algorithms that sort internally, that is, that do not use external storage such as disks and tapes. Most operating systems provide efficient sorting utilities, such as *sort* with Unix™. You should use such facilities for large files. Very few programmers should ever need to write programs for external sorting.

Merging of arrays is so simple that specific algorithms have not been provided in this book. Suppose you want to merge arrays A and B, which contain NA and NB elements respectively, with elements numbered from 1. Assume that array A is large enough to contain the merged arrays. One approach (Gonnet and Baeza-Yates 1991) is as follows:

```
loop until NB = 0
    if NA = 0 or A[NA] < B[NB] then
        let A[NA+NB] = B[NB]
        let NB = NB – 1
    else
        let A[NA+NB] = A[NA]
        let NA = NA – 1
    end if
end loop
```

Clearly, the double test can be eliminated by putting a sentinel such as *–maxinteger* into unused element A[0]. You may also wish to examine the Merge~Sort algorithm in Section 5.7, which uses a merge process to sort data maintained in list structures. Again, the merging of sorted lists is straightforward, and the code may be found embedded in the Merge~Sort algorithm. Disk and tape files may be merged using the *sort* facility under Unix™.

6.1 SEQUENCING

Putting a fixed number of items into sorted sequence

Example

The variables A, B, C, D, and E contain the values A = 15, B = –15, C = 0, D = 5, E = 10. The following code produces the results A = –15, B = 0, C = 5, D = 10, E = 15.

```
call Sort~5 (A, B, C, D, E)
```

Subprograms

6.1.1 Sort~2 (updates X1, X2)
6.1.2 Sort~3 (updates X1, X2, X3)
6.1.3 Sort~4 (updates X1, X2, X3, X4)
6.1.4 Sort~5 (updates X1, X2, X3, X4, X5)
6.1.5 Sort~6 (updates X1, X2, X3, X4, X5, X6)
6.1.6 Sort~7 (updates X1, X2, X3, X4, X5, X6, X7)
6.1.7 Sort~8 (updates X1, X2, X3, X4, X5, X6, X7, X8)

Usage

Each procedure is used by listing the variables to be sorted. The example above shows how five variables are sorted by listing the five variable names. Thus Sort~2 through Sort~8 have two through eight nicknames respectively.

Although the code operates on integers, the procedures may be altered to operate on other types merely by changing the type descriptions of the nicknames.

The test program refers only to Sort~5 through Sort~8. Sort~2 through Sort~4 are used by these procedures and so are tested indirectly. In order to keep the test program simple, all procedures except Sort~8 are tested more than once on identical data.

Analysis

The efficiency of sequencing algorithms is independent of the values being sorted. The same amount of code is executed for all possible values of the input variables. With certain arrangements of the data values the sequencing algorithms may be less efficient than sorting algorithms. For example, Insertion~Sort will "sort" an array of eight integers already in ascending sequence faster than will Sort~8. In general, for haphazard distributions of values the sequencing algorithms will be superior in efficiency.

The test program checks that the procedures operate correctly for all possible combinations of zeros and ones. It is left to mathematically inclined readers to prove that the procedures will consequently work with any combinations of values.

IMPLEMENTATION

Exported Names

Sort~2	Sorts 2 integers using a sorting network (6.1.1)
Sort~3	Sorts 3 integers using a sorting network (6.1.2)
Sort~4	Sorts 4 integers using a sorting network (6.1.3)
Sort~5	Sorts 5 integers using a sorting network (6.1.4)
Sort~6	Sorts 6 integers using a sorting network (6.1.5)
Sort~7	Sorts 7 integers using a sorting network (6.1.6)
Sort~8	Sorts 8 integers using a sorting network (6.1.7)

Nicknames

X1, X2, ..., X8	Variables to be sorted

6.1.1 Sort~2 (updates X1, X2)

Code

```
procedure Sort~2 (X1, X2 are integers)
    if X1 > X2 then
        call swap (X1, X2)
    end if
end Sort~2
```

6.1.2 Sort~3 (updates X1, X2, X3)

Code

```
procedure Sort~3 (X1, X2, X3 are integers)
    call Sort~2 (X1, X2)
    call Sort~2 (X1, X3)
    call Sort~2 (X2, X3)
end Sort~3
```

6.1.3 Sort~4 (updates X1, X2, X3, X4)

Code

```
procedure Sort~4 (X1, X2, X3, X4 are integers)
    call Sort~2 (X1, X2)
    call Sort~2 (X3, X4)
    call Sort~2 (X1, X3)
    call Sort~2 (X2, X4)
    call Sort~2 (X2, X3)
end Sort~4
```

6.1.4 Sort~5 (updates X1, X2, X3, X4, X5)

Code

```
procedure Sort~5 (X1, X2, X3, X4, X5 are integers)
    call Sort~3 (X1, X2, X3)
    call Sort~2 (X4, X5)
    call Sort~2 (X1, X4)
    call Sort~2 (X3, X4)
    call Sort~2 (X2, X5)
    call Sort~2 (X2, X3)
    call Sort~2 (X4, X5)
end Sort~5
```

6.1.5 Sort~6 (updates X1, X2, X3, X4, X5, X6)

Code

```
procedure Sort~6 (X1, X2, X3, X4, X5, X6 are integers)
    call Sort~3 (X1, X2, X3)
    call Sort~3 (X4, X5, X6)
    call Sort~2 (X1, X4)
    call Sort~2 (X3, X6)
    call Sort~2 (X3, X4)
    call Sort~2 (X2, X5)
    call Sort~2 (X2, X3)
    call Sort~2 (X4, X5)
end Sort~6
```

6.1.6 Sort~7 (updates X1, X2, X3, X4, X5, X6, X7)

Code

```
procedure Sort~7 (X1, X2, X3, X4, X5, X6, X7 are integers)
    call Sort~4 (X1, X2, X3, X4)
    call Sort~3 (X5, X6, X7)
    call Sort~2 (X1, X5)
    call Sort~2 (X3, X7)
    call Sort~2 (X3, X5)
    call Sort~2 (X2, X6)
    call Sort~2 (X4, X6)
    call Sort~2 (X2, X3)
    call Sort~2 (X4, X5)
    call Sort~2 (X6, X7)
end Sort~7
```

6.1.7 Sort~8 (updates X1, X2, X3, X4, X5, X6, X7, X8)

Code

```
procedure Sort~8 (X1, X2, X3, X4, X5, X6, X7, X8 are integers)
    call Sort~4 (X1, X2, X3, X4)
    call Sort~4 (X5, X6, X7, X8)
    call Sort~2 (X1, X5)
    call Sort~2 (X3, X7)
    call Sort~2 (X3, X5)
    call Sort~2 (X2, X6)
    call Sort~2 (X4, X8)
    call Sort~2 (X4, X6)
    call Sort~2 (X2, X3)
    call Sort~2 (X4, X5)
    call Sort~2 (X6, X7)
end Sort~8
```

TEST PROGRAM

Local Names

X Array of 8 integers to be sorted
K Bit pattern for initializing variables to be sorted

Pseudo Code

```
for k = 0 to 255
    set up bits of k in separate variables and sort them
    check that the values of the variables are in the correct sequence
end for
```

Code

```
variable X is array 1 to 8 of integers
variable K is integer
for k = 0 to 255                                   Cycle through all possible
    for i = 5 to 8                                 combinations of eight bits
        let K = k
        for j = 1 to i                             Set up a pattern of zeros and ones
            let X[j] = K mod 2                     for sorting
            let K = K ÷ 2
        end for
        if i = 5 then
            call Sort~5 (X[1], X[2], X[3], X[4], X[5])
        else-if i = 6 then
            call Sort~6 (X[1], X[2], X[3], X[4], X[5], X[6])
        else-if i = 7 then
            call Sort~7 (X[1], X[2], X[3], X[4], X[5], X[6], X[7])
        else-if i = 8 then
            call Sort~8 (X[1], X[2], X[3], X[4], X[5], X[6], X[7], X[8])
        end if
        for j = 2 to i                             Check that pattern has been sorted
            check X[j–1] < X[j]
        end for
    end for
end for
```

6.2 ARRAY SORTING

Sorting the elements of an array, using a variety of methods

Example

An array A of integers held in locations A[L] to A[U] is sorted into ascending sequence, using one of the sorting algorithms Quick~Sort as an example, by:

call Quick~Sort (A, L, U)

Subprograms

6.2.1 Bubble~Sort (updates Items; receives Lower, Upper)
6.2.2 Selection~Sort (updates Items; receives Lower, Upper)
6.2.3 Insertion~Sort (updates Items; receives Lower, Upper)
6.2.4 Shell~Sort (updates Items; receives Lower, Upper)
6.2.5 Heap~Sort (updates Items; receives Lower, Upper)
6.2.6 Quick~Sort (updates Items; receives Lower, Upper)
6.2.7 Radix~Sort (updates Items; receives Lower, Upper)
6.2.8 Merge~Sort (updates Items; receives Lower, Upper; supplies Temp)
6.2.9 Linear~Sort (updates Items; receives Lower, Upper; supplies Temp)

Usage

All nine subprograms may be used to sort any segment of an array of integers. Frequently, one will want to sort the whole array. In all cases the lower and upper bounds of the elements to be sorted must be specified. The nicknames Lower and Upper represent the lowest and highest subscripts of the particular segment of the array to be sorted. Programmers with a Fortran, Cobol, or Basic background will typically choose Lower = 1, while those using C will probably find it more convenient if Lower = 0. However, Lower may have any value less than Upper.

All subprograms generate the same end result, the elements of the array being in sorted sequence. Merge~Sort and Linear~Sort differ from the other subprograms in that they require an additional array Temp, used by the subprograms for temporary storage. The temporary array must have available the same subscripted locations as are sorted in the primary array. For example, if you wish to sort array A by calling Merge~Sort (A, L, U, B), the locations of array B that are used by the algorithm will range from B[L] to B[U]. The sorted array ends up back in A as with the other algorithms, and not in B.

Subprogram Linear~Sort reserves storage for an array of 256 counts C[0] to C[255]. Otherwise, all subprograms are coded in a straightforward manner. Note that several make use of the sequencing algorithms defined in the previous section. It is recommended that these be coded in line for greatest efficiency, thereby eliminating nested procedure calls. In particular, the three calls to Sort~4 in Radix~Sort can be improved considerably. They have been coded as calls to Sort~4 to illustrate the symmetries in the algorithm, and to simplify understanding, testing, and debugging.

In order to make a suitable choice of sorting algorithm you will need to consider the following analysis. If you are in a hurry, and are prepared to use a good, if not necessarily optimal algorithm, follow these guidelines for choosing a method that is simple to implement. Use Selection~Sort or Insertion~Sort for small arrays (10 items), Shell~Sort for medium-sized arrays (1,000 items), Quick~Sort or Merge~Sort for large arrays (100,000 items), and Linear~Sort for very large arrays. Use a less efficient sort for one-off jobs, because it will be simpler to implement, and efficiency is not likely to be of major concern.

The test program initializes the array to a descending sequence of integers, usually the worst case for sorting algorithms.

Analysis

First, you will need to know how each of the algorithms works. For consistency, all algorithms use the nickname Items for the array to be sorted, with subscripts ranging from Lower to Upper. The number of items to be sorted is N, where N = Upper – Lower + 1.

Bubble Sort

Bubble~Sort makes successive passes through the array, exchanging adjacent items if they are in the wrong sequence with respect to each other. The algorithm terminates when no exchanges are made in a given pass. It can be guaranteed that after k iterations the last k items in the array will be in their final positions. Depending on the initial distribution of array elements, in excess of k of the last elements of the array may be in their final positions after k iterations. The best case occurs when the array is in sorted sequence initially, for the algorithm makes just one pass. The worst case occurs when the array is in reverse sequence initially, when the algorithm makes N passes.

Selection Sort

Selection~Sort searches the array for the smallest item, which is then exchanged with Items[Lower]. The algorithm then searches Items[Lower+1] through Items[Upper] for the second-smallest item, which is exchanged with Items[Lower+1], and so on. The algorithm always makes N–1 passes through the array, successively putting the k-th smallest item into Items[Lower+k–1]. The k-th iteration leaves Items[Lower] through Items[Lower+k] in their final positions.

Insertion Sort

Insertion~Sort has something in common with Selection~Sort. In the k-th iteration it also leaves Items[Lower] through Items[Lower+k] sorted. However, Insertion~Sort does not inspect all successive elements in the array each time. It considers only the next element Items[Lower+k] in the k-th iteration. It moves the elements prior to it into one higher subscript position in order to insert Items[Lower+k] into the correct position. This is similar to the way a hand of playing cards is typically sorted. Thus, while Selection~Sort inspects all remaining elements in the array and moves one of them, Insertion~Sort inspects one of them and moves from 0 to k–1 of the elements already sorted.

Shell Sort

The Shell~Sort algorithm is named after D.L. Shell, who first published the idea. It operates by using a more sophisticated version of the insertion sort concept. The problem with insertion sorting is that many elements must be moved when inserting an array element that is a long way from its final position. Shell~Sort starts by insertion sorting all elements that are a fixed distance apart. In the first pass the distance chosen is large, so that elements a long way from their final positions are quickly moved closer to home. In successive passes the distance is reduced, until a final pass is made with the distance equal to one, equivalent to the normal insertion sort.

Heap Sort

The Heap~Sort algorithm makes use of a heap data structure, as described in Section 5.3. The heap is built in the array to be sorted itself, rather than in a separate array.

Heap~Sort requires one less than N iterations to create the heap, and then the same number of iterations to create the sorted array from the heap. Initially, it is assumed that Items[Lower] comprises a heap of 1 element. In the first iteration Items[Lower+1] is inserted into the heap, which now occupies the two elements Items[Lower] and Items[Lower+1]. In the k-th iteration, when element Items[Lower+k] is inserted, the heap will occupy elements Items[Lower] through Items[Lower+k]. Once the heap has been constructed, the removal process starts. The largest element is removed from Items[Lower]. The remainder of the heap is rearranged so that it now occupies Items[Lower] through Items[Upper–1]. The largest element that was extracted is now conveniently stored in Items[Upper]. In the k-th iteration of the removal process elements Items[Upper–k+1] through Items[Upper] are in their final positions.

Quick Sort

The Quick~Sort algorithm chooses one element of the array to act as a dividing fence, say Items[Middle]. It then moves elements of the array greater than Items[Middle] into elements Items[Middle+1] through Items[Upper], and elements less than Items[Middle] into elements Items[Lower] through Items[Middle–1]. The position of Items[Middle] itself is changed in most instances to suit the actual numbers of elements discovered to be less than or greater than Items[Middle]. The process is then applied recursively to the two partitions of the array on either side of the element Items[Middle]. For each such pair of partitions the smaller partition is sorted immediately and (pointers to) the longer one saved on a stack for sorting later. This device keeps the stack size less than the logarithm to base 2 of the size of the whole array being sorted. When all partitions are small, no further partitioning is done, and the cleanup is done by Insertion~Sort.

Radix Sort

The Radix~Sort algorithm is very similar to Quick~Sort. The important difference is that the dividing fence is not one of the elements of the array. Instead, Radix~Sort focuses on individual bit positions of the items to be sorted. In the first pass all items with a zero bit in the most significant bit position are moved to Items[Lower] through Items[Middle], and those with a one bit are moved to Items[Middle+1] through Items[Upper]. In the next pass each partition is considered separately, and each is further partitioned on the second-most significant bit position. The process is applied to successive bit positions on all partitions generated. As with Quick~Sort, it is more efficient to use Insertion~Sort for a final cleanup when the partitions are small.

Merge Sort

The Merge~Sort algorithm sorts Items[Lower] and Items[Lower+1] into the correct sequence. Then it does the same with Items[Lower+2] and Items[Lower+3], and so on through the entire array. In the second pass it merges the subarray consisting of Items[Lower] and Items[Lower+1] with the subarray consisting of Items[Lower+2] and Items[Lower+3] to produce a sorted subarray consisting of Items[Lower] through Items[Lower+3]. The whole array is treated in this way, merging subarrays of two elements into subarrays of four elements. The process is applied repeatedly, doubling the length of the subarrays at each iteration, until the entire list is in a single subarray.

Linear Sort

The Linear~Sort algorithm sorts the array first on the least significant 8-bit byte, then on the second-least significant byte, and so on until the sort is carried out on the most significant byte. For a 32-bit word four iterations are required. In order to sort on any given byte, one pass is made through the array to count the number of records having each byte value. These counts are maintained in a count array C, which has elements from C[0] to C[255]. The cumulative counts are then obtained, so that C[k] contains the position in Items of the last occurrence of the byte with value k (in that byte position within a word). Working backward through the array, the algorithm then places each element in the position Items[C[k]], decrementing C[k] by one to allow for the other occurrences of the same byte.

Efficiency

Now you can appreciate the variations in efficiency among the algorithms. Table 6.1 provides a comparison. It shows the performance of each algorithm under four different assumptions about the ordering of the N items in the array. Extreme cases are used, none of which is likely to occur in practice, but which illustrate the performance of the algorithms in various circumstances. The four cases are (1) random integers, (2) an ascending sequence of integers, (3) a descending sequence of integers, and (4) all items with the same value.

Table 6.1

Method	*Random*	*Ascending*	*Descending*	*Equal*	*Stable*
Bubble~Sort	O (N^2)	O (N)	O (N^2)	O (N)	Yes
Selection~Sort	O (N^2)	O (N^2)	O (N^2)	O (N^2)	Yes
Insertion~Sort	O (N^2)	O (N)	O (N^2)	O (N)	Yes
Shell~Sort	O $(N^{1.25})$	O (N *log* N)	O $(N^{1.5})$	O (N *log* N)	No
Heap~Sort	O (N *log* N)	O (N *log* N)	O (N *log* N)	O (N)	No
Quick~Sort	O (N *log* N)	O (N *log* N)	O (N *log* N)	O (N *log* N)	No
Radix~Sort	O (N *log* N)	O (N^2)	O (N^2)	O (N^2)	No
Merge~Sort	O (N *log* N)	O (N *log* N)	O (N *log* N)	O (N *log* N)	Yes
Linear~Sort	O (N)	O (N)	O (N)	O (N)	Yes

A sorting algorithm is "stable" if the relative positions of equal keys are undisturbed by the sorting process. Stability is irrelevant when our only consideration is merely getting an array of items into sorted sequence. In those circumstances equal items are indistinguishable. Stability is important when there is a data record associated with each item to be sorted. For example, suppose you have an array of names and birth dates in alphabetical order. If you sort the array into order of birth dates, you would like the names of people with identical birth dates to remain in alphabetical order. Stable methods will achieve this, but unstable methods will not.

Superficial examination of the table indicates that Linear~Sort, implemented by a key-counting algorithm, is the most efficient. It requires a time proportional to the size of the array being sorted. For very large arrays Linear~Sort is likely to run faster than any other method. Further, its running time (proportional to the size of the array) increases more slowly than that of any other method as the size of the array increases. The algorithm is also stable. The main disadvantage is that linear sorting requires a temporary array equal in size to the array being sorted. There is also more code in the algorithm than with several other methods. If limited memory size does not militate against use of a temporary array, Linear~Sort is the method of choice for large arrays.

The table is quite misleading when small arrays are considered. When N is small, the amount of overhead in algorithms (looping, counting, testing, etc.) is more significant than the number of exchanges carried out. Insertion~Sort and Selection~Sort are more efficient than all other methods in these circumstances. Bubble~Sort, sometimes called shuttle sort, is a poor general-purpose algorithm, and is provided here so that if you are using it you may recognize it and consider using an alternative. A bidirectional, or cocktail shaker, version of Bubble~Sort is excellent for arrays in which only a few elements are out of place (Gonnet and Baeza-Yates 1991). For ten or twenty items in random sequence Insertion~Sort seems to be marginally more efficient than Selection~Sort. Insertion~Sort is considerably better if the array is already partially sorted or if there are many equal keys. Selection~Sort is better than insertion for arrays in reverse sequence.

Surprisingly, Insertion~Sort is usually implemented without optimization of the inner loop. There is typically a double test as shown below (e.g., Gonnet and Baeza-Yates 1991), or even more complex code if the programming is done in Pascal (e.g., Sedgewick 1988).

```
loop until J < Lower or Items[J] ≤ T
    let Items[J+1] = Items[J]
    let J = J – 1
end loop
```

The "J < Lower" part is rarely true but is executed in every iteration of the loop. Observe that all elements in the array before the J-th are in sorted sequence. Therefore, our algorithm checks before entering the loop whether T is less than Items[Lower]. If so, it exchanges the two values and proceeds with the new value of T. The loop is then guaranteed to terminate without the necessity for testing J against Lower in the loop. A similar improvement can be made in Shell~Sort.

The analysis of Shell~Sort is complex and not fully developed. Empirical evidence (Gonnet and Baeza-Yates 1991; Weiss 1991) supports the estimates of efficiency provided in Table 6.1. Shell~Sort is simple to implement and is recommended for general-purpose use in a variety of applications. It is reasonably efficient for several thousand records, although slower than all algorithms below it in the table, except Heap~Sort. Its principal disadvantage is that it is not stable. The best choice of distances between elements is an area of active research. Our choice, recommended by Gonnet and Baeza-Yates (1991), is superior to that found in other references.

Insertion~Sort and Shell~Sort can apparently be improved by using binary search to locate the position in which to insert the item currently being considered. The "improvement" may be more apparent than real. In practice, in the applications for which they are intended, the two methods need to search only short sequences of sorted elements in order to find the correct insertion point. The extra overhead in implementing the binary insertion search method is probably not warranted.

Heap~Sort is theoretically as efficient as Quick~Sort and Merge~Sort, requiring O (N *log* N) execution time. The constant of proportionality seems to be higher for

Heap~Sort than for other methods. We were unable to implement it efficiently enough to compete effectively with the other algorithms, a finding supported by Gonnet and Baeza-Yates (1991). Improvements suggested by Xunrang and Yuzhang (1990) seem to be less helpful than eliminating the double tests in the inner loops of Heap~Sort. Unfortunately, the double test cannot be eliminated without using location Items[Lower–1]. Doing that destroys the generality of the algorithm. Heap~Sort also suffers from the disadvantage that it is not stable.

Quick~Sort, on the other hand, is a very efficient algorithm, beaten only by Linear~Sort (when large files are sorted). Quick~Sort is not stable, although a more complex stable version has been proposed (Motzkin 1981). The other disadvantage is that there is a remote possibility that Quick~Sort can be as slow as Selection~Sort, with O (N^2) performance. The various devices that have been proposed for dealing with this problem (Sedgewick 1978) are included in our version. Other improvements have been suggested (e.g., Motzkin 1983), but while these reduce the number of comparisons and exchanges, the additional code increases the running time. The worst-case performance has negligible probability of occurring in any practical use of the algorithm. We tested Quick~Sort with 1,000 sets of data, each containing 200 elements, with all kinds of patterns, including randomness. There was an acceptable maximum deviation of ± 22% from the average number of comparisons, and ± 6% from the average number of exchanges. This means that Quick~Sort can be confidently used for large sorting applications. If you have any lingering doubt, replace "*let* Middle = (Lower + Upper) ÷ 2" by "*call* Integer~Initialize (Lower, Upper)" followed by "*call* Random~Integer (Middle)".

Radix~Sort is not recommended unless the data to be sorted are known to be randomly distributed. In those circumstances Radix~Sort compares very favorably with Quick~Sort (and can probably be optimized to exceed the performance of Quick~Sort). However, one can rarely expect the luxury of randomly distributed data. The performance of Radix~Sort deteriorates with increasing regularity in the sequencing of the array elements. Radix~Sort should not, for example, be used generally for sorting text. The algorithm also performs badly when many keys have equal values.

Radix~Sort does not require bit manipulation, although the textbook implementation usually uses functions that extract bits from words (Sedgewick 1988). For any given partition being sorted on the k-th most significant bit, the preceding bits of all items in that partition are identical. The dividing fence is constructed from those identical bits, and all bits following the k-th bit are set to zeros. The largest possible integer *maxinteger* plus one, successively divided by two, provides the required sequence of bits.

Radix~Sort is usually implemented with a double test in the inner loop, in a manner similar to that discussed concerning Insertion~Sort above. The double test is eliminated by ensuring that Items[Lower] and Items[Upper] contain the lowest and highest items respectively. This is done by saving the original contents of those locations temporarily, and replacing them in the right places after the partitioning process has been completed. These operations are carried out by the three calls to Sort~4. The position of Middle is also adjusted after this process to compensate for there being zero, one, or two one-bits in the two locations temporarily saved. Although this complicates the code in the partitioning procedure, there appears to be no alternative for making the inner loop of the algorithm as efficient as possible, without using locations outside the range Lower to Upper.

Both the Radix~Sort and Quick~Sort algorithms halt the partitioning process when the subarrays become small. In both algorithms the cutoff point is a subarray of size 10, as suggested by the literature. At the end of the partitioning process the list will consist of a sorted sequence of unsorted subarrays, none of which has more than ten items. Insertion~Sort is used to carry out the final sorting process, this being more efficient than using the Radix~Sort or Quick~Sort methods on small subarrays. This raises a potential programming problem. You can make a mistake in transcription, but the algorithm will still work, albeit slowly! Insertion~Sort will repair the damage done by the bug in the partitioning code. The only evidence of a problem will be O (N^2) behavior rather than the expected O (N *log* N). Caveat emptor!

By way of contrast, Merge~Sort is a safe and secure algorithm, although it appears to be marginally slower than Quick~Sort. Merge~Sort has the disadvantage that it requires a temporary storage array equal in size to the array to be sorted. The algorithm has the property of stability, which is highly desirable for many practical applications. Merge~Sort is simple to implement, although the literature contains amazingly complex attempts to code it (e.g., Knuth 1973). The simplicity of Merge~Sort is secured by capitalizing on the fact that the merged array is placed in temporary storage. The original array can therefore be overwritten. As each key is selected from the source array it is replaced by a value higher than any actual key. This replacement eliminates much extraneous testing and produces clean code. The algorithm ensures that at the end of the process the merged array is put back in the original array.

Linear~Sort can be improved in efficiency by using a larger array of counts, at present set to 256 items. With simple modifications the size of the array can be increased to 256^2, or 65,536 locations, and the sorting process completed in two passes instead of four.

You may be concerned with sorting very long records. There are two kinds of potential problem. The keys may be long or the associated data records may be long (or both). Radix~Sort is theoretically the best algorithm for long keys, because it inspects only enough bits of the keys to produce sorted subarrays smaller than ten items. It will be necessary to test individual bits of long keys rather than use our whole-word comparison method. The latter is efficient only for short keys. Selection~Sort and Linear~Sort may be the best for long data records, because they minimize the amount of record exchanging, for small and large arrays respectively. There is another way of dealing with long data records that allows any sorting method to be used without negative implications for efficiency.

For a large number of long records you should modify the algorithms to sort indirectly. This requires an additional auxiliary array, say P. Initialize P[I] to contain I, where Items[I] is the I-th item to be sorted. Thus, P contains "pointers" to the array elements. You sort these pointers to the items rather than the items themselves. Whenever Items[I], say, is referred to (but not moved), replace the reference by Items[P[I]]. All movements, such as exchanging Items[I] and Items[J], are modified to exchange P[I] and P[J] instead.

Note again that all algorithms are written for sorting lists of integers. However, not much effort is required other than changes to data types to permit the algorithms to work on other types of data. Linear~Sort requires a number of calls to Partial equal to the number of bytes in a key. Keys of unequal length can be handled by calling Partial sufficient times to deal with the maximum key size, zero being used as the "value" of any nonexistent bytes when comparing keys.

Obviously, these algorithms are "internal" methods, which implies that they are designed for sorting within the computer's main memory. Other methods beyond the scope of this book are used for efficient sorting of very large files using disk storage. Standard software such as the Unix™ *sort* utility will be adequate for most practical applications. Nevertheless, if your programming language has a "virtual memory" capability for arrays, you can use the sorting algorithms presented here for very large sets of data. It is up to you to check the efficiency of the algorithms in those circumstances, although Merge~Sort and Linear~Sort are likely to be the most promising.

IMPLEMENTATION

<u>Exported Names</u>

Bubble~Sort	Sorts array of integers using bubble method (6.2.1)
Heap~Sort	Sorts array of integers using heap method (6.2.5)
Insertion~Sort	Sorts array of integers using insertion method (6.2.3)
Linear~Sort	Sorts array of integers using radix/counting method (6.2.9)
Merge~Sort	Sorts array of integers using merge method (6.2.8)
Quick~Sort	Sorts array of integers using "quicksort" method (6.2.6)
Radix~Sort	Sorts array of integers using radix method (6.2.7)
Selection~Sort	Sorts array of integers using selection method (6.2.2)
Shell~Sort	Sorts array of integers using Shell's method (6.2.4)

<u>Imported Names</u>

Sort~2	Sorts two items (6.1.1)
Sort~3	Sorts three items (6.1.2)
Sort~4	Sorts four items (6.1.3)
Stack~Initialize	Initializes the stack (5.1.3)
Stack~Pop	Removes an item from the stack (5.1.2)
Stack~Push	Inserts an item into the stack (5.1.1)

<u>Local Subprograms</u>

Partial	Carries out one pass of a multipass sorting algorithm
Partition	Inserts a fence between smaller and larger items
Pop	Removes several values from the stack
Push	Inserts several values into the stack

<u>Nicknames</u>

Fence	Partitioning value greater than some items and less than others
Items	Array of items, from Items[Lower] to Items[Upper], to be sorted
Lower	Position of first relevant item in Items array, i.e., Items[Lower]
Middle	Position of partitioning element, i.e., Items[Middle], in sublist
N	Number of items in sublist to be merged with another sublist
Ones	Word containing contiguous one bits following contiguous zeros
Pass	Byte number to be processed in this pass through the array
Temp	Array of temporary storage, from Temp[Lower] to Temp[Upper]
Upper	Position of last relevant item in Items array, i.e., Items[Upper]

<u>Local Names</u>

C	Array of counts of number of occurrences of each byte value
Child	Item below parent in heap
Divisor	Power of two used for obtaining required byte by division
Done	Flag to indicate whether sorting process is complete

EndItem	Position of the last item in the second sublist
Fence	Partitioning value greater than some items and less than others
I	Distance between Items items chosen as candidates for exchanging
J	Loop counter and array index
K	Byte value
L	Position of lowest item in current sublist being partitioned
List1	Position of the first item in the first sublist
List2	Position of the first item in the second sublist
M	Position of partitioning item in current sublist being partitioned
Max	Initially larger than any item in the sublist
Min	Initially smaller than any item in the sublist
N	Number of items in sublist to be merged with another sublist
One	Word containing a single one bit
Parent	Item above child in heap
Small	Position of smallest item so far
T	Temporary variable for holding largest sublist item so far
U	Position of uppermost item in current sublist being partitioned

6.2.1 Bubble~Sort (updates Items; receives Lower, Upper)

Pseudo Code

```
loop
    for i = Lower to (Upper – 1)
        sort Items[i] and Items[i+1]
    end for
end loop when no exchanges took place
```

Code

```
procedure Bubble~Sort (Items is array of integers, Lower, Upper are integers)
    variable J is integer
    variable Done is true-false
    let J = 1
    loop
        let Done = true
        for i = Lower to (Upper – J)
            if Items[i] > Items[i+1] then
                call swap (Items[i], Items[i+1])
                let Done = false
            end if
        end for
        let J = J + 1
    end loop when Done = true
end Bubble~Sort
```

6.2.2 Selection~Sort (updates Items; receives Lower, Upper)

Pseudo Code

```
for i = Lower to (Upper – 1)
    find position Small of smallest item from i+1 through Upper
    exchange Items[i] and Items[Small]
end for
```

Code

```
procedure Selection~Sort (Items is array of integers, Lower, Upper are integers)
    variable Small is integer
    for i = Lower to (Upper – 1)
        let Small = i
        for j = (i + 1) to Upper
            if Items[j] < Items[Small] then
                let Small = j
            end if
        end for
        call swap (Items[i], Items[Small])
    end for
end Selection~Sort
```

6.2.3 Insertion~Sort (updates Items; receives Lower, Upper)

Pseudo Code

```
for i = Lower to (Upper – 1)
    sort Items[Lower] and Items[i+1]
    scan backward to find position J of first item Items[J] ≤ Items[i+1]
    move Items[J+1] through Items[i] to Items[J+2] through Items[i+1]
    save original value of Items[i+1] in Items[J+1]
end for
```

Code

```
procedure Insertion~Sort (Items is array of integers, Lower, Upper are integers)
    variables J, T are integers
    for i = Lower to (Upper – 1)
        let T = Items[i+1]
        call Sort~2 (Items[Lower], T)
        let J = i
        loop until Items[J] ≤ T
            let Items[J+1] = Items[J]
            let J = J – 1
        end loop
        let Items[J+1] = T
    end for
end Insertion~Sort
```

6.2.4 Shell~Sort (updates Items; receives Lower, Upper)

Pseudo Code

```
compute starting value of increment
loop until increment I ≤ 1
    update value of increment I
```

```
    for k = Lower to (Upper – I)
        sort Items[J] and Items[k+I], where J is first position in array relevant to this
                increment
        scan backward to find position J of first item Items[J] ≤ Items[k+1]
        move Items[J+I] through Items[k] to Items[J+(2*I)] through Items[k+I]
        save original value of Items[k+I] in Items[J+I]
    end for
end loop
```

Code

```
procedure Shell~Sort (Items is array of integers, Lower, Upper are integers)
    variables I, J, T are integers
    let I = Upper – Lower + 1                    Get next value of increment
    loop until I ≤ 1
        let I = maximum (1, ((I * 5) – 1) / 11)
        for k = Lower to (Upper – I)
            let T = Items[k+I]
            let J = ((k – Lower) mod I) + Lower  Ensure lowest item is smaller than
            call Sort~2 (Items[J], T)            next one considered
            let J = k
            loop until Items[J] ≤ T              Insertion sort elements separated
                let Items[J+I] = Items[J]        by increment
                let J = J – I
            end loop
            let Items[J+I] = T
        end for
    end loop
end Shell~Sort
```

6.2.5 Heap~Sort (updates Items; receives Lower, Upper)

Pseudo Code

```
for k = (Lower + 1) to Upper
    insert Items[k] into heap, i.e., Items[Lower] through Items[k–1], using
            Heap~Insert process
end for
for decreasing k = (Upper – 1) to Lower
    remove top of heap using Heap~Remove process and place it in Items[k]
end for
```

Code

```
procedure Heap~Sort (Items is array of integers, Lower, Upper are integers)
    variables Big, Child, Parent are integers
    for k = (Lower + 1) to Upper                 Transform the array elements into
        let Child = k                            a heap
        let Parent = (Child + Lower – 1) ÷ 2
```

```
        loop until Parent < Lower or Items[Parent] ≥        Double test can be
                Items[Child]                                eliminated if
            call swap (Items[Parent], Items[Child])         List[Lower–1] used as
            let Child = Parent                              per heap data
            let Parent = (Child + Lower – 1) ÷ 2            structure algorithm
        end loop
    end for
    for decreasing k = (Upper – 1) to Lower            Remove array elements from the
        let Big = Items[Lower]                         heap
        let Items[Lower] = Items[k+1]
        let Items[k+1] = –maxinteger                   Set up low key temporarily to
        let Parent = Lower                             eliminate double test in loop
        let Child = Lower + 1
        loop until Child > k
            if Items[Child] < Items[Child+1] then           Select largest of the
                let Child = Child + 1                       two children
            end if
            if Items[Parent] ≥ Items[Child] then            Check for the end of
                let Child = k                               the process
            else
                call swap (Items[Parent], Items[Child])
            end if
            let Parent = Child
            let Child = (Parent * 2) – Lower + 1
        end loop
        let Items[k+1] = Big                           Replace temporary key with
    end for                                            largest element
end Heap~Sort
```

6.2.6 Quick~Sort (updates Items; receives Lower, Upper)

Pseudo Code

```
push the limits of the whole array, L and U, onto the stack
loop
    divide the partition so that Items[L] … Items[M–1] ≤ Items[M],
        and Items[M+1] … Items[U] ≥ Items[M]
    push the limits of the largest partition onto the stack
    set L and U to be the limits of the smallest partition
    repeatedly pop the limits of a partition from the stack until a partition has more
            than 10 items
end loop when there are no more partitions on the stack
insertion sort the whole array
```

Code

```
procedure Quick~Sort (Items is array of integers, Lower, Upper are integers)
    variables L, M, U are integers
    check Upper – Lower > 10
```

```
        call Stack~Initialize
        call Push (Lower, Upper)                    Used to terminate inner loop
        let L = Lower
        let U = Upper
        loop
            call Partition (Items, L, M, U)
            if M < (L + U) ÷ 2 then                 Put largest sublist on stack and
                call Push (M + 1, U)                partition the other
                let U = M – 1
            else
                call Push (L, M – 1)
                let L = M + 1
            end if
            loop until U – L > 10                   Ignore small sublists
                call Pop (L, U)
            end loop
        end loop when Stack~Size ( ) = 0
        call Insertion~Sort (Items, Lower, Upper)
    end Quick~Sort
```

Local **Partition** (updates Items; receives Lower; supplies Middle; receives Upper)

```
    procedure Partition (Items is array of integers, Lower, Middle, Upper are integers)
        variables Fence, L are integers
        let Middle = (Lower + Upper) ÷ 2
        call Sort~3 (Items[Middle], Items[Upper],   Median goes into Upper position
                Items[Lower])                       initially, to be swapped into
        let Fence = Items[Upper]                    Lower later
        let L = Lower
        let Middle = Upper
        loop
            call swap (Items[L], Items[Middle])     Swap array elements where both
            loop                                    on wrong side of fence
                let L = L + 1
            end loop when Items[L] ≥ Fence
            loop
                let Middle = Middle – 1
            end loop when Items[Middle] ≤ Fence
        end loop when L ≥ Middle
        call swap (Items[Lower], Items[Middle])     Put median into its proper posi-
    end Partition                                   tion in the middle
```

Local **Push** (receives Lower, Upper)

```
    procedure Push (Lower, Upper are integers)
        call Stack~Push (Lower)
        call Stack~Push (Upper)
    end Push
```

```
Local    Pop (supplies Lower, Upper)
    procedure Pop (Lower, Upper are integers)
            call Stack~Pop (Upper)
            call Stack~Pop (Lower)
    end Pop
```

6.2.7 Radix~Sort (updates Items; receives Lower, Upper)

Pseudo Code

```
determine the first Fence
push the limits of the whole array, L and U, onto the stack
loop
    divide the partition so that Items[L] … Items[M] ≤ Fence,
        and Items[M+1] … Items[U] > Fence
    push the limits of the largest partition onto the stack, with fence information
    set L and U to be the limits of the smallest partition
    repeatedly pop the limits of a partition from the stack until a partition has more
            than 10 items
end loop when there are no more partitions on the stack
insertion sort the whole array
```

Code

```
procedure Radix~Sort (Items is array of integers, Lower, Upper are integers)
    variables Fence, L, M, One, U are integers
    check Upper – Lower > 10
    let One = (maxinteger ÷ 2) + 1
    let Fence = One
    call Stack~Initialize
    call Push (One, Fence, Lower, Upper)           Used to terminate inner loop
    let L = Lower
    let U = Upper
    loop
        call Partition (Items, L, M, U, Fence)
        let One = One ÷ 2
        if M < (L + U) ÷ 2 then                    Put largest sublist on stack and
            call Push (One, Fence + One,           partition the other
                    M + 1, U)
            let U = M – 1
            let Fence = Fence – One
        else
            call Push (One, Fence – One, L, M – 1)
            let L = M + 1
            let Fence = Fence + One
        end if
        loop until U – L > 10                      Ignore small sublists
            call Pop (One, Fence, L, U)
        end loop
```

```
        end loop when Stack~Size ( ) = 0
        call Insertion~Sort (Items, Lower, Upper)
    end Radix~Sort
```

Local **Partition** (updates Items; receives Lower; supplies Middle; receives Upper, Fence)

```
    procedure Partition (Items is array of integers, Lower, Middle, Upper, Fence are
            integers)
        variables L, Max, Min are integers
        let Min = 0
        let Max = maxinteger
        call Sort~4 (Items[Upper], Min, Max, Items[Lower])   Save first and last ele-
        let L = Lower                                        ments in Min and Max,
        let Middle = Upper                                   replacing them with 0
        loop until L ≥ Middle                                and maxinteger
            call swap (Items[L], Items[Middle])          Swap array elements where both
            loop until Items[L] > Fence                  on wrong side of fence
                let L = L + 1
            end loop
            loop until Items[Middle] ≤ Fence
                let Middle = Middle – 1
            end loop
        end loop
        call Sort~4 (Min, Items[Middle],                 Replace saved array elements at
                Items[Middle+1], Max)                    fence position and remove
        call Sort~4 (Min, Items[Lower],                  dummies 0 and maxinteger
                Items[Upper], Max)
        if Items[Middle] ≥ Fence then
            let Middle = Middle – 1
        else-if Items[Middle+1] < Fence then             Adjust position of fence for
            let Middle = Middle + 1                      zero, one, or two 1-bits in saved
        end if                                           elements
    end Partition
```

Local **Push** (receives One, Fence, Lower, Upper)

```
    procedure Push (One, Fence, Lower, Upper are integers)
        call Stack~Push (One)
        call Stack~Push (Fence)
        call Stack~Push (Lower)
        call Stack~Push (Upper)
    end Push
```

Local **Pop** (supplies One, Fence, Lower, Upper)

```
    procedure Pop (One, Fence, Lower, Upper are integers)
        call Stack~Pop (Upper)
        call Stack~Pop (Lower)
        call Stack~Pop (Fence)
        call Stack~Pop (One)
    end Pop
```

6.2.8 Merge~Sort (updates Items; receives Lower, Upper; supplies Temp)

Pseudo Code

```
initialize the subarray size N to 1
loop until N > number of items being sorted
    call Partial to sort subarrays of size N from array Items into array Temp
    call Partial to sort subarrays of size N*2 from array Temp into array Items
    let N = N * 4
end loop
procedure Partial
    for i = 1 to total number of pairs of subarrays
        merge subarrays from source array into destination array
    end for
end Partial
```

Code

```
procedure Merge~Sort (Items is array of integers, Lower, Upper are integers, Temp
        is array of integers)
    variable N is integer
    let N = 1
    loop until N > Upper – Lower + 1
        call Partial (Items, Lower, Upper, Temp, N)
        call Partial (Temp, Lower, Upper, Items, N * 2)
        let N = N * 4
    end loop
end Merge~Sort
```

Local **Partial** (updates Items; receives Lower, Upper; supplies Temp; receives N)

```
procedure Partial (Items is array of integers, Lower, Upper are integers, Temp is
    array of integers, N is integer)
    variables EndItem, List1, List2 are integers
    let List1 = Lower
    let List2 = minimum (Lower + N, Upper)
    for i = 1 to ((Upper – Lower + 1) ÷ (N * 2)) + 1
        let EndItem = minimum (List2 + N – 1, Upper)        Cycle through pairs of
        for k = List1 to EndItem                            sublists
            if Items[List1] ≤ Items[List2] then        Merge the sublists at First and
                let Temp[k] = Items[List1]             Second
                let Items[List1] = maxinteger
                let List1 = List1 + 1
            else
                let Temp[k] = Items[List2]
                let Items[List2] = maxinteger
                let List2 = minimum (List2 + 1, EndItem)
            end if
        end for
        let List1 = EndItem + 1
        let List2 = minimum (List1 + N, Upper)     Determine positions of next two
    end for                                        sublists
end Partial
```

6.2.9 Linear~Sort (updates Items; receives Lower, Upper; supplies Temp)

Pseudo Code

```
call Partial to sort array Items into array Temp on successively less significant bytes
procedure Partial
    initialize byte count array C to zeros
    scan entire array, counting the number of occurrences of each byte
    replace each element of C by cumulative counts
    scan array backward, moving source elements to destination positions given by
            byte value
end Partial
```

Code

```
procedure Linear~Sort (Items is array of integers, Lower, Upper are integers, Temp
        is array of integers)
    for i = 1 to (ceiling (log2 (maxinteger)) ÷ 16)       Upper limit is 2 for a
        call Partial (Items, Lower, Upper, Temp, (i * 2) – 2)   32-bit word size,
        call Partial (Temp, Lower, Upper, Items, (i * 2) – 1)   suitable for sorting
    end for                                                on 8-bit bytes
end Linear~Sort
```

Local **Partial** (updates Items; receives Lower, Upper; supplies Temp; receives Pass)

```
procedure Partial (Items is array of integers, Lower, Upper are integers, Temp is
        array of integers, Pass is integer)
    constant Divisor = power (256, Pass)
    variable C is array 0 to 255 of integers
    variable K is integer
    for j = 0 to 255                          Initialize count for each possible
        let C[j] = 0                          byte
    end for
    for i = Lower to Upper                    Count occurrences of each byte
        let K = (Items[i] ÷ Divisor) mod 256
        let C[K] = C[K] + 1
    end for
    for j = 1 to 255                          Develop cumulative counts
        let C[j] = C[j] + C[j–1]
    end for
    for decreasing i = Upper to Lower         Place array elements in positions
        let K = (Items[i] ÷ Divisor) mod 256  given by cumulative counts
        let Temp[C[K]] = Items[i]
        let C[K] = C[K] – 1
    end for
end Partial
```

TEST PROGRAM

<u>Local Names</u>

A	The array to be sorted
B	The array used for temporary storage
L, U	Lower and upper bounds of the test arrays

Pseudo Code

```
for each method in turn
    initialize array of integers in reverse sequence
    sort array
    check that array elements are correctly sequenced
end for
```

Code

```
constants L = 1, U = 100
variable A, B are arrays L to U of integers
for k = 1 to 27
    if k mod 3 = 1 then
        for i = L to U                      Initialize array to decreasing
            let A[i] = U – i + L            sequence of integers
        end for
    else-if k = 2 then                      Select sorting method
        call Bubble~Sort (A, L, U)
    else-if k = 5 then
        call Selection~Sort (A, L, U)
    else-if k = 8 then
        call Insertion~Sort (A, L, U)
    else-if k = 11 then
        call Shell~Sort (A, L, U)
    else-if k = 14 then
        call Heap~Sort (A, L, U)
    else-if k = 17 then
        call Quick~Sort (A, L, U)
    else-if k = 20 then
        call Radix~Sort (A, L, U)
    else-if k = 23 then
        call Merge~Sort (A, L, U, B)
    else-if k = 26 then
        call Linear~Sort (A, L, U, B)
    else-if k mod 3 = 0 then
        for i = L to U                      Check that array is in ascending
            check A[i] = i                  sequence
        end for
    end if
end for
```

7 Text Processing

A large part of the world's computing budget is spent on processing text. Word processing is now commonplace. With the proliferation of networking, there are central file servers that channel large quantities of text back and forth among many end users. A great deal of the work of organizations of all kinds involves processing information, much of it textual information. It is therefore appropriate that you should have readily available some algorithms that are particularly suitable for text manipulation.

Two algorithms in this chapter are concerned with the matching of names, or more generally with comparing one representation of a word or text string with another. There are many useful applications for these algorithms. To take just one example, consider the problem facing telephone information operators. A caller wishes to know the telephone number corresponding to a given name. It is relatively easy to look up a computerized directory to find a specific word or name. But how about finding *approximate* matches, which are needed frequently? For example, suppose you are trying to find McLaughlan, but the directory contains MacLaughlan. Is that a match or is it not? The telephone operator may not spell the name correctly, just as the caller may have an incorrect spelling.

There are two main approaches to deal with the problem caused by minor differences in spelling. One approach is to measure the degree of similarity between the words or names. The Text Similarity Algorithm in Section 7.2 assesses the similarity of McLaughlan and MacLaughlan at just over 95%. Names can be displayed on the screen in decreasing order of the extent to which they match the specified name. The other approach is the Soundex method described in Section 7.1. The idea behind Soundex is to convert the names to codes that contain the phonetic quality of the names. Both

McLaughlan and MacLaughlan have the same Soundex code, and so they are judged to be phonetically similar.

Word processing programs usually have a *find* facility. This permits the user to search through a document to find a particular word or text string. It is important that the facility operate efficiently, for obvious reasons. The pattern-matching algorithm presented in Section 7.3 is a relatively recent development that is claimed to be the fastest yet developed. In addition, you will find some ideas for optimization of the inner loop.

A frequent requirement is to search an array of data to find a particular item. For example, if you have a program that accesses names in a sorted or unsorted array, you will need to find the location in which a particular name occurs. The searching algorithms discussed in Section 7.4 address the issue, providing algorithms for sequential and binary search. Both implementations are better than the rather simplistic approaches frequently seen in introductory textbooks. Some work has been done to ensure that they operate efficiently.

In order to choose between the sequential and binary search methods you need to consider two matters, the time required to insert items into the array and the time required to access specific items. Sequential search with an unsorted array is superior with respect to the first criterion. Binary search with a sorted array is superior with respect to the second. Insertion times for sequential and binary searches are O (1) and O (N) respectively. Times required for searching are O (N) and O (*log* N) respectively. This would suggest that sequential searching in large unsorted arrays and inserting items into large sorted arrays should be avoided.

Insertion and access times can be improved by using hashing or a trie. The hashing method, discussed in Section 7.5, is very fast indeed, generally providing O (1) performance. It suffers from the disadvantage that you cannot extract records in sorted sequence from a hashed file. Also, the maximum number of records must be known in advance. The performance of the hashing method deteriorates markedly as the maximum number of records is approached.

The trie is also fast, although its performance is O (*log* N). The trie, described in Section 7.6, has the advantage that records are kept in sorted sequence. In addition, a trie can grow to potentially any size without the need for reformatting the entire set of records as occurs with hashing. The trie algorithm requires access to particular bits of words.

Generally speaking, hashing and trie searching may be considered advanced methods, because they are trickier to implement correctly than array-searching algorithms. However, the key implementation problems have been addressed in this chapter and the algorithms are suitable for general-purpose use, even if you are not familiar with searching theory.

7.1 SOUNDEX

Coding a name by its phonetic quality

Example

The Soundex code N620 corresponding to “New York” is calculated and displayed by:

output Soundex~Code (“New York”)

Subprograms

7.1.1 Soundex~Code (receives *text* Name; *result text*)

Usage

The idea behind Soundex is to convert a name to a code that contains the phonetic quality of the name. A Soundex code is a mixture of letters and digits. The digits are codes for major categories of sound. The Soundex code for a name approximates the way the name sounds. Both McLaughlan and MacLaughlan have a Soundex code of M242, and are therefore judged to be phonetically similar.

A typical application for Soundex involves telephone inquiry. For example, suppose you dial Information and ask for the telephone number for McLaughlan in a particular city. The operator will type the surname (plus initials or first name) and city into the computer, and a number of possible matches will be displayed on the screen. The key benefit of the Soundex system is that neither you nor the operator needs to spell the name correctly (most of the time). All the spellings McLaughlan, MacLaughlan, McLochlan, M'Glaghlin, and Nagloky produce the same Soundex code M242. The sounds of these names are very similar and could easily be misunderstood for each other over the telephone. Provided that the computer retrieves the information by Soundex code, all these matching names will be displayed, no matter which one was typed in.

The system is not perfect, however. Similar names such as Rogers and Rodgers have different Soundex codes. Names that are very different, such as Shogun and Kassim, have the same codes. Nevertheless, the system is in widespread use and greatly improves the chances of finding a particular name when the spelling is known only approximately.

Analysis

The algorithm always uses the first letter of the name as the first letter of the code. Three digits in the range zero to six are appended to the first letter. The digits are chosen so as to bring together letters that have a similar sound. Vowels are dropped, so that Soundex codes reflect the consonants only. Double letters are compressed, so that only one of the letters is reflected in the code. The algorithm is described by Knuth (1973) and Hall and Dowling (1980).

The Soundex system is highly oriented toward English, and should not be used in other languages without major modification. For example, the letters *l* and *r* are regarded as major and distinct categories of sound, although they are virtually indistinguishable to Japanese ears. Similarly, it does not make sense to treat the German *w* as a vowel, because it is pronounced rather like the English *v*. On the other hand, the German *j* should be processed like the English *y*. The Spanish *ll* should be handled like a vowel also. There are many other examples.

The test program checks several specific Soundex codes, exercising all main sections of the code, but not every letter of the alphabet.

Very high processing efficiency is not usually a necessity for Soundex implementations. However, there is considerable room for improvement in the efficiency of the Numeric subprogram if speed is critical. The subprogram can be eliminated entirely by creating a 256-element array called Numeric, one location for each possible argument value. Most of the locations will contain zero. If memory space is a problem, note that the values of Numeric require only three bits each. The entire array can be packed into just 26 32-bit words. More elegantly, and perhaps more efficiently, in implementing the algorithm with shift instructions, each digit can be stored in four bits in a 32-element array.

The implementation assumes that the binary codes for uppercase letters have smaller values than those for lowercase letters. It also assumes that the codes for all 26 letters are contiguous binary numbers. This assumption is supported by standards such as ASCII and ISO 7. If you are using a nonstandard or *de facto* standard character set such as EBCDIC, the implementation may require modification.

IMPLEMENTATION

Exported Names

Soundex~Code	Finds the Soundex code corresponding to a given name (7.1.1)

Local Subprograms

Numeric	Converts a letter to a Soundex digit in the range 0 to 6

Nicknames

Letter	One letter from name for which Soundex code is required
Name	Name for which Soundex code is required

Local Names

Code	Soundex code
PrevCode	Numeric code for previous character in name
ThisCode	Numeric code for current character in name

7.1.1 Soundex~Code (receives Name; *result text*)

Pseudo Code

```
let Code = first letter of Name
for current letter = second letter of Name to last letter of Name
    if Numeric (current letter) ≠ Numeric (preceding letter) then
        if Code has fewer than 4 characters in it then
            append Numeric (current letter) to end of Code
        end if
    end if
end for
loop until Code has 4 characters in it
    append '0' to end of Code
end loop
function Numeric (Letter)
    convert Letter to a digit in the range 0 to 6
        (aehiouwy = 0, bfpv = 1, cgjkqsxz = 2, dt = 3, l = 4, mn = 5, r = 6)
end Numeric
```

Code

```
function Soundex~Code (Name is text) is text
    variable Code is text
    variable PrevCode, ThisCode are integers
    check length (Name) > 0
    let PrevCode = Numeric (byte (Name, first))
    for i = first+1 to last (Name)
        let ThisCode = Numeric (byte (Name, i))
        if ThisCode ≠ PrevCode and ThisCode ≠ '0' and length (Code) < 4 then
            call append (Code, ThisCode)
        end if
        let PrevCode = ThisCode
    end for
    loop until length (Code) = 4
        call append (Code, '0')
    end loop
    result Code
end Soundex~Code
```

Local **Numeric** (receives Letter; *result integer*)

```
function Numeric (Letter is integer) is integer
    constant Digit is array 0 to 25 of integers =
        0, 1, 2, 3, 0, 1, 2, 0, 0, 2, 2, 4, 5, 5, 0, 1, 2, 6, 2, 3, 0, 1, 0, 2, 0, 2
    if Letter < 'A' then
        result '0'
    else-if Letter ≤ 'Z' then
        result Digit(Letter – 'A') + '0'
    else-if Letter < 'a' then
        result '0'
    else-if Letter ≤ 'z' then
        result Digit(Letter – 'a') + '0'
    else
        result '0'
    end if
end Numeric
```

TEST PROGRAM

Pseudo Code

check the Soundex codes for several names are the expected codes

Code

```
check Soundex~Code ("New York") = "N620"
check Soundex~Code ("Tokyo") = "T200"
check Soundex~Code ("Mexico City") = "M222"
check Soundex~Code ("Llangollen") = "L524"
```

7.2 TEXT SIMILARITY

Determining whether two text strings are the same or similar

Example

The text strings "contraception" and "conceptualize" have "con", "cept", and "i" in common. The total number of characters in common (eight) is calculated and displayed by:

output Similarity~Characters ("contraception", "conceptualize")

Subprograms

7.2.1 Common~String (receives Text1, Text2; supplies Pos1, Pos2, Max)
7.2.2 Common~Characters (receives Text1, Text2; *result integer*)

Usage

The Common~Characters function is useful for spelling checkers, telephone inquiry software, and similar applications, where it is desired to find which words are most similar to a given word. The function counts how many characters in one word match characters in the other. For example, if "Manchester" is misspelled as "Mancester", the value of Common~Characters ("Manchester", "Mancester") will be 9. This is equal to the number of letters in "Mancester", and is one short of the ten letters in "Manchester".

An "index" of similarity may be computed as twice the number of letters in common divided by the sum of the numbers of characters in the two strings. The index will always lie somewhere in the range 0 to 1, where 0 indicates no matching characters and 1 indicates that the two strings are identical.

Common~Characters makes use of the procedure Common~String, which finds the longest common substring. In the example used above, "Mancester" and "Manchester" have "ester" as the longest common substring. Common~String returns via Pos1 and Pos2 the positions in "Mancester" and "Manchester" where "ester" occurs, and also returns via Max the number of characters in "ester" (five in this example).

Analysis

In calculating the number of characters in common in two words (or more generally in two text strings) the algorithm Common~Characters initially uses Common~String to find the longest common string of characters. In our example "cept" is the longest string of characters that occurs in both "contraception" and "conceptualize". The algorithm then treats the characters to the left of "cept" in both words in the same way, finding the longest common string by using Common~String again. In the example there are three characters in common in "contra" and "con". The characters to the right of "cept" are also compared in the same way by Common~String. The longest string in common in "ion" and "ualize" is "i". Further checks are made on the strings "on" and "ze", which have no characters in common. The required similarity measure is equal to the sum of the numbers of characters in common determined for each of the substrings. Putting it more technically, the algorithm finds the longest string in common and then applies the process recursively to the substrings on the left and right of the longest common string. This is the so-called Gestalt algorithm developed by Ratcliff and Obershelp. A readable account of the algorithm, together with assembly language code, is given by Ratcliff and Metzener (1988). It is shown diagramatically in Figure 7.1.

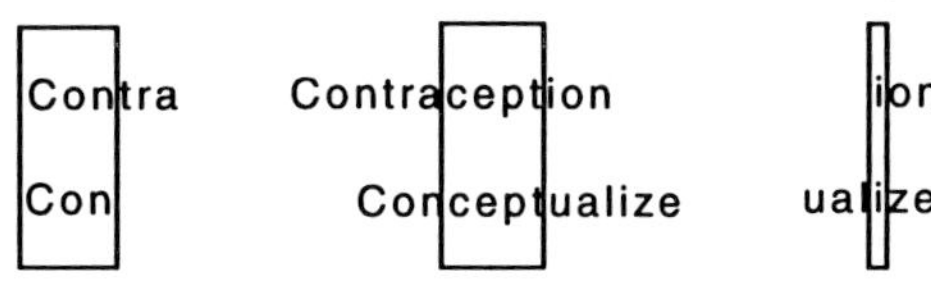

Figure 7.1

Caution! Take care in using Common~Characters with long text strings. The Common~String algorithm has a double loop that considers almost every character position of one text string against almost every character position of the other text string. Within that double loop is a further loop that finds the number of matching characters. The algorithm will be slow when used with long text strings, its running time being O (N^3), where N is the length of the text string.

In order to optimize the inner loop of Common~String, a unique character (with binary code 377_8 or 255_{10} in our implementation) has been appended to the end of one of the strings. The algorithms in this book typically avoid increasing the length of input text arguments, because of the problems this causes in some programming languages. To remove this difficulty, the algorithm can simply take a copy of the string and alter the copy instead of appending a character directly to the value of the nickname. If this is not desirable, it will be necessary to create a double test, which terminates the inner loop in the following manner:

```
let L = minimum (last (Text2) – 1, last (Text1) + J – I)
loop until K > L or byte (Text1, I + K – J) ≠ byte (Text2, K + 1)
    let K = K + 1
end loop
```

This modification requires that you also remove the calls to the subprograms *append* and *shorten.*

IMPLEMENTATION

Exported Names

Common~Characters	Finds the total number of characters in common in two *text* strings (7.2.2)
Common~String	Finds the longest string in common in two *text* strings (7.2.1)

Imported Names

Stack~Initialize	Initialize stack (5.1.3)
Stack~Pop	Pop item from stack (5.1.2)
Stack~Push	Push item onto stack (5.1.1)
Stack~Size	Examine stack size (5.1.4)

Nicknames

Max	Computed number of characters in common in Text1 and Text2
Pos1, Pos2	Computed character position in Text1 or Text2 respectively
Text1, Text2	Text strings to be compared

Global Names

Unique	Character not found anywhere in input text strings

Local Names

A, B	Temporary text strings
Apos, Bpos	Positions in text strings A and B respectively
I, J, K	Loop counters and text string indexes
Max	Number of characters in common in A and B
Sum	Total number of characters in common in Text1 and Text2

Code

```
constant Unique = 255
```

7.2.1 Common~String (receives Text1, Text2; supplies Pos1, Pos2, Max)

Pseudo Code

```
let maximum string length so far = 0
for i = first to last usable character of Text1
    for j = first to last usable character of Text2
        calculate number of matching characters from positions i and j respectively
        if number of matching characters > maximum so far then
            let maximum string length so far = number of matching characters
            save positions i and j
        end if
    end for
end for
```

Code

```
procedure Common~String (Text1, Text2 are text, Pos1, Pos2, Max are integers)
    variables I, J, K are integers
    call append (Text1, Unique)
    let Max = 0                                   Put a unique character at the end
    let I = first – 1                             of one string
    loop until I ≥ last (Text1) – Max
        let I = I + 1                             Loop through Text1
        let J = first – 1
        loop until J ≥ last (Text2) – Max
            let K = J                             Loop through Text2
            loop until byte (Text1, I + K – J) ≠
byte (Text2, K + 1)                                         Find the length
                let K = K + 1                               of matching
            end loop                                        substring
            let K = K – J
```

```
            let J = J + 1
            if K > Max then                  Keep track of the longest match-
                let Max = K                  ing substring
                let Pos1 = I
                let Pos2 = J
            end if
        end loop
    end loop
    call shorten (Text1)                     Remove the unique character
end Common~String
```

7.2.2 Common~Characters (receives Text1, Text2; *result integer*)

Pseudo Code

```
let similarity = 0
initialize the stack
push Text1 and Text2 onto the stack
loop until the stack is empty
    pop two strings A and B from the stack
    find the longest substring A and B have in common
    let similarity = similarity + number of characters in common
    push nonempty substrings from each string preceding the common substring
            onto the stack
    push nonempty substrings from each string following the common substring
            onto the stack
end loop
```

Code

```
function Common~Characters (Text1, Text2 are text) is integer
    variables A, B are text
    variables Apos, Bpos, Max, Sum are integers
    let Sum = 0
    call Stack~Initialize
    call Stack~Push (Text1)                  Put both strings on the stack
    call Stack~Push (Text2)
    loop until Stack~Size = 0
        call Stack~Pop (B)                   Remove two strings from the stack
        call Stack~Pop (A)
        call Common~String (A, B, Apos,      Find position of longest common
                Bpos, Max)                   substring
        let Sum = Sum + Max
        if Apos > first and Bpos > first then
            call Stack~Push (substring (A,   Put substrings preceding common
                    first, Apos – 1))        substring on stack
            call Stack~Push (substring (B, first, Bpos – 1))
        end if
```

```
        if Apos + Max ≤ last (A) and Bpos + Max ≤ last (B) then
            call Stack~Push (substring (A, Apos + Max, last (A)))     Put substrings
            call Stack~Push (substring (B, Bpos + Max, last (B)))     following
        end if                                                        common sub-
    end loop                                                          string on stack
    result Sum
end Common~Characters
```

TEST PROGRAM

Local Names

- M Number of characters in common
- P1 Position of common substring in first text string
- P2 Position of common substring in second text string

Pseudo Code

check the similarity of a string with itself is the number of characters in the string
check the similarity of strings with no characters in common is zero
check the longest common substring in "Mancester" and "Manchester" is "ester"
check the total number of characters in common in "Mancester" and "Manchester" is 9
check the total number of characters in common in "contraception" and "conceptualize" is 8

Code

```
variables P1, P2, M are integers
call Common~String ("Alfie", "Alfie", P1, P2, M)
check P1 = first and P2 = P1 and M = 5
call Common~String ("Alfie", "Norm", P1, P2, M)
check M = 0
call Common~String ("Mancester", "Manchester", P1, P2, M)
check P1 = 5 and P2 = 6 and M = 5
check Common~Characters ("Mancester", "Manchester") = 9
check Common~Characters ("Contraception", "Conceptualize") = 8
```

7.3 PATTERN MATCHING

Finding a word in a document

Example

The character position of the first character of "stu" in "pqrstuvwxyz" is calculated and output by the following code. The result is *first* + 3.

```
call Pattern~Match ("stu", "pqrstuvwxyz", P)
output P
```

Subprograms

7.3.1 Pattern~Match (updates Word; receives Document; supplies Position)

Usage

The algorithm searches for a "word" text string within a "document" text string. In practice, the "word" may be any string of characters at all, with embedded spaces and punctuation if required. Similarly, the "document" may be a string of characters of any length, from zero to the size of the available memory.

If the string of characters being searched for does not exist in the text string, the value –1 is returned as the result. Otherwise, the character position is returned of the first character in the document at which the word being searched for is embedded.

Analysis

The algorithm operates by stepping along to successive positions in the document. At each position each character of the word is compared with contiguous characters in the document. If all characters match, the job is done. Otherwise, the algorithm steps to the next character position in the document. Before the search the algorithm builds a table in which the last occurrence of each letter in the word is recorded. The table allows the algorithm to skip more than one character position in the document when a mismatch is encountered.

This algorithm was shown by Sunday (1990) to be superior to earlier competing algorithms such as the Boyer–Moore and Knuth–Morris–Pratt methods. Nevertheless, it requires processing time proportional to the product of the lengths of the pattern and text strings. In addition, the initialization substantially impairs the performance of the algorithm when it is used for short documents.

A "naive" algorithm, which does not require initialization, can be obtained simply by deleting some code. The naive algorithm is slower for long documents, but faster with short documents. A simple description of the naive algorithm is given by Baase (1988). The changes required are as follows:

- Delete the definition of the array Shift.
- Delete the call to Initialize.
- Replace:
  let J = *minimum* (*last* (Document), D + *length* (Word) + 1)
  let D = D + Shift[*byte* (Document, J)]
  by:
  let D = D + 1

The performance of the algorithm has been enhanced here by treating the first character of the word as a special case. Sunday's algorithm is entered only when there is a match between the first character of the word and the current position in the document. This change is in itself helpful because most comparisons during the scan of a document will in fact result in a mismatch at the first character of the word. It is worthwhile optimizing the code for this likely eventuality.

The algorithm as presented by Sunday (1990) has a double test in the inner loop. The change just described permits optimizing the inner loop by removing one of these tests. This is accomplished by temporarily replacing the first character of the word by a character known to be absent from the document (binary value 377_8 or 255_{10} in the current implementation). The original character is replaced in the word after the search has been completed.

IMPLEMENTATION

<u>Exported Names</u>

Pattern~Match	Finds the position of a given substring within a *text* string (7.3.1)

<u>Local Subprograms</u>

Initialize	Sets up an array of character positions in the word
Sentinel	Puts a sentinel in the first character position of the word

<u>Nicknames</u>

Document	String to be searched for given substring
Letter	One byte, to be inserted at beginning of word
Position	First character in document at which substring match is found
Word	Given substring

<u>Global Names</u>

Shift	Position in the word of the last occurrence of each letter
Unique	Character not found anywhere in document

<u>Local Names</u>

D	Current character position in document
End	Last possible position in document for first character of word
Initial	First character of word
J	Loop counter

Code

constant Unique = 255
variable Shift *is array* 0 *to* 255 *of integers*

7.3.1 Pattern~Match (updates Word; receives Document; supplies Position)

Pseudo Code

```
let Shift[i] = last position in Word of character with binary value i
replace first character of Word by a sentinel
loop until end of Document is reached
    if original first character of Word = current position in Document then
        if remainder of Word matches Document from current position + 1 then
            let Position = current position
            move to end of Document
    else
            move to position in Document determined by first character beyond last
                    matched with Word
    end if
```

```
        else
            increment current position in document by 1
        end if
    end loop
    restore first character of Word
```

Code

```
procedure Pattern~Match (Word, Document are text, Position is integer)
    variables D, End, Initial, J are integers
    check length (Word) > 0
    call Initialize (Word)
    let Position = –1
    let D = first
    let End = last (Document) – length (Word) + 1
    let Initial = byte (Word, first)              Put a sentinel in the first character
    call Sentinel (Word, Unique)                  of Word
    loop until D > End
        if Initial = byte (Document, D) then      See if first character matches
            let J = length (Word) – 1
            loop until byte (Word, first+J) ≠      Match Word at current
                    byte (Document, D+J)          position in document
                let J = J – 1
            end loop
            if J = 0 then
                let Position = D                  Sentinel found, job done
                let D = End + 1
            else
                let J = minimum (last (Document), D + length (Word) + 1)
                let D = D + Shift[byte (Document, J)]    Sentinel not found, try
            end if                                       again
        else
            let D = D + 1
        end if
    end loop
    call Sentinel (Word, Initial)                 Restore initial character of Word
end Pattern~Match
```

Local **Initialize** (receives Word)

```
procedure Initialize (Word is text)               Set up Shift array with last usage
    for i = 0 to 255                              of each character in Word
        let Shift[i] = length (Word) + 1
    end for
    for i = first to last (Word)
        let Shift[byte (Word, i)] = length (Word) – i + 1
    end for
end Initialize
```

Local **Sentinel** (updates Word; receives Letter)

```
procedure Sentinel (Word is text, Letter is integer)    Replace first character of
    call reverse (Word)                                 Word
    call shorten (Word)
    call append (Word, Letter)
    call reverse (Word)
end Sentinel
```

TEST PROGRAM

Local Names

Doc	Document
P	Position determined by algorithm
W	Word to be searched for

Pseudo Code

```
for i = 1 to length of Document
    let W = a substring of variable size extracted from Document starting from
            position i
    call Pattern~Match to find position P of W in Doc
    check P = i
end for
call Pattern~Match to find position P of a nonexistent character in Doc
check P = –1
```

Code

```
constant Doc = "abcdefghijklmnopqrstuvwxy"
variable W is text
variable P is integer
for i = first to last (Doc)
    let W = substring (Doc, i, minimum (last (Doc), i * 2))
    call Pattern~Match (W, Doc, P)
    check P = i
end for
call Pattern~Match ("z", Doc, P)
check P = –1
```

7.4 ARRAY SEARCHING

Finding a particular word in an array of words

Example

To find an item in an array Table of items in locations Table[L] to Table[U], which is in no particular sequence:

```
call Search~Sequential (Table, L, U, Item, Location, Found)
```

The user supplies the lower and upper limits L and U of the array Table, the array of values itself, and the value of the Item to be found. If Found is set equal to *true* by Search~Sequential, the item is at Table[Location], otherwise the item is not in the list.

To find an item in a large sorted array:

call Search~Binary (Table, L, U, Item, Location, Found)

The item is either at Table[Location] or is missing but should be at Table[Location].

Subprograms

7.4.1 Search~Sorted (updates Table; receives Lower, Upper; supplies Sorted)
7.4.2 Search~Sequential (updates Table; receives Lower, Upper, Item; supplies Location, Found)
7.4.3 Search~Binary (receives Table, Lower, Upper, Item; supplies Location, Found)
7.4.4 Search~Insert (updates Table; receives Lower; updates Upper; receives Item, Location)

Usage

Search~Sequential carries out a sequential search for a specified item in an array. The items in the array may be in any sequence. The subprogram returns the position of the item in the array, as described for the example above. The *true-false* variable Found is set to *true* if the item is in the array, and *false* otherwise.

Search~Binary carries out a binary search for a specified item in a sorted array. The items in the array must be in ascending sequence, although a simple modification will allow a search on an array sorted in descending sequence. The subprogram returns values of the same variables as Search~Sequential.

Search~Insert inserts a missing item at the location given by Search~Sequential or Search~Binary. Search~Sorted is a function that tests whether an array is in sorted sequence.

The code assumes that the array items and specified item are *text* strings, but the logic is identical if other data types are to be used.

Analysis

As a generalization, binary search is more efficient than sequential search, although it requires a presorted array. In some applications requiring only a few searches, it may be more efficient to use an unsorted array for sequential searching, rather than to sort the array and use binary search.

Search~Sequential operates by examining each array element in turn until the desired element is found, or until the end of the array is reached. There are therefore two conditions that may terminate the search. This leads to a double test in the inner loop unless some extra effort is made to optimize the code. The usual approach is to put a "sentinel" at the end of the array, that is, an extra array item containing the value to be searched for. The inner loop does not then need to test for the end of the array because the item being searched for will always be found. An efficient implementation employs a sentinel that is a null string. The *byte* subprogram obtains bytes of value zero from this string, ensuring that the null string has a value at least as low as that of any string in the input array.

However, the generality of the algorithm is compromised by assuming that an extra location can be used for the null string. Assuming that either Table[Lower–1] or Table[Upper+1] is available may be inconvenient for some implementations. Instead, we place the sentinel in the last location Table[Upper], and replace the original element at the end of the search. Although this makes the code a little more complicated, it is almost equally efficient and is more general. Despite these improvements, the algorithm has to examine half of the array elements on average, and has O (N) running time.

For some purposes Search~Sequential can be improved by rearranging the elements of the table as each search is performed. The objective is to move the most frequently used items toward the beginning of the array. The best approach for a simple self-organizing search algorithm is to interchange the found element with its immediate predecessor (Gonnet and Baeza-Yates 1991). Over time the most frequently used items will tend to drift toward the beginning of the array. You should also consider implementing the algorithm using a linked list rather than an array. A found element is moved to the front of the list. This move-to-front heuristic adapts much more rapidly to changes in the probabilities of occurrence of the keys.

The binary search algorithm is not easy to program correctly, although it is easy to describe. Search~Binary operates by dividing the array in half. A test is made to see if the required item is in the first half or the second half. Once that has been determined, the correct half is then treated as if it were the entire array, and the process is repeated. The algorithm very quickly zeros in on the correct position. The number of iterations is not greater than the logarithm to base two of the number of items in the array, giving O (*log* N) running time.

There are a couple of nice features of the binary search algorithm as it is programmed here. Search~Binary handles in a tidy way multiple occurrences of items in the array. The algorithm always finds the first item in the array equal to the specified Item, as described by Bentley (1984). The second feature is that the algorithm locates the position at which the item should appear if it is not found in the array. It is then a simple matter to insert the item, if required, by moving all elements from Table[Location] through Table[N] one place to the locations Table[Location+1] through Table[N+1]. Insertion in this manner is carried out by the procedure Search~Insert.

Search~Sorted checks whether an array is in sorted sequence. It is programmed like Search~Sequential so that the inner loop is as efficient as possible.

The test program does a thorough job, testing every possible list size up to a specified limit. It searches for every possible item in the array and for items not in the array between every pair of existing items and at the beginning and end of the array. Multiple occurrences of items are checked. The use of Insert to construct the test list is not an efficient way of building such arrays in general. It is done this way in the test program to exercise the Insert procedure.

IMPLEMENTATION

Exported Names

Search~Binary	Binary searches a sorted array for a given item (7.4.3)
Search~Insert	Inserts an item at a given location in an array (7.4.4)

Search~Sequential	Sequentially searches an array for a given item (7.4.2)
Search~Sorted	Tests if elements of array are in sorted sequence (7.4.1)
<u>Nicknames</u>	
Found	*true* if item is at Table[Location], otherwise *false*
Item	User-specified item to be searched for in Table
Location	Table[Location] is where item is found, or should be found
Lower	Position of first relevant item in Table array, i.e., Table[Lower]
Sorted	*true* if list is in sorted sequence, otherwise *false* (7.4.1)
Table	Array of items, from Table[Lower] to Table[Upper]
Upper	Position of last relevant item in Table array, i.e., Table[Upper]
<u>Local Names</u>	
I	Loop counter and array index
L	Lower limit of segment of array being searched
Save	Temporary variable for holding list element
U	Upper limit of segment of array being searched

7.4.1 Search~Sorted (updates Table; receives Lower, Upper; supplies Sorted)

Pseudo Code

let Save = lowest possible key (a null string)
swap Save and item at end of array Table[Upper]
search the array to find the first point I at which Table[I–1] > Table[I]
replace Table[Upper] by swapping it again with Save
array is sorted if I = Upper

Code

```
procedure Search~Sorted (Table is array of text, Lower, Upper are integers,
        Sorted is true-false)
    variable I is integer
    variable Save is text
    check Upper > Lower
    let Save = ""                          Swap null substring with last
    call swap (Save, Table[Upper])         array element
    let I = Lower + 1
    if Table[Upper–1] ≤ Save then
        loop until Table[I–1] > Table[I]   Search for adjacent elements in
            let I = I + 1                  wrong sequence
        end loop
    end if
    call swap (Save, Table[Upper])         Restore last array element
    if I < Upper then
        let Sorted = false
    else
        let Sorted = true
    end if
end Search~Sorted
```

7.4.2 **Search~Sequential** (updates Table; receives Lower, Upper, Item; supplies Location, Found)

Pseudo Code

```
save Table[Upper], and replace it by Item being searched for
search the array to find the first point I at which Table[I] = Item
if I = Upper then
    the item is found only if the saved Table[Upper] = Item, otherwise it is not
        found
else
    the item is found at location Table[I] < Upper
end if
replace Table[Upper]
```

Code

```
procedure Search~Sequential (Table is array of text, Lower, Upper are integers,
        Item is text, Location is integer, Found is true-false)
    variable Save is text                          Put sentinel (item being searched
    let Save = Table[Upper]                        for) in last array element
    let Table[Upper] = Item
    let Location = Lower
    loop until Table[Location] = Item              Scan array until item matches
        let Location = Location + 1                input item
    end loop
    if Location = Upper and Item ≠ Save then       Check whether item was really
        let Location = Location + 1                found or we just hit sentinel
        let Found = false
    else
        let Found = true
    end if
    let Table[Upper] = Save                        Restore last array element
end Search~Sequential
```

7.4.3 **Search~Binary** (receives Table, Lower, Upper, Item; supplies Location, Found)

Pseudo Code

```
initialize L and U to the first locations of Table beyond Lower and Upper
        respectively
loop until L and U are adjacent
    find the midpoint Location between L and U
    if Item lies beyond Table[Location] move the lower limit L to Location,
            otherwise move the upper limit U to Location
    if Table[U] contains the item it is found, otherwise it is not found
end loop
```

Code

```
procedure Search~Binary (Table is array of text, Lower, Upper are integers,
        Item is text, Location is integer, Found is true-false)
    variables L, U are integers
    let L = Lower – 1                          Initial limits are outside bounds
    let U = Upper + 1                          of array
    loop until U = L + 1
        let Location = (L + U) ÷ 2             Choose midpoint between lower
        if Item > Table[Location] then         and upper limits
            let L = Location
        else
            let U = Location
        end if
    end loop
    let Location = U                           Handles equal keys
    if Location > Upper then                   Check whether or not item was
        let Found = false                      found
     else-if Table[Location] = Item then
        let Found = true
    else
        let Found = false
    end if
end Search~Binary
```

7.4.4 **Search~Insert** (updates Table; receives Lower; updates Upper; receives Item, Location)

Pseudo Code

```
move items one place in the array, starting with Table[Upper], finishing with
        Table[Location]
insert the new item at Table[Location]
increment the upper limit of the array
```

Code

```
procedure Search~Insert (Table is array of text, Lower, Upper are integers,
        Item is text, Location is integer)
    for decreasing i = Upper to Location
        let Table[i+1] = Table[i]
    end for
    let Table[Location] = Item
    let Upper = Upper + 1
end Search~Insert
```

TEST PROGRAM

Local Names

A The array to be searched

F Set to *true* if and only if search finds item in array

K Location of key being searched for
L Location in key array
M Size of test array specified by user
N Location determined by insert or search process
U Upper bound of the array

Pseudo Code

```
set up array of letters of the alphabet
for i = 1 to M
    append a letter to search array
    locate letter known to be in array using Sequential~Search
    check that letter was found
    locate letter known not to be in array using Sequential~Search
    check that letter was not found
    append a letter to search array
    locate letter known to be in array using Binary~Search
    check that letter was found
    locate letter known not to be in array using Binary~Search
    check that letter was not found
end for
```

Code

```
constants M = 10, U = 2 * M
variables A, Key are arrays 1 to U of text
variables K, N are integers
variable F is true-false
let N = 0
for i = 1 to U
    let Key[i] = ""                              Set up array of keys as successive
    call append (Key, i + 'a' – 1)               letters
end for
for i = 1 to M
    let L = i * 2
    call Search~Insert (A, 1, N, Key[L], L – 1)  Increase size of array to be
    for j = 1 to i                               searched
        let L = j * 2
        call Search~Sequential (A, 1, N, Key[L–1], K, F)   Check sequential
        check F = false and K = N + 1                      search, successful and
        call Search~Sequential (A, 1, N, Key[L], K, F)     unsuccessful
        check F = true and K = L – 1
    end for
    call Search~Insert (A, 1, N, Key, K)         Increase size of array to be
    for j = 1 to i                               searched
        let L = j * 2
        call Search~Binary (A, 1, N, Key[L–1], K, F)       Check binary search,
        check F = false and K = L – 1                      successful and
        call Search~Binary (A, 1, N, Key[L], K, F)         unsuccessful
        check F = true and K = L – 1
    end for
end for
```

check N = U	Ensure that insertion has worked correctly
call Search~Sorted (A, 1, U, F)	
check F = *true*	

7.5 HASHING

Maintaining a table for finding particular words rapidly

Example

The location A[Loc] of "abc" in the array A (inserting the string if it is not already in the array) is found by:

call Hash~Search (A, L, U, "abc", Loc)

where L and U are the lower and upper bounds of the array.

Subprograms

7.5.1 Hash~Search (updates Table; receives Lower, Upper, Word; supplies Location)

7.5.2 Hash~Initialize (updates Table; receives Lower, Upper)

Usage

The algorithm maintains a table of text strings. On each call to Hash~Search the algorithm determines whether or not the specified text string Word is in the array Table. If it is not, the algorithm inserts it. In either case Hash~Search returns the location of the specified string. It is necessary to call Hash~Initialize to clear all locations of the table initially.

Care should be taken not to fill the table completely. As discussed more fully in the analysis below, the efficiency of the algorithm declines as more entries are put into the table. The efficiency is excellent for a table that is only half full, and very good when it is 75% full. The efficiency drops to that of Search~Sequential when the table is almost full.

The number of elements in the table must remain fixed. That is, the table cannot merely be extended in size when it is getting full. A new table with larger dimensions must be constructed by reinserting all existing items into the new table. Items will occupy different positions in the new table.

The user specifies the lower and upper bounds Lower and Upper for the array Table. The number of elements in the table is therefore given by N = Upper – Lower + 1. The algorithm requires that the prime factors of N be known. The user must set the value of the constant Factors equal to the product of the prime factors of N. For example, if N = 600, the prime factors of N are 2, 3, and 5, because $600 = 2^3 * 3 * 5^2$. In this case it is necessary to set Factors = 30.

One solution is to choose N as a prime number, as recommended by many textbooks. In that case Factors = 1, and the line of code in the implementation of the algorithm that uses the value of Factors reduces to a null operation. However, this is often inconvenient in practice. The test program uses what is usually regarded as a poor choice of table size: a power of two. Nevertheless, the algorithm operates perfectly happily because of the suitable choice of hash functions as described below.

The test program allows the table to become completely full. Although this is not recommended in practical use of the algorithm, it demonstrates that the hashing process fails to get the program stuck in a loop (one likely outcome of a poor choice of hashing method).

Analysis

A readable view of the hashing process is given by Sedgewick (1988). Detailed performance information is provided by Gonnet and Baeza-Yates (1991). A good and practical algorithm uses the method of "double hashing". The hashing process develops a number from the text string key that can be used as an index of the array holding the text table. The aim is that different text strings produce different indexes, implying that the hash function must be carefully chosen. (A hash function is simply the method by which the numeric index is computed from the text key.) It is theoretically impossible, as Knuth (1973) has pointed out, for all possible text strings to produce different indexes, and so "collisions" are inevitable. In other words, it will happen that the index for one text string may be equal to the index for an entirely different text string. Nevertheless, the primary hash function must be as efficient as possible, minimizing the number of collisions.

When there is a collision, the simplest approach is to compute a secondary hash function from the key, and use it to produce another table index. Again, the aim is that the second table index will not result in a collision. If the secondary hash function is well chosen, the number of collisions will be minimized, but collisions will inevitably occur again. The algorithm skips sequentially through the table, the index incrementing in steps equal to the value of the secondary hash function. It "wraps around" from the end of the table to the beginning whenever necessary.

We tested the algorithm on simulated English and on successive segments of Chapter 4 of this book. For the former tests we filled an empty 256-location hash table 724 times. (Why 724? Because we had a clear result at that point. Still, 724 is vaguely logical, in that it is the geometric mean of 512 and 1024—powers of two). The pseudo-English words were text strings of length 1–9 characters (uniformly distributed), with letter distribution conforming to a well-known board game that uses English words. The average number of probes (for unsuccessful searches, which require an insertion) was computed for each table size. In the second test we extracted all contiguous strings of letters (only) from Chapter 4 and repeatedly filled the hash table, again computing the average number of probes. The results from both tests were virtually identical.

The literature suggests that the expected number of probes for unsuccessful searches is inversely proportional to the amount of free space in the list. Suppose you have a fraction f of the table free at any given time. Then the number of probes should average out at $1/f$. Indeed, the tests got exactly that result for tables that were up to 95% full. Between 95% and 100% full the number of probes declines uniformly to $1/2f$. Given that tables would not be allowed to become as full in practice, this deviation can be ignored. Thus, on average one probe is required for an empty table, two probes for a table that is half full, four probes for a table that is three-quarters full, and eight probes for a table that is seven-eighths full. Successful searches are much more efficient, requiring about $-log_e(f)/(1-f)$ probes. For example, when a table has one-eighth of its locations free, a successful search requires three probes on average.

The variability of these figures is quite high. It is not all that unusual to require ten probes in a table that is barely half full. Thus the above conclusions must be seen for what they are—averages.

Many hash functions have been proposed. The code has a function that is simple to implement and that operates efficiently. To understand how the function operates, you must think of the characters in the text string as 8-bit binary integers, as obtained by the *byte* function. The primary function sums these integers weighted by powers of two. For example, consider "abc", which has three 8-bit binary components 01100001, 01100010, and 01100011. Multiply the first by 4, the second by 2, and the third by 1, and add up the products. Multiplication by 2 is simply a shift left. Divide the result by the table size and keep the remainder. In the test program the table size is 256, and so the modulus operation results in keeping the last eight bits, or 10101011. In decimal this produces 171 as the index into the table. Gonnet and Baeza-Yates (1991) recommend a function in which the multiplication by 2 in our algorithm is replaced by multiplication by 131_{10}.

The secondary hash function is even simpler to compute. You merely form the total of the numbers without any shifting. In this example 01100001 + 01100010 + 01100011 = 100100110, or 294 in decimal. In the first application of the secondary function the index is (171 + 294) *mod* 256, which equals 209. If necessary, another probe takes us to (209 + 294) *mod* 256, which equals 247, another takes us to 29, another to 67, and so on.

The reason it is important to get the value of Factors right is as follows. If the value of the secondary hash function and the table size have a factor greater than unity in common, the visits to successive elements in the table will not potentially reach many of the table elements. Only when the two quantities are relatively prime can you be assured that the secondary hash function can reach all table elements.

Pearson (1990) has cautioned against using our secondary hash function as the primary hash function, a point with which we agree. The simple sum of the letters in a word will not separate anagrams such as "no" and "on" or "eat", "ate", and "tea", for example. Our primary hash function will produce different table addresses for such anagrams. Indeed, in a table of size 2^N the algorithm will produce different addresses for 2^N "words" that are just N-character words containing all possible combinations of two letters. In our tests, Pearson's more complex algorithm was marginally slower than the method given here.

IMPLEMENTATION

Exported Names

Hash~Initialize	Initializes the hash table (7.5.2)
Hash~Search	Finds a text string in a table (7.5.1)

Imported Names

Factors	Product of prime factors of size of hash table array

Nicknames

Location	Table[Location] is where item is found

Lower	Position of first relevant item in Table array, i.e., Table[Lower]
Table	Hash table array, from Table[Lower] to Table[Upper]
Upper	Position of last relevant item in Table array, i.e., Table[Upper]
Word	User-specified word to be searched for or inserted in Table
<u>Local Names</u>	
Character	ASCII value of one character from Word
N	Number of items in hash table
Primary	Primary hash value, computed from characters in Word
Secondary	Secondary hash value, computed from characters in Word

7.5.1 Hash~Search (updates Table; receives Lower, Upper, Word; supplies Location)

Pseudo Code

```
compute primary and secondary hash codes from Word
ensure secondary hash code is relatively prime to table size
loop
    compute probe position
    if table position is empty insert Word there
    update probe increment using secondary hash code
end loop when Word found
```

Code

```
procedure Hash~Search (Table is array of text, Lower, Upper are integers, Word is
        text, Location is integer)
    variables Character, N, Primary, Secondary are integers
    let N = Upper – Lower + 1
    let Primary = 0
    let Secondary = 0
    for i = first to last (Word)
        let Character = byte (Word, i)
        let Primary = ((Primary * 2) + Character) mod N
        let Secondary = Secondary + Character
    end for
    let Secondary = Secondary – (Secondary mod Factors) + Factors – 1
    loop
        let Location = Lower + Primary
        if length (Table[Location]) = 0 then
            let Table[Location] = Word
        end if
        let Primary = (Primary + Secondary) mod N
    end loop when Word = Table[Location]
end Hash~Search
```

7.5.2 Hash~Initialize (updates Table; receives Lower, Upper)

Pseudo Code

```
initialize hash table to null text strings
```

Code

```
procedure Hash~Initialize (Table is array of text, Lower, Upper are integers)
    for i = Lower to Upper
        let Table[i] = ""
    end for
end Hash~Initialize
```

TEST PROGRAM

Local Names

A	Array in which the hash table is constructed
B	Array of "words" inserted into hash table
Factors	Product of prime factors of size of hash table array
K	Location in hash table of current word
L	Lower bound of the array
M	Size of test array specified by user
N	Location determined by insert or search process
T	Word currently being used
U	Upper bound of the array

Pseudo Code

```
insert increasingly long text strings into array
find each inserted string using Hash~Search
check the reported position of each string
```

Code

```
constant Factors = 5
constants L = 1, U = 25
variables A, B are arrays L to U of text
variable T is text
variable K is integer
call Hash~Initialize (A, L, U)
let T = ""
for i = L to U
    call append (T, i – L + 'a')
    let B[i] = T
    call Hash~Search (A, L, U, T, K)
end for
for i = L to U
    call Hash~Search (A, L, U, B[i], K)
    check A[K] = B[i]
end for
```

7.6 TRIE

Maintaining an efficient index for a table of words

Example

The location A[Loc] of "abc" in the array A (inserting the string if it is not already in the array) is found by:

call Trie~Insert (T, A, L, "abc", Loc)

where T is an array providing space for a "trie" and L is the lower bound of the arrays.

Subprograms

7.6.1 Trie~Search (updates Trie, Table; receives Lower, Word; supplies Location)
7.6.2 Trie~Initialize (supplies Trie, Table; receives Lower)

Usage

The algorithm maintains a table of text strings, using a trie data structure (with nickname Trie) as an index for locating each text string. On each call to Trie~Search the algorithm determines whether or not the specified text string Word is in the table with nickname Table. If it is not, the algorithm inserts it. In either case Trie~Search returns via the nickname Location the position of Word in Table. Trie~Initialize must be called to initialize the trie.

The user must provide arrays to contain both the table of text strings and the list of integer pointers maintained as a trie. The algorithm can be used without understanding how a trie data structure operates. The user needs to specify only the lower bound of the arrays, it being assumed that (a) both arrays have the same lower bound, and (b) sufficient space is allocated for both arrays. If the text table is in array locations Lower through Upper, the trie must have available at least the locations from Lower through (Upper + 1) * 3.

The algorithm requires access to individual bits of computer words. Unless such access is reasonably efficient the algorithm will run more slowly than is desirable. Nevertheless, the user may simulate bit access using integer division if necessary. Consider accessing the N-th bit of a text string, where the first bit is numbered zero. The character C in which the bit will be found is character number *first* + (N ÷ 8). You need to access bit number N *mod* 8 in character C. Put powers of two in an eight-element array as follows: P[7] = 1, P[6] = 2, P[5] = 4, ..., P[0] = 128. The value of the required bit from character C (represented by its binary value) is (C ÷ P[N *mod* 8]) *mod* 2.

Analysis

This is a simple algorithm that is efficient and easy to implement. It is possible to implement the algorithm as a more general data structure along the lines of the balanced tree algorithm in Section 5.8. The data structures here are maintained in arrays rather than lists, thus requiring that the maximum number of text strings to be processed be known in advance.

A trie is a binary tree in which paths from parent records to child records are determined by successive bit positions in the key. Consider, for example, a trie containing the words in the sentence "the quick brown fox jumps over the lazy dog". All words consist of lowercase letters, and as it turns out, each word begins with a different letter. The word "the" occurs twice. The placing of the words in the trie will be determined only by the initial letter in this particular example. Lowercase letters have ASCII codes that range from 97 for 'a' to 122 for 'z', or 01100001 to 01111010 in binary. The words are represented in Figure 7.2.

The binary codes for each letter are at the so-called external nodes of the trie, that is, those containing text strings. Follow the path from the root of the trie at the top to any word, and the bits on the links connecting each of the internal nodes on the way down will trace out the binary code for the first letter of that word. At least, it will trace out enough bits of the letter to find a unique place in the trie for the word in question. The numbers in the boxes representing the internal nodes are the bit positions you need to examine at that point.

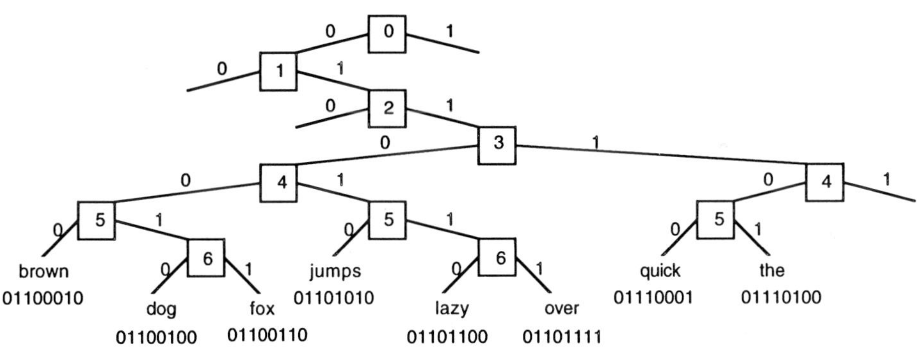

Figure 7.2

If you add the word "up" to the trie, you need to examine the binary code for the letter 'u', which is 01110101. Tracing out this value on the way down the trie, you bump into the word "the". You have to add two additional nodes to separate "the" and "up" as shown in Figure 7.3.

Although such a trie is easy to maintain, note that it contains a number of nodes that have only one useful path emanating from them. For certain distributions of data the proliferation of such nodes makes searching considerably less efficient and requires more memory than is needed. An elegant solution to the problem was developed by D.R. Morrison and is discussed by Knuth (1973) and Sedgewick (1988). With a simple trie the bit numbers shown in the boxes are not actually stored. Using Morrison's algorithm, which he called Patricia (Practical Algorithm To Retrieve Information Coded In Alphanumeric), the bit positions are stored in the trie array, along with the left and right pointers. Then it is possible to eliminate the redundant nodes. The Patricia trie is shown in Figure 7.4.

The algorithm presented here uses the Patricia method. It is suitable for any distribution of text data, with very long keys if necessary. One of its advantages is that only one full key comparison is done for any one search. This is much better than hashing, for which a key comparison must be done with every probe. Therefore, it is conceivable that the keys for a Patricia search could be in a disk file rather than in memory, with no loss in efficiency.

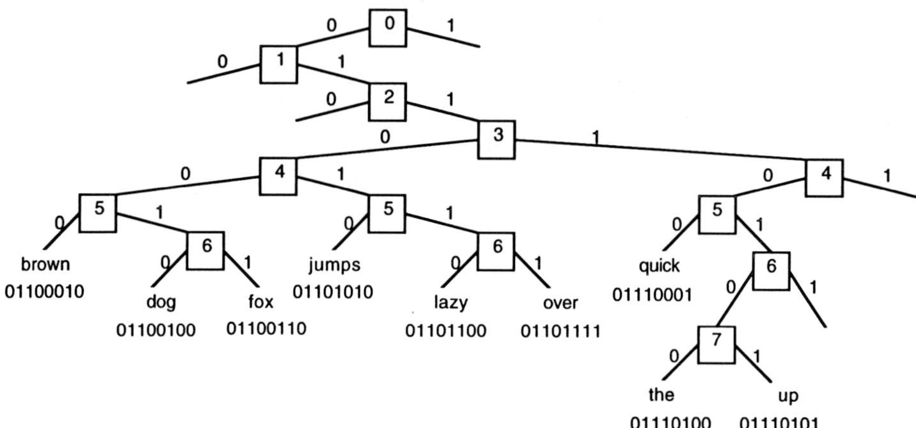

Figure 7.3

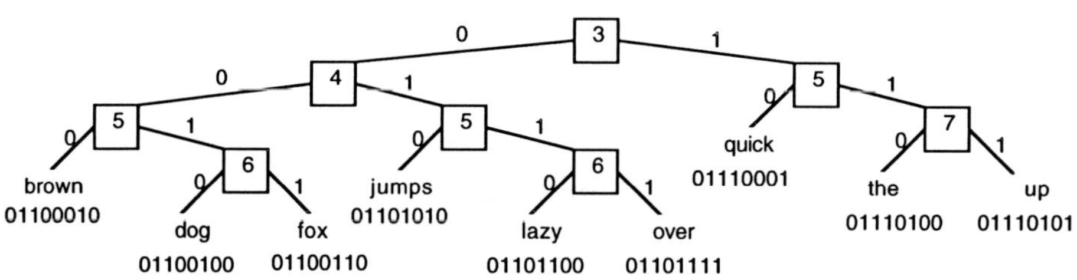

Figure 7.4

The important property of a Patricia trie is that there is a one-to-one correspondence between paths through the trie and particular text strings. Each string corresponds to one path and vice versa. The way to detect a missing text string is to follow the tree down to the position where the item *could* be, and then to check whether it actually *is* there. If it is not there, the item is inserted and the trie adjusted to preserve the Patricia property.

In adding nodes into the tree there are two cases to consider. The node may need to be added between an existing internal node and an external node, or between two internal nodes. These two cases result in a double test in one of the internal loops that cannot be eliminated.

In the coding of the algorithm the convention has been used that positive pointers point from one trie node to another, and negative pointers point to the table of text strings. This simple device avoids confusion resulting from the intermixing of the text table and trie, usually found in textbooks. The algorithm employs the header record approach (used, for example, in the balanced tree algorithm in Section 5.8) to avoid having to provide code for special cases such as an empty tree.

Although it is possible to access keys in a trie in key sequence, a subprogram for that purpose is not provided here. To implement such a facility you will need to provide either (a) an "up" pointer in each trie record to point from a child record to a parent, or (b) a separate stack in which the locations of successive parent records are recorded as the program proceeds down through the tree. The approach taken in the Tree~Next subprogram (5.8.2) should generally be followed.

IMPLEMENTATION

Exported Names

Trie~Initialize	Initializes trie data structure (7.6.2)
Trie~Search	Finds a word in the trie, or inserts it if it cannot be found (7.6.1)

Imported Names

To~Integer	Converts an integer in *text* form to an *integer* (2.1.1)
To~Text	Converts an *integer* number to *text* form (2.1.2)

Nicknames

Location	Table[Location] is current word
Lower	Position of first item in Table and Trie arrays, e.g., Table[Lower]
Table	Table containing distinct words
Trie	Array containing trie data structure
Word	User-specified word to be searched for and/or inserted in Trie

Global Names

Left	Position of left pointer in node
Position	Position of word table pointer or bit position in node
Right	Position of right pointer in node

Local Names

Count	Bit position of first difference in two words
Character	ASCII value of one character from Word
Current	Pointer to current trie record
Direction	Value that signals left or right exit from node
N	Number of items in hash table
Next	Pointer to next trie record down the tree
Ntrie	Number of integer locations used in Trie array
Nwords	Number of words in word table Table

Code

```
constant Left = 0
constant Right = 1
constant Position = 2
```

7.6.1 **Trie~Search** (updates Trie, Table; receives Lower, Word; supplies Location)

Pseudo Code

```
obtain the current sizes of the text table and trie from the lowest elements of the
        arrays
initialize trie pointer to header node
initialize current bit position to zero, i.e., the leftmost bit
loop until pointer points to an external node (is negative)
    obtain bit from key in current bit position
    let trie pointer = left or right pointer from current node (for 0 or 1 bit respectively)
end loop
if key = text string pointed to by trie pointer then
    item is found
else
    insert text string at next available table location
    initialize new bit position to zero
    loop until new text string and string pointed to by current pointer differ at new
            bit position
        increment new bit position
    end loop
    initialize trie pointer to header node
    initialize current bit position to zero
    loop until trie pointer points to an external node or bit position of next node is
            higher than new position
        obtain bit from key in current bit position
        let trie pointer = left or right pointer from current node (for 0 or 1 bit
                respectively)
    end loop
    create new node in trie array and update pointers
end if
restore the current sizes of the text table and trie into the lowest elements of the
        arrays
```

Code

```
procedure Trie~Search (Trie is array of integers, Table is array of text, Lower is
        integer, Word is text, Location is integer)
    variables Count, Direction, Current, Next, Nwords, Ntrie are integers
    let Ntrie = Trie[Lower]
    let Nwords = To~Integer (Table[Lower])
    let Table[Lower] = “”                           Temporary zero key to act as key
    let Current = Lower + 1                         for header node
    let Direction = 0
    loop until Current ≤ 0                                      Move down trie based
        let Direction = bit (Word, Trie[Current+Position])      on bits in key being
        let Current = Trie[Current+Direction]                   searched for
    end loop
```

```
    let Current = –Current
    if Word = Table[Current] then              Check whether search key is in
        let Location = Current                 trie
    else
        let Nwords = Nwords + 1
        let Location = Lower + Nwords
        let Table[Location] = Word
        let Count = 0
        loop until bit (Word, Count) ≠         Find where search key and item at
                bit (Table[Current], Count)    external node differ
            let Count = Count + 1
        end loop
        let Current = Lower + 1
        let Direction = 0
        let Next = Trie[Current]
        loop until Next ≤ Lower or             Find correct position in trie for
                Trie[Next+Position] > Count    new node
            let Current = Next
            let Direction = bit (Word, Trie[Current+Position])
            let Next = Trie[Current+Direction]
        end loop
        let Next = Lower + Ntrie               Insert bit position and pointers in
        let Trie[Next+Position] = Count        new node
        let Trie[Next–bit (Word, Count)+1] =
                Trie[Current+Direction]
        let Trie[Next+bit (Word, Count)] = –(Lower + Nwords)
        let Trie[Current+Direction] = Next     Update pointer from parent node
        let Ntrie = Ntrie + 3
    end if
    let Table[Lower] = To~Text (Nwords)
    let Trie[Lower] = Ntrie
end Trie~Search
```

7.6.2 Trie~Initialize (supplies Trie, Table; receives Lower)

Pseudo Code

```
initialize header node
initialize word table
```

Code

```
procedure Trie~Initialize (Trie is array of integers, Table is array of text, Lower is
        integer)
    variable Current is integer
    let Current = Lower + 1
    let Trie[Current+Left] = –Lower            Pointers to zero key in header
    let Trie[Current+Right] = –Lower           node
```

```
        let Trie[Current+Position] = 0
        let Trie[Lower] = 4
        let Table[Lower] = 0
    end Trie~Initialize
```

TEST PROGRAM

Local Names

- A Array of words pointed to by trie
- B Table of words inserted into trie, for checking accuracy of array A
- K Location in word table of current word
- L Lower bound of the arrays
- T Array in which the trie is constructed
- U Upper bound of the word array

Pseudo Code

insert increasingly long text strings into array
find each inserted string using Trie~Search
check the reported position of each string

Code

```
constant L = 0
constant U = 25
variables A, B are arrays L to U of text
variable T is array L to (U+1)*3 of integers
variable K is integer
call Trie~Initialize (T, A, L)
for i = (L + 1) to U
    let B[i] = 'a' + i – L
    call Trie~Search (T, A, L, B[i], K)
end for
for i = (L + 1) to U
    call Trie~Search (T, A, L, B[i], K)
    check A[K] = B[i]
end for
```

NOTES—DATA COMPRESSION

Compressing text by a simple new method

As defined by Lelewer and Hirschberg (1987), "the aim of data compression is to reduce redundancy in stored or communicated data". It is an advanced topic for which we can provide only an introduction in this book. Fortunately, many programmers will not have to write data compression algorithms. The increasingly popular Unix™ operating system provides data compression utilities.

Data compression is used in practice for two different purposes: data storage and data transmission. The amount of disk storage required for large files can be reduced, typically by around 30–50%, by compression. The time required to transmit data from one place to another over a channel with a limited bandwidth can be reduced by compressing the data before transmission and decompressing it at the receiving end. The same algorithms are used, whether the application is data storage or data transmission. We will pretend that compressed information is sent from a sender to a receiver, although it may be merely stored and then retrieved.

To give an example, let us compress English text using the following algorithm. Delete vowels from words, subject to the restriction that the abbreviated words are unique compressions. The sentence:

The quick brown fox jumps over the lazy dog

then becomes (say):

Th qck brwn fx jmps ovr th lzy dg

The original sentence has been compressed by 23% from 43 characters to 33. A decompression algorithm is required to recover the original words from the abbreviations. In practice, this particular algorithm is not very convenient, because of the large number of contingencies that must be considered, and the evolving nature of human languages.

The remainder of this discussion assumes you need to compress text, and are unable to use the Unix™ utilities for one reason or another. We do not claim to present the *best* approach, but our method is simple and efficient. It is based on the relatively new BSTW algorithm developed by Bentley et al. (1986) and Elias (1987).

First, we need to emphasize that algorithms that employ bit manipulation strategies can achieve better compression than those that do not. We restrict ourselves to text algorithms that manipulate characters only. Our algorithm can be made more efficient by encoding integers using Elias codes, but the discussion of Elias codes is beyond the scope of this book. These restrictions result in about 35% compression by our algorithm, while perhaps as much as 50% is achievable by working in binary. You should consult the survey by Lelewer and Hirschberg (1987) if greater efficiency is required.

The BSTW algorithm is based on the simple idea of numbering the words as they are encountered, and keeping them in a table. When a new word is encountered, it is transmitted in full and also entered into the table. If the word is encountered again, its position in the table is transmitted instead of the word itself. Suppose, for example, we have a ten thousand word document containing one thousand unique words. Any one word can be represented by at most a four-digit integer. If the average word size is, say, five characters, we achieve a small degree of compression by representing words by four digits.

The developers of the algorithm improved upon this basic idea by realizing that the positions at the beginning of the table are represented by only one or two digits. Their aim was to keep the most frequently used words at the beginning of the table, so that the transmitted positions had as few digits as possible. The BSTW scheme achieves this by moving a word to the top of the table every time it is used, pushing all the other words down one place. Obviously, the receiver has to maintain a table identical to that of the sender, so that the table movements keep in step. The move-to-front idea tends to ensure that frequently used words remain near the top of the table.

An additional important advantage of BSTW is that the algorithm is "locally adaptive". Many documents are organized into sections that address different topics.

Frequently used words in one section will be rarely used in another. It is not difficult to see that the move-to-front scheme tends to keep recent frequently used words near the top of the table, allowing less recent frequently used words to slip down the table. To take an example, the sentence:

The best algorithm is best in theory and best in practice

is compressed by the BSTW algorithm into:

The best algorithm is 3 in theory and 4 4 practice

As the algorithm proceeds through a document it will typically encounter fewer and fewer new words, so that the end of the document is usually encoded mostly by integer codes rather than the original words themselves. Any given word is transmitted only once.

The key practical problem with BSTW is that it is difficult to implement efficiently. It is hard to move words to the top of the table quickly and also simply. A naive implementation, literally moving words in an array, takes an unacceptably long O (N) running time. To get O (*log* N) performance, Bentley et al. (1986) used two interlinked tree structures. They used a tree structure to simplify computation of word positions, requiring a time proportional to the length of the word being encoded. A trie was used to maintain the words table. The trie and the tree needed to be interlinked with pointers in both directions. In the authors' words "this implementation, though theoretically efficient, is more complicated than one would like". They recommended using a hash table in place of the tree and a so-called self-adjusting search tree for the word list. Although a hash table operates in O (1) time, a self-adjusting search tree is thought to require O (*log* N) time.

We appear to be stuck with O (*log* N) processing time at best and so we sought an alternative algorithm. We would agree that hashing is the best way to implement the word table. Our experiments revealed that an alternative and simpler strategy is almost as effective as the move-to-front scheme. When a previously used word is encountered, we move it toward the front the table by a distance equal to half the number of items between it and the front. Instead of pushing the intervening items one place away from the front, requiring O (N) time, we merely exchange the current item and the item at the new position. For example, if the word is found at position 2, it is exchanged with the item at position 1. The item at position 7 is exchanged with the item at position 4, and so on. We tested the two methods by compressing Chapter 4 of this book. The move-to-front scheme achieved a compression of 37.3%, and the half-distance exchange method achieved a compression of 36.3%.

You will need to think about some implementation details. Remember that the sender sends a combination of words and word positions. The most important issue to resolve is how the receiver can distinguish between word positions and text. This issue is more complicated than it seems, because we have conveniently omitted to define so far what we mean by "words". Usually, you want to transmit not just letter groups but also punctuation and formatting information. In more precise terminology, you must segment the text into "tokens". In our tests we defined tokens as (1) strings of letters (i.e., words delimited by nonletters), and (2) single nonletter characters (such as space, digit, full stop, hyphen, etc.). We transmitted raw text, omitting formatting codes.

The sender transmits a special character (binary 377_8 or 255_{10} in our tests) before every token, and the same character to terminate every token. All other characters transmitted are assumed to be positions in an array that holds all the tokens. Characters with binary values in the range 1 to 127_{10} represent counts. Characters with binary values in the range 128_{10} to 254_{10} signal that two characters will be used for the token position—the current character and the one immediately following. Let C and D be the ASCII values of the two adjacent characters. The token position is represented as 256 * (C – 128) + D. This arrangement allows for approximately 30,000 token positions to be encoded, enough for quite large practical applications. Obviously, the coding system could be extended, if required, to allow for an even larger number of tokens.

A second array, the same size as the token table, is needed to contain addresses. For each token the address table contains the address of the corresponding tree, trie, or hash table record. This address table is used when exchanging tokens, to enable quick access to the tree, trie, or hash table record for the token halfway up the table with which the exchange takes place. If the table occupies positions Lower to N of an array, the "top" of the table is position N, not position Lower. An item at position *i* has code N – *i* + Lower, not *i*.

We will now summarize the main ideas behind the compression algorithm in pseudo code and code. We won't go into the details of decompression, but it operates very similarly to the compression process. Don't forget the pointers from the word table back to the trie. You must exchange the pointers in the trie when two items in the word table are swapped. These and other details are omitted below.

Pseudo Code

```
loop
    get next token
    if token has been used previously then
        encode and transmit position as one or two characters
        exchange current token with token halfway toward top of table
    else
        transmit 255₁₀, token, 255₁₀
    end if
end loop
```

Code

```
constants L = 1, U = 1000
variable W is array L to U of text
variable T is array L to (U + 1) * 3 of integers
variables I, J, N are integers
variables Character, Sentinel, Token are text
let Sentinel = ""
call append (Sentinel, 255)
call Trie~Initialize (T, W, L)
input Token
loop
    let Character = ""
    let N = W[L]
    call Trie~Search (T, W, L, Token, I)
```

```
    if I > N then
        output Sentinel, Token, Sentinel
    else
        let J = N – I + 1
        if J < 128 then
            call append (Character, J)
            output Character
        else
            call append (Character, (J ÷ 256) + 128)
            call append (Character, J mod 256)
            output Character
        end if
        let J = J ÷ 2
        call swap (W[I], W[I+J])
    end if
    input Token
end loop
```

8: Random Numbers

Doing things "at random" would seem to be very easy to accomplish. With a computer it is actually quite difficult to do it well. Webster's Dictionary defines "random" as "lacking a definite plan, purpose, pattern". The computer is a precise and totally predictable piece of machinery (hardware failures excluded), with its plan and purpose being the program it executes. How, then, can a computer generate randomness?

Perhaps you would first ask why. Why would a computer need to do things at random? There are lots of examples. A computer can be programmed to play many games, such as blackjack, poker, and craps, only if it can simulate shuffling cards or throwing dice. Telephone companies "simulate" telephone traffic through exchanges by randomly generating "calls" that mimic the behavior of real users. One implementation of the sorting algorithm Quick~Sort uses a random number for choosing the dividing fence in partitioning an array.

Random numbers generated by a computer are not really random, but are carefully calculated to look as if they have no "plan, purpose, [or] pattern". For this reason, they are called "pseudorandom". If you look at a sequence of pseudorandom numbers, you will not be able to predict the next one in sequence, no matter how many numbers there are in the sequence.

The usual method used for generating random numbers is very simple. You can get the idea using a desk calculator. Take a suitable constant multiplier, say 238. Start with any "seed" number, say 238 again. Multiply by 238 and keep only the last three digits of the answer. Since 238 times 238 is 56644, you keep 644. Put a decimal point in front and you have your first "random" number, 0.644. Now multiply 644 by 238 and keep the last three digits to give 0.272. Continue this process to obtain 0.736, 0.168, 0.984,

0.192, 0.696, and so on. That is how a computer can generate pseudorandomness, using the "linear congruential" method. This particular example is an inferior implementation, and the Random~Number algorithm in this section is far superior.

The linear congruential method generates "uniformly distributed" numbers within the range 0 to 1. The notion of "distribution" is fundamental to random numbers, and some explanation of the term is needed. Using everyday terms, a distribution is a description of the likelihood of any particular random number being equal to a given value, or lying within a specified range. A uniform distribution is one in which any given value is as likely to occur as any other.

Random numbers are typically introduced in textbooks using dice throwing or coin tossing as examples. In rolling an unbiased six-sided die one expects each of the numbers 1 to 6 to come up equally often. In tossing an unbiased coin, the number of heads is expected to equal the number of tails, on average. Both these are examples of uniform distributions. You can accurately describe the *average* behavior of dice and coins even though you cannot predict the outcome of any *particular* roll or toss.

If you consider, for example, the number of heads likely to occur in two tosses of a coin, you are dealing with a nonuniform distribution. There are four possible occurrences, all of which are equally likely, namely, HH, HT, TH, TT. There is one chance in four of getting two heads, two chances of getting one head, and one chance in four of getting no head. More technically, the event consisting of two heads has a probability of 0.25, one head a probability of 0.5, and no heads a probability of 0.25. This is an example of the "binomial" distribution. The binomial random number generator Random~Binomial applied to this situation will generate 0, 1, or 2 (representing the number of heads) with probabilities 0.25, 0.5, and 0.25 respectively.

There are several random number generators in Section 8.1. All rely on Random~Number to generate firstly numbers with a uniform distribution. The non-uniform generators twist and manipulate the uniform distribution so that it has other shapes, just like the binomial distribution above.

Random~Integer can be used to generate a random integer in the range 1 to 52 for drawing simulated cards from a deck or for generating spins of a simulated roulette wheel. Random integers are uniformly distributed, but restricted to having integral values. If you want to be the Dice Man (Reinehart 1971) and live your life by choosing actions at random from a list of six possibilities, you'll need Random~Integer also.

If you are writing a program to mimic the way cosmic rays strike your house, you will need to space out the simulated arrival times appropriately by using Random~Exponential. This same procedure can be used to simulate arrival times of people at checkout points within a given steady period of demand, or to depict vehicles passing through an intersection at a given time of day. To turn this around another way, you can calculate randomly the number of events in a given period of time using Random~Poisson.

Perhaps you run a manufacturing business, and you want to simulate the number of attempts required to make a product fail given a known average rate of failure. The procedure Random~Geometric can help you there. You need to tell the procedure the probability of failure, and it will generate a random number that simulates the number of attempts required to make the product fail.

Perhaps you want to simulate the behavior of a bowler in a tenpin bowling alley. The person always aims at the nearest pin but owing to small uncontrollable factors never exactly hits the pin in the same spot. Frequently the ball is close to dead center, but occasionally it is wide of the mark. Use the convention that the error is positive or negative according to whether the ball went to the left or right of the pin. The number generated by Random~Normal will give the "error" on each simulated occasion. If the random number is positive the ball went to the right, otherwise it went to the left. (The distribution is called "normal" because most real-life processes involving many small uncontrollable factors operating at the same time can be described by it.)

Section 8.2 contains random selection algorithms, which use Random~Number to generate arrays containing uniformly distributed random integers. There are three procedures: Random~Shuffle, Random~Sequence, and Random~Set. Random~Shuffle will rearrange an array of items into random sequence, all items having equal probabilities of occurring in any given location of the array. The validity of the procedure is easy to prove mathematically, but shuffling an array many times will demonstrate that a given item may be found anywhere within the array on different occasions.

If you are writing a program to play blackjack, you will need a procedure to shuffle a deck of 52 electronic cards. If an array contains the integers 1–52 to represent the cards, they may be shuffled by calling Random~Shuffle. The cards may be "dealt" simply by taking them one at a time in sequence from successive elements of the array.

Auditors are often faced with a large set of numbered documents, say invoices. They want to choose some of them at random for checking. Let's say there are N = 15,000 invoices and you need to choose K = 100. Random~Sequence and Random~Set will both provide a list of K random integers between 1 and N. The list produced by Random~Sequence is sorted, but that produced by Random~Set is not. Random~Set is faster when K is small and N is relatively large. Random~Sequence is preferred when N is small and K is relatively large.

NOTES—THE LAW OF AVERAGES

Answering the question: Is the law of averages a reality or a myth?

The cavernous room has a feeling of hushed expectancy against a background of an audible hum of muted conversation. Several hundred people are clustered in groups of five or ten around dozens of tables of varying shapes and sizes. The polished timbers radiate a regal and timeless atmosphere, while the green baize seeks to calm and soothe some frazzled nerves. Croupiers deal cards, turn wheels, and deftly move plastic chips about, and occasionally force folded banknotes through narrow slots into security boxes.

At several roulette tables players are marking numbers on cards provided by the casino. Standing behind one player, you see the small white ball fall into a numbered slot on the slowly rotating horizontal wheel. The player writes down the number and also notes whether it was black or red, even or odd. Why does the player do this? Are the numbers selected at random by the white ball really "random", or is there some pattern to them? Clearly, the player does not believe the numbers are truly "random". The player assumes there is some sort of pattern to be understood, so that he or she can win!

Many gamblers believe in the "law of averages". This "law" says that, over a sufficiently long period of time, each number on the roulette wheel should come up equally often. Our player records each throw of the white ball in order to identify the numbers that have not appeared yet.

The law of averages says, according to the believers, that the numbers that have not appeared for some time have a higher probability of occurring than those that have appeared more often. The argument that is advanced is that this must happen, otherwise the averages will be incorrect. Our player is a believer who will bet on numbers that have not come up recently.

You move to one of the tables where cards are being dealt. The game is blackjack. Six decks of 52 cards are shuffled together. (The number of decks varies among casinos.) The croupier puts the shuffled cards in a "shoe" and inserts a red marker card about two-thirds of the way through the deck. The cards are dealt one at a time from the top, bets are placed, winnings and losses are calculated, chips change hands. Many such cycles occur until the red marker card is reached. The current hand is completed and the cards are shuffled again.

Why does the casino not deal the entire deck before shuffling the cards? The reason is that a person with either a very good memory, or a system on a computer to keep track of the numbers of aces, kings, queens, and so on, would be more likely to beat the bank as the game progresses. For example, if by chance many aces have appeared from the cards at the front of the shoe, the player will know that the chances of obtaining "blackjack" (ace and a picture card) are reduced below the theoretical average. The law of averages would enable a skilled player to beat the bank if all cards in the deck were played out. That is why the casino shuffles the deck well before the end of the shoe, to prevent people with good memories from taking advantage.

Despite its intuitive appeal, the law of averages as applied to a fair roulette wheel is useless for predictive purposes, although it works for blackjack. Why is roulette different from blackjack? The difference is subtle, but important. In blackjack there are only 312 cards that can be drawn from the shoe. For example, there are six aces of spades. Once a particular ace of spades has been dealt, it cannot be drawn again until the deck is shuffled. That ace of spades goes into the discard pile. By contrast, the numbers on the roulette wheel stay in play for every turn. There is no discard pile that prevents a given number from coming up again. In statistical jargon, blackjack uses sampling *without* replacement. Roulette uses sampling *with* replacement, because each number on the wheel is able to be selected regardless of whether it has been selected recently or not.

There is a popular game called lotto, which is played in a number of countries. It is a public game similar to the game of keno played in casinos. Players submit entries that try to predict six numbers in a given range, say 1 to 45, to be drawn by a special machine. The machine contains 45 numbered ping-pong balls that are allowed to emerge one at a time after being thoroughly mixed. The first six balls to emerge provide the winning numbers. Each weekend the newspapers publish tables giving the number of weeks since each number was drawn as a winning lotto number, the number of times each number has been drawn since the series of games started, the twelve most frequently drawn numbers, and the twelve least frequently drawn numbers.

Is there any real point to these lists? Does the law of averages work for lotto and keno, or does it not? It seems there are two ways of applying the law of averages to lotto. The "orthodox averagists", as we might call them, insist that one should bet on the least frequently drawn numbers, because these must come up soon in order to even up the averages. The "radical averagists" assert that one should bet on the most frequently drawn numbers because these are on a "run", or because there is some form of bias toward frequently drawn numbers in the machines. The radical averagists will bet on such numbers until the run appears to have finished, then switch to other frequently drawn numbers, knowing that in the longer term a run cannot last for ever.

The organizers of gambling games believe that the law of averages does *not* apply to lotto and keno. Otherwise, they would be in danger of losing significant amounts of money to people who beat the system. The only money made out of these games is by people who write books with titles like "Winning at Keno". Lotto and keno use sampling *with* replacement from game to game. In any one game the balls are drawn *without* replacement to ensure that a number is never drawn twice. All the ping-pong balls are replaced for the next game. If the ping-pong ball machine is not faulty, the method of sampling with replacement ensures that the newspaper lists are valueless.

Any truly random process using sampling *with* replacement gives you no information at all that is of value in improving your predictive ability. Sampling *without* replacement, on the other hand, gives you the certain knowledge that the items that have been selected so far cannot possibly be selected again. To win at roulette, lotto, or keno you need to discover a bias or lack of symmetry in the wheel or drawing machine. Such asymmetries *may* exist, but one should not bet on it.

Pseudorandomness

To produce a computerized version of European roulette you need to be able to generate numbers in the range 0 to 36 *with* replacement. That is, on any turn of the wheel *any* of the 37 numbers should be equally likely to come up, including the one that appeared in the previous turn. (American roulette has a 00 as well as a 0, requiring a number in the range 0 to 37.) For lotto and keno the computer must select numbers *without* replacement in any given game. Of course, in subsequent games all numbers are replaced, and so you should think of lotto and keno as games that are based on sampling *with* replacement.

Now what about blackjack? It seems to depend on whether you are a recreational card player or a casino player, because there are different answers for the two groups. In playing blackjack at home with friends you are likely to use one or two decks of cards. The cards will be shuffled and dealt, effectively using sampling *without* replacement. Casinos don't like this system because of the information you get that helps you to predict what cards are due to come up. By using a large number of decks and the red marker card a casino is trying to get a good approximation to sampling *with* replacement.

Computerizing a game of chance requires an extremely good random number generator. From the discussion above you will have gathered that the most desirable random number generator will be one that produces an unpredictable and patternless sequence of numbers using sampling *with* replacement. That is, each number produced by Random~Number should provide no information that could make it easy to predict what the next number is. Indeed, it could well be argued that our Random~Number algorithm is quite suitable for casinos, because it is generally agreed to be a very good random number generator.

The absolutely astonishing fact about Random~Number is that every number it produces is easily predicted from the previous number. If it is called repeatedly billions of times, the algorithm generates every possible integer in the range 1 to $2^{31}-2$, each integer being divided by $2^{31}–1$ to give a fraction greater than zero and less than one. Each integer is determined by, and only by, the previous number in the sequence. Any given integer is used only once in a succession of $2^{31}–2$ such integers. When all $2^{31}–2$ integers have been used, the cycle starts again, generating all numbers in exactly the same sequence.

The other astonishing truth of the matter is that Random~Number uses sampling *without* replacement! If you had a good enough memory to remember the first $2^{31}–3$ numbers (this is an extraordinarily large number, greater than two billion), you would be able to predict the last number without even knowing the formula that is used to derive it from the second last number. With the first $2^{31}–3$ numbers known, there is only one remaining number in the total cycle of $2^{31}–2$. How then, and in what sense, can one possibly say that Random~Number is a good random number generator?

To answer that question, consider briefly a bad random number generator. Desk calculators frequently have a random number generator that generates a fraction between zero and one. For example, on my calculator the first five "random" numbers given to me were 0.708, 0.290, 0.229, 0.287, and 0.601. The three numbers in the middle look decidedly nonrandom taken in isolation, so I obtained another five: 0.845, 0.436, 0.050, 0.161, 0.708. These numbers look more random, don't they? But wait! The last number, 0.708, is the same as the first of the ten numbers I have obtained so far. Does that mean I am stuck in a loop? Let's try another five: 0.299, 0.878, 0.202, 0.665, 0.299. It's not a loop but, oh dear, we have three more numbers starting with 0.2 as in the first set of five, and two of them are identical. Let's try another five: 0.899, 0.678, 0.596, 0.709, 0.309. These seem OK, except that four of them are larger than 0.5, the average. One more run of five, 0.120, 0.777, 0.885, 0.367, and 0.463, doesn't have any obvious flaws. The question of whether these numbers are "random" or not is not easy to resolve. Suffice it to say that there should be no pattern or predictability in the numbers produced by a random number generator.

In just about every *use* to which Random~Number can be put the algorithm generates numbers that appear "random" according to every test that has been devised. The fundamental reason is that only the first few digits after the decimal point are ever used. Programs effectively discard or ignore all remaining digits that, with your super-memory, you could use for prediction purposes. For example, is it likely that three of the first five numbers generated by Random will start with 0.2? More generally, is it likely that in the first five numbers three will have the same first digit after the decimal point? The answer is "no" in both cases. Many scientific tests have been devised. Will there be approximately equal numbers of numbers in all intervals of, say, one-tenth, between 0 and 0.1, 0.1 and 0.2, and so on? Or any given intervals for that matter? Yes, these pseudorandom numbers have that property. Are there too many, or too few, ascending or descending "runs"? No! Are the run lengths distributed as one would expect for random numbers? Yes!

Although the numbers are calculated without replacement, they are all different from each other only when spelled out to ten decimal places. No one uses *random* numbers with that kind of precision. If you work with a list of random numbers rounded off to, say, three decimal places, you'll find numbers being repeated in the list with just the right expected frequency. For all practical uses these three-digit pseudorandom numbers appear random, patternless, and unpredictable, but with averages and the variabilities expected of truly random numbers. They appear to be sampled *with* replacement when rounded to only a few decimal places.

Caveat

Caution is advised, however. At any one point in time there are no doubt millions of people struggling to find ways to beat the odds in horse racing, lotteries, poker games, the stock market, and just about every gambling system ever devised. Let's suppose you decide to enter the market for gaming machines as a manufacturer. Would you trust the linear congruential random number generator to be the brains behind your electronic versions of roulette and blackjack?

The problem you have is that *really*, in all honesty, the numbers produced by Random~Number are *not* random at all. They are very good pseudorandom numbers, which are essentially unpredictable for almost all practical purposes. But even these numbers are not good enough for a foolproof electronic casino. If you, a wily customer intent on breaking the bank, know that the casino is using Random~Number, you can use your ingenuity to win. The key to making the essentially unpredictable totally predictable is your knowledge of the algorithm used in the random number generator. Let's look at how you could break the bank at roulette.

You'll need to plan on having another computer to sit alongside you as you try to defeat the casino. Conceptually, it is not at all difficult. The practical difficulty is to program the process efficiently so that it can be implemented and operational in real time in the electronic casino. Generate and store all possible $N = 2^{31}-2$ numbers in the sequence generated by Random~Integer. Better still, save the random number "seed" that produces each random integer. A random integer in the range 0–36 is generated by Random~Integer by taking the integer part of R * 37, where R is generated by Random~Number. Copy the first six values of R into the first row of a two-dimensional array T(1, 1) through T(1, 6). Now "shift left" one place, copying T(1, 2) through T(1, 6) into T(2, 1) through T(2, 5). Generate the next value of R and store it in T(2, 6). Shift left again, putting T(2, 2) through T(2, 6) into T(3, 1) through T(3, 5), and put the next value of R into T(3, 6). Continue this process until all *maxinteger*–1 rows of T are filled. Now sort the array T, not on the seed values themselves, but on the random integers derived from them by truncating the product of each with 37.

Type in each number as it appears from the electronic roulette table and it is possible to build up enough information to find where Random~Number is in its sequence. As each roulette number appears it's just a matter of looking it up in the sorted list using binary search. In the first lookup, requiring at most 31 probes, you will find *maxinteger* / 37 consecutive entries containing the seed for the current roulette number in the first column of T. Search these *maxinteger* / 37 entries to match the second roulette number in the second column, requiring about 26 probes. There will be *maxinteger* / (37 * 37) consecutive matching entries. The third number will require about 21 probes to find a list of *maxinteger* / (37 * 37 * 37), or about 42,400 matching entries. Do this several more times. After only half a dozen electronic spins there will be only one possible matching entry. Now you know where Random~Number is in its sequence. You can predict all following "random" numbers! You're rich! Well, conceptually anyway.

This hypothetical example shows just how dangerous sampling without replacement can be. The law of averages as espoused by the orthodox averagists is indeed a valid law when sampling without replacement is used.

8.1 RANDOM NUMBER GENERATORS

Generating random numbers with a variety of distributions

Examples

An ordinary (uniformly distributed) random number R in the interval 0 to 1, and a normally distributed random number U with mean 0 and standard deviation 1, are generated by:

call Random~Number (R)
call Random~Normal (U)

Both subprograms require initialization, as the following example shows:

call Random~Initialize (*maxinteger* – 1)
call Normal~Initialize (0, 1)

Subprograms

8.1.1a Random~Number (supplies Random)
8.1.1b Random~Initialize (receives NewSeed)
8.1.2 Random~Number (supplies Random)
8.1.3 Random~Number (supplies Random)
8.1.4a Random~Integer (supplies Random)
8.1.4b Integer~Initialize (receives Lower, Upper)
8.1.5a Random~Normal (supplies Random)
8.1.5b Normal~Initialize (receives Mean, StdDev)
8.1.6a Random~Exponential (supplies Random)
8.1.6b Exponential~Initialize (receives Mean)
8.1.7a Random~Poisson (supplies Random)
8.1.7b Poisson~Initialize (receives Mean)
8.1.8a Random~Geometric (supplies Random)
8.1.8b Geometric~Initialize (receives Probability)
8.1.9a Random~Binomial (supplies Random)
8.1.9b Binomial~Initialize (receives N, Probability)

Usage

Each of the nine methods is implemented by a call to a procedure that has just one nickname, the name of the variable into which the random number is placed. Each procedure is accompanied by an initialization procedure that should be called only when a change is required in the parameters of the distribution. To get a different sequence of random numbers each time the program is run, call Random~Initialize with NewSeed set to different values each time. For example, use the computer clock time hhmmss as a six-digit number for initializing the random number generator.

Note that the test program assumes that all random number generators produce a *real* result. In fact, several of them generate *integers*. To keep the test program simple, we modified each integer generator to produce a *real* result while testing the algorithms.

It is a simple matter to restore the *integer* type without endangering the correctness of the code. The Initialize procedure for some of the algorithms does little more than copy the values of the nicknames to local storage. This is done to give each generator exactly one nickname, and to ensure that the random number generation is as fast as possible, minimizing the use of nicknames on each call to the generators themselves.

The methods implemented here are efficient, require few constants, and use no arrays. The choice of algorithms was based on ease of implementation, as well as on efficiency. More efficient but more complicated methods exist in some cases, as discussed below. These methods are not recommended for occasional use, because they typically require very careful programming and extremely rigorous testing.

It is useful to understand several technical terms when dealing with random numbers. The term "distribution" was introduced at the beginning of this chapter. The distribution of a set of random numbers describes the likelihood, or probability, of a given random number being equal to a specified value, or of its lying within a specified range of values. Probability is a number lying between zero and one. An event that will never occur has a probability of zero. An event that is certain to occur has a probability of one. Tossing a fair coin will result in heads with probability one-half and tails with probability also one-half.

The "mean" is the average of an infinite number of random numbers generated for the distribution under discussion. The "standard deviation" is a measure of the spread of the values generated. If the mean is M and the random numbers are R, the standard deviation is simply the square root of the average value of $(R - M)^2$, again averaged over an infinite number of random numbers.

Statisticians tend to use the square of the standard deviation frequently. The square of the standard deviation is called the "variance". It is just the average value of $(R - M)^2$. "Skewness" is a measure of the asymmetry of the distribution, and is calculated as the average value of $(R - M)^3$. "Kurtosis" measures the peakedness of the distribution. It is calculated as the average value of $(R - M)^4$. Clearly, there is an infinite number of these quantities, with successively higher powers of $(R - M)$, which are called "moments" of the distribution.

The test program makes use of the first two moments, mean and variance. It checks that the means and variances are about right for each distribution, using a sample of 1,000 random numbers from each. If a more stringent test is required, you should also check that the skewness is about right. Kurtosis and higher moments may also be included in the tests, but much larger samples are required as the order of the moment increases, owing to the raising of the deviations to larger powers. Formulas for higher moments are provided in standard reference books, such as the classic work of Kendall and Stuart (1963).

To explain the terms simply without providing a treatise on statistics, think about the distribution of numbers when rolling two dice. What is the probability of getting zero, one, or two values of a particular number? Suppose you are interested in the five for some reason. There is one chance in six of getting a five when rolling one of the dice, and the same probability of getting a five when rolling the other. Because the two events are independent, the chance of both occurring is the product, or one in 36. There are five chances in six of not getting a five with one roll, and five chances in six of not getting a five in the second roll. Again the events are independent and the probabilities are multiplicative. There are therefore 25 chances in 36 of not getting a five when both dice are rolled. The remaining 10 chances in 36 apply to getting just one five from both rolls.

This is an example of the binomial distribution, with the number of events N = 2 and the probability P of one event (a five) being P = 1/6. There are three possible outcomes: 0, 1, or 2 fives. In an infinite number of rolls of the dice you will get 0 fives in 25 out of 36 cases, 1 five in 10 out of 36, and 2 fives in 1 out of 36. On average then, in 36 rolls you will get 0×25 plus 1×10 plus 2×1 fives, or 12 fives. That is, the average number of fives in one roll is 12/36 or 1/3. This is the mean of the binomial distribution with N = 2 and P = 1/6. It can be shown mathematically that the mean is always equal to $N \times P$.

To calculate the variance, look at 36 rolls again. For 25 rolls the number of fives is zero, or –1/3 below the mean. For 10 rolls it is 2/3 above the mean, and for 1 roll it is 1 + (2/3) above the mean. The variance is then $25 \times (-1/3)^2$ plus $10 \times (2/3)^2$ plus $(1 + (2/3))^2$ all divided by 36, or 10/36. The skewness is calculated using cubes instead of squares, and is $25 \times (-1/3)^3$ plus $10 \times (2/3)^3$ plus $(1 + (2/3))^3$ all divided by 36, or 10/54. The positive value for skewness means that there is a longer "tail" of the distribution above the mean (1/3) than below it. Indeed, the tail stretches out to 2 above the mean and only down to 0 below it.

Random~Number

The procedure Random~Number generates a uniformly distributed random number, which is greater than zero and less than one. The probability that a generated random number is less than a particular value X, where $0 \le X \le 1$, is just X. The initialization procedure Random~Initialize should be called once to initialize the seed of the random number generator. The seed should be set to any positive integer value between 1 and (*maxinteger* – 1). Initialization is required only at the beginning of the program, and whenever the user needs different sequences of random numbers in successive executions of the program.

There are three random number generation procedures with the same name and all three produce identical results if properly implemented. The novice user should implement 8.1.1 unless the correct conditions can be established for the use of 8.1.2 or 8.1.3 as described in the analysis below.

All the other random number generators rely on this one, which generates a number between 1/*maxinteger* and (*maxinteger*–1)/*maxinteger*. All possible values within that range may occur. It is assumed that the calling program "knows" nothing about the random number generation algorithm, and so all values appear equally likely. From the calling program's point of view the probability of any one particular random number being generated is therefore 1/(*maxinteger*–1), a very small value indeed.

Random~Integer

The range in which the random integer is required is specified by a call to Integer~Initialize. For example, if the lower and upper limits are L and U respectively, Random~Integer will generate an integer greater than or equal to L and less than or equal to U. The random integers are uniformly distributed. The probability of any given number being generated is 1/(U – L + 1).

Random~Normal

The "normal" distribution is completely specified by its mean and standard deviation. The mean and standard deviation are given to Normal~Initialize. All subsequent calls to Random~Normal produce numbers with the specified distribution. The probability that a number approximately equal to R is generated, when the mean and standard deviation are M and S respectively, is proportional to *exp* $(-(R - M)^2 / (2 * S^2))$.

Random~Exponential

The exponential distribution is completely specified by its mean, its standard deviation always being equal to the mean. Only one parameter needs to be supplied to Exponential~Initialize. All subsequent calls to Random~Exponential produce numbers with the specified distribution. The probability that a number approximately equal to R is generated, when the mean of the distribution is M, is proportional to *exp* (–R / M).

Random~Poisson

The Poisson distribution is also completely specified by its mean, its variance always being equal to the mean. Only one parameter needs to be supplied to Poisson~Initialize. All subsequent calls to Random~Poisson produce numbers with the specified distribution. The method is slow when the mean is large. Random~Poisson generates an integer R, the probability of which for a distribution with mean M is *exp* $(-M) * M^R / R!$, where R! is the factorial of R.

Random~Geometric

In common with the above two distributions the geometric distribution is completely specified by its mean. However, it is usual to think about the distribution in terms of the inverse of its mean, which is equal to the probability of one event occurring, say P. The mean is then 1/P. The parameter supplied to Geometric~Initialize is the probability P. All subsequent calls to Random~Geometric produce numbers with the specified distribution. Random~Geometric generates an integer R, the probability of any specific value of which is $P * (1 - P)^{R-1}$.

Random~Binomial

As mentioned earlier, the binomial distribution is specified by a probability P and a number of events N. These parameters are supplied to Binomial~Initialize. All subsequent calls to Random~Binomial produce numbers with the specified distribution. Random~Binomial generates an integer R, the probability of any specific value of which is ${}^{N}C_{R} * P^{R} * (1 - P)^{N-R}$. The notation ${}^{N}C_{R}$ refers to the number of combinations of R things taken from N defined in Section 4.1.

The binomial generation method slows down to unacceptable levels when N * P becomes large. In these circumstances the normal distribution provides a good approximation. Siegel (1956) suggests that N * P * (1 – P) should be greater than 9 before the normal approximation is used. Initialize the normal generator with mean equal to N * P and standard deviation equal to *square~root* (N * P * (1 – P)). Then use the numbers supplied by Random~Normal, rounded to the nearest integer, as if they had been supplied by Random~Binomial. This approximation is good, but it does not converge to exactness as N * P increases in size. The skewness of the normal distribution is zero, but that of the binomial distribution is always nonzero and equal to the variance multiplied by (1 – (2 * P)).

Analysis

It is vital that the test program be used carefully for checking the code of random number generators, which are intrinsically difficult to test. The test program checks whether the values of the first two moments of the distribution of the generated numbers conform with theory. The values of the moments in the test program for each of the distributions are derived from Kendall and Stuart (1963). With a sample size of 1,000 all distributions should generate approximations to the moments with at least three bits of accuracy.

For most of the random number generators the reasoning behind each method is difficult to explain rigorously without higher mathematics. The explanations here demonstrate how the algorithms work, and do not set out to prove that they work. Nevertheless, the explanations should be found reassuring to you, particularly if you are not familiar with statistical methods. You should consult the literature, starting with Knuth (1969), if a mathematical proof for a particular method is required. On a point of programming style, all algorithms are implemented as procedures rather than functions, so as to avoid side effects involved with manipulating the random number seed.

Random~Number

In the introduction to this chapter there was an illustratration of how the linear congruential method operates. The three subprograms for producing uniformly distributed random numbers are all equivalent. They produce exactly the same results using the "minimal standard" method (Park and Miller 1988). The second, 8.1.2, is a faster and more straightforward method that gives the same result as 8.1.1. However, it should be implemented only in a language that permits the arithmetic for Seed * 16807 and the remaindering to be done to at least 48 bits of accuracy. The 32-bit implementation in 8.1.1 makes use of the fact that *maxinteger* = (16807 * 127773) + 2836. The properties of arithmetic using the *mod* operator ensure that the implementations of 8.1.1 and 8.1.2 are equivalent (Park and Miller 1988).

The third subprogram, 8.1.3, is an even faster way to implement the algorithm, suggested by Carta (1990). It will require implementation in assembly language, or a low-level language that provides access to hardware facilities. Assume you get the product Seed * 16807 in two 32-bit registers. Call the registers A and B, where A contains the most significant part of the product and B contains the least significant 31 bits, the sign of B being ignored. Now add A and B together to produce the new value of the seed. Very occasionally this sum will cause integer overflow. When that happens, ignore the overflow but add 1 to the sum, that is, to the new seed. Then divide the new seed by *maxinteger*, as with the other versions of the algorithm, to obtain the result.

Random~Integer

The Random~Integer procedure is in essence simply a multiplication by the range and a truncation to an integer. It is preferable to code the procedure in line, and one would normally do so in preference to calling a subprogram for this very simple algorithm.

Random~Normal

The random normal deviate generator uses the Box–Muller method, as described by Knuth (1969). Random~Normal generates two random numbers simultaneously, one and then the other being returned on two successive calls. The method is actually faster than Teichroew's approximate method that was proposed as a way of avoiding using logarithms. Most programmers tend to use high-level languages. Standard functions tend to be written in assembly language, and are usually very efficient. The inefficiencies of high-level languages appear to outweigh any apparent savings from avoiding the use of standard functions.

The method generates two random numbers at the same time, although this fact is transparent to the user. The algorithm starts with two uniform random numbers, which define a random point inside a unit circle. Now you have to think in polar coordinates, the two uniform random numbers being represented by a radius and an angle. Radii greater than or equal to 1.0 are discarded. The discard loop is executed on average about 1.27 times, and is therefore quite efficient. The angle is uniformly distributed and remains constant in the key transformation of the radius R_1. To simplify this discussion, assume that the mean is zero and the standard deviation is one. The algorithm generates two new polar coordinates with radius R_2, where R_2 = *square~root* (–2 * log_e (R_1^2)). Inverting this relationship we see that R_1^2 = *exp* (–R_2^2 / 2). In general terms, you will see the form of the normal distribution here. Two independent normal random numbers are obtained by converting back to Cartesian coordinates. See Knuth (1969) for a proof of the method.

Random~Exponential

The exponential distribution has the property, called its cumulative distribution function, that the probability that any number is less than, say, X is 1 – *exp* (–X / Mean). The algorithm generates a random number equal to –log_e (Random) * Mean. If you divide by –Mean and take exponentials of both quantities, you see that the probability that –log_e (Random) * Mean is less than X is equal to the probability that Random is greater than *exp* (–X / Mean), which is equal to the probability that Random is less than 1 – *exp* (–X / Mean). This demonstrates that the algorithm achieves the desired result.

Random~Poisson

The Poisson distribution requires that the probability of generating an integer I must be equal to *exp* (–Mean) * $Mean^I$ / I!, where I! is the factorial of I. These paragraphs will look at the probabilities of generating random numbers equal to zero and one, and indicate how the computations are carried out for larger numbers. The algorithm generates zero as the result only if the loop is not executed at all. By examining the code, you see that the probability of the loop not being executed is equal to the probability that a uniform random number is less than *exp* (–Mean). This is equal to the desired result *exp* (–Mean) * $Mean^0$/0!.

The algorithm generates a one if the loop is executed once. Two uniform random numbers S and R are generated, and S is modified during the loop. To avoid confusion, call the two vanilla random numbers R_1 and R_2. The algorithm sets S equal to R_1, then R is set equal to R_2, and S is modified to be equal to R_1*R_2. The probability of the loop exiting after one iteration is equal to the probability that R_1 is greater than *exp* (–Mean) and R_1*R_2 is less than *exp* (–Mean). This is best represented in diagrammatic form. Suppose you plot R_1 and R_2 as the X and Y axes respectively. This is done in Figure 8.1. The shaded area represents the required probability. Using integral calculus, the area under the curve R_2 = *exp* (–Mean) / R_1 is found to be *exp* (–Mean) * Mean, which is equal to the desired result *exp* (–Mean) * $Mean^1$ / 1!.

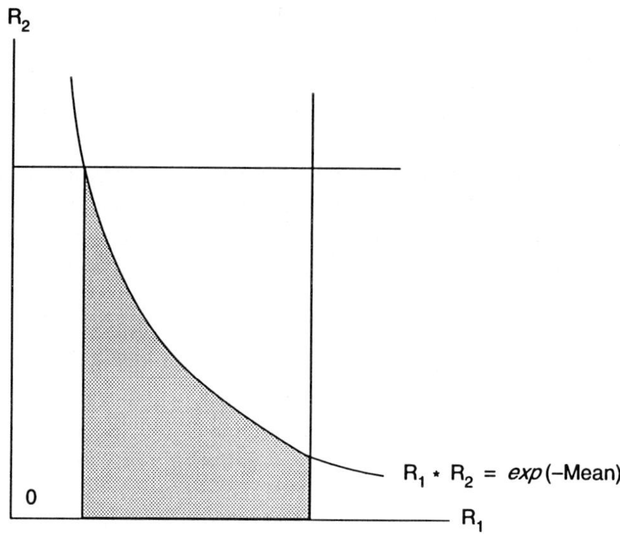

Figure 8.1

The probability that the algorithm will generate the number two is obtained by finding the volume of a solid bounded by two hyperboloid curves and three planes, and the complexity increases for larger-valued random numbers. An alternative method of proving the effectiveness of the algorithm, which requires greater mathematical sophistication, is given by Knuth (1969).

Random~Geometric

The algorithm generates an integer I by taking the *ceiling* of a *real* quantity Random = *ceiling* (log_e (R) / LogProbability). Note that I = *ceiling* (Random) is equivalent to $I - 1 < \text{Random} \leq I$. When this is rewritten using the computed value of Random, the probability that Random is in this range is equal to the probability that $I - 1 < log_e (R) / \text{LogProbability} \leq I$. Multiplying all terms by the value of LogProbability and then taking the exponential *exp* of all terms, this is equivalent to the probability that $(1 - P)^{I-1} < R \leq (1 - P)^I$, where P is the specified probability. The probability that the value of the uniform random number R is in that range is $P * (1 - P)^{I-1}$, as required.

Random~Binomial

The binomial algorithm uses the inverse transformation described by Kachitvichyanukul and Schmeiser (1988). The formula for the distribution indicates that a random integer R must have a probability of ${}^{N}C_{R} * P^{R} * (1 - P)^{N-R}$. For example, R = 0 and 1 have probabilities $(1 - P)^N$ and $N * P * (1 - P)^{N-1}$ respectively. These are the first two terms in the expansion of $((1 - P) + P)^N$. The algorithm is similar to that for Random~Poisson, in that the result is equal to the number of times the loop is executed. The probability that the loop is executed zero times is just the probability that a uniform random number is less than Q, which is equal to $(1 - P)^N$. The probability that a uniform random number is less than a value between 0 and 1 is just that value itself, and so the probability that the loop is executed zero times is $(1 - P)^N$ as required.

The loop is executed once when the uniform random number is greater than Q, but less than Q plus N * (1 – P) / P * Q. The term N * P / (1 – P) * Q is equal to N * P * $(1 - P)^{N-1}$, which is the second term in the expansion of $((1 - P) + P)^N$. Thus the random integer 1 is produced with the correct probability. Probabilities for other random integers are determined in the same way.

Because the number of iterations of the loop is equal to the random number generated, the mean number of iterations is equal to the mean of the distribution, or N * P. This is the reason for the increasing inefficiency of the algorithm as N * P grows in size. This problem led to the modification evident in the algorithm to take account of a symmetry in the distribution, in that if R is a binomially distributed integer with probability P, then N – R is also binomial with probability N – P. The maximum number of iterations of the loop is therefore N / 2 rather than N.

Rectangle-Wedge-Tail Methods

There is a faster method for generating normally distributed numbers, described by Knuth (1969) as the "rectangle-wedge-tail" method. This ingenious method developed by Marsaglia and McLaren has been avoided here because it is so difficult to test. The algorithm contains hundreds of constants that must be specified accurately to sixteen decimal places (for full machine accuracy with 64-bit real numbers). The simple code in the algorithm is executed the most often, and the most complex code is executed the least often. Very complex code is used very rarely. This makes it likely that hidden bugs will remain hidden until Murphy's Law takes over. The test program, which checks the values of moments of the distribution as a whole, is unlikely to detect bugs in the least-used code.

Similar comments apply to other distributions for which these rectangle-wedge-tail methods have been developed, such as the binomial, exponential, and Poisson. The algorithm for the exponential distribution developed by Ahrens and Dieter (1988) is less complex, but has similar undesirable properties. Our tests show that it is slower than algorithm 8.1.6 when coded in a high-level language. This could be due to the efficiency with which the logarithm is implemented in modern language libraries. The authors suggest that their algorithm be implemented in assembly language.

No apology is needed for typically using simple if somewhat slower algorithms. Some uses of random number generators are tied to business decisions involving millions of dollars. Computer time is relatively inexpensive. You should not use rectangle-wedge-tail methods in such programs unless you face the prospect of using vast amounts of computer time. Given the difficulty of testing complex random number generators, the correct business decision is usually to avoid the rectangle-wedge-tail methods. It is likely that only the writers of specialized random-number generator packages, or programmers embarking on large and costly simulations, could justify the time and cost of implementing such methods.

IMPLEMENTATION

Exported Names

Binomial~Initialize	Initializes random binomial generator (8.1.9b)
Exponential~Initialize	Initializes random exponential generator (8.1.6b)

Geometric~Initialize	Initializes random geometric generator (8.1.8b)
Integer~Initialize	Initializes random integer generator (8.1.4b)
Normal~Initialize	Initializes random normal generator (8.1.5b)
Poisson~Initialize	Initializes random Poisson generator (8.1.7b)
Random~Binomial	Computes a geometrically distributed number (8.1.9a)
Random~Exponential	Computes an exponentially distributed number (8.1.6a)
Random~Geometric	Computes a geometrically distributed number (8.1.8a)
Random~Initialize	Initializes uniform random number generator (8.1.1b)
Random~Integer	Computes a random integer in a specified range (8.1.4a)
Random~Normal	Computes a random normally distributed number (8.1.5a)
Random~Number	Computes a uniform random number using 32-bit arithmetic (8.1.1a)
Random~Number	Computes a uniform random number using 48-bit arithmetic (8.1.2)
Random~Number	Computes a uniform random number using 64-bit arithmetic (8.1.3)
Random~Poisson	Computes an exponentially distributed number (8.1.7a)

<u>Nicknames</u>

Lower	Start of inclusive range in which random integer will lie
Mean	Mean of distribution
N	Size of population
NewSeed	Positive integer seed
Probability	Probability for geometric distribution
Random	Random number generated by procedure
StdDev	Standard deviation of distribution
Upper	End of inclusive range in which random integer will lie

<u>Global Names</u>

Bottom	Lowest integer in range
ExpMean	Transformed mean
G	Indicator that probability is greater than 0.5
Interval	Magnitude of the range of integers
LogProbability	Transformed probability
M	Value one greater than N
Mu	Mean
Q	Probability of event not occurring
Saved	Intermediate result for Random~Normal
Seed	Random number generator "seed" or multiplier
Sigma	Standard deviation
T	Broadly, the ratio Probability / (1 – Probability)
Z	Probability of zero events occurring

<u>Local Names</u>

C	Count of successes, to become result
DoubleRegister	64-bit register, comprising HighRegister and LowRegister
HighRegister	32-bit register, containing upper bits of product
LowRegister	32-bit register, containing lower 31 bits of product
NewSeed	Newly calculated value for Seed
Probability	Probability of a single event
R, S	Intermediate random numbers

8.1.1a **Random~Number** (supplies Random)

Pseudo Code (32-bit method)

multiply seed by 7^5
divide result by *maxinteger*, discarding quotient and retaining remainder as new seed
divide new seed by *maxinteger*, giving a result between 1 and *maxinteger* – 1

Code

```
variable Seed is integer
procedure Random~Number (Random is real)
    variable NewSeed is integer
    let NewSeed = (16807 * (Seed mod 127773)) – (2836 * (Seed ÷ 127773))
    if NewSeed > 0 then
        let Seed = NewSeed
    else
        let Seed = NewSeed + maxinteger
    end if
    let Random = Seed / maxinteger
end Random~Number
```

8.1.1b **Random~Initialize** (receives NewSeed)

```
procedure Random~Initialize (NewSeed is integer)
    check NewSeed > 0
    let Seed = NewSeed
end Random~Initialize
```

8.1.2 **Random~Number** (supplies Random)

Pseudo Code (48-bit method)

multiply seed by 7^5
divide result by *maxinteger*, discarding quotient and retaining remainder as new seed
divide new seed by *maxinteger*, giving a result between 1 and *maxinteger* – 1

Code

```
variable Seed is integer
procedure Random~Number (Random is real)
    let Seed = (Seed * 16807) mod maxinteger
    let Random = Seed / maxinteger
end Random~Number
```

8.1.3 **Random~Number** (supplies Random)

Pseudo Code (64-bit method)

multiply seed by 7^5
divide result by *maxinteger*, discarding quotient and retaining remainder as new seed
divide new seed by *maxinteger*, giving a result between 1 and *maxinteger* – 1

Code

```
variable Seed is integer
procedure Random~Number (Random is real)
    variables DoubleRegister, HighRegister, LowRegister are integers
    let DoubleRegister = Seed * 16807
    let HighRegister = DoubleRegister ÷ (maxinteger + 1)
    let LowRegister = DoubleRegister mod (maxinteger + 1)
    let Seed = LowRegister + HighRegister
    if Seed > maxinteger then
        let Seed = Seed – maxinteger
    end if
    let Random = Seed / maxinteger
end Random~Number
```

8.1.4a Random~Integer (supplies Random)

Pseudo Code

multiply Interval by a random number, and truncate to an integer
result is integer plus lower end of interval

Code

```
variables Bottom, Interval are integers
procedure Random~Integer (Random is integer)
    variable R is real
    call Random~Number (R)
    let R = R * Interval
    let Random = Bottom + truncate (R)
end Random~Integer
```

8.1.4b Integer~Initialize (receives Lower, Upper)

```
procedure Integer~Initialize (Lower, Upper are integers)
    check Lower ≤ Upper
    let Bottom = Lower
    let Interval = magnitude (Upper – Lower) + 1
end Integer~Initialize
```

8.1.5a Random~Normal (supplies Random)

Pseudo Code

```
if number was not saved in the previous iteration
    generate a random point in a unit circle
    transform radius from uniform to exponential distribution
    transform to two points with normal distribution
    return one of the points and save the other
```

```
else
    return number saved in previous iteration
end if
```

Code

```
variables Mu, Saved, Sigma are real
procedure Random~Normal (Random is real)
    variables R, S are real
    if Saved = 0 then
        loop
            call Random~Number (R)
            let R = (R * 2) – 1
            call Random~Number (S)
            let S = (S * 2) – 1
            let Random = (R * R) + (S * S)
        end loop when Random < 1
        let Random = square~root (–2 * log_e (Random) / Random)
        let Saved = (S * Random * Sigma) + Mu
        let Random = (R * Random * Sigma) + Mu
    else
        let Random = Saved
        let Saved = 0
    end if
end Random~Normal
```

8.1.5b Normal~Initialize (receives Mean, StdDev)

```
procedure Normal~Initialize (Mean, StdDev are real)
    let Mu = Mean
    let Sigma = StdDev
    let Saved = 0
end Normal~Initialize
```

8.1.6a Random~Exponential (supplies Random)

Pseudo Code

```
generate random number, and transform it directly by inverse of distribution
        function
```

Code

```
variable Mu is real
procedure Random~Exponential (Random is real)
    call Random~Number (Random)
    let Random = –log_e (Random) * Mu
end Random~Exponential
```

8.1.6b Exponential~Initialize (receives Mean)

```
procedure Exponential~Initialize (Mean is real)
    let Mu = Mean
end Exponential~Initialize
```

8.1.7a Random~Poisson (supplies Random)

Pseudo Code

```
let count of iterations Random = 0
generate random number S
loop until S < exp (–Mean)
    increment iteration count Random
    transform S to product of itself and another random number
end loop
result is iteration count Random
```

Code

```
variable ExpMean is real
procedure Random~Poisson (Random is integer)
    variables R, S are real
    let Random = 0
    call Random~Number (S)
    loop until S < ExpMean
        let Random = Random + 1
        call Random~Number (R)
        let S = S * R
    end loop
end Random~Poisson
```

8.1.7b Poisson~Initialize (receives Mean)

```
procedure Poisson~Initialize (Mean is real)
    let ExpMean = exp (–Mean)
end Poisson~Initialize
```

8.1.8a Random~Geometric (supplies Random)

Pseudo Code

```
generate random number Random
result is smallest integer not greater than log_e (Random) / log_e (1 – P)
```

Code

```
variable LogProbability is real
procedure Random~Geometric (Random is integer)
    variable R is real
    call Random~Number (R)
    let Random = ceiling (log_e (R) / LogProbability)
end Random~Geometric
```

8.1.8b Geometric~Initialize (receives Probability)

```
procedure Geometric~Initialize (Probability is real)
    let LogProbability = log_e (1 – Probability)
end Geometric~Initialize
```

8.1.9a Random~Binomial (supplies Random)

Pseudo Code

```
let iteration counter C = 0
generate random number R
loop until R ≤ probability of C events occurring out of N
    increment iteration counter C
    adjust R to deal with exactly C events instead of number of events from 0 to C
end loop
select correct tail of distribution
```

Code

```
variables G, M are integers
variables Q, T, Z are real
procedure Random~Binomial (Random is integer)
    variable C is integer
    variable R is real
    let C = 0
    let Q = Z
    call Random~Number (R)
    loop until R ≤ Q
        let R = R – Q
        let C = C + 1
        let Q = ((M / C) – 1) * T * Q
    end loop
    if G ≥ 0 then
        let Random = M – C – 1
    else
        let Random = C
    end if
end Random~Binomial
```

8.1.9b Binomial~Initialize (receives N, Probability)

```
procedure Binomial~Initialize (N is integer, Probability is real)
    let Q = maximum (Probability, 1 – Probability)
    let T = minimum (Probability, 1 – Probability) / Q
    let Z = power (Q, N)
    let G = sign (Probability – 0.5)
    let M = N + 1
end Binomial~Initialize
```

TEST PROGRAM

<u>Imported Names</u>

Similarity~Bits	Finds the number of bits in common in two numbers (2.3.1)

<u>Local Subprograms</u>

Test	Checks calculated mean and variance of distribution

<u>Nicknames</u>

Distribution	Name of procedure that generates random number
Mean	Theoretically calculated exact mean of distribution
Variance	Theoretically calculated exact variance of distribution

<u>Local Names</u>

Deviate	Deviation of a random number from the distribution mean
Emean	Total for estimating distribution mean
Evariance	Total for estimating distribution variance
N	Number of iterations
Random	A uniformly distributed random number

Pseudo Code

```
for n = 2 to 12
    for each distribution to be tested
        initialize parameters of distribution
        call Test to check that mean and variance conform with distribution
                parameters
    end for
end for
procedure Test
    let sum and sum of squares = 0
    for i = 1 to 1000
        generate a random number from the required distribution
        subtract the theoretical mean from the random number
        accumulate sum and sum of squares
    end for
    check that sum/1000 is close to zero
    check that sum of squares/1000 is close to theoretical variance
end Test
```

Code

```
for n = 2 to 12
    call Random~Initialize (maxinteger – n)
    call Test (Random~Number, 1 / 2, 1 / 12)
    call Integer~Initialize (0, 6 * n)
    call Test (Random~Integer, 3 * n, n * ((3 * n) + 1))
    call Normal~Initialize (n, n)
    call Test (Random~Normal, n, n * n)
    call Exponential~Initialize (n)
    call Test (Random~Exponential, n, n * n)
    call Poisson~Initialize (n)
```

```
        call Test (Random~Poisson, n, n)
        call Geometric~Initialize (1 / n)
        call Test (Random~Geometric, n, n * (n – 1))
        call Binomial~Initialize (n * n, 1 / n)
        call Test (Random~Binomial, n, n – 1)
    end for

Local Test (receives Distribution, Mean, Variance)
    procedure Test (Distribution is procedure, Mean, Variance are real)
        constant N = 1000
        variable Deviate, Emean, Evariance, Random are real
        let Emean = 0
        let Evariance = 0
        for i = 1 to N
            call Distribution (Random)
            let Deviate = Random – Mean
            let Emean = Emean + Deviate
            let Evariance = Evariance + (Deviate * Deviate)
        end for
        check Similarity~Bits ((Emean / N) + Mean, Mean, 0) ≥ 3
        check Similarity~Bits (Evariance / N, Variance, 0) ≥ 3
    end Test
```

8.2 RANDOM SELECTION

Shuffling, and choosing a number of items randomly from a larger set

Examples

A list of 100 integers in array locations List[1] to List[100] is shuffled into random order by:

```
call Random~Shuffle (List, 1, 100)
```

A list of 50 integers selected randomly from the range 1 to 10,000 is produced by:

```
call Random~Set (List, 10000, 50)
```

Subprograms

8.2.1 Random~Shuffle (updates Items; receives Lower, Upper)
8.2.2 Random~Sequence (updates Items; receives Lower, Upper, N)
8.2.3 Random~Set (updates Items; receives Lower, Upper, N)

Usage

Random~Shuffle assumes that the array to be shuffled has been initialized. If the user is simply looking for a shuffled set of the first N integers, it will be necessary to initialize the elements of the array with nickname Item to the integers 1 to N.

Random~Sequence assumes that the user wants a random selection of the first N integers. This selection is stored in sorted sequence in the array with nickname Item. The size of the selection is determined by the lower and upper limits of the array, Lower and Upper.

Random~Set also assumes that the user wants a random selection of the first N integers. The selection is stored in Item, but the elements of the selection are not in sorted sequence. Again, the size of the selection is determined by the lower and upper limits of the array.

The test program operates in two parts. The first part exercises Random~Set, and checks that the sample is a suitably random set of integers in the required range. The second part exercises Random~Sequence. Because the latter produces a sorted sample, the sample is shuffled using Random~Shuffle, and the degree of randomness is again checked. The check is carried out against an expected uniform distribution using Pearson's chi-squared statistic. If you want to learn more about the test, you may wish to consult the classic text on nonparametric statistics by Siegel (1956), a more modern text on the subject, or Knuth (1969).

Analysis

Random~Shuffle deals with the elements of the array one by one. The first element is swapped with an element chosen at random. The first element itself is given an equal probability of being chosen. There is a constant probability that the element in the first array location will be swapped into any particular array location. The part of the array following the first element is then treated as if it were the whole array, and the process is then repeated for the entire array. At every stage every element has an equal opportunity of occupying an array position, and so the process is unbiased. The algorithm is very efficient, running in O (N) time. It has been rediscovered many times and is described by Knuth (1969).

Random~Sequence selects K integers at random from the sequence 1 to N. This algorithm also has been rediscovered frequently, and is explained by Knuth (1969). The algorithm appears at first sight to fail to terminate correctly, a fact that no doubt gave rise to the less elegant, but apparently safer, version developed by Pike (1979). The algorithm is convenient, in that the sample of integers is produced in sorted sequence. However, it is inefficient when N is large compared with K, because it always cycles through its loop N times.

The essence of the method is that it keeps up to date the ratio needed / left, where "needed" is the number of integers still needed for the sample and "left" is the number of integers still to be considered in the loop from 1 to N. A random number is produced in each iteration of the loop. If the random number is less than needed / left, the current integer is added to the sample. When the array is empty and the loop begins, it is obvious that the probability of selection of the first integer is correctly equal to needed / left, which is K / N. If the first integer is selected, the probability of selecting the second integer is (K / N) * ((K – 1) / (N – 1)), because "needed" reduces by one and "left" reduces by one. The probability of not selecting the first integer is 1 – (K / N). If the first integer is not selected, the probability of selecting the second integer is (1 – (K / N)) * (K / (N – 1)), because "needed" stays constant, and "left" again reduces by one. The probability of selecting the second element regardless of what happens to the first element is the sum of these two probabilities, which reduces to K / N. Continuing in this manner, it is easy to demonstrate that every integer has the same probability K / N of selection for the sample.

To assure oneself that the process actually works, it is useful to consider what happens in the extreme cases (a) if the sample is completed before N is reached, and (b) if N – k iterations of the loop are completed and exactly k integers are still needed for the sample. In the former case, needed / left = 0 and no further integers are selected. In the latter case needed / left = 1 and every integer is selected.

Random~Set is attributed to R. Floyd by Bentley (1987). The algorithm is more efficient than Random~Sequence, in that its loop is executed only K times rather than N. But it is less efficient when K is relatively large, because the algorithm has to search the current sample every time a new item is selected. This can be overcome by using an array of N marker elements (set to *true* when the corresponding integer is selected for the sample) instead of an array of K integers. Such an array may be inconvenient and may complicate the processing of the sample. Its other disadvantage, that the selection is not a sorted sequence, can be overcome by the use of a sorting algorithm if necessary. The relative efficiencies of the two algorithms are clearly data-dependent and implementation-dependent, and neither can be recommended exclusively.

Random~Set chooses its first item for the sample from the first N – K + 1 integers. Its second item is chosen from the first N – K + 2 integers, and in general its *i*-th choice is from the first N – K + *i* integers. The second and subsequent choices may select a number previously chosen, hence the need to check whether that is the case. If a previously chosen number is selected again, the selection is revised to choose N – K + *i* instead. It is not easily seen that the process selects each integer with equal probability.

Any given integer less than or equal to N – K + 1, say 1, has a probability of selection of 1 / (N – K + 1) in the first iteration. Its probability of not being selected is (N – K) / (N – K + 1). In the second iteration the integer has a probability of selection of 1 / (N – K + 2), if it was not selected in the first iteration. Its net probability of selection in the second iteration is (N – K) / ((N – K + 1) * (N – K + 2)). The total probability for selection of the item in the first two iterations is the sum of the two probabilities, which reduces to 2 / (N – K + 2). The argument extends easily to demonstrate that the probability of selection of any integer less than N – K + 1 in K iterations is K / (N – K + K), which equals the required K / N.

The probability of selection of any integer greater than N – K + 1 in the first iteration is zero. The integer N – K + 2 has its first opportunity to be selected in the second iteration. It is chosen with probability 1 / (N – K + 2) in its own right, or is used as a replacement if the integer selected is the same as the integer chosen in the first iteration. The probability of this occurring is also 1 / (N – K + 2). Thus the total probability of N – K + 2 being selected in the second iteration is the sum of the two probabilities, which equals 2 / (N – K + 2). The argument in the previous paragraph now applies. When it is extended to all iterations, the probability of selection of any item is shown to be K / N.

IMPLEMENTATION

Exported Subprograms

Random~Shuffle	Shuffles the elements of an array (8.2.1)
Random~Sequence	Produces a sorted random selection of integers (8.2.2)
Random~Set	Produces a random selection of integers (8.2.3)

Imported Names

Random~Number	Computes a uniform random number (8.1.1)

Nicknames

Items	Array of items to be shuffled or selected
Lower	Lower limit of elements of array Items
N	Number of items from which selection is to be made
Upper	Upper limit of elements of array Items

Local Names

I, J	Array indexes and loop counters
Random	Uniformly distributed random number

8.2.1 Random~Shuffle (updates Items; receives Lower, Upper)

Pseudo Code

```
for i = first array item to second last item
    generate random number J in the range i to the last item of the array
    swap array items at locations i and J
end for
```

Code

```
procedure Random~Shuffle (Items is array of integers, Lower, Upper are integers)
    variable Random is real
    variable J is integer
    for i = Lower to Upper – 1
        call Random~Number (Random)
        let J = truncate (Random * (Upper – i + 1))
        call swap (Items[i], Items[Lower+J])
    end for
end Random~Shuffle
```

8.1.2 Random~Sequence (updates Items; receives Lower, Upper, N)

Pseudo Code

```
let I = 0
loop until needed = 0
    let I = I + 1
    generate random number Random
    if Random < needed/left then
        add I to the sample
    end if
end loop
```

Code

```
procedure Random~Sequence (Items is array of integers, Lower, Upper, N are
        integers)
    variable Random is real
    variables I, J are integers
```

```
        let I = 0
        let J = Lower
        loop until J > Upper
            let I = I + 1
            call Random~Number (Random)
            if ((N – I + 1) * Random) < (Upper – J + 1) then
                let Items[J] = I
                let J = J + 1
            end if
        end loop
    end Random~Sequence
```

8.1.3 Random~Set (updates Items; receives Lower, Upper, N)

Pseudo Code

```
    for i = (N – K + 1) to N
        choose random integer J in the range 1 to i for possible inclusion in sample
        if J is already in sample then
            include i in the sample
        else
            include J in the sample
        end if
    end for
```

Code

```
    procedure Random~Set (Items is array of integers, Lower, Upper, N are integers)
        variable Random is real
        variables J, M are integers
        for i = (N – Upper + Lower) to N
            let M = Upper + i – N
            call Random~Number (Random)
            let Items[M] = truncate (Random * i) + 1
            let J = Lower
            loop until Items[J] = Items[M]
                let J = J + 1
            end loop
            if J ≠ M then
                let Items[M] = i
            end if
        end for
    end Random~Set
```

TEST PROGRAM

Imported Names

Random~Initialize	Initializes uniform random number generator (8.1.1b)

Local Subprograms

Clear	Clears totals in array T
Chi~Squared	Calculates deviation of observed distribution from expected

Local Names

Deviation	Measure of deviation of observed distribution from expected
Difference	Difference between observed and expected counts
Expected	The count expected on average in every element of T
Items	Array of integers to contain random sample
L	Lower bound of array Items
N	Size of population from which sample is selected
T	Array of counts of usage of each integer in sample
U	Upper bound of array Items

Pseudo Code

```
clear array of total frequencies
generate 100 random sets of 10 integers using Random~Set
accumulate frequencies of each possible integer
perform chi-squared test to check for uniform distribution
clear array of total frequencies
generate 100 random sets of 10 integers in sorted sequence using
        Random~Sequence
accumulate frequencies of each possible integer
perform chi-squared test to check for uniform distribution
clear array of total frequencies
generate an array of integers
shuffle the array 100 times using Random~Shuffle
accumulate frequencies for each possible integer position
perform chi-squared test to check for uniform distribution
```

Code

```
constant L = 1, U = 10, N = 100
variable Items is array L to U of integers
variable T is array 1 to N of integers
call Random~Initialize (maxinteger – 1)
call Clear
for k = 1 to N
    call Random~Set (Items, L, U, N)
    for i = L to U
        let T[Items[i]] = T[Items[i]] + 1
    end for
end for
check Chi~Squared ( ) < N + (4.66 * square~root (N – 1)) + 5.57
call Clear
for k = 1 to N
    call Random~Sequence (Items, L, U, N)
    for i = L to U
        let T[Items[i]] = T[Items[i]] + 1
    end for
end for
check Chi~Squared ( ) < N + (4.66 * square~root (N – 1)) + 5.57
```

```
call Clear
for i = L to U
    let Items[i] = i
end for
for k = 1 to N
    call Random~Shuffle (Items, L, U)
    for i = L to U
        let T[Items[i]] = T[Items[i]] + 1
    end for
end for
check Chi~Squared ( ) < N + (4.66 * square~root (N – 1)) + 5.57
```

Local **Clear**

```
procedure Clear
    for i = 1 to N
        let T[i] = 0
    end for
end Clear
```

Local **Chi~Squared** (*result real*)

```
function Chi~Squared ( ) is real
    variables Deviation, Difference, Expected are real
    let Expected = U – L + 1
    let Deviation = 0
    for i = 1 to N
        let Difference = T[i] – Expected
        let Deviation = Deviation + (Difference * Difference / Expected)
    end for
    result Deviation
end Chi~Squared
```

9 Finance

According to Timothy, the love of money is the root of all evil. It is not surprising, then, that this chapter makes considerable use of an algorithm for finding the root of equations involving money. Seriously, though, this chapter provides several important algorithms at the root of much of the world of finance.

There is probably a greater variety of accounting packages on the market than any other category of software, including word processors. Such packages range from very simple, costing about a day's wages, to extremely sophisticated, costing a thousand times as much or more. The aim of all such packages is to keep track of what a person or an organization does with its money. At the heart of even the most complex accounting software is an algorithm known as double-entry bookkeeping. In Section 9.1 you will find the simplest implementation of the algorithm we could devise. Editing is assumed to be carried out using a word processor with data presented in the easiest form possible. The double-entry program produces a balance sheet (statement of what the enterprise owns and owes) and an income statement (summary of the components of the profit or loss made by the enterprise) with as little code as we could get away with.

The effects of compound interest and inflation over a period of years are not easy to assess intuitively, unless you have a background in finance. Ordinary people are usually shocked when they calculate how much interest is paid over the life of a house mortgage loan. Some people will put money into savings accounts for many years, pay tax on the interest, and realize far too late that their nest egg has all but evaporated because of inflation. The long-term effects of interest rates and inflation can be quite dramatic. Estimating just how good is an investment can be difficult, particularly when there are cash inflows and outflows over a number of months or years.

The best general method for assessing loans and cash flows is to use a spreadsheet program. Spreadsheets usually have a number of facilities specifically tailored to financial calculations. For example, the one on my desk allows me to compute future values, internal rates of return, net present values, and the relationships between typical loan parameters such as repayments, interest rate, period, and principal.

It is not always convenient to use a spreadsheet, particularly when the calculations form part of another program. For this reason Section 9.2 contains a set of important algorithms involving interest rates, which enable you to compute one parameter of a loan proposition given the other parameters. Section 9.3 deals with the evaluation of a cash flow over a number of periods, calculating useful measures such as the net present value and the internal rate of return.

Sections 9.2 and 9.3 make use of the algorithm in Section 9.4 for computing a "root" of a function. The algorithm is a basic mathematical tool that has wide application. For example, it is used for computing the internal rate of return on a cash flow. Suppose CF is an array containing the net cash in each period. The internal rate of return is the value of the interest rate R for which Net~Present~Value (CF, R) = 0. This value of R is called a "root" of the equation.

9.1 FINANCIAL STATEMENTS

Efficiently generating a balance sheet and income statement

Example

See the input and output files in the following implementation for a specific example of the books of account for an enterprise.

Subprograms

9.1.1 Financial~Statements (receives AccountFile, NewFile, TransactionFile; disk input-output)

Usage

If you are not familiar with the elements of bookkeeping you should familiarize yourself with the detailed explanation in the notes following this section.

Two files are input to the procedure and one file is output. The input files consist of AccountFile, the account codes and associated balances, and TransactionFile, the financial transactions for the period. A file NewFile, of updated account balances, is output by the procedure. In addition, the net worth and net profit are calculated. The input files may be produced using any word processor compatible with the language in which the procedure is written.

The sequencing of the accounts is important. It is assumed that asset and liability accounts precede income and expense accounts. Asset and liability accounts may be intermingled among themselves. The distinction between assets and liabilities is determined purely by the signs of the balances. Similarly, income and expense accounts need not be in any sorted sequence. The distinction between income and expenses is also determined by the signs of the balances. Note that income balances are shown as negative and expense account balances as positive. The net profit has the correct sign, a profit being positive and a loss being negative.

A pseudoaccount "Net-Worth" must follow the asset and liability accounts. A pseudoaccount "Net-Profit" must follow the income and expense accounts. These two pseudoaccounts are used as delimiters, and to contain the totals corresponding to their names. An account with a name such as "Errors" must be at the end to catch any transactions with invalid account codes. The account codes may be chosen to suit the user. The program does not make use of the description in each transaction. Only the debit and credit account codes, and the transaction amount are processed. The left (right) hand account in every transaction is the debit (credit) account code.

Most elementary accounting textbooks and introductory books on bookkeeping for businesspeople will provide further useful information about double-entry bookkeeping. However, traditional texts such as Sheff (1938) were oriented toward manual bookkeeping and tend to obscure the intrinsic simplicity and elegance of the double-entry algorithm.

Analysis

The program ensures that the accounting invariant is preserved by requiring that each transaction contain just three components: the accounts to be debited and credited, and the transaction amount. Every debit is accompanied by a matching credit and so the "balance" is always preserved.

IMPLEMENTATION

Exported Names

Financial~Statements	Produces financial statements (9.1.1)

Local Subprograms

Search	Finds a specified account code in the array of account codes

Nicknames

AccountFile	Integer containing the file number for the file of accounts
Accounts	Array of account codes
Code	An account code to be searched for in the array of account codes
N	Number of accounts
NewFile	Integer containing the file number for the updated file of accounts
TransactionFile	Integer containing the file number for the transactions

Local Names

Accounts	Array of account codes
Amount	Dollar value of a transaction
Balance	Array of current balances corresponding to Accounts array
Credit	Account code for crediting transaction amount
Debit	Account code for debiting transaction amount
J, K	Array indexes
MaxAccounts	Maximum number of accounts
N	Number of accounts

9.1.1 Financial~Statements (receives AccountFile, NewFile, TransactionFile, disk input-output)

Pseudo Code

```
read existing accounts and balances
loop until there are no more transactions
    input next transaction
    find debit code in account array
    add transaction amount to account balance
    find credit code in account array
    subtract transaction amount from account balance
end loop
initialize pseudoaccount "Net-Worth" balance to zero
loop until "Net-Worth" is reached
    select next account
    add account balance to "Net-Worth" balance
    output account code and balance to new accounts file
end loop
output "Net-Worth" code and balance
initialize pseudoaccount "Net-Profit" balance to zero
loop until "Net-Profit" is reached
    select next account
    add account balance to "Net-Profit" balance
    output account code and balance to new accounts file
end loop
output "Net-Profit" code and balance
output "Errors" code and balance to capture any transaction account codes not
        recognized
```

Code

```
procedure Financial~Statements (AccountFile, NewFile, TransactionFile are
        integers)
    constant MaxAccounts = 100
    variable Accounts is array 1 to MaxAccounts of text
    variable Balance is array 1 to MaxAccounts of real
    variables Debit, Credit are text
    variables J, K, N are integers
    variable Amount is real
    let N = 0
    input from AccountFile into Accounts[N+1], Balance[N+1]        Input account
    loop until end~of~file (AccountFile)                          codes and
        let N = N + 1                                             balances
        input from AccountFile into Accounts[N+1], Balance[N+1]
    end loop
    input from TransactionFile into Debit, Credit, Amount      Input transactions
    loop until end~of~file (TransactionFile)                   and update account
        let K = Search (Accounts, N, Debit)                    balances
        let Balance[K] = Balance[K] + Amount
        let K = Search (Accounts, N, Credit)
        let Balance[K] = Balance[K] – Amount
        input from TransactionFile into Debit, Credit, Amount
    end loop
```

```
    let K = Search (Accounts, N, "Net-Worth")
    let Balance[K] = 0
    for i = 1 to (K – 1)                                        Output asset and
        let Balance[K] = Balance[K] + Balance[i]                liability account codes
        output into NewFile from Accounts[i], Balance[i]        and balances
    end for
    output into NewFile from Accounts[K], Balance[K]
    let J = K
    let K = Search (Accounts, N, "Net-Profit")
    let Balance[K] = 0
    for i = (J + 1) to (K – 1)                                  Output income and
        let Balance[K] = Balance[K] – Balance[i]                expense account codes
        output into NewFile from Accounts[i], Balance[i]        and balances
    end for
    output into NewFile from Accounts[K], Balance[K]
    output into NewFile from Accounts[K+1], Balance[K+1]
  end Financial~Statements
```

```
Local Search (receives Accounts, N, Code; result integer)
  function Search (Accounts is array of text, N is integer, Code is text) is integer
    variable Location is integer
    let Location = 1                                            Find account code in
    loop until Code = Accounts[Location] or Location = N        array of account
        let Location = Location + 1                             codes
    end loop
    result Location
  end Search
```

TEST PROGRAM

Local Names

- AF File number for existing account file
- NF File number for new account file
- TF File number for transaction file

Pseudo Code

```
  open the three files
  call Financial~Statements
```

Code

```
  variables AF, NF, TF are integers
  open AF file "Accounts"                                 Open files
  open TF file "Transactions"
  create NF file "New Accounts"
  call Financial~Statements (AF, NF, TF)
```

Accounts

Cash	350.00	Asset accounts
Debtors	250.00	
Equipment	0.00	
Amex	–120.00	Liability accounts
Creditors	0.00	
Loan	0.00	
Tax	0.00	
Net-Worth	480.00	Balance sheet net worth
Sales	0.00	Income accounts
Interest	0.00	
Materials	0.00	Expense accounts
Running	0.00	
Wages	0.00	
Net-Profit	0.00	Income statement net profit
Errors	0.00	

Transactions

Cash	Loan	2000.00	July 1, Loan to business
Materials	Cash	787.50	July 1, Purchase raw materials
Running	Cash	83.00	July 3, Insurance
Amex	Cash	120.00	July 3, Pay credit card balance
Debtors	Sales	300.00	July 4, Credit sale to XYZ Company
Debtors	Tax	60.00	July 4, Sales tax on sale to XYZ Company
Cash	Sales	500.00	July 5, Cash sale, tax exempt
Cash	Debtors	250.00	July 5, Payment of debt by ABC Inc.
Running	Cash	88.00	July 8, Telephone bill
Equipment	Amex	815.00	July 11, Purchase press by credit card
Debtors	Sales	900.00	July 12, Sale to ABC Company
Debtors	Tax	150.00	July 12, Sales tax on sale to ABC Company
Materials	Cash	850.00	July 19, Purchase raw materials
Cash	Debtors	360.00	July 22, Payment of debt by XYZ Company
Wages	Cash	750.00	July 26, Casual help
Amex	Cash	400.00	July 29, Part pay credit card
Cash	Debtors	1050.00	July 29, Payment of debt by ABC Inc.
Cash	Sales	1200.00	July 29, Cash sale
Cash	Tax	240.00	July 29, Tax on cash sale
Cash	Interest	37.50	July 30, Bank interest
Cash	Sales	1500.00	July 30, Cash sale, tax exempt
Tax	Cash	450.00	July 30, Pay sales tax office

New Accounts

Cash	3959.00
Debtors	0.00
Equipment	815.00
Amex	–415.00
Creditors	0.00

Loan	–2000.00
Tax	0.00
Net-Worth	2359.00
Sales	–4400.00
Interest	–37.50
Materials	1637.50
Running	171.00
Wages	750.00
Net-Profit	1879.00
Errors	0.00

NOTES—GENERAL LEDGER

Keeping the books of account for an enterprise

Double-entry bookkeeping is an ancient procedure for keeping track of the financial state of an enterprise. Before the widespread use of computers, most businesses had a "bookkeeper", whose job was to record all the financial transactions of a business enterprise in "journals", and to summarize them in "ledgers". There was considerable pride in producing these books, which were not infrequently leather-bound and filled with exceptionally neatly handwritten entries. At the end of each week, month, or year the bookkeeper would produce a "trial balance" to prove that transactions had been correctly entered. Computer technology has brought about the demise of physical journals and ledgers, although the terms have survived to describe similar computer-based records of financial information.

The basic principles of double-entry bookkeeping are simple to understand. The financial records of a business are called the "books of account". Let's look at the fundamental concepts of bookkeeping before discussing the procedure for keeping the books up to date. The most basic concept is that of the "transaction". Anything a business enterprise does relating to money must be recorded in the books of account. The record of any particular event is called a transaction. Examples of transactions include paying bills, sending invoices, purchasing goods by credit card, lending or borrowing money, allowing for wear and tear of assets (called "depreciation"), and so on. In the past, lists of transactions were written up in journals. Nowadays transactions can be listed using a word processor or a spreadsheet program.

Every transaction refers to categories of money called "accounts". In everyday language we have become used to talking about checking accounts, expense accounts, and credit card accounts. For bookkeeping purposes accounts include all of these, but also all other categories of money useful to the business enterprise. There is an element of choice in deciding which categories of money to use. For convenience, accounts are typically grouped under subheadings and major headings. In a very large organization there may be several levels of headings and subheadings. In a very small business there may be no subheadings at all. The point is that a business needs to keep track of the balance (amount of money at a given time) of each account. The "general ledger" is the mechanism for keeping these account balances, and the algorithm for maintaining it is described above.

There are four major account groups in the ledger. These are universally adopted, and every bookkeeper must understand them. Two of the account groups are called "assets" and "liabilities". Assets are what the enterprise owns and liabilities are what it owes. For example, cash, equipment, real estate, and debts owed to it are all assets. A business might usefully have asset accounts such as a cash account, an equipment account, a real estate account, and a debtors account. Liabilities might be recorded in a mortgage account, a credit card account, and a bills payable or creditors account.

The net worth of a business at any point in time is the difference between its total assets and total liabilities. Some transactions will affect assets and some will affect liabilities. As the transactions are recorded over time the net worth of the business will increase or decrease. Increases or decreases in assets will cause increases or decreases in net worth respectively. Increases or decreases in liabilities will cause decreases or increases in net worth respectively.

The other two major groups of accounts are "income" and "expenditure", or "revenue" and "expenses". The terms used to describe these groups are not completely standardized. In fact, it would be better if the groups were called "production" and "consumption", to reflect more accurately the purposes of the two groups of accounts. Whatever the enterprise produces is recorded in a production or income account. Examples include sales of goods and services, interest on money in the bank, and reimbursement of expenses incurred on behalf of someone else. Whatever the enterprise consumes is recorded in a consumption or expense account. Examples include payments for electricity, telephone, postage, raw materials, wages, and tax.

If the enterprise produces more than it consumes, it makes a "profit", and if it consumes more than it produces, it makes a "loss". The difference between production and consumption, or income and expenses, measures the profit or loss made by the business. Any profit or loss affects the net worth of the business. If there is a profit, the net worth increases; if there is a loss, it decreases. The fundamental principle of double-entry bookkeeping is that the change in net worth from one point in time to another is always equal to the difference between the production and consumption over that period of time. The method of bookkeeping ensures that the principle is never violated. Books of account may be inspected at any time, and it will always be true that the profit or loss in any period of time is equal to both the change in net worth and the difference between income and expenses.

This is achieved by the "double-entry" part of bookkeeping. Every transaction affects at least two accounts, and the net effect is always zero. That is, every transaction must always "balance". The increase or decrease in net worth caused by a transaction must always be exactly matched by an identical increase or decrease in the difference between income and expenses. Let's see how this operates in practice.

You lend your business $2,000 as working capital. The cash asset of the business has increased to $2,000. At the same time the business has incurred a liability. It owes you $2,000. This particular transaction affects assets and liabilities, but not income or expenses. The change to assets minus the change to liabilities is $2,000 – $2,000, which is zero, and so the transaction balances.

Now suppose you buy raw materials to be used for the goods you will be selling. The business pays $787.50 for the raw materials. This reduces the cash asset of the business, and hence the net worth, by $787.50. This must be reflected by a similar decrease in the difference between income and expenses. The transaction is recorded as increasing an expense account for raw materials by $787.50. Once again the transaction balances.

The example may be continued in this way, adding more transactions. The transaction file in the above implementation shows how the financial activity of the business over one month might look. At the beginning of the month there was $350 in the bank and the business was owed $250 for previous work done. It also owed $120 on its credit card. The net worth of the business was therefore $350 + $250 – $120, or $480. At the end of the month the business had made a profit of $1,879 and its net worth had increased to $2,359. The change in net worth, from $480 to $2,359, is $1,879, which equals the profit of $1,879, as it should.

You may like to see the above discussion recast in more formal language. The net worth of an enterprise at a point in time is the sum of its assets minus the sum of its liabilities, or A – L. During any accounting period the profit or loss the enterprise makes is equal to the sum of its income minus expenses, I – E. The fundamental concept in accounting is that a change in profit is mirrored by an equal change in net worth. In other words, the accounting "invariant" can be expressed as A – L = I – E. Every transaction must preserve this invariant, which is written in the more convenient but equivalent form A – L – I + E = 0.

Positive and negative signs are typically not used as such by accountants. The terms "debit" and "credit" are used instead, and have been used for hundreds of years. The A and E accounts that have positive signs in the invariant are called "debit" accounts, and the L and I accounts are called "credit" accounts. In the computer, debit figures are kept as positive numbers and credit figures as negative numbers.

Acquisition of an asset is "debited" to an asset account. That is, it is added to the total for that account. The incurring of a liability is recorded by "crediting" the amount to a liability account. That is, the amount is subtracted from the total for that account, creating a negative total. Sale of an asset is credited to an asset account, the amount being subtracted from the account total. Paying out a liability is recorded by debiting a liability account, the amount being added to the negative account total, reducing its magnitude.

Because of the signs in the accounting invariant, income is credited to an income account, and expenses are debited to a debit account. It seems strange that income should be recorded as a negative figure, and expenses as a positive figure, but this ensures that the accounting invariant can be preserved with respect to every transaction. To make this easier to understand, the explanation is usually given that debit accounts record what comes in to the enterprise, and credit accounts record what goes out. For example, sales go out and cash comes in. Therefore, sales is a credit account with a negative total and cash on hand is a debit account with a positive total.

The displaying of account totals with negative signs will be seen as an abomination by accountants. A more accountant-friendly approach is to use two columns for the account balances. The left-hand column should contain debit (positive) balances and the right-hand column should contain credit (negative) balances with negative signs removed. Dropping the negative signs also makes the report easier for the nonspecialist to understand, although the novice will wonder why the income and expense totals appear in their particular columns. The new account balances from our example should be displayed as follows:

Cash	3959.00		Balance sheet, or statement of net worth
Debtors	0.00		
Equipment	815.00		
Amex		415.00	
Creditors		0.00	
Loan		2000.00	
Tax		0.00	
Net-Worth	2359.00		
Sales		4400.00	Income statement, or profit and loss statement
Interest		37.50	
Materials	1637.50		
Running	171.00		
Wages	750.00		
Net-Profit		1879.00	

Now that manual bookkeeping has been replaced by computer processing the distinction between debit and credit accounts is not strictly necessary, although accounting traditions die hard. The important distinction is between the net worth accounts and the net profit accounts. Assets and liabilities can be distinguished among themselves by the signs of their balances. If the account balance is positive, the enterprise owns something, and if it is negative, the enterprise owes something. Similarly, there is no need for a distinction between income and expense accounts.

9.2 CASH FLOW

Calculating internal rates of return and net present values

Example

The effective interest rate (16.25%) earned on an investment of $800 that returns $500 in a year's time and another $500 a year later is calculated by:

variable Cash *is array* 0 *to* 2 *of real*
let Cash[0] = –800
let Cash[1] = 500
let Cash[2] = 500
output Internal~Return~Rate (Cash, 2)

Subprograms

9.2.1 Net~Present~Value (receives Cash, Periods, Rate; *result real*)
9.2.2 Internal~Return~Rate (receives Cash, Periods; *result real*)

Usage

The internal rate of return is the effective interest rate earned on an investment. The net present value of a cash flow is the sum of the net cash figures in each period, with each being "discounted" at a specified interest rate per period. The relationship between the two measures is quite straightforward. In the above example, the net present value of $500 received next year and the year after, using the internal rate of return as the interest rate, is $800.

Consider a typical case, such as purchase of an investment property. The cash flow is specified in the array with nickname Cash, each array element corresponding to a time period. The initial investment is made at time 0. The net cash inflow or outflow at the end of each period is specified in successive array elements, with the expected sale price of the investment in the last period. There is therefore one more array element than there are periods. The internal rate of return is calculated by Internal~Return~Rate. If you want to calculate the net present value using interest rates supplied by you, use the function Net~Present~Value.

Take care with unusual cash flows. The normal pattern with an investment is to pay for it in year zero, to have annual expenses or income that are small compared with the size of the investment itself, and then to sell it at some future time. Such a pattern will give a unique and meaningful internal rate of return. However, if there are large negative figures in later periods interspersed with positive figures at earlier times, it is sometimes possible for there to be multiple solutions to the problem, and hence any calculated internal rate of return will be meaningless.

The subprograms do not assume that the periods for analysis are years. Any convenient period such as weeks, months, or years may be assumed. Remember that the interest rate or internal rate of return is calculated on the same basis. For example, if you use months, the internal rate of return will be the effective interest rate per month, and the rate of interest used for calculating the net present value must be a monthly rather than a yearly figure.

Internal~Return~Rate calls the Function~Root subprogram (Section 9.4), which has to be supplied with the name of the function that computes the net present value for any interest rate. Function~Root is a general algorithm that assumes that only the independent variable, typically thought of as the X value, needs to be supplied to the function in order to calculate the net present value, or Y value. In fact X, or R in this case, is insufficient, because the cash flow and number of periods are also required. To preserve the generality of Function~Root, an Evaluate subprogram is defined in Internal~Return~Rate. Evaluate takes just one argument, the X value, and is the function supplied to Function~Root. Evaluate calls Net~Present~Value as its only useful task.

It is difficult to define Evaluate simply, so that it can easily be implemented in most programming languages. The simplest possible presentation is given, which will be easier to implement in C or Pascal than Basic or Cobol. The Evaluate function is defined inside the code that defines Internal~Return~Rate. The code will be more complicated in languages that do not permit functions to be defined inside functions. Some versions of Fortran that do not enforce the restrictions of ANSI X3.9 or ISO 1539 will permit Evaluate to be defined as a statement function within the code for Internal~Return~Rate.

Analysis

The algorithms use compound interest formulas. It is assumed that the compounding takes place at the end of each period. Very different results may be obtained by changing the time periods used. In the example given earlier, suppose the financial returns consisted of $250 in each half year instead of $500 per year. The internal rate of return becomes 9.56% per six months, which is equivalent to 20% per annum compound. The internal rate of return is higher when returns are received six monthly, because the investment is recovered sooner on average. The money is outstanding for an average of 18 months in the yearly case and 15 months in the half-yearly case.

Suppose the interest rate used in computing the net present value of a cash flow is in variable R, expressed as a fraction rather than as a percentage. One dollar invested at that interest rate will be worth 1 + R dollars at the end of the next period, $(1 + R)^2$ after two periods, and $(1 + R)^N$ after N periods. Another way of saying it is that to receive one dollar at the end of one period you have to invest $1 / (1 + R)$ dollars at time 0. To receive one dollar at the end of N periods you need to invest $1 / (1 + R)^N$ dollars at time 0. Thus the net present value of one dollar obtained after N periods is $1 / (1 + R)^N$ dollars. The net present value of a cash flow is obtained by summing for each value of N the net cash at period N multiplied by $1 / (1 + R)^N$.

With regard to the internal rate of return, you have exactly the same logic as for the net present value, except that the value of R is unknown. The algorithm operates by trying various values of R until the one is found that makes the net present value of the entire cash flow, including the initial investment, zero. This is equivalent to finding the interest rate that makes the net present value of all cash inflow and outflow after time 0 become equal to the initial investment at time 0. The Function~Root algorithm is used to find the unknown value of R using a systematic method.

Function~Root is supplied with two "bounds" for R, being values of R known to give net present values with opposite signs. The initial estimates for R are calculated in a loop that considers increasingly large intervals. The internal rate of return for a non-pathological cash flow, including almost all cash flows likely to be analyzed in practice, will be greater than –1. The algorithm tests whether $R_1 = 0$ and $R_2 = 1$ give net present values on either side of zero. For almost all practical uses of the algorithm these values will turn out to be satisfactory, R_1 giving a positive net present value and R_2 giving a negative figure. If not, the distance between R_1 and –1 is halved, and the value of R_2 doubled. This process is iterated until a suitable range is found. The algorithm terminates without a result in pathological cases.

IMPLEMENTATION

Exported Names
- Net~Present~Value — Computes the net present value of a cash flow (9.2.1)
- Internal~Return~Rate — Calculates the internal rate of return of a cash flow (9.2.2)

Imported Names
- Function~Root — Computes a "root" of a specified function (9.4.1)
- Similarity~Test — Tests the similarity of two numbers (2.3.2)

Local Subprograms
- Evaluate — Calculates net present value

Nicknames
- Cash — Array of net cash inflows
- Periods — Number of periods
- Rate — Rate of interest per period

Local Names
- Discount — Factor by which amount of money is discounted (divided)
- Lower — Lower initial estimate for internal rate of return
- Sum — Total of monetary amounts
- Upper — Upper initial estimate for internal rate of return

9.2.1 Net~Present~Value (receives Cash, Periods, Rate; *result real*)

Pseudo Code

```
initialize total and discount factor
sum the discounted elements of the Cash array
result is the discounted sum
```

Code

```
function Net~Present~Value (Cash is array of real, Periods is integer, Rate is real)
        is real
    variables Discount, Sum are real
```

```
        let Sum = 0.0
        let Discount = 1.0
        for i = 0 to Periods
            let Sum = Sum + (Cash[i] / Discount)
            let Discount = Discount * (1 + Rate)
        end for
        result Sum
    end Net~Present~Value
```

9.2.2 Internal~Return~Rate (receives Cash, Periods; *result real*)

Pseudo Code

```
    initialize Lower and Upper bounds for R to 0 and 1 respectively
    loop until net present value for Lower has the opposite sign to the net present value
            for Upper
        let Lower = value halfway between Lower and –1
        let Upper = Upper * 2
    end loop
    result is the root of the net present value function
```

Code

```
    function Internal~Return~Rate (Cash is array of real, Periods is integer) is real
        function Evaluate (Rate is real) is real
            result Net~Present~Value (Cash, Periods, Rate)
        end Evaluate
        variables Lower, Upper are real
        let Lower = 0
        let Upper = 1
        loop until sign (Evaluate (Lower)) ≠ sign (Evaluate (Upper))
            let Lower = (Lower – 1) / 2
            let Upper = Upper * 2
            check Similarity~Test (Lower, –1, 1) = false
        end loop
        result Function~Root (Evaluate, Lower, Upper)
    end Internal~Return~Rate
```

TEST PROGRAM

<u>Imported Names</u>

Similarity~Test	Tests the similarity of two numbers (2.3.2)

<u>Local Names</u>

C	Array of net cash inflows
M	Maximum number of periods
R	Interest rate
V	Value of net present value

Pseudo Code

```
initialize initial investment to M
for i = 1 to M
    initialize financial return in year i to i
    calculate R as internal rate of return for periods 0 to i
    calculate V as net present value of cash flow using interest rate R
    check calculated net present value is close to zero
end for
```

Code

```
constant M = 10
variable C is array 0 to M of real
variables R, V are real
let C[0] = –M
for i = 1 to M
    let C[i] = i
    let R = Internal~Return~Rate (C, i)
    let V = Net~Present~Value (C, i, R)
    check Similarity~Test (V, 0, 1) = true
end for
```

9.3 LOANS

Determining interest rates, terms, and repayments of loans

Example

Suppose a loan of $100,000 is taken out over 10 years at 15% interest. The monthly repayments are calculated by:

```
output 100000 / Loan~Annuity (0.15 / 12, 10 * 12)
```

Subprograms

9.3.1 Loan~Annuity (receives Rate, Periods; *result real*)
9.3.2 Loan~Periods (receives Instalment, Rate; *result real*)
9.3.3 Loan~Rate (receives Instalment, Periods; *result real*)

Usage

The fundamental concept required for loan calculations is the "annuity". Broadly speaking, an annuity is thought of as a payment one makes to an insurance company in return for specified regular payments in the future. You need to think in terms of annuities that are calculated as the number of dollars loaned now equivalent to instalments of $1 per period for a specified number of periods at a specified interest rate. For example, $5 will last 10 years if invested at 15% and withdrawn in yearly amounts of $1. Any principal amount other than $1 can be applied to the annuity formula by scaling up; for example, $5,000 will last 10 years at 15% with yearly instalments of $1,000. Loan~Annuity calculates the annuity value from the interest rate and number of periods.

There is a simple relationship between the repayments for a loan and the principal amount that is borrowed. The periodic repayment is equal to the principal divided by the annuity. Switching the equation around you can determine the amount that can be borrowed if the repayment figure is given. The principal is equal to the repayment multiplied by the annuity.

The example at the beginning of this section makes use of the annuity calculation. Note that any convenient period, such as week, month, or year, may be used. However, all figures will be assumed to be calculated with respect to the same period. For example, if a monthly repayment is used, the interest rate must be per month and the number of periods must be months.

Sometimes you know how much you have to borrow and at what interest rate, and you want to determine how long it will take to pay off the loan given a specific repayment. The number of periods is calculated by Loan~Periods. This function is supplied with the interest rate and the ratio of the repayment to the principal.

In other circumstances, such as when you are offered a deal by a finance company, you know the principal, the repayments, and the period of the loan but not the effective interest rate. Loan~Rate calculates the rate from the number of periods and the ratio of the repayment to the principal.

Loan~Rate calls the Function~Root subprogram (Section 9.4), which has to be supplied with the name of the function that computes the annuity for any interest rate. Function~Root is a general algorithm that assumes that only the independent variable, typically thought of as the X value, needs to be supplied to the function in order to calculate the annuity, or Y value. In fact X, or R in this case, is insufficient, because the number of periods is also required. To preserve the generality of Function~Root, a Residual subprogram is defined in Loan~Rate. Residual takes just one argument, the X value, and is the function supplied to Function~Root. Residual calls Loan~Annuity as its primary useful task.

It is difficult to define Residual simply, so that it can easily be implemented in most programming languages. The simplest possible presentation is given here, which will be easier to implement in C or Pascal than Basic or Cobol. The Residual function is defined inside the code that defines Loan~Rate. The code will be more complicated in languages that do not permit functions to be defined inside functions. Some versions of Fortran that do not enforce the restrictions of ANSI X3.9 or ISO 1539 will permit Residual to be defined as a statement function within the code for Loan~Rate.

Analysis

To see how the annuity calculation works, let us start with a principal amount P, periodic instalments I, and an interest rate R. At the end of the first period the principal has grown to $P * (1 + R)$, where R is expressed as a fraction and not as a percentage. The instalment is deducted, leaving a residual amount of $P * (1 + R) - I$. At the end of the second period you add the interest and deduct the instalment, giving a residual amount of $(P * (1 + R) - I) * (1 + R) - I$, which is equivalent to $(P * (1 + R)^2) - (I * (1 + (1 + R)))$. This type of calculation is repeated, so that after N periods the residual is $(P * (1 + R)^N) - (I * (1 + (1 + R) + \ldots + (1 + R)^{N-1}))$. Setting this equal to zero and rearranging terms, you find that P/I is equal to the value calculated by Loan~Annuity, or $((1 + R)^N - 1) / (R * (1 + R)^N)$. Thus if you deal with the ratio of the instalment to the principal, you have a formula that involves only the interest rate and the number of periods.

Suppose the annuity value and interest rate are known and you want to find the number of periods. You need to determine the value of N that makes the annuity formula $((1 + R)^N - 1) / (R * (1 + R)^N)$ produce the known annuity value. Some high-school algebra is required to rearrange the formula so that N can be calculated as is done by Loan~Periods.

When the interest rate is very close to zero, the calculation involves dividing two quantities that are nearly zero, and so the accuracy of the result diminishes. The formula simply will not work when the interest rate is equal to zero. A similar problem arises in the annuity calculation itself. To deal with all these cases, simpler calculations are carried out when the interest rate is close to zero. They rely on the fact that the regular repayment on a loan at a zero interest rate is just the principal amount divided by the number of periods.

Now consider the case when the interest rate is unknown. Again, you use the annuity formula. You want to know what interest rate R will make $((1 + R)^N - 1) / (R * (1 + R)^N)$ equal to the known annuity amount, given a known number of periods N. The formula is impossible to unravel using algebra, and you have to resort to a trial-and-error method. The algorithm operates by trying various values of R until the one is found that produces the correct annuity figure. The Function~Root algorithm is used to find the unknown value of R using a systematic method.

Function~Root is supplied with two "bounds" for R, being values of R known to give annuity values above and below the known amount. The initial estimates for R are calculated in a loop that considers increasingly large intervals. The rate of interest must be greater than –1 to make any sense. The algorithm tests whether $R_1 = 0$ and $R_2 = 1$ give annuity values on either side of the known figure. For almost all practical uses of the algorithm these values will turn out to be satisfactory. If not, the distance between R_1 and –1 is halved, and the value of R_2 doubled. This process is iterated until a suitable range is found. The algorithm terminates without a result in pathological cases.

IMPLEMENTATION

Exported Names

Loan~Annuity	Calculates an annuity for an interest rate and time period (9.3.1)
Loan~Periods	Calculates the number of periods required to repay a loan (9.3.2)
Loan~Rate	Calculates the effective interest rate on a loan (9.3.3)

Imported Names

Function~Root	Computes a "root" of a specified function (9.4.1)
Similarity~Test	Tests the similarity of two numbers (2.3.2)

Local Subprograms

Residual	Calculates the difference between known and calculated annuities

Nicknames

Instalment	Ratio of loan repayment to principal amount
Periods	Number of periods
Rate	Rate of interest per period

Local Names

Difference	Excess of (ratio of repayment to principal amount) over interest rate

Discount	Interest compounded over specified number of periods
Lower	Lower initial estimate for interest rate
Upper	Upper initial estimate for interest rate

9.3.1 Loan~Annuity (receives Rate, Periods; *result real*)

Pseudo Code

```
if interest rate is close to zero then
    result is the number of periods
else
    result is value determined by the annuity formula
end if
```

Code

```
function Loan~Annuity (Rate, Periods are real) is real
    variable Discount is real
    check Rate > –1
    if Similarity~Test (Rate, 0, 1) = true then
        result Periods
    else
        let Discount = power (1 + Rate, Periods)
        result (Discount – 1) / (Discount * Rate)
    end if
end Loan~Annuity
```

9.3.2 Loan~Periods (receives Instalment, Rate; *result real*)

Pseudo Code

```
if interest rate is zero then
    result is inverse of difference between instalment rate and interest rate
else
    result is value determined from the formula
end if
```

Code

```
function Loan~Periods (Instalment, Rate are real) is real
    variable Difference is real
    let Difference = Instalment – Rate
    check Difference > 0
    if Similarity~Test (Rate, 0, 1) = true then
        result 1 / Difference
    else
        result log_e (Instalment / Difference) / log_e (1 + Rate)
    end if
end Loan~Periods
```

9.3.3 Loan~Rate (receives Instalment, Periods; *result real*)

Pseudo Code

```
initialize Lower and Upper bounds for R to 0 and 1 respectively
loop until annuities for Lower and Upper are on opposite sides of known annuity
    let Lower = value halfway between Lower and –1
    let Upper = Upper * 2
end loop
result is the root of the function that calculates the difference between the known
        and estimated annuities
```

Code

```
function Loan~Rate (Instalment, Periods are real) is real
    function Residual (Rate is real) is real
        result Instalment – (1 / Loan~Annuity (Rate, Periods))
    end Residual
    variables Lower, Upper are real
    let Lower = 0
    let Upper = 1
    loop until sign (Residual (Lower)) ≠ sign (Residual (Upper))
        let Lower = (Lower – 1) / 2
        let Upper = Upper * 2
        check Similarity~Test (Lower, –1, 0) = false
    end loop
    result Function~Root (Residual, Lower, Upper)
end Loan~Rate
```

TEST PROGRAM

<u>Imported Names</u>

Similarity~Test	Tests the similarity of two numbers (2.3.2)

<u>Local Names</u>

I	Instalment
N	Number of periods
R	Interest rate

Pseudo Code

```
for i = –1 to 4
    calculate instalment based on interest rate of i / 20 over 10 periods
    calculate interest rate that would produce this instalment
    calculate number of periods that is required for this instalment and interest rate
    check calculated number of periods is close to 10
end for
```

Code

```
variables I, N, R are real
for i = –1 to 4
    let I = 1 / Loan~Annuity (0.05 * i, 10)
    let R = Loan~Rate (I, 10)
    let N = Loan~Periods (I, R)
    check Similarity~Test (N, 10, 1) = true
end for
```

9.4 FUNCTION ROOT

Finding the point at which a curve crosses the X axis

Example

A bank offers to lend $100,000 in return for 12 yearly payments of $12,500. Suppose the effective annual interest rate is R. The formula that links R with paying off 0.125 times the principal per year is $R / (1 - (1 / (1 + R)^{12})) = 0.125$. The value of R (estimated to be between 1% and 30%) is computed by:

```
output Function~Root (Formula, 0.01, 0.30)
function Formula (R is real) is real
    result 0.125 – R / (1 – (1 / power (1 + R, 12)))
end Formula
```

Subprograms

9.4.1 Function~Root (receives Subprogram, Lower, Upper; *result real*)

Usage

So that you can see what the algorithm does, consider an example. In order to find the number of degrees Fahrenheit corresponding to 20° Celsius you could simply apply the formula F = (C * 1.8) + 32. To illustrate the usage of Function~Root let's do it the hard way, assuming that you cannot simply "invert" the defining function C = (F – 32) / 1.8. You supply Function~Root with the name of a function that computes (F – 32) / 1.8 – 20, and Function~Root does the rest, finding the value of F (68°) that results in this formula having the value zero.

The algorithm was described by Gorn (1960), and is a well-known bisection method reminiscent of binary search. It is necessary to provide the algorithm with two values of the unknown quantity, one of which is known to give a function value greater than zero, and the other a value less than zero. The algorithm bisects this interval and determines whether the result is greater than or less than zero. Using this information it then has a smaller interval in which the result lies. The algorithm iterates until a sufficiently accurate result is obtained. As it is programmed here the result is accurate to within 3 bits of full machine accuracy. The user should adjust the required accuracy to the circumstances of the problem to which the algorithm is applied.

Analysis

The algorithm is guaranteed to give a result if the initial estimates are correctly supplied. If the function has multiple roots, the algorithm will home in on one of them. If the lower and upper limits given to the algorithm are narrow enough to enclose only one root, the algorithm will find that root. The algorithm is not the most efficient known, but it is reliable, works for any one-to-one or many-to-one function such as polynomials, and is easy to implement.

IMPLEMENTATION

<u>Exported Names</u>

Function~Root	Computes a "root" of a specified function (9.4.1)

<u>Imported Names</u>

Similarity~Bits	Finds the number of bits in common in two numbers (2.3.1)

<u>Nicknames</u>

Lower	Lower limit of independent variable
Subprogram	Subprogram that computes value of specified function
Upper	Upper limit of independent variable

<u>Local Names</u>

Flower	Value of the function at the current lower limit
Fmiddle	Value of the function at the current midpoint
L	Current lower limit of the independent variable
Middle	Midpoint between L and U
U	Current upper limit of the independent variable

9.4.1 Function~Root (receives Subprogram, Lower, Upper; *result real*)

Pseudo Code

```
check given X bounds Lower and Upper have Y values of opposite sign
loop
    let Middle = half way between Lower and Upper
    if Y value for Middle has same sign as Y value for Lower then
        let Lower = Middle
    else
        let Upper = Middle
    end if
end loop when Lower = Upper
```

Code

```
function Function~Root (Subprogram is function, Lower, Upper are real) is real
    variables Flower, Fmiddle, L, Middle, U are real
    let Flower = Subprogram (Lower)
    let Fmiddle = Subprogram (Upper)
    check sign (Flower) ≠ sign (Fmiddle)
```

```
let L = Lower
let U = Upper
loop
    let Middle = (L + U) / 2
    let Fmiddle = Subprogram (Middle)
    if sign (Fmiddle) = sign (Flower) then
        let L = Middle
        let Flower = Fmiddle
    else
        let U = Middle
    end if
end loop when Similarity~Bits (L, U, magnitude (Upper – Lower)) ≥ maxbits – 3
result Middle
end Function~Root
```

TEST PROGRAM

Imported Names

Similarity~Test	Tests the similarity of two numbers (2.3.2)

Local Subprograms

S	Subprogram that computes function of which root is required

Nicknames

X	Independent variable in function

Local Names

R	Root of function

Pseudo Code

```
compute root of function known to have root R satisfying R = –log_e (R)
check R has correct value
```

Code

```
variable R is real
let R = Function~Root (S, 0.1, 1)
check Similarity~Test (R, –log_e (R), 1) = true
```

Local **S** (receives X; *result real*)

```
function S (X is real) is real
    result log_e (X) + exp (–X)
end S
```

10 File Updating

A fundamental function in data processing is the maintenance of files of information (or, perhaps, data). Most organizations have such requirements. Banks have "accounts" for their customers. The master files of accounts need updating whenever customers open or close accounts. Mailing lists are kept by hundreds of different institutions. There is a need to keep them up to date whenever names and addresses change. Thousands of business firms keep files of information about their customers or suppliers. These need to be altered whenever a customer or supplier changes any of the information kept on file by the firm.

The ubiquity of the requirement for file updating has prompted the development of file-handling tools. Fourth-generation languages have lessened the need for programmers to construct file updating programs. Nevertheless, there are many circumstances in which you may find it necessary to carry out file updating. It is frequently more efficient to do it with a third-generation language, the application may not be suited to a fourth-generation language, and other factors may dictate that specially tailored file-updating algorithms be provided.

Banks, insurance companies, and similar large organizations have been reluctant to allow on-line updating of their master files. There are very good reasons for this. In such applications it is important to keep very good records, or audit trails, of every change that is made in master files. Organizations cannot afford to risk losing information because of a hardware or software bug, or a power failure. With large systems involving thousands of simultaneous on-line users, file integrity must be preserved at all costs.

Traditionally, this has been ensured by accumulating "transactions" during the day. Overnight, the transactions are merged with the master files to create the updated master files. Backup copies of the files, printouts, and microfiche listings are made to ensure that there is no ambiguity about the state of the master files on any day. If an update run crashes for any reason, that is, if it does not run to completion successfully, the whole process can be started again when the problem causing the crash has been rectified. The advantage of updating in this manner is that it provides a high level of security. Such off-line processing provides opportunities for creating very efficient file-updating programs based on the general methods examined particularly in Sections 10.1 and 10.2.

There are three algorithms for updating files. Section 10.1 provides an algorithm for updating "serial" files. A serial file is the kind that could have been produced by a word processor or text editor. A master file is maintained in sorted sequence with respect to a "key", which is just a data item within each record of the file. During the updating process a sorted file of transactions, or requested changes, is passed against the master file. The transaction file and master file keys are matched up, and creations, deletions, or additions performed as required. The output consists of the updated master file in sorted sequence, and an error file containing any transactions that were invalid.

In Section 10.2 there is an algorithm for updating "indexed" files. There is no need to keep the master file in sorted sequence when you have an index. New master file records are appended to the end of the file in arbitrary order. When a record is deleted it is replaced by the last record in the master file, so that the file shrinks automatically (provided that the master file records are of uniform size). Records are located by means of an index file that is maintained in sorted key sequence. The index entry for each key contains a pointer to (disk address of) a master file record. Much of the updating logic is the same for serial and indexed files, and this is reflected in the way the algorithms are presented here.

Section 10.3 presents a dynamic hashing algorithm that can be used instead of the indexed updating algorithm for maintaining a general master file. The advantages and disadvantages are discussed below. The algorithm is used by the indexed updating algorithm in Section 10.2 for maintaining the master file index. Records in a dynamically hashed file are located by means of a directory that contains pointers to (addresses of) master file records. The directory is directly accessed using a portion of the "hash code" computed from the key as the directory file address.

Serial file updating has the advantage that only one disk input and one disk output are required per master file record processed. With the other methods several input-output accesses may be required in order to locate and update the required record. Serial updating has the disadvantage that the transaction file must be presorted, the entire master file must be read and written no matter how few transactions there are, and separate storage space must be allocated for the new and old master files simultaneously.

Indexed file updating has the principal advantage that the only master file records that are accessed are those for which transactions exist. The file is updated *in situ* and so there is no need for additional storage space during the updating process. Although the algorithm is more efficient when the transactions are presorted, it is easily adapted to handle an unsorted transaction file.

Dynamic hashing attempts to gain the efficiencies of hashing while overcoming the prime disadvantage of having to prespecify a maximum file size. You may wish to consult Section 7.5 for a discussion of basic hashing. The dynamic algorithm has the advantage that no maximum file size needs to be prespecified. The directory and the main file grow or shrink dynamically to accommodate any number of records. For most read and write operations there is a guaranteed upper maximum of two disk accesses per record. The main disadvantage of dynamic hashing is that the amount of disk space required for the directory may grow unacceptably large if the hashing function is poorly chosen. Another disadvantage is that response time may be unacceptably poor on the few occasions when the directory has to be expanded. You may have to build in special code to prevent terminals locking up if the directory is expanded on-line.

10.1 SERIAL UPDATE

Updating a serial master file with a file of transactions

Example

The test program shows how the algorithm is used. Once the transaction, old master, new master, and error files (TF, OF, NF, EF respectively) have been opened, the update is done by:

call Serial~Update (TF, OF, NF, EF)

Following the test program are the listings of four files. The transaction and old master files are inputs to the algorithm; the new master and error files are the outputs.

Subprograms

10.1.1 Serial~Update (receives Tfile, Ofile, Nfile, Efile)

Usage

The subprogram passes a file Tfile of "transactions" against an "old" master file Ofile, producing a "new" master file Nfile, and a log of errors in file Efile.

Each file record is assumed to have three fields, although the code is easy to modify for other cases. There is a status code/transaction type, a key, and a description. The first field contains a status code in the master file and a transaction type in the transaction file. The master file may have a status of Exists or Frozen. A record is frozen if an erroneous transaction is detected, to prevent further updating until the record is released. A transaction record may have a transaction type of Create, Modify, Delete, or Release.

When a record is created by a transaction type Create, the master file status is set to Exists and the master file key and description are copied from the transaction file. When a master file record is modified by a transaction type Modify, the master file description is replaced by the transaction file description. In most practical applications the modifications will need to be more complicated than this simple replacement. When a record is deleted by a transaction type Delete, the old master file record is not copied to the new master file. When a record is released by a transaction type Release, the status of the master file record is changed from Frozen to Exists.

The test program tries all possible combinations of valid and erroneous transactions. The new master file and error file generated by the test program are listed here to demonstrate what the correct output should look like.

Analysis

The algorithm is relatively straightforward, but contains many nested tests to examine the various alternatives that can arise. The approach taken here is explained in detail by Dwyer (1981) and Inglis (1981).

Note that it is sometimes necessary to freeze a master file record to eliminate ambiguities. For example, a user might attempt to create a record that already exists. If modification transactions then follow, it is ambiguous whether the existing or new master file record should be updated.

IMPLEMENTATION

<u>Exported Names</u>

Serial~Update	Updates a serial master file (10.1.1)

<u>Local Subprograms</u>

Input~Record	Inputs one record from a specified file
Output~Record	Outputs one record to a specified file

<u>Nicknames</u>

Efile	File number for file of erroneous transactions
File	File number for input-output of a record
Nfile	File number for new (updated) master file
Ofile	File number for old master file
Rdata	Data field for File record
Rkey	Key field for File record
Rtype	Type field for File record
Tfile	File number for transaction file

<u>Local Names</u>

Ndata	Data field for new master file record
Nkey	Key field for new master file record
Ntype	Record type field for new master file record
Odata	Data field for old master file record
Okey	Key field for old master file record
Otype	Record type field for old master file record
Sentinel	High value code used to provide end of file indication
Tdata	Data field in transaction file record
Tkey	Key field in transaction file record
Ttype	Transaction type field in transaction file record

10.1.1 Serial~Update (receives Tfile, Ofile, Nfile, Efile)

Pseudo Code

input first record of transaction file and old master file
let new master file key = lesser of the keys of the transaction file and old file records
loop until new master file key is the end of file sentinel
    if new master file key = old master file key *then*
        let new master file record = old master file record
        input next old master file record
    end if

```
        loop until transaction key ≠ new master file key
            update new master file record according to transaction type
            input next transaction record
        end loop
        if new master file record has not been deleted then
            output new master file record
        end if
        let new master file key = lesser of the keys of the transaction file and old file
                records
    end loop
```

Code

```
    constant Sentinel = "|"
    procedure Serial~Update (Tfile, Ofile, Nfile, Efile are integers)
        variables Ntype, Nkey, Ndata are text
        variables Otype, Okey, Odata are text
        variables Ttype, Tkey, Tdata are text
        call Input~Record (Tfile, Ttype, Tkey, Tdata)
        call Input~Record (Ofile, Otype, Okey, Odata)
        let Nkey = minimum (Tkey, Okey)
        loop until Nkey = Sentinel
            if Nkey = Okey then
                let Ntype = Otype
                let Ndata = Odata
                call Input~Record (Ofile, Otype, Okey, Odata)
            else
                let Ntype = "Missing"
            end if
            loop until Tkey ≠ Nkey
                if Ttype = "Create" then
                    if Ntype = "Missing" then
                        let Ntype = "Exists"
                        let Ndata = Tdata
                    else
                        let Ntype = "Frozen"
                        call Output~Record (Efile, Ttype, Tkey, Tdata)
                    end if
                else-if Ttype = "Delete" then
                    if Ntype = "Exists" then
                        let Ntype = "Missing"
                    else
                        call Output~Record (Efile, Ttype, Tkey, Tdata)
                    end if
                else-if Ttype = "Modify" then
                    if Ntype = "Exists" then
                        let Ndata = Tdata
                    else
                        call Output~Record (Efile, Ttype, Tkey, Tdata)
                    end if
```

```
            else-if Ttype = "Release" then
                if Ntype = "Frozen" then
                    let Ntype = "Exists"
                else
                    call Output~Record (Efile, Ttype, Tkey, Tdata)
                end if
            end if
            call Input~Record (Tfile, Ttype, Tkey, Tdata)
        end loop
        if Ntype ≠ "Missing" then
            call Output~Record (Nfile, Ntype, Nkey, Ndata)
        end if
        let Nkey = minimum (Tkey, Okey)
    end loop
end Serial~Update
```

Local **Input~Record** (receives File; supplies Rtype, Rkey, Rdata)

```
procedure Input~Record (File is integer, Rtype, Rkey, Rdata are text)
    if end~of~file (File) = true then
        let Rkey = Sentinel
    else
        input from File into Rtype, Rkey, Rdata
    end if
end Input~Record
```

Local **Output~Record** (receives File, Rtype, Rkey, Rdata)

```
procedure Output~Record (File is integer, Rtype, Rkey, Rdata are text)
    output into File from Rtype, Rkey, Rdata
end Output~Record
```

TEST PROGRAM

Local Names

EF	Error file number
NF	New master file number
OF	Old master file number
TF	Transaction file number

Pseudo Code

```
open the four files
call Serial~Update
```

Code

```
variables EF, NF, OF, TF are integers
open TF file "Transaction File"
open OF file "Old Master File"
```

create NF *file* "New Master File"
create EF *file* "Error File"
call Serial~Update (TF, OF, NF, EF)

Transaction File

Create	1	"Transaction error"
Modify	1	"Transaction error"
Release	1	"Transaction OK"
Modify	1	"Transaction OK"
Modify	2	"Transaction OK"
Modify	3	"Transaction error"
Delete	3	"Transaction error"
Release	3	"Transaction error"
Delete	4	"Transaction OK"
Create	4	"Transaction OK"

Old Master File

Exists	1	"Master record"
Exists	2	"Master record"
Exists	4	"Master record"

New Master File

Exists	1	"Master record"
Exists	2	"Transaction OK"
Exists	4	"Transaction OK"

Error File

Create	1	"Transaction error"
Modify	1	"Transaction error"
Modify	3	"Transaction error"
Delete	3	"Transaction error"
Release	3	"Transaction error"

10.2 INDEXED UPDATE

Updating an indexed master file with a file of transactions

Example

The test program shows how the algorithm is used. Once the transaction, master, and error files (TF, MF, EF respectively) have been opened, the update is done by:

call Indexed~Update (TF, MF, EF, LM)

The variable LM contains the position of the end of file in the master file. Following the test program are the listings of two files. The transaction and master files are inputs to the algorithm; the master and error files are the outputs.

Subprograms

10.2.1 Indexed~Update (receives Tfile, Mfile, Efile; supplies LastMaster)

Usage

The subprogram inputs a file Tfile of "transactions" for updating an indexed master file Mfile, any errors being logged in file Efile. The character position of the last character in the master file is returned as LastMaster.

Each file record is assumed to have three fields, although the code is easy to modify for other cases. There is a status code/transaction type, a key, and a description. The first field contains a status code in the master file and a transaction type in the transaction file. The master file may have a status of Exists or Frozen. A record is frozen if an erroneous transaction is detected, to prevent further updating until the record is released. A transaction record may have a transaction type of Create, Modify, Delete, or Release.

When a record is created by a transaction type Create, the master file status is set to Exists and the master file key and description are copied from the transaction file. When a master file record is modified by a transaction type Modify, the master file description is replaced by the transaction file description. In most practical applications the modifications will need to be more complicated than this simple replacement. When a record is deleted by a transaction type Delete, the record is removed from the master file. When a record is released by a transaction type Release, the status of the master file record is changed from Frozen to Exists.

The test program tries all possible combinations of valid and erroneous transactions. The master file is initially empty and is left as empty after all transactions have been processed. The error file output by the test program is listed here to demonstrate what the error output should look like.

Analysis

The algorithm is relatively straightforward, but contains many nested tests to examine the various alternatives that can arise. The approach taken here is explained in detail by Dwyer (1981) and Inglis (1981).

Note that it is sometimes necessary to freeze a master file record to eliminate ambiguities. For example, a user might attempt to create a record that already exists. If modification transactions then follow, it is ambiguous whether the existing or new master file record should be updated.

Keeping an index to a master file is in itself a nontrivial task. The index needs to be efficiently organized so that any specific master file record can be easily located. The master file records are typically arranged in the master file in no particular sequence. The index keeps track of each one, recording the master file address, or location, at which the record is to be found. The index file has to keep all the keys and the corresponding master file locations in an easily accessible form. The dynamic hashing algorithm presented in Section 10.3 is used for that purpose.

IMPLEMENTATION

<u>Exported Names</u>

Indexed~Update   Updates a serial master file (10.2.1)

<u>Imported Names</u>

Hash~Close   Closes master file and directory (10.3.6)

Hash~Insert	Inserts key and associated data item into master file (10.3.1)
Hash~Open	Opens existing master file and directory (10.3.4)
Hash~Remove	Removes specified key from master file (10.3.3)
Hash~Search	Searches for specified key, retrieving associated data item (10.3.2)
To~Integer	Converts an integer in *text* form to an *integer* (2.1.1)
To~Text	Converts an *integer* number to *text* form (2.1.2)
Local Subprograms	
Input~Record	Inputs one record from a specified file
Output~Record	Outputs one record to a specified file
Nicknames	
Efile	File number for file of erroneous transactions
File	File number for input-output of a record
Mfile	File number for master file
Rdata	Data field for File record
Rkey	Key field for File record
Rtype	Type field for File record
Tfile	File number for transaction file
Global Names	
Dsize	Size of data field on disk in bytes
Isize	Size of a binary integer on disk in bytes
Ksize	Size of key field on disk in bytes
Rsize	Size of record on disk in bytes
Ssize	Size of status field on disk in bytes
Local Names	
CurrentKey	Key field for current transaction record
LastMaster	End of file position in master file
Location	Address of master file record
Mdata	Data field for master file record
Mkey	Key field for master file record
Mtype	Record type field for master file record
Sentinel	Arbitrary code used to provide end of file indication
Tdata	Data field in transaction file record
Tkey	Key field in transaction file record
Ttype	Transaction type field in transaction file record

Code

constants Dsize = 20, Isize = 4, Ksize = 4, Ssize = 8
constant Rsize = Ssize + Ksize + Dsize
constant Sentinel = "End File"

10.2.1 Indexed~Update (receives Tfile, Mfile, Efile; supplies LastMaster)

Pseudo Code

obtain position of end of master file
if file is empty, initialize position of end of file after record containing master file size

```
input first record of transaction file
loop until transaction file key is the end of file sentinel
    look up master file address for transaction key in index
    read master file record, or note that it is missing
    loop until transaction key changes
        update new master file record according to transaction type
        if master record is to be deleted, move last master record to current master
                record
        input next transaction record
    end loop
    if master file record has not been deleted then
        insert key in index if it is not already there
        output master file record
    end if
end loop
save position of end of master file
```

Code

```
procedure Indexed~Update (Tfile, Mfile, Efile, LastMaster are integers)
    variables Mtype, Mkey, Mdata are text
    variables Ttype, Tkey, Tdata are text
    variable CurrentKey is text
    variables LastMaster, Location are integers
    seek Mfile position 0                          Get position of end of master file
    if end~of~file (Mfile) then
        let LastMaster = Isize
        write into Mfile from LastMaster size Isize
    else
        read from Mfile into LastMaster size Isize
    end if
    call Hash~Open
    call Input~Record (Tfile, Ttype, Tkey, Tdata)
    loop until Tkey = Sentinel
        call Hash~Search (Tkey, CurrentKey)        Find current transaction key in
        let Location = To~Integer (CurrentKey)     index, and retrieve master file
        if Location = 0 then                       record
            let Mtype = "Missing"
        else
            seek Mfile position Location
            read from Mfile into Mtype size Ssize, Mkey size Ksize, Mdata
                    size Dsize
        end if
        let CurrentKey = Tkey
        loop until Tkey ≠ CurrentKey               Process all transactions with the
            if Ttype = "Create" then               same key value
```

```
        if Mtype = "Missing" then
            let Mtype = "Exists"
            let Mkey = Tkey
            let Mdata = Tdata
        else
            let Mtype = "Frozen"
            call Output~Record (Efile, Ttype, Tkey, Tdata)
        end if
    else-if Ttype = "Delete" then
        if Mtype = "Missing" then
            call Output~Record (Efile, Ttype, Tkey, Tdata)
        else
            let Mtype = "Missing"
            call Hash~Remove (Mkey)
            let LastMaster = LastMaster – Rsize
            if LastMaster ≠ Location then          Overwrite current
                seek Mfile position                 record with last master
                        LastMaster
                read from Mfile into Mtype size Ssize, Mkey size Ksize,
                        Mdata size Dsize
                seek Mfile position Location
                write into Mfile from Mtype size Ssize, Mkey size Ksize,
                        Mdata size Dsize
                call Hash~Insert (Mkey, To~Text (Location))
            end if
        end if
    else-if Ttype = "Modify" then
        if Mtype = "Missing" then
            call Output~Record (Efile, Ttype, Tkey, Tdata)
        else
            let Mdata = Tdata
        end if
    else-if Ttype = "Release" then
        if Mtype = "Frozen" then
            let Mtype = "Exists"
        else
            let Mtype = "Frozen"
            call Output~Record (Efile, Ttype, Tkey, Tdata)
        end if
    end if
    call Input~Record (Tfile, Ttype, Tkey, Tdata)
end loop
if Mtype ≠ "Missing" then
    if Location = 0 then                    If this is a new key, insert it in the
        let Location = LastMaster           index and get a new master file
        call Hash~Insert (Mkey,             record position
                To~Text (Location))
        let LastMaster = LastMaster + Rsize
    end if
```

```
            seek Mfile position Location
            write into Mfile from Mtype size Ssize, Mkey size Ksize, Mdata size
                Dsize
        end if
    end loop
    seek Mfile position 0                           Save the size of the master file
    write into Mfile from LastMaster size Isize
    call Hash~Close
end Indexed~Update
```

Local **Input~Record** (receives File; supplies Rtype, Rkey, Rdata)

```
procedure Input~Record (File is integer, Rtype, Rkey, Rdata are text)
    if end-of-file (File) = true then
        let Rkey = Sentinel
    else
        input from File into Rtype, Rkey, Rdata
    end if
end Input
```

Local **Output~Record** (receives File, Rtype, Rkey, Rdata)

```
procedure Output~Record (File is integer, Rtype, Rkey, Rdata are text)
    output into File from Rtype, Rkey, Rdata
end Output
```

TEST PROGRAM

Local Names

- EF Error file number
- LM Last master file record, i.e., end of file
- MF Master file number
- TF Transaction file number

Pseudo Code

open the three files
call Indexed~Update

Code

```
open TF file "Transaction File"
create MF file "Master File"
create EF file "Error File"
call Indexed~Update (TF, MF, EF, LM)
check LM = Isize
```

Transaction File

```
Create   1   "Master record"
Create   2   "Master record"
Create   4   "Master record"
```

Create	1	"Transaction error"
Modify	1	"Transaction error"
Release	1	"Transaction OK"
Modify	1	"Transaction OK"
Modify	2	"Transaction OK"
Modify	3	"Transaction error"
Delete	3	"Transaction error"
Release	3	"Transaction error"
Delete	4	"Transaction OK"
Create	4	"Transaction OK"
Delete	1	"Transaction OK"
Delete	2	"Transaction OK"
Delete	4	"Transaction OK"

Error File

Create	1	"Transaction error"
Modify	1	"Transaction error"
Modify	3	"Transaction error"
Delete	3	"Transaction error"
Release	3	"Transaction error"

10.3 DYNAMIC HASHING

Maintaining an index in a variable-size file

Example

To insert into the master file a key and its associated data held in the text strings Key and Data:

call Hash~Insert (Key, Data)

To search the master file for a Key and to obtain the associated Data:

call Hash~Search (Key, Data)

Subprograms

10.3.1 Hash~Insert (receives Key, Data)
10.3.2 Hash~Search (receives Key; supplies Data)
10.3.3 Hash~Remove (receives Key)
10.3.4 Hash~Open (receives MasterName, DirectoryName)
10.3.5 Hash~Create (receives MasterName, DirectoryName)
10.3.6 Hash~Close

Usage

Before the master file is used it must be initialized by a call to Hash~Create, specifying the names to be given to the master file and a directory file. Records are inserted into the file by calling Hash~Insert with the key and associated data provided as text strings. Records may be retrieved randomly by calling Hash~Search with the required key. If the key is found in the master file, the associated data field is returned, otherwise the data will be a null text string.

Records are removed from the master file by calling Hash~Remove, specifying the required key. The algorithm will ignore an attempt to remove a nonexistent key. When the updating is finished, the files must be closed by a call to Hash~Close in order to preserve information about the structure of the file. An existing master file may be accessed by a call to Hash~Open instead of Hash~Create.

The amount of disk space required for the directory depends greatly on the effectiveness of the local subprogram Hash~Function. The function computes a binary integer called a hash code from the text string key. It is important that the bits of the hash code be fairly randomly distributed. The hash functions used in Section 7.5, while quite suitable for the purposes of that section, are not as good for dynamic hashing. The hash function used here calculates a weighted sum of the bytes of the key, using a sequence of integers as weights. Despite this improvement, the very badly distributed keys in the test program cause nine directory expansions, with 512 directory entries addressing just 48 (very small-sized) master file blocks containing 64 keys. The function of Gonnet and Baeza-Yates (1991), with multiplier 131, causes 12 expansions. You should experiment with hashing functions for the particular application being considered, before starting to implement this algorithm. A survey of hashing methods is provided by Maurer and Lewis (1975).

The test program generates keys of various lengths, inserting them into an empty file and then removing them all. The master and directory files grow, and then shrink to their original sizes. Although the disk block size is defined here as 32 bytes, the algorithm is much more effective if a larger block is used, say 512 bytes. The test program has a small block size merely to exercise the algorithm thoroughly.

Analysis

You should be familiar with the analysis in Section 7.5 before proceeding further. The key difference is that Section 7.5 deals with hashing to array subscripts, while this section deals with hashing to disk addresses. Our aim is to generate as few disk accesses as possible. The dynamic hashing algorithm is essentially that of Fagin et al. (1979), following the description given by Enbody and Chu (1988). The details of the removal process were developed by the present author. Although no proof is available for the algorithm, extensive testing suggests that the removal process is effective and reliable.

In Section 7.5 the hash code was calculated *mod* the size of the array containing the keys. This modulo process produced a subscript within the limits of the array. In the dynamic hashing algorithm the modulus is always taken with respect to a power of two. Typically only the last few bits of the hash code are used, the precise number of bits being held in the variable Depth. Thus, to obtain the last three bits of the hash code the algorithm takes the value of the hash code *mod* 2^3. The term "index" is used to describe the last few bits of the hash code currently being used, and the term "depth" to describe the number of bits in the index.

There are two main kinds of dynamic hashing schemes, those that use a directory and those that do not. With a nondirectory scheme, the index points to a master file block. With a directory scheme, it points to a directory entry that contains the address of a master file block. The nondirectory schemes suffer from the disadvantage of having to deal with overflow blocks to take account of collisions, which the directory scheme does not have to do. (Only a primary hash function is used, there being no secondary hash function that could be very inefficient, requiring many disk accesses.) The performance of a nondirectory scheme degrades in a nonuniform way as overflows occur, is more complicated to implement, and has less predictable performance than the directory scheme. For these reasons a directory scheme is provided. At best a nondirectory scheme requires one disk access where a directory scheme requires two. At worst, when there are many overflows, the nondirectory scheme can be many times less efficient than the directory scheme. There is a rare exception—the necessary doubling in size of the directory slows the directory scheme down hugely for a few transactions. The chosen algorithm provides mostly stable performance, and a few suggestions are provided about how to handle directory expansion.

Consider now the details of implementation of a directory scheme. Each master file block contains three fields: the depth, index, and bucket fields. The bucket field is the largest and contains keys and data items concatenated together as a single text string. This arrangement is simply for convenience of presentation, and other methods may suit particular applications. The depth and index fields are just binary integers.

Every master file block has a depth, an index, and zero or more text strings in its bucket. The depths of blocks may vary throughout the file. To see how these fields are updated, consider how an empty file copes with a sequence of calls to Hash~Insert. Initially there is just one block for each of the directory and master files. The directory block is numbered zero. The master file block has a depth of zero and an index of zero. When a master file record is read into memory, its fields are stored, naturally enough, in the variables Depth, Index, and Bucket. As keys are processed the hash function is computed and its last Depth bits (Index) are considered. This value of Index is used to access a directory entry. At the beginning, when Depth is zero, directory entry zero is always accessed, and it points to the first master file block. Keys are appended to the bucket, which is rewritten to the first master file block.

Thirty-five integers used for control purposes are stored at the beginning of the master file, requiring 140 bytes. The first available master file block therefore starts at byte position 140. Byte positions are numbered from zero rather than from one, in order to simplify the presentation, which relies substantially on modulo arithmetic. Counting from one requires much cluttering up of the code, although programmers using certain languages such as Basic and Cobol will be forced to make a conversion. (See Figure 10.1.)

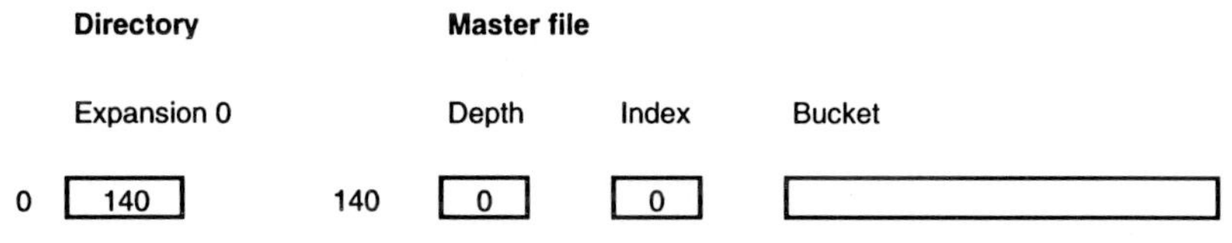

	Directory		Master file		
	Expansion 0		Depth	Index	Bucket
0	140	140	0	0	

Figure 10.1

The process of inserting keys happens smoothly until the bucket in the first master file block becomes full. At this stage the algorithm doubles the directory in size, appending all its records to the end of itself. Now it has two pointers to the first master file block, in directory blocks zero and one. At this point we have to describe the difference between the "global" depth and the "local" depth. The global depth has just increased from zero to one, and is recorded in the variable Expansion, but the local depth of the sole master file block remains at zero. (See Figure 10.2.)

	Directory		Master file		
	Expansion 1		Depth	Index	Bucket
0	140	140	0	0	
1	140				

Figure 10.2

The variable Expansion tells you how many bits of the hash code to use in accessing the directory. With Expansion equal to one, the last bit of the hash code is used to find out the master file address for the required bucket. The size of the directory having just been doubled, with both entries pointing to the same master file block, it is immaterial whether the last bit of a hash code is zero or one. The same master file block is obtained. However, that is about to change. The full bucket is split into two buckets. One of the buckets contains all the keys that have zero as the last bit of their hash codes. The other bucket contains all those that have one as the last bit. The former are rewritten into the first master file block and a new master file block is allocated for the latter. The local depth of each block will also have increased to one, signifying that its index is equal to the last bit in the hash code. The directory is adjusted so that its block number one points to the master filc block just allocated. The two blocks are called "buddies". Their indexes differ in the most significant bit. (See Figure 10.3.)

	Directory		Master file		
	Expansion 1		Depth	Index	Bucket
0	140	140	1	0	
1	172	172	1	1	

Figure 10.3

As more keys are received the algorithm continues to look at the last Expansion bits of their hash codes, at present their last bit. If the last bit is zero, it accesses block zero of the directory to obtain the address of the first master file block. If the last bit of the hash code is one, it accesses block one of the directory to obtain the address of the second master file block. It continues to append keys to either of the master file buckets until one of them overflows, say the block at address 172. Now it has to double the directory in size again, setting Expansion equal to two. The directory has four blocks, pointing to the first, second, first, and second blocks of the master file respectively. (See Figure 10.4.)

	Directory		**Master file**		
	Expansion 2		Depth	Index	Bucket
0	140	140	1	0	
1	172	172	1	1	
0	140				
1	172				

Figure 10.4

At this point two buddies are created from the master file block at address 172. This is done by increasing the depth of the block from one to two, and expanding each index from one to two bits, differing in the most significant bit. As before, a new master file block is allocated to one of the buddies. (See Figure 10.5.)

	Directory		**Master file**		
	Expansion 2		Depth	Index	Bucket
00	140	140	1	0	
01	172	172	2	01	
10	140	204	2	11	
11	204				

Figure 10.5

That explains, in an intuitive way, the main features of the insertion algorithm. The removal algorithm, generally speaking, reverses the process. As keys are deleted they are removed from the buckets in which they reside. The buddy of the block is inspected and if the total size of the buckets of the two buddies will allow it the two buckets are combined, provided that the two buddies have the same depth. The directory entries are adjusted so that pointers to the second buddy are replaced by pointers to the first buddy. The depth is reduced by one, and each index has its most significant bit removed.

The vacant master file block is filled by copying the last master file block into the vacant location. All directory entries pointing to that block are updated. There are a couple of special cases. If the last block in the file happens to be the second buddy, no copying is done. If the last block happens to be the first buddy, you need to remember that the first buddy has been moved when you come to update the master file block. We can now explain why the index needs to be stored in the master file record. The last block in the file might happen to be empty as a result of removals. Therefore, the algorithm cannot compute the index from the depth and the hash code computed from one of the keys in the block. The index needs to be stored explicitly.

When there are many deletions, it may happen that all the depths of the master file records will become less than the current value of Expansion. When this occurs, the first half of the directory will be identical to the second half. The algorithm then cuts the directory in half. In order to manage this process efficiently counts are maintained of the number of blocks having each possible depth. The halving of the directory can then be accomplished without any disk accesses. The counts are stored at the beginning of the master file by Hash~Close.

A subtle problem can occur with this algorithm in splitting a bucket that has a depth equal to the current expansion. The directory must be doubled, but it may happen that all the keys in the current bucket hash to just one of the two buddies that have been created. If this occurs, the solution implemented is to double the directory again, and perhaps repeatedly until the index is long enough to separate some of the keys in the bucket. This is why such an emphasis is placed on ensuring that the hashing function produces approximately uniformly distributed hash codes. The penalty paid for a poor hashing function is a huge directory.

There is one trap for programmers who want to allow multiple equal keys in their file. The algorithm fails if there are more equal keys than can fit in a bucket. The algorithm will get stuck in a loop, doubling the directory each time, being unable to find a bit position in which the new key differs from the keys in the bucket! Many applications deal only with unique keys, and the algorithm is presented in its simplest form for the more common case. If you want the algorithm to handle multiple equal keys, you will need to enhance it along the following lines. These enhancements have the side effect of keeping the directory size lower than it would otherwise be, at the cost of an increased average number of disk accesses per key. Even if you do not use equal keys, these enhancements will minimize the directory size, and at the same time address the problem referred to in the previous paragraph.

First, the directory must not be automatically doubled when a bucket is full and Depth is equal to Expansion. Check whether one doubling will enable the keys in the bucket plus the new key to be split across two buckets. If so, proceed as with the current algorithm; otherwise, create an overflow bucket in a new block. Change the index of the current block into a pointer to the new block, making it easily identifiable by giving it a negative sign. Put the new key into this overflow block. If there are many equal keys, there will be several overflow blocks in a chain, the last one being identified by the positive value of its index field.

In general terms, the whole algorithm must now be upgraded to examine overflow blocks. When one is searching for a key, all blocks in a chain must be examined with a *loop until* the index is non-negative. When attempting to insert a key, all blocks through the last overflow block in the chain must be examined. If the new key cannot be inserted in any block in the chain, you proceed as in the current algorithm, comparing the values of Depth and Expansion. If Depth is less than Expansion, you split the chain of blocks into two chains, whereas at present the algorithm merely splits one block into two blocks.

In the removal algorithm you have a choice. You can delete a key from the block it occupies and then either compress the whole overflow chain or leave the rest of the chain as it is. In order to keep the file size under control, we recommend compacting the whole overflow chain whenever a key is deleted. Although it is possible to leave the compaction until, say, a block becomes empty, a great deal of file space can be wasted by this alternative. Leaving an overflow chain of partly used blocks also makes it difficult to know when to join buckets together, and hence may delay halving the directory much longer than is necessary. As a general rule of thumb, you should get rid of overflow blocks as soon as possible, because they have a negative impact on search times. The decision, however, involves a number of positive and negative factors in the classic trade-off between processing time and file storage space.

Different operating systems handle files in different ways. These procedures should be adapted to the idiosyncrasies of particular operating systems. For example, the doubling of the directory can be made much more efficient under the Unix™ operating system by using the *cat* command to concatenate the directory with itself. You must think carefully about directory doubling, which is the most time-consuming part of the algorithm. Fortunately, the number of doublings required is proportional to the logarithm of the number of keys in the file. When the expansion number exceeds 10–15, however, doubling can take a significant amount of time. You must ensure that terminals do not freeze up while waiting for doubling to be completed.

IMPLEMENTATION

Exported Names

Hash~Close	Closes master file and directory (10.3.6)
Hash~Create	Creates new master file and directory (10.3.5)
Hash~Insert	Inserts key and associated data item into master file (10.3.1)
Hash~Open	Opens existing master file and directory (10.3.4)
Hash~Remove	Removes specified key from master file (10.3.3)
Hash~Search	Searches for specified key, retrieving associated data item (10.3.2)

Imported Names

To~Integer	Converts an integer in *text* form to an *integer* (2.1.1)
To~Text	Converts an *integer* number to *text* form (2.1.2)

Local Subprograms

Append~String	Append character count and text string to bucket
Extract~String	Extract character count and text string from bucket
Get~Master	Get master file block

Hash~Function	Compute hash code for specified key
Join~Buckets	Join two buckets to make a single bucket
Split~Bucket	Split a bucket into two buckets using one hash code bit
Update~Directory	Update all directory entries pointing to specified master file block

<u>Nicknames</u>

Address	Disk address of master file block
Bucket	Collection of key values and associated data items
BucketA	First bucket of a pair
BucketB	Second bucket of a pair
Buddy	Address of master file block for buddy of current block
Data	Data associated with current key
Depth	Number of bits of hash code used for indexing
DirectoryName	Name of directory file
Hash	Hash code computed from supplied key
Index	Portion of hash code containing Depth least significant bits
K	Character counter or position indicator
Key	Current key value
MasterName	Name of master file
String	Text string

<u>Global Names</u>

Bsize	Size of a bucket on disk in bytes
Count	Array of counts of blocks having particular depths
Directory	File number for directory file
EndDirectory	Position of end of directory file
EndMaster	Position of end of master file
Expansion	Number of times directory has been doubled in size
Isize	Size of a binary integer on disk in bytes
Master	File number for master file
MaxDepth	Maximum number of bits usable in hash code
Rsize	Size of a block on disk in bytes

<u>Local Names</u>

Address	Disk address of master file block
Bdata	Data item retrieved from disk block
Bkey	Key value retrieved from disk block
Bucket	Collection of key values and associated data items
BucketA	First bucket of a pair
BucketB	Second bucket of a pair
Depth	Number of bits of hash code used for indexing
Done	Indication whether loop is to be terminated
Hash	Hash code computed from supplied key
Index	Portion of hash code containing Depth least significant bits

Code

constants Isize = 4, Rsize = 32, MaxDepth = 31, Bsize = Rsize – (Isize * 2)
variables Directory, EndDirectory, EndMaster, Expansion, Master *are integers*
variable Count *is array* 0 *to* MaxDepth *of integers*

10.3.1 Hash~Insert (receives Key, Data)

Pseudo Code

```
get hash code for specified key
loop until specified key and data have been written to master file
    get master file block corresponding to key
    if key and data will fit into bucket from block then
        append key and data to bucket
        rewrite block into master file
    else-if number of bits used of hash code for this bucket < number of doublings then
        split bucket into buddies, based on most significant bit of index
        rewrite block with first buddy over current block
        rewrite block with second buddy at end of master file
        update directory to point to second buddy
    else
        copy whole directory to end of directory, doubling its size
    end if
end loop
```

Code

```
procedure Hash~Insert (Key, Data are text)
    variables Address, Depth, Hash, Index are integers
    variables Bucket, BucketA, BucketB are text
    variable Done is true-false
    let Hash = Hash~Function (Key)
    let Done = false
    loop until Done = true
        call Get~Master (Hash mod shift (1, Expansion), Address, Depth, Bucket)
        if length (Key) + length (Data) + length (Bucket) ≤ Bsize – 2 then
            call Append~String (Bucket, Key)        Append key and data to current
            call Append~String (Bucket, Data)       bucket; rewrite block
            let Index = Hash mod shift (1, Depth)
            seek Master position Address
            write into Master from Depth size Isize, Index size Isize, Bucket size
                    Bsize
            let Done = true
        else-if Depth < Expansion then
            call Split~Bucket (Bucket, BucketA, BucketB, Depth)   Split bucket
            let Count[Depth] = Count[Depth] – 1                   into two
            let Depth = Depth + 1                                 buddies
            let Count[Depth] = Count[Depth] + 2
            let Index = Hash mod shift (1, Depth – 1)
            seek Master position Address
            write into Master from Depth size Isize, Index size Isize, BucketA size
                    Bsize
            let Index = Index + shift (1, Depth – 1)   Double the size of the directory
            let Index = Index mod shift (1, Depth)
            seek Master position EndMaster
            write into Master from Depth size Isize, Index size Isize, BucketB size
                    Bsize
            call Update~Directory (Depth, Index, EndMaster)
            let EndMaster = EndMaster + Rsize
```

```
        else
            for i = 0 to (shift (1, Expansion) – 1)
                seek Directory position i * Isize
                read from Directory into Address size Isize
                seek Directory position EndDirectory
                write into Directory from Address size Isize
                let EndDirectory = EndDirectory + Isize
            end for
            let Expansion = Expansion + 1
        end if
    end loop
end Hash~Insert
```

10.3.2 Hash~Search (receives Key; supplies Data)

Pseudo Code

```
get master file block corresponding to hash code for specified key
if bucket in block contains key then
    obtain associated data from bucket
else
    return null text string
end if
```

Code

```
procedure Hash~Search (Key, Data are text)
    variables Address, Depth, Index, K are integers
    variables Bdata, Bkey, Bucket are text
    let Index = Hash~Function (Key) mod shift (1, Expansion)
    call Get~Master (Hash, Address, Depth, Bucket)
    let Data = ""
    let K = first
    loop until K > length (Bucket)
        call Extract~String (Bucket, K, Bkey)
        call Extract~String (Bucket, K, Bdata)
        if Bkey = Key then
            let Data = Bdata
            let K = length (Bucket) + 1
        end if
    end loop
end Hash~Search
```

10.3.3 Hash~Remove (receives Key)

Pseudo Code

```
get master file block corresponding to hash code for specified key
remove key and associated data from bucket in block
loop until block and its buddy cannot be merged
```

```
if same number of bits are used for indexing current block and its buddy then
    join the buddies with a view to writing the joined block over the first buddy
    move the last record in the file to overwrite the second buddy
    update the associated directory entries
    let the first buddy be used as the current block
    if all master file blocks are indexed by fewer bits than size of directory
            permits then
        halve the directory
    end if
end if
end loop
write the master file block
```

Code

```
procedure Hash~Remove (Key is text)
    variables Address, Buddy1, Buddy2, Depth, Depth1, Done, Hash, Index, K are
            integers
    variables Bdata, Bkey, Bucket, BucketA, BucketB are text
    let Hash = Hash~Function (Key)
    let Index = Hash mod shift (1, Expansion)
    call Get~Master (Hash, Address, Depth, BucketB)    Remove key from bucket
    let Bucket = ""                                    in which it is located
    let K = first
    loop until K > length (BucketB)
        call Extract~String (BucketB, K, Bkey)
        call Extract~String (BucketB, K, Bdata)
        if Bkey ≠ Key then
            call Append~String (Bucket, Bkey)
            call Append~String (Bucket, Bdata)
        end if
    end loop
    let Done = Depth
    loop until Done = 0
        let Index = Hash mod shift (1, Depth)          Get buddy of current block
        if shift (Hash, –(Depth – 1)) mod 2 = 0 then
            let Buddy1 = Address
            let BucketA = Bucket
            call Get~Master (Hash + shift (1, Depth – 1), Buddy2, Depth1, BucketB)
        else
            let Buddy2 = Address
            let BucketB = Bucket
            call Get~Master (Hash – shift (1, Depth – 1), Buddy1, Depth1, BucketA)
        end if
        if Depth = Depth1 and length (BucketA) + length (BucketB) ≤ Bsize then
            call Join~Buckets (Bucket, BucketA, BucketB)    Join buckets into
            let Count[Depth] = Count[Depth] – 2              one bucket
            let Depth = Depth – 1
```

```
            let Count[Depth] = Count[Depth] + 1
            let Index = Index mod shift (1, Depth)
            let Index = Index + shift (1, Depth)
            call Update~Directory (Depth + 1, Index, Buddy1)
            let EndMaster = EndMaster – Rsize     Move last block to overwrite sec-
            if EndMaster ≠ Buddy2 then            ond buddy
                seek Master position EndMaster
                read from Master into Depth1 size Isize, Index size Isize, BucketB
                        size Bsize
                seek Master position Buddy2
                write into Master from Depth1 size Isize, Index size Isize, BucketB
                        size Bsize
                call Update~Directory (Depth1, Index, Buddy2)
            end if
            if EndMaster = Buddy1 then            Determine current block on the
                let Address = Buddy2              basis of whether last block was
            else                                  first buddy or not
                let Address = Buddy1
            end if
            if Count[Expansion] = 0 then
                let Expansion = Expansion – 1             Halve size of directory
                let EndDirectory = EndDirectory ÷ 2
            end if
            let Done = Depth
        else
            let Done = 0
        end if
    end loop
    let Index = Hash mod shift (1, Depth)         Write block containing current
    seek Master position Address                  bucket
    write into Master from Depth size Isize, Index size Isize, Bucket size Bsize
end Hash~Remove
```

10.3.4 Hash~Open (receives MasterName, DirectoryName)

Pseudo Code

open master file and directory file
obtain number of doublings, and end of file positions for both files from master file
obtain frequency counts of number of hash code bits used by each master file record

Code

```
procedure Hash~Open (MasterName, DirectoryName are text)
    open Master file MasterName
    open Directory file DirectoryName
    seek Master position 0
    read from Master into Expansion size Isize, EndDirectory size Isize, EndMaster
            size Isize
```

```
        for i = 0 to MaxDepth
            seek Master position (i + 3) * Isize
            read from Master into Count[i] size Isize
        end for
    end Hash~Open
```

10.3.5 Hash~Create (receives MasterName, DirectoryName)

Pseudo Code

```
    create directory file
    insert first available master file position into first directory entry
    open master file
    initialize number of doublings, and end of file positions for both files
    initialize frequency counts of number of hash code bits used by each master file
            record
    save initialized values in master file
```

Code

```
    procedure Hash~Create (MasterName, DirectoryName are text)
        variables Address, Index are integers
        variable Bucket is text
        let Address = Isize * (MaxDepth + 4)
        create Directory file DirectoryName
        seek Directory position 0
        write into Directory from Address size Isize
        let Expansion = 0
        let EndDirectory = Isize
        let EndMaster = Address + Rsize
        create Master file MasterName
        seek Master position 0
        write into Master from Expansion size Isize, EndDirectory size Isize, EndMaster
                size Isize
        for i = 0 to MaxDepth
            let Count[i] = 0
            seek Master position (i + 3) * Isize
            write into Master from Count[i] size Isize
        end for
        let Bucket = ""
        let Index = 0
        write into Master from Expansion size Isize, Index size Isize, Bucket size Bsize
    end Hash~Create
```

10.3.6 Hash~Close

Pseudo Code

```
    save number of doublings and end of file positions in master file
    save frequency counts of number of hash code bits used by each master file record
            in master file
    close file
```

Code

```
procedure Hash~Close
    seek Master position 0
    write into Master from Expansion size Isize, EndDirectory size Isize, EndMaster
            size Isize
    for i = 0 to MaxDepth
        seek Master position (i + 3) * Isize
        write into Master from Count[i] size Isize
    end for
    close Master
    close Directory
end Hash~Close
```

Local **Hash~Function** (receives Key; *result integer*)

```
function Hash~Function (Key is text) is integer
    variable Sum is integer
    let Sum = 0
    for i = first to last (Key)
        let Sum = Sum + (byte (Key, i) * (i – first + 1))
    end for
    result Sum
end Hash~Function
```

Local **Split~Bucket** (receives Bucket; supplies BucketA, BucketB; receives Depth)

```
procedure Split~Bucket (Bucket, BucketA, BucketB are text, Depth is integer)
    variable K is integer
    variables Bdata, Bkey are text
    let BucketA = “”
    let BucketB = “”
    let K = first
    loop until K > last (Bucket)
        call Extract~String (Bucket, K, Bkey)
        call Extract~String (Bucket, K, Bdata)
        if shift (Hash~Function (Bkey), –Depth) mod 2 = 0 then
            call Append~String (BucketA, Bkey)
            call Append~String (BucketA, Bdata)
        else
            call Append~String (BucketB, Bkey)
            call Append~String (BucketB, Bdata)
        end if
    end loop
end Split~Bucket
```

Local **Join~Buckets** (supplies Bucket; receives BucketA, BucketB)

```
procedure Join~Buckets (Bucket, BucketA, BucketB are text)
    variable K is integer
    variable String is text
```

```
        let Bucket = BucketA
        let K = first
        loop until K > last (BucketB)
            call Extract~String (BucketB, K, String)
            call Append~String (Bucket, String)
        end loop
    end Join~Buckets

Local  Update~Directory (receives Depth, Index, Buddy)
    procedure Update~Directory (Depth, Index, Buddy are integers)
        for i = 0 to (shift (1, Expansion – Depth) – 1)
            seek Directory position (Index + (i * shift (1, Depth))) * Isize
            write into Directory from Buddy size Isize
        end for
    end Update~Directory

Local  Append~String (updates Bucket; receives String)
    procedure Append~String (Bucket, String are text)
        call append (Bucket, length (String))
        for i = first to last (String)
            call append (Bucket, byte (String, i))
        end for
    end Append~String

Local  Extract~String (receives Bucket; updates K; supplies String)
    procedure Extract~String (Bucket is text, K is integer, String is text)
        let String = ""
        for i = (K + 1) to (K + byte (Bucket, K))
            call append (String, byte (Bucket, i))
        end for
        let K = K + byte (Bucket, K) + 1
    end Extract~String

Local  Get~Master (receives Hash, Address, Depth, Bucket)
    procedure Get~Master (Hash, Address, Depth are integers, Bucket is text)
        variable Index is integer
        seek Directory position (Hash * Isize)
        read from Directory into Address size Isize
        seek Master position Address
        read from Master into Depth size Isize, Index size Isize, Bucket size Bsize
    end Get~Master
```

TEST PROGRAM

<u>Local Names</u>

Data	Data item associated with key
Key	Current key

N	Size of test problem
StartDirectory	Position of end of directory when directory is empty
StartMaster	Position of end of master file when master file is empty

Pseudo Code

```
for i = 1 to N
    insert N strings of i contiguous characters
end for
for i = 1 to N
    remove N strings of i contiguous characters
end for
check master file and directory file have been returned to their original state
```

Code

```
variables Key, Data are text
variables StartDirectory, StartMaster are integers
constant N = 8
call Hash~Create ("Master", "Directory")
let StartDirectory = EndDirectory
let StartMaster = EndMaster
for i = 0 to (N – 1)
    let Key = ""
    for j = 0 to (N – 1)
        call append (Key, i + j + 'a')          Insert keys into empty file
        call Hash~Insert (Key, Key)
    end for
end for
call Hash~Close
call Hash~Open ("Master", "Directory")
call Hash~Search ("z", Data)                    Check that key not inserted can-
check Data = ""                                 not be found
for i = 0 to (N – 1)
    let Key = ""
    for j = 0 to (N – 1)
        call append (Key, i + j + 'a')          Check that inserted keys can be
        call Hash~Search (Key, Data)            found
        check Data = Key
        call Hash~Remove (Key)                  Remove keys and check their
        call Hash~Search (Key, Data)            removal
        check Data = ""
    end for
end for
call Hash~Close
check EndDirectory = StartDirectory             Check that file sizes are the same
check EndMaster = StartMaster                   as their original values
```

11 Matrices

A matrix is just a two-way table of numbers. A table or matrix is frequently a convenient way in which to organize the data relevant to a particular problem. For certain kinds of problems specific algorithms have been developed that perform rather complex numerical feats in order to obtain a solution.

One of the most successful algorithms of this kind is "linear programming". It is poorly named, in that the algorithm has nothing to do with writing computer programs in a straight line, or setting up radio programs to follow each other in a strictly determined sequence. Linear programming carries out "constrained optimization". What "programming" means in this context is examining a range of alternatives in a methodical manner and determining the best alternative that is consistent with restrictions set out in tabular form. The algorithm has been used with great success by the oil industry, saving the industry millions of dollars by choosing the best ways in which to transport its product around the world. It is used in the livestock industry, ensuring that animals receive adequate nutrition while keeping costs as low as possible. In the financial sector linear programming can be used to allocate investments subject to various requirements. The algorithm is discussed in Section 11.3.

When the number of variables in a linear programming problem is equal to the number of independent constraints, the problem reduces to a simpler form. All that is required is to solve a set of simultaneous linear equations. Such linear equations arise in other ways. For example, in least squares statistical analysis it is often necessary to solve simultaneous linear equations to obtain summary information about experimental data. In fitting a spline curve through a set of points (Section 12.2) it is necessary to solve simultaneous linear equations to obtain the coefficients of a cubic polynomial for each interval between the points. There are many other applications for this algorithm, which is presented in Section 11.1.

The two algorithms above make use of a fundamental tool called the "pivot step" or "pivotal transformation". This tool is also used in computing the inverse of a matrix. The pivot step has been included as a separate algorithm in Section 11.2 for two reasons. First, it will help you to understand more fully the workings of the algorithms for linear programming and simultaneous linear equations. Second, the algorithm is useful in its own right for a number of applications. You will find an example of unraveling the cross-ownerships of companies by each other. The algorithm is employed in economic analyses that make use of input-output matrices. It also forms the basis of the multiple regression analysis algorithm discussed in Section 12.4.

There is a decision-making technique that helps in conflict resolution, and in getting some quantitative information about largely qualitative issues. We have used it frequently in obtaining management input regarding tender evaluations for information technology equipment. Management can be rather reticent about having a say, because of limited knowledge of the technology. The process builds commitment and ensures that decisions are made on organizational, rather than purely technological, grounds.

The technique involves comparing evaluation criteria two at a time and deciding on the relative weighting of those two with respect to each other. This produces a table, or matrix, of pairwise comparisons from which overall weights for all criteria need to be computed. Condensing the pairwise weights into a single weight for each criterion requires that the first "eigenvalue" and "eigenvector" of the matrix be computed. The algorithm in Section 11.4 does this job. This particular application is discussed more fully in that section.

In order to test the algorithms in Sections 11.1, 11.2, and 11.4 effectively a matrix, or set of equations, is needed that has known properties. It is best to have a matrix that is "difficult" to work with numerically, so that inherent weaknesses in the algorithms can be easily identified. Such a matrix is obtained from the potentially infinite Hilbert matrix, named after one of history's most able mathematicians. When you encounter the matrix in those three sections you will recognize it as having elements X(I, J) = 1 / (I + J – 1). For example, the 4 x 4 segment of the Hilbert matrix is as follows:

$$\begin{matrix} 1 & {}^1/_2 & {}^1/_3 & {}^1/_4 \\ {}^1/_2 & {}^1/_3 & {}^1/_4 & {}^1/_5 \\ {}^1/_3 & {}^1/_4 & {}^1/_5 & {}^1/_6 \\ {}^1/_4 & {}^1/_5 & {}^1/_6 & {}^1/_7 \end{matrix}$$

11.1 LINEAR EQUATIONS

Solving a set of simultaneous linear equations

Example

Company A owns 30% of company B, and B owns 60% of A. A's assets other than shares in B are valued at $1 million, and B's assets other than shares in A are valued at $2 million. To be consistent, the valuations of A and B inclusive of shares must be related by the equations:

A = 1.0 + (0.3 * B)
B = (0.6 * A) + 2.0

These equations can be rearranged to have A and B on the same side of the equals signs:

A – (0.3 * B) = 1.0
–(0.6 * A) + B = 2.0

If the array of coefficients:

 1.0 –0.3
–0.6   1.0

is in the two-dimensional array X, the right-hand sides are in the array R, the value of N is equal to 2, and variables are provided for D and S, the equations are solved using:

call Equations~Solve (X, R, N, D, S)

The computed valuations of companies A and B ($1.95 million and $3.17 million) replace the right-hand sides R[1] and R[2] respectively.

Subprograms

11.1.1 Equations~Solve (updates X, R; receives N; supplies Determinant, Significance)

Usage

As shown in the example, the coefficients of the variables must be set up in the matrix with nickname X. The number of equations, equal to the number of variables, is given the nickname N. The right-hand sides of the equations are in the one-dimensional array with nickname R. The values of X[I, J] and R[I], for J taking the values 1 to N, comprise the specification for the I-th equation, for I taking the values 1 to N. The value of the J-th variable determined by the algorithm is returned in R[J].

The algorithm returns two values, Determinant and Significance, which provide information about the matrix of coefficients. As its name implies, Determinant contains the determinant of the coefficient matrix. Significance contains an estimate of the number of bits of significance that remain in the solution. Interpretation of this estimate is discussed more fully in the analysis below. Suffice it to say here that unless the significance of the results is more than a few bits, the results will be misleading.

Analysis

This algorithm is an efficient implementation of Gaussian elimination, along the lines of the subprogram of Moler (1972). The triangularization process and back substitution used in this algorithm are considerably more efficient than complete elimination. Nevertheless, the algorithm requires processing time proportional to the cube of the number of variables, requiring O (N^3) execution time.

To see how the algorithm works it is worthwhile tracing the solution of just two equations. As in the example above, there is a 2×2 matrix of coefficients and an array containing two right-hand sides. Using symbols, the coefficient and right-hand side arrays are as follows:

```
X[1, 1]   X[1, 2]   R[1]
X[2, 1]   X[2, 2]   R[2]
```

There is some code that rearranges the order of the equations. Ignore this code for now. It merely ensures that in any column under consideration the element on the main diagonal of the matrix has as large a magnitude as possible. This is done only to improve the numerical stability of the process (Wilkinson 1967). Rearranging the order of equations makes no difference to the solution produced.

The matrix is transformed by the code at the end of the first rather long *for* loop as follows. The element X[1, 1] is the divisor, and is called the "pivot". The pivot is always on the main diagonal having subscripts that are equal (perhaps after rearranging the order of the equations).

```
 X[1, 1]               X[1, 2]
–X[2, 1] / X[1, 1]     X[2, 2] – (X[2, 1] * X[1, 2] / X[1, 1])
```

Because the matrix is only 2 × 2 in size, no further work is done by the first part of the algorithm. The forward and backward substitutions now take place, using the right-hand sides. The matrix itself is not changed any further, but the right-hand sides are transformed. At the end of the forward substitution only the second right-hand side has been changed:

```
R[1]
R[2] – (R[1] * X[2, 1] / X[1, 1])
```

The backward substitution carries out the bulk of the work for this simple example. The second pivot, the transformed value of X[2, 2], is used here. Before simplifying the expressions, but letting Pivot = X[2, 2] – (X[2, 1] * X[1, 2] / X[1, 1]) for simplicity of presentation, you obtain:

```
R[1] / X[1, 1] – X[1, 2] / X[1, 1] * (R[2] – R[1] * X[2, 1] / X[1, 1]) / Pivot
(R[2] – R[1] * X[2, 1] / X[1, 1]) / Pivot
```

Simplifying these expressions you end up with:

```
(R[1] * X[2, 2] – R[2] * X[1, 2]) / (X[1, 1] * Pivot)
(R[2] * X[1, 1] – R[1] * X[2, 1]) / (X[1, 1] * Pivot)
```

You can check by alternative calculation that these are the correct solutions for two equations. Although this does not prove that the method works for a larger system of equations, it increases one's confidence in the correctness of the algorithm.

The algorithm may be split easily into two separate parts if multiple right-hand sides must be processed for a given matrix of coefficients. The early part of the algorithm before the forward substitution does not use the right-hand sides. The later part of the algorithm makes no further changes to the matrix and processes only the right-hand sides. Therefore the later part of the algorithm may be used repeatedly, and applied to multiple right-hand sides.

The accuracy of the solution is very much determined by the "condition" of the equations. If any of them is actually redundant, because it is just a combination of the other equations, they are said to be "singular". There is no unique solution to singular equations. The algorithm returns Determinant = 0 in this case. In practice, you rarely find equations being exactly singular. It is more usual to find that some of the equations are "almost" linear combinations of the others. Gaussian elimination applied blindly to such equations will generate a result that may be very different from the true solution, while providing no warning to the user.

The problem with many published Gaussian elimination algorithms is that they give no indication of near-singularity. In the *Collected Algorithms from ACM* alone there are eight algorithms (16, 43, 107, 126, 135, 195, 423, 576), of which only one (McKeeman 1962) provides an approximate measure of the condition of the equations. That algorithm and the later one of Barrodale and Stuart (1981) incorporate a refinement process, in which the initial solution determined by Gaussian elimination is improved iteratively. This ensures that a meaningful result is obtained even with poorly conditioned equations. The disadvantage with these algorithms is that they are lengthy, being unlikely to be attractive to busy programmers.

In many practical applications there is no point in trying to get a correct solution to poorly conditioned equations. Equation coefficients are normally measurements taken from some kind of industrial, commercial, scientific, or agricultural process and are subject to error. Minor changes in equation coefficients will produce major fluctuations in the solution when the equations are ill-conditioned. Poor conditioning is often, but not always, a symptom of underlying problems. Frequently the correct remedy is changing the specification of the problem or using an alternative solution framework rather than pursuing numerical accuracy. For example, one might use stepwise linear regression or linear programming instead of direct solution of linear equations. If you are willing to accept one of a large or infinite set of solutions to a near-singular system of equations, chosen according to certain criteria, you should consult Barrodale and Stuart (1981).

You do not have to specify a "tolerance" figure in advance. A "tolerance" is a small number that provides the algorithm with a cutoff point beyond which values of pivots are assumed to be zero, and therefore that indicate singularity. You inevitably have to experiment with various tolerances in order to obtain a usable solution to the problem at hand. You may have little knowledge of the range in which suitable tolerance figures should lie. The algorithm is written in such a way that specification of a tolerance is unnecessary.

The chosen algorithm is relatively simple, but it provides safeguards against poor conditioning for programmers who may not be specialists in numerical analysis. From a practical point of view the effect of poor conditioning is manifested in the loss of significance during subtraction of numbers that are nearly equal. When the result of such a subtraction is used as a pivot, the loss of significance is propagated through the entire matrix of coefficients. For example, suppose element X[3, 3] is to be used as the next pivot, and its value was calculated in the previous iteration by subtracting 4.178326 from 4.179022. Its value is now 0.000696, which has just three significant digits. The pivoting process will result in all matrix elements being downgraded as a result, from seven significant digits to only three.

Our algorithm examines each pivot before it is used, and compares the two numbers that were subtracted to produce it during the previous pivot step. The similarity of the two figures, as measured by Similarity~Bits, gives an approximate measure of the loss of significance. This loss will be propagated in the current pivot step. The solution to the equations has a potential maximum significance of *maxbits*. This is reduced by the pivot similarity on each iteration, giving an approximate upper bound to the significance of the final result. Very little extra code is required for this measure and it has a negligible impact on the efficiency of the algorithm. The usefulness of Significance is attested to by the fact that it is within a couple of bits of the accuracy of the known solution developed by the test program. Tests with a variety of other matrices show that our measure is within the ballpark of the logarithm to base two of the matrix condition numbers.

IMPLEMENTATION

Exported Names

Equations~Solve	Solves simultaneous equations by Gaussian elimination (11.1.1)

Imported Names

Similarity~Bits	Finds the number of bits in common in two numbers (2.3.1)

Nicknames

Determinant	Determinant of matrix of coefficients
N	Number of equations and unknowns
R	Array of right-hand sides and solution of equations
Significance	Total number of bits of significance lost by all pivots
X	Array of equation coefficients and decomposed matrix

Local Names

Index	Array of pointers to rows used as pivot rows
P1, P2	Values that were subtracted to give current pivot
Pivot	Current pivot

11.1.1 Equations~Solve (updates X, R; receives N; supplies Determinant, Significance)

Pseudo Code

```
initialize Determinant to 1
for k = 1 to N
    find the position Index[k] of the largest value (Pivot) in column k at or below
            row k
    let Determinant = Determinant * Pivot
    check Pivot ≠ 0
    if pivot row is not on main diagonal, exchange it to main diagonal and negate
            determinant
    calculate loss of significance in Pivot and subtract it from Significance
    carry out elimination to right of and below Pivot
end for
carry out forward substitution
carry out backward substitution
```

Code

```
procedure Equations~Solve (X is matrix of real, R is array of real, N is integer,
        Determinant is real, Significance is integer)
    variable Index is array 1 to N of real
```

```
variables P1, P2, Pivot are real
let Determinant = 1
for k = 1 to N
    let Pivot = 0
    for i = k to N                                  Find pivot as largest column
        if magnitude (X[i, k]) > magnitude          element
(Pivot) then
            let Index[k] = i
            let Pivot = X[i, k]
        end if
    end for
    let Determinant = Determinant * Pivot           Update progressive determinant
    check Pivot ≠ 0                                 value
    if Index[k] ≠ k then
        let Determinant = –Determinant
        for j = k to N                              Move pivot to main diagonal
            call swap (X[Index[k], j], X[k, j])
        end for
    end if
    if k = 1 then                                   Calculate loss of significance in
        let Significance = maxbits                  pivot
    else
        let P1 = –X[Index[k], k–1] * X[k–1, k]
        let P2 = X[k, k] + P1
        let Significance = Significance – Similarity~Bits (P1, P2, 0)
    end if
    for i = (k + 1) to N
        let X[i, k] = –X[i, k] / Pivot
    end for
    for j = (k + 1) to N                            Carry out elimination using
        for i = (k + 1) to N                        current pivot
            let X[i, j] = X[i, j] + (X[i, k] * X[k, j])
        end for
    end for
end for
for j = 1 to (N – 1)                                Carry out forward substitution
    call swap (R[j], R[Index[j]])
    for i = (j + 1) to N
        let R[i] = R[i] + (X[i, j] * R[j])
    end for
end for
for decreasing j = N to 1                           Carry out backward substitution
    let R[j] = R[j] / X[j, j]
    for i = 1 to (j – 1)
        let R[i] = R[i] – (X[i, j] * R[j])
    end for
end for
end Equations~Solve
```

TEST PROGRAM

Imported Names

Similarity~Bits	Finds the number of bits in common in two numbers (2.3.1)

Local Names

D	Determinant
M	Number of equations
R	Right-hand sides
S	Significance
X	Matrix of equation coefficients

Pseudo Code

```
initialize coefficients of the ill-conditioned Hilbert matrix
compute right-hand sides for a solution equal to consecutive integers
call Equations~Solve
check similarity of solution to correct solution is about equal to Significance
```

Code

```
constant M = 10
variable X is matrix 1 to M, 1 to M of real
variable R is array 1 to M of real
variables D, S are real
for n = 1 to M
    for i = 1 to n
        let R[i] = 0
        for j = 1 to n
            let X[i, j] = 1 / (i + j – 1)
            let R[i] = R[i] + (X[i, j] * j)
        end for
    end for
    call Equations~Solve (X, R, n, D, S)
    for i = 1 to n
        check Similarity~Bits (R[i], i, 1) ≥ S – 2
    end for
end for
```

11.2 PIVOT STEP

Carrying out one step of a matrix inversion operation

Example

To invert a diagonally dominant N × N matrix X (one with relatively large elements on the main diagonal):

```
for k = 1 to N
    call Pivot~Step (X, N, N, k, k)
end for
```

Subprograms

11.2.1 Pivot~Step (updates X; receives Nrows, Ncols, Row, Col)
11.2.2 Symmetric~Pivot (updates X; receives N; updates Used; receives Piv)

Usage

Pivot~Step carries out a pivotal transformation on any matrix (provided that the chosen pivot element is nonzero). The nickname X is the matrix on which the pivotal transformation is to be carried out. The next two nicknames, Nrows and Ncols, indicate the number of rows and columns in the matrix. The first row and column is assumed to be numbered 1. The last two nicknames, Row and Col, specify the row and column numbers of the pivot element itself. In the example, Pivot~Step is applied to the main diagonal element of a square matrix, which explains the provision of N and *k* twice in the example.

Symmetric~Pivot also carries out a pivotal transformation, but makes use of only the lower triangle of the matrix. The assumption is that the full matrix is symmetric, with X[I, J] = X[J, I]. This algorithm is useful for least squares applications, which typically generate a symmetric matrix. Such applications need generate only the lower triangle, thereby increasing their efficiency. The algorithm is restricted to carrying out pivots using elements on the main diagonal of the matrix. The *true-false* array Used indicates which elements have been used as pivots. Call the subprogram initially with Piv = 0 to initialize Used, and then subsequently specify Piv as the pivot row/column.

The use of Symmetric~Pivot may permit an application to save memory space. If the programming language you are using allows a matrix to be declared as *symmetric*, storing only one triangle, the subprogram will work as is. Otherwise, it is easy to simulate this feature. An N × N matrix requires N * (N + 1) ÷ 2 memory locations for one triangle. Allocate this amount of storage in a one-dimensional array. Then access elements X[I, J] using a single subscript, written as X[Index (I, J)]. The function Index returns a value equal to the position of element X[I, J] in the one-dimensional array. Index is programmed as follows, and is almost as efficient as the usual subscript calculation process. Both require a multiplication and an addition. Index also requires a subtraction and a shift right to divide by two.

```
function Index (I, J are integers) is integer
    result (((I – 1) * I) ÷ 2) + J
end Index
```

Analysis

A matrix inversion algorithm was first made widely available by Orden (1960), and the algorithm relies on his description. A pivotal transformation is in essence one of N steps required to invert an N × N matrix. The key idea is that whatever operations transform a matrix to the unit matrix will transform a unit matrix to the inverse of the original matrix. To see how this works, look at a 3 × 3 matrix in the array X alongside a unit matrix. Subscripts such as X[1, 2] are abbreviated to X_{12} for simplicity of presentation.

$$\begin{matrix} X_{11} & X_{12} & X_{13} & 1 & 0 & 0 \\ X_{21} & X_{22} & X_{23} & 0 & 1 & 0 \\ X_{31} & X_{32} & X_{33} & 0 & 0 & 1 \end{matrix}$$

First, divide the top row throughout by X[1, 1]:

$$\begin{array}{llllll} 1 & X_{12}/X_{11} & X_{13}/X_{11} & 1/X_{11} & 0 & 0 \\ X_{21} & X_{22} & X_{23} & 0 & 1 & 0 \\ X_{31} & X_{32} & X_{33} & 0 & 0 & 1 \end{array}$$

Now subtract X[2, 1] times the top row from the second row, and X[3, 1] times it from the third row:

$$\begin{array}{llllll} 1 & X_{12}/X_{11} & X_{1}\ /X_{11} & 1/X_{11} & 0 & 0 \\ 0 & X_{22} - X_{21}*X_{12}/X_{11} & X_{23} - X_{21}*X_{13}/X_{11} & -X_{21}/X_{11} & 1 & 0 \\ 0 & X_{32} - X_{31}*X_{12}/X_{11} & X_{33} - X_{31}*X_{13}/X_{11} & -X_{31}/X_{11} & 0 & 1 \end{array}$$

That completes the first of three pivot steps required to invert the 3 × 3 matrix. Note that there are still three unit columns in the six columns. This suggests a compact way of storing the information. You don't have to store the unit matrix at all, because its elements are known and easily computable if required. In the above example, move the fourth column into the first column, which gives:

$$\begin{array}{lll} 1/X_{11} & X_{12}/X_{11} & X_{13}/X_{11} \\ -X_{21}/X_{11} & X_{22} - X_{21}*X_{12}/X_{11} & X_{23} - X_{21}*X_{13}/X_{11} \\ -X_{31}/X_{11} & X_{32} - X_{31}*X_{12}/X_{11} & X_{33} - X_{31}*X_{13}/X_{11} \end{array}$$

This provides you with a specification for the pivotal transformation, or pivot step, using element X[1, 1] as the pivot element. The process is easily generalized to use other pivot elements. The main diagonal elements must be larger than all other elements, otherwise a general-purpose inversion algorithm such as that given by Boothroyd (1964) should be used.

The steps that transform a matrix to the unit matrix will transform a unit matrix to the inverse of the original matrix. The inverse of the inverse of a matrix is the matrix itself. Therefore, going through the same pivot steps again will restore the original matrix, degraded by the effects of any loss of significance as discussed in Section 11.1.

Symmetric~Pivot makes use of the observation that after a number of pivots on a full symmetric matrix the matrix is still symmetric apart from changes of sign. X[I, J] is always equal to plus or minus X[J, I]. The sign of an element depends on whether or not its row and column correspond with a row or a column previously used as a pivot. A straightforward modification of Pivot~Step results in a complicated series of tests in the final matrix transformation. For this reason, two additional one-dimensional arrays, Rpiv and Cpiv, are used to contain the pivot row and column. These arrays simplify, and make very efficient, the matrix transformation process. The algorithm is described by Rutishauser (1963).

IMPLEMENTATION

<u>Exported Names</u>

Pivot~Step	Carries out a pivotal transformation (11.2.1)
Symmetric~Pivot	Carries out a pivot step on a symmetric matrix (11.2.2)

<u>Nicknames</u>

Col	Column number of pivot element
N	Number of rows and columns in matrix

Ncols	Number of columns in matrix
Nrows	Number of rows in matrix
Row	Row number of pivot element
Used	Array of *true false* indicators of rows/columns used as pivots
X	Matrix

Local Names

Cvalue	Element in pivot column
Rpiv	Pivot row
Pivot	Pivot element
Cpiv	Pivot column

11.2.1 Pivot~Step (updates X; receives Nrows, Ncols, Row, Col)

Pseudo Code

```
invert pivot element
for i = 1 to Nrows
    if i is not the index of the pivot row then
        transform all elements in the row
    end if
end for
transform all elements in the pivot row
replace the inverted pivot in the matrix
```

Code

```
procedure Pivot~Step (X is matrix of real, Nrows, Ncols, Row, Col are integers)
    variables Cvalue, Pivot are real
    check 0 < Row and Row ≤ Nrows
    check 0 < Col and Col ≤ Ncols
    check X[Row, Col] ≠ 0
    let Pivot = 1 / X[Row, Col]
    for i = 1 to Nrows
        if i ≠ Row then
            let Cvalue = – X[i, Col] * Pivot
            for j = 1 to Ncols
                let X[i, j] = X[i, j] + (X[Row, j] * Cvalue)
            end for
            let X[i, Col] = Cvalue
        end if
    end for
    for j = 1 to Ncols
        let X[Row, j] = X[Row, j] * Pivot
    end for
    let X[Row, Col] = Pivot
end Pivot~Step
```

11.2.2 Symmetric~Pivot (updates X; receives N; updates Used; receives Piv)

Pseudo Code

```
initialize Used indicators if pivot row/column is zero
invert pivot element, initializing pivot row/column values of Rpiv and Cpiv
```

```
calculate Rpiv and Cpiv values for elements preceding pivot row/column
calculate Rpiv and Cpiv values for elements following pivot row/column
for i = 1 to N
    transform all elements in row i up to main diagonal
end for
```

Code

```
procedure Symmetric~Pivot (X is matrix of real, N is integer, Used is array of true-
        false, Piv is integer)
    variables Rpiv, Cpiv are arrays 1 to N of real
    if Piv = 0 then                                  Initialize array, specifying pivots
        for i = 1 to N                               used so far
            let Used[i] = false
        end for
    else-if Piv > 0 and Piv ≤ N
        let Used[Piv] = not Used[Piv]                Set up current pivot
        let Cpiv[Piv] = 1 / X[Piv, Piv]
        let Rpiv[Piv] = 1
        let X[Piv, Piv] = 0
        for j = 1 to (Piv – 1)                       Transform the pivot column
            let Rpiv[j] = X[Piv, j]                  before the pivot
            let Cpiv[j] = X[Piv, j] * Cpiv[Piv]
            if Used[j] ≠ Used[Piv] then
                let Cpiv[j] = –Cpiv[j]
            end if
            let X[Piv, j] = 0
        end for
        for i = (Piv + 1) to N                       Transform the pivot row after the
            let Rpiv[i] = X[i, Piv]                  pivot
            if Used[i] = Used[Piv] then
                let Rpiv[i] = –Rpiv[i]
            end if
            let Cpiv[i] = –X[i, Piv] * Cpiv[Piv]
            let X[i, Piv] = 0
        end for
        for i = 1 to N                               Transform matrix elements
            for j = 1 to i
                let X[i, j] = X[i, j] + (Cpiv[i] * Rpiv[j])
            end for
        end for
    end if
end Symmetric~Pivot
```

TEST PROGRAM

Imported Names

Similarity~Test   Tests the similarity of two numbers (2.3.2)

<u>Local Names</u>

N	Number of rows and columns
U	Indicators of pivot row/columns used
X	Matrix

Pseudo Code

```
generate ill-conditioned matrix X
use Pivot~Step to invert matrix
use Symmetric~Pivot to invert inverse
check that all matrix elements are equal to their original values
```

Code

```
constant N = 5
variable X is matrix 1 to N, 1 to N of real
variable U is array 1 to N of true-false
for i = 1 to N                                    Set up ill-conditioned Hilbert
    for j = 1 to N                                matrix
        let X[i, j] = 1 / (i + j – 1)
    end for
end for
for i = 1 to N                                    Invert matrix
    call Pivot~Step (X, N, N, i, i)
end for
call Symmetric~Pivot (X, N, U, 0)
for i = 1 to N                                    Invert matrix again
    call Symmetric~Pivot (X, N, U, i)
end for
for i = 1 to N                                    Check lower triangle of original
    for j = 1 to i                                matrix restored
        check Similarity~Test (X[i, j], 1 / (i + j – 1), 1) = true
    end for
end for
```

NOTES—COMPANY VALUATION

Finding the real value of companies linked by cross-ownerships

Unraveling complex cross-ownerships among companies is quite a difficult process. In an address by a member of the Australian Stock Exchange (*Australian*, November 27, 1990) an example was given of five core companies, each of which owned 15% of two others. In addition, there were five joint venture companies, each owned 50/50 by pairs of core companies. Each joint venture company owned 30% of one of the core companies. Such an arrangement is perfectly legal, although it provides an opportunity for companies to hide information about the strengths and weaknesses of the group of interrelated companies as a whole. What does a shareholder in one of these companies actually own?

It is difficult to know what any one company in this web is really worth. The share price does not necessarily give a good indication, because the share price of any one of them is used in the evaluation of the others. If the share price of any one of them falls, this will drag down the value of the others, which will in turn affect the first one negatively. There is a way to unravel this maze, and it provides a practical case study for use of the pivot step algorithm.

The simultaneous equations algorithm Equations~Solve gives you a specific solution to the problem when you know precisely what the nonpaper assets of each company are worth, as well as the extent of ownership of each company by the others. Pivot~Step gives a more general solution as the inverse of a certain matrix, which is useful even when you don't know precisely the values of the nonpaper assets of each company. The example discussed in Section 11.1 will be used here also.

The solution obtained in Section 11.1 tells you that, for consistency, the valuations of A and B must be \$1.95 million and \$3.17 million respectively. It does not tell you that these *are* the valuations, just that there is some kind of problem in the structuring of the companies or in their assessment by the share market if the value of B is not half as much again as that of A.

Now invert the coefficient matrix, using the process given in the example at the start of this Section 11.2. The inverse is:

1.22	0.37
0.73	1.22

Use Company A as an example in understanding what these numbers mean. Remember that shareholders other than related companies hold 40% of it. The interpretation is that Company A has a paper valuation of 1.22 times its own nonpaper assets plus 0.37 times B's nonpaper assets, of which 40% or \$0.78 million is held by these shareholders. Similarly, you can work out that 70% of company B is worth \$2.22 million, the nonpaper assets in effect held by shareholders other than related companies. Note that 0.78 + 2.22 = 3, which is, as you would expect, the total of the nonpaper assets of the two companies, which are 1 and 2 million dollars.

The inverse matrix is useful by itself, in that it unravels the cross-ownerships and tells you exactly how each company is related to the nonpaper assets of the others. This simple example involved only two companies. Relationships of any complexity can be analyzed with this approach. Note that the matrix always has unity on the main diagonal, and negative entries less than one elsewhere. This ensures that Pivot~Step can be used safely to compute the inverse.

11.3 LINEAR PROGRAMMING

Finding the best way of doing something subject to certain constraints

Example

See the discussion below.

Subprograms

11.3.1 Simplex~Optimize (updates X; receives Nrows, Ncols)

Usage

It is necessary to construct a tableau (matrix of data) with nickname X, specifying a number of quantities. The tableau format is best described by a hypothetical example. Suppose you have up to $100,000 to invest and you want to decide among fixed interest securities, shares, and property. Assume you are able to achieve net returns of 4%, 3%, and 5% on the three types of investment respectively. You want the greatest overall return. You could put the money entirely into the highest-yielding investment, but that would not provide a satisfactory spread of risk. You have stipulated that you want at least half as much money in shares, the lowest performer, as in property. How much do you invest in each of the alternatives?

Let the variables F, S, and P represent the number of dollars you spend on fixed interest securities, shares, and property respectively. These values are unknown at present, but you have some constraints that can be specified symbolically. You cannot spend more than your budget, and so the sum of F, S, and P must be less than $100,000. Your other requirement, that you balance shares and property, is summarized by saying that P must always be less than 2 * S. These requirements can be written more formally as linear inequalities:

Constraint 1: $1 * F + 1 * S + 1 * P \leq 100{,}000$
Constraint 2: $0 * F - 2 * S + 1 * P \leq 0$

The return you get on your investment is 4% of whatever number of dollars is represented by F, plus 3% of S, plus 5% of P. In the jargon of linear programming, you wish to maximize the following "objective function":

Maximize: $0.04 * F + 0.03 * S + 0.05 * P$

You now have numbers that can be arranged in a consistent form, in a matrix X with three rows and four columns (Nrows = 3, Ncols = 4). Now, you will see how to use linear programming to solve the problem. The bottom right-hand corner element X[Nrows, Ncols] is set to zero by convention, and has a use soon to be discussed. Leave out the three variables F, S, and P as such, and think of them as being associated with the first three columns of the matrix.

1	1	1	100,000
0	–2	1	0
0.04	0.03	0.05	0

Attach labels to the rows and columns by adding row 0 and column 0 to the matrix X. To keep the presentation of the algorithm as simple as possible, numeric labels are used. The rows are numbered with negative integers and the columns with positive integers. The variables F, S, and P are now indicated by labels 1, 2, and 3 respectively.

0	1	2	3	0
–1	1	1	1	100,000
–2	0	–2	1	0
0	0.04	0.03	0.05	0

The zeros in the top row and left-hand column, (X[0, 0], X[Nrows, 0], and X[0, Ncols]), have been added to make the matrix easier to input with some simple code. They play no part in the solution process. With this matrix in X, and with Nrows = 3 and Ncols = 4, you call Simplex~Optimize (a "simplex" is an abstract mathematical object related to linear programming), which returns the transformed matrix:

0	–1	1	–2	0
2	0.3333	0.3333	–0.3333	33,333
3	0.6667	0.6667	0.3333	66,667
0	–0.0433	0.0033	–0.0067	–4,333

The algorithm has exchanged some of the row and column identifiers. To interpret the output, you look first for column numbers appearing in the row number positions. There are two such column numbers, 2 and 3, corresponding to S and P. From the right-hand column in the same rows you read the amounts to be invested, namely, $33,333 in shares and $66,667 in property. Any variables associated with column numbers still in the top row are assumed to be zero. Thus no money is to be invested in fixed interest securities, associated with variable number 1. The total amount of interest you earn is shown in the bottom right-hand corner element X[Nrows, Ncols] as a negative figure, which must be negated to give $4,333. This is equivalent to an average interest rate of 4.333%.

The algorithm assumes that the constraints are specified as *less than* inequalities. You may wish to use constraints that are equalities or *greater than* inequalities. It is easy to convert both of the latter into the former type of inequality. A constraint such as $A \geq B$, for example, is equivalent to $-A \leq -B$. Just multiply all coefficients by –1 to turn a *greater than* inequality into a *less than* inequality. A constraint such as $A = B$ is replaced by two constraints $A \leq B$ and $-A \leq -B$.

Some problems require that the objective function be minimized subject to *greater than* constraints, rather than maximized, as is assumed here, subject to *less than* constraints. A minimum can be obtained by specifying the tableau as the transpose of the form outlined above. The constraints, as *greater than* inequalities, should form the columns and the costs should be given as the last column. This takes advantage of the "dual" property of the simplex algorithm.

The test program inputs a file of test data and outputs the resulting final tableau to a file. The result obtained on your computer may validly differ in nonessential ways from our results, because of different random number sequences produced on the two machines. The test program is discussed more fully in the analysis below.

Analysis

Linear programming was developed in the 1940s, largely by Dantzig, with significant developments in the 1950s by Ford, Fulkerson, Kuhn, and Tucker. A summary of that work was produced in the late 1950s by Arden (1960). Generally speaking, the literature on linear programming is highly mathematical and abstract, although two- or three-dimensional geometric explanations are common. The account given here uses an alternative and simpler approach, illustrating the main concepts and making extensive use of the small example.

With some sleight of hand, the inequalities in the specification have been turned into equalities in the tableau. This has been sneakily done by associating the row numbers with dummy variables called "slack" variables. Each constraint has a corresponding slack variable. In the first tableau, slack variable numbered –1 has the value 100,000, and slack variable numbered –2 has the value zero. Now go back to the original specification of the problem and rewrite the inequalities in the form of equalities, using C_1 and C_2 to represent the slack variables numbered –1 and –2 respectively.

Constraint 1: $1 * F + 1 * S + 1 * P + 1 * C_1 + 0 * C_2 = 100{,}000$
Constraint 2: $0 * F - 2 * S + 1 * P + 0 * C_1 + 1 * C_2 = 0$

The actual variables F, S, and P are assumed to be zero at the beginning of the simplex algorithm. The slack variables "take up the slack" in the inequalities, leaving nothing unaccounted for. In order to achieve this they initially have values equal to the right-hand sides of the equations. In other words, C_1 = 100,000 and C_2 = 0. Thus you have what is called in the jargon an initial "feasible" solution involving only slack variables. The simplex algorithm produces a number of feasible solutions until it finds the one that is optimal.

From the final tableau you note that you invested in only two of the three possibilities. This illustrates an important property of linear programming. The total number of actual and slack variables in any feasible solution is always equal to the number of constraints. The number of actual, as opposed to slack, variables in a solution is at most equal to the number of constraints. In the example there are two constraints, and therefore you require at most two of the variables F, S, and P to be nonzero.

This fact immediately suggests a combinatorial method for finding the optimum: Take all possible combinations of Nrows variables from all actual and slack variables available. For each combination solve the set of Nrows of simultaneous linear equations given by the constraints. Evaluate the "objective function" using the values of the variables, and choose its largest value.

In the example there are five variables (three actual and two slack). There are ${}^5C_2$ possible combinations of two variables taken from five, or 10. This requires solving 10 sets of simultaneous equations. The first set, involving C_1 and C_2, is implicit in the initial tableau. F, S, and P are zero initially, and so you can ignore the part played by the coefficients of those variables in the constraints. In the initial tableau you have in effect the two simultaneous equations:

$$1 * C_1 + 0 * C_2 = 100{,}000$$
$$0 * C_1 + 1 * C_2 = 0$$

Choosing another set of equations at random as an example, the set involving P and C_1 is:

$$1 * P + 1 * C_1 = 100{,}000$$
$$1 * P + 0 * C_1 = 0$$

You can use Equations~Solve (Section 11.1) to generate the solutions for each such set of equations. The total interest earned by each solution is calculated by multiplying the computed value of each variable by its corresponding interest rate. Slack variables will earn zero interest, of course. The following table shows the results of all of this calculation:

Set 1: C_1 = \$100,000, C_2 = 0, Interest earned = 0
Set 2: F = \$100,000, S = 0, Interest earned = \$4,000
Set 3: F = \$100,000, P = 0, Interest earned = \$4,000

Set 4: F = ?, C_1 = ?, Indeterminate solution
Set 5: F = $100,000, C_2 = 0, Interest earned = $4,000
Set 6: S = $33,333, P = $66,667, Interest earned = $4,333
Set 7: S = 0, C_1 = $100,000, Interest earned = 0
Set 8: S = $100,000, C_2 = $200,000, Interest earned = $3,000
Set 9: P = 0, C_1 = $100,000, Interest earned = 0
Set 10: P = $100,000, C_2 = –$100,000, Negative value of a variable

Set 6 produces the best result, agreeing with the solution in the final tableau produced by the simplex algorithm. Some other features of linear programming are evident in this table. No solution was produced for Set 4, because the two equations contained insufficient information, or were "singular". You simply ignore such occurrences and focus on the sets for which solutions can be determined. The result for Set 10 is unacceptable because one of the variables has a negative value. Although we have not said so until now, there has been an implicit requirement that all variables have non-negative values. Again, you just ignore this set.

Quite clearly, you have carried out a lot of calculation on this very small problem. With a typical practical case, involving several hundred constraints and variables, the number of sets of equations to be solved becomes astronomical. The simplex algorithm reduces the amount of computation to a realistic level by providing several important shortcuts.

The simplex algorithm allows a change of one variable at a time, removing one from the current set and adding a new one. This is a very efficient process, using the pivot step algorithm discussed in Section 11.2. You never have to solve a full set of simultaneous equations. You start with the initial set, technically called the starting "basis", of slack variables, for which the solution consists of the right-hand sides of the constraints. Using one pivot step at a time you produce a new solution, with a basis that has one variable different from the previous basis.

The second important feature of the simplex algorithm is that it lets you know ahead of time which new variables will give a better solution and which ones will not. You avoid computing the values of variables for sets that end up giving an inferior solution. When you remove a variable from the basis and add a new one, you know ahead of time that you are not going backward in terms of your objective function. The third feature is that you do not create sets of variables that have indeterminate solutions, or that have negative variable values. These features of the simplex algorithm dramatically improve the process.

Now refer back to the final tableau produced by the algorithm. The interest rates in the last row have been transformed, and can be given a useful interpretation. They tell you the change in the net interest rate if the solution were to contain the variable associated with the column in question. For example, slack variable –1, or C_1, has the figure –0.0433 at the bottom of its column. This indicates that bringing C_1 into the basis would result in a net decrease in interest earned, at the rate of 4.33%. The figure for C_2 is 0.67%, and for F is 0.33%.

Why do the figures for these variables differ from their specified interest rates? The reason is that these figures take into account the changes that would occur in the values of all the variables in order to keep the constraints satisfied. If F were brought into the basis, for example, you find that the values of S and P would have to plummet to zero.

You change from investing \$33,333 at 3% and \$66,667 at 5% to investing \$100,000 at 4%. This is a net change in interest earned from \$4,333 to \$4,000, or an effective interest rate reduction of 0.33%. Thus, at any stage of the algorithm, the figures in the bottom row provide the information about which variables will move the objective function in the right direction.

At this point, you should become familiar with the pivot step algorithm. We discussed in Section 11.2 how to store the matrix in a compact form. Notice that the coefficients of C_1 and C_2 in the set of equalities at the top of this analysis form a "unit matrix", with a single 1 in each column and zeros otherwise. Every pivot step destroys one of the unit matrix columns and creates another in a different place. The unit matrix is always associated with variables that are in the current solution set, or basis. When you pivot, you remove a variable associated with one of the unit matrix columns and insert a variable that is currently not associated with a unit matrix column.

You use storage more efficiently when you do not store the unit matrix explicitly. That is where the row and column identifiers become useful. The identifiers in column 0 tell you which variables are currently in the basis. The identifiers in row 0 tell you which variables are not in the basis. When you carry out a pivot operation, you exchange one of the variables in the basis with one of the variables outside it. This is mirrored by simply exchanging the corresponding variable identifiers in row 0 and column 0.

The simplex algorithm iterates until it is unable to find a variable to bring into the basis that will improve the objective function. The vitally important part of the simplex algorithm is correctly choosing the matrix element to use as the pivot in each iteration. Remember that the row in which the pivot element is situated has an identifier in column 0 of the associated variable currently in the basis. The column in which the pivot element is situated has an identifier in row 0 of the associated variable currently not in the basis. The pivot operation will exchange the basis memberships of these two variables.

Every constraint coefficient is given the opportunity to become the pivot element in each iteration. Several checks are made to determine the best pivot. The first step is to eliminate unsuitable columns for the current iteration. Only columns that have a positive figure in the last row are acceptable, because these are the only ones that will result in an improvement in the objective function. The algorithm examines every element in the suitable columns. Elements that are negative or zero are rejected. Negative elements would result in the right-hand sides becoming negative, and that contravenes our requirement that the values of all variables be non-negative. Zero elements cannot be used as pivot elements because they specify no relationship between the variable associated with the column and the variable associated with the constraint row in which the element lies. You would end up trying to divide by zero.

In a given column, the algorithm selects the element that has the smallest ratio of the right-hand side to the element. If an element with a larger ratio were selected, you would find that other variables would illegally be driven to have negative values. At this point you have a suitable pivot element. The algorithm could go ahead and use it, but there may be better pivots in other columns.

Consider the set of all eligible pivot elements found by the process described in the previous paragraphs. There are various methods for choosing a pivot from this set. The algorithm uses the "steepest descent" criterion. It selects the pivot that makes the greatest change in the objective function. If there are several equal candidates, it chooses one at random. The code for choosing is simple and efficient, and gives all candidates equal chances of being selected. The current pivot is selected if a random integer between 1 and the number of candidates so far is equal to 1. This selection may be overridden by any new equal candidates.

Many linear programming problems are "degenerate", in the sense that in one or more iterations the best possible pivot makes a difference of zero in the objective function. Such problems may exhibit cycling if special precautions are not taken. This means that it is possible for the algorithm to keep removing and inserting the same variables in an endless loop. The random choice method fortunately eliminates the possibility of cycling. Nevertheless, very degenerate problems may be intractable to linear programming because of the very large number of combinations of variables involved. This means that large numbers of iterations can take place until any improvement in the objective function occurs.

The test program provides, as a kind of algorithmic joke, a solution to the "four queens" problem. This is a scaled-down version of the "eight queens" problem, in which it is required to place eight nonattacking queens on a chessboard with 64 squares. Queens are pieces that can attack vertically, horizontally, or diagonally. The requirement is that no two queens occupy the same row, column or diagonal. The "four queens" problem involves a board of sixteen squares.

The specification of the problem uses sixteen variables, which must be zero or one, to represent the sixteen squares. A variable has a value of one if a queen occupies that square and a value of zero otherwise. The constraints on placements in the rows, columns, and diagonals are then simple inequalities involving the relevant squares. The problem is highly degenerate, and useful as a test for the algorithm. Strictly speaking, the problem requires integer programming, because normal linear programming can result in fractional results, whereas zero-one results are required. However, the test program obtains a solution in eight iterations as shown below. You may have fun investigating how the algorithm could be tricked into giving integral variable values. One solution to the problem is shown in Figure 11.1.

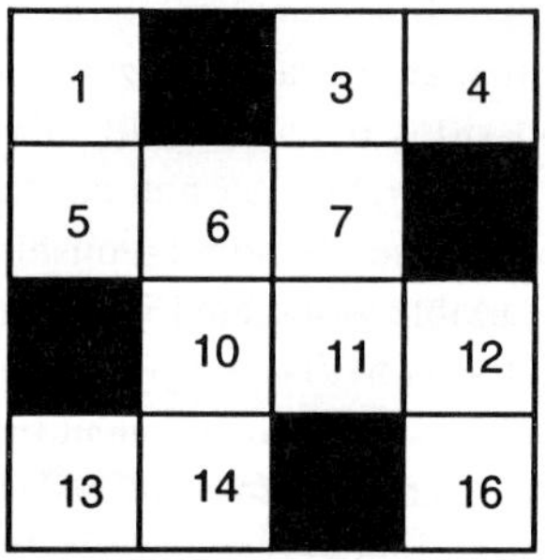

1		3	4
5	6	7	
	10	11	12
13	14		16

Figure 11.1

The question of efficiency is not an easy one to answer. Each iteration of the simplex algorithm requires O (Nrows * Ncols) running time. It is difficult to determine ahead of time how many iterations will be required for a given problem. It is generally believed that nondegenerate problems require O (Nrows) iterations. Degenerate problems may require running time that is either a high-degree polynomial function, or an exponential function, of Nrows.

IMPLEMENTATION

Exported Names	
Simplex~Optimize	Performs the simplex method (11.3.1)
Imported Names	
Integer~Initialize	Initializes random integer generator (8.1.4)
Pivot~Step	Carries out a pivotal transformation (11.2.1)
Random~Integer	Computes a random integer in a specified range (8.1.4)
Nicknames	
Ncols	Number of columns in the matrix X
Nrows	Number of rows in the matrix X
X	Linear programming tableau
Local Names	
Change	Amount by which objective function would change with this pivot
Col	Column in which a suitable pivot has been found
Csave	Column number of element intended for use as a pivot
MaxChange	Maximum value of Change
MinRatio	Minimum value of Ratio
Npivots	Number of potential pivots with equal validity to be selected
Ratio	Ratio of matrix element to right-hand side value
Row	Row in which a suitable pivot has been found
Rsave	Row number of element intended for use as a pivot
Select	Selects one of multiple potential pivots

11.3.1 Simplex~Optimize (updates X; receives Nrows, Ncols)

Pseudo Code

```
initialize indicator of pivot selection to ensure loop is entered
loop until no pivots were selected
    for j = 1 to (Ncols – 1)
        if element in last row for column j > 0 then
            save Row and Col positions of element with minimum ratio
        end
        if change in objective function due to element X[Row, Col] is maximum so
                far then
            initialize count of equal candidates
        end if
        if change in objective function due to element X[Row, Col] equals current
                maximum then
            choose element X[Rsave, Csave] as the pivot with probability 1 / number
                    of eligible pivots
        end if
    end for
```

```
        if pivot has been selected then
            call Pivot~Step to perform pivotal transformation
            exchange variable identifiers
        end if
    end loop
```

Code

```
procedure Simplex~Optimize (X is matrix of real, Nrows, Ncols are integers)
    variables Row, Rsave, Col, Csave, Npivots, Select are integers
    variables Change, MaxChange, Ratio, MinRatio are real
    let Select = –1
    loop until Select = 0                         Iterate until no pivot has been
        let Select = 0                            selected
        let MaxChange = –maxreal
        for j = 1 to (Ncols – 1)                  Select eligible column
            if X[Nrows, j] > 0 then
                let MinRatio = maxreal
                for i = 1 to (Nrows – 1)          Select eligible rows in the column
                    if X[i, j] > 0 then
                        let Ratio = X[i, Ncols] / X[i, j]
                        if Ratio ≥ 0 and Ratio < MinRatio then    Find row and
                            let MinRatio = Ratio                  column with
                            let Row = i                           minimum ratio
                            let Col = j
                        end if
                    end if
                end for
                if MinRatio < maxreal then
                    let Change = MinRatio * X[Nrows, j]
                    if Change > MaxChange then    Get candidate with maximum
                        let Npivots = 0           change in objective function
                        let MaxChange = Change
                    end if
                    if Change = MaxChange then    Deal with candidates having equal
                        let Npivots = Npivots + 1 impact on objective function
                        call Integer~Initialize (1, Npivots)
                        call Random~Integer (Select)
                        if Select = 1 then
                            let Rsave = Row
                            let Csave = Col
                        end if
                    end if
                end if
            end if
        end for
```

```
        if Select > 0 then                                If a pivot has been
           call Pivot~Step (X, Nrows, Ncols, Rsave, Csave)   selected, carry out
           call swap (X[Rsave, 0], X[0, Csave])          pivot step
        end if
     end loop
  end Simplex~Optimize
```

TEST PROGRAM

Imported Names

Random~Initialize	Initializes uniform random number generator (8.1.1)

Local Names

D	Data file number
M	Number of rows in matrix
N	Number of columns in matrix
R	Output results file number
X	Matrix used as linear programming tableau

Pseudo Code

```
open the data and results disk files
input the data file into matrix X from disk
call Simplex~Optimize
output the resulting matrix X to disk
```

Code

```
variable X is matrix 0 to 20, 0 to 20 of real
variables M, N, D, R are integers
call Random~Initialize (maxinteger – 1)
open D file "Test Data"
open R file "Results"
input from D into M, N
for i = 0 to M
   for j = 0 to N
      input from D into X[i, j]
   end for
end for
call Simplex~Optimize (X, M, N)
for i = 0 to M
   for j = 0 to N
      output into R from X[i, j]
   end for
end for
```

Test Data

```
19 17
  0  1  2  3  4  5  6  7  8  9 10 11 12 13 14 15 16  0
 -1  1  1  1  1  0  0  0  0  0  0  0  0  0  0  0  0  1
 -2  0  0  0  0  1  1  1  1  0  0  0  0  0  0  0  0  1
 -3  0  0  0  0  0  0  0  0  1  1  1  1  0  0  0  0  1
 -4  0  0  0  0  0  0  0  0  0  0  0  0  1  1  1  1  1
 -5  1  0  0  0  1  0  0  0  1  0  0  0  1  0  0  0  1
 -6  0  1  0  0  0  1  0  0  0  1  0  0  0  1  0  0  1
 -7  0  0  1  0  0  0  1  0  0  0  1  0  0  0  1  0  1
 -8  0  0  0  1  0  0  0  1  0  0  0  1  0  0  0  1  1
 -9  1  0  0  0  0  1  0  0  0  0  1  0  0  0  0  1  1
-10  0  1  0  0  0  0  1  0  0  0  0  1  0  0  0  0  1
-11  0  0  1  0  0  0  0  1  0  0  0  0  0  0  0  0  1
-12  0  0  0  0  1  0  0  0  0  1  0  0  0  0  1  0  1
-13  0  0  0  0  0  0  0  0  1  0  0  0  0  1  0  0  1
-14  0  1  0  0  1  0  0  0  0  0  0  0  0  0  0  0  1
-15  0  0  1  0  0  1  0  0  1  0  0  0  0  0  0  0  1
-16  0  0  0  1  0  0  1  0  0  1  0  0  1  0  0  0  1
-17  0  0  0  0  0  0  0  1  0  0  1  0  0  1  0  0  1
-18  0  0  0  0  0  0  0  0  0  0  0  1  0  0  1  0  1
  0  2  1  2  1  2  1  2  1  2  1  2  1  2  1  2  1  0
```

Results

```
  0 -5 -7  3 -1  5  6 -2 -8 -3 10 11 12 13 14 -4 16  0
  2 -1 -1  0  1  0  1  1 -1  1  1  0  0  0  1  1  0  1
  7  0  1  1  0  0  0  0  0  0  0  1  0 -1 -1 -1 -1  0
  9  0  0  0  0  0  0  0  0  1  1  1  1  0  0  0  0  1
 15  0  0  0  0  0  0  0  0  0  0  0  0  1  1  1  1  1
  1  1  0  0  0  1  0  0  0 -1 -1 -1 -1  1  0  0  0  0
 -6  1  1  0 -1  0  0 -1  1 -1  0  0  0  0  0 -1  0  0
  4  0  1  1  0 -1 -1 -1  1  0  0  1  1 -1 -1 -1  0  0
  8  0 -1 -1  0  1  1  1  0  0  0 -1  0  1  1  1  1  1
 -9 -1  0  0  0 -1  1  0  0  1  1  2  1 -1  0  0  1  1
-10  1  0 -1 -1  0 -1 -1  1 -1 -1 -1  1  1  0  0  1  0
-11  0  1  2  0 -1 -1 -1  0  0  0  1  0 -1 -1 -1 -1  0
-12  0  0  0  0  1  0  0  0  0  1  0  0 -1 -1 -1 -1  0
-13  0  0  0  0  0  0  0  0 -1 -1 -1 -1  0  1  0  0  0
-14  1  1  0 -1  1 -1 -1  1 -1 -1  0  0  0 -1 -1  0  0
-15  0  0  1  0  0  1  0  0 -1 -1 -1 -1  0  0  0  0  0
-16  0 -2 -2  0  1  1  1 -1  0  1 -2 -1  3  2  2  1  1
-17  0  1  1  0 -1 -1 -1  0  0  0  2  0 -1  0 -1 -1  0
-18  0  0  0  0  0  0  0  0  0  0  0  1 -1 -1 -1 -1  0
  0 -1 -1  0 -1  0  0 -1  0 -1  0  0  0  0  0 -1  0 -6
```

11.4 MATRIX ROOT

Finding the dominant eigenvalue and eigenvector of a matrix

Example

Assuming N = 2, and the N by N matrix X contains the following numbers:

1.00 0.81
0.64 1.00

the code:

call Eigen~Find (X, N, Root, V, A)

produces the eigenvalue 1.72 in Root, the eigenvector values 0.75 and 0.66 in V[1] and V[2], and a measure of accuracy in the variable A.

Subprograms

11.4.1 Eigen~Find (receives X, N; supplies Root, V, Accuracy)
11.4.2 Eigen~Deflate (updates X; receives N, Root, V)

Usage

This algorithm is intended as a "quick and dirty" procedure for obtaining the largest eigenvalue and its associated eigenvector from a matrix. The example above describes the use of the algorithm fairly well. The matrix elements X[I, J] are assumed to be stored with subscripts I and J both ranging from 1 to N. Similarly, the eigenvector array has elements from V[1] to V[N]. The eigenvalue computed by the algorithm is stored in Root.

If the matrix is symmetric, the algorithm may be used to find any number of eigenvalues and their associated eigenvectors. This is accomplished by calling Eigen~Deflate after each has been found. Eigen~Deflate "deflates" the matrix by the current eigenvalue and eigenvector, making the next largest eigenvalue available for extraction.

The matrix given to Eigen~Find need not be symmetric. Nonsymmetric matrices may have complex eigenvalues. If the root is complex, only its magnitude will be returned. The eigenvector returned by the algorithm will be meaningless if the root is complex.

The nickname Accuracy refers to a variable that receives an estimate of the minimum number of significant bits in the elements of the eigenvector. Accuracy will be high (around *maxbits*) for well-conditioned symmetric matrices, and for the first eigenvector of a reciprocal matrix. It will be zero for an eigenvector associated with a complex eigenvalue.

There are more efficient methods for general use when all eigenvalues of a large matrix are required (Ortega 1967). This algorithm is best when only the largest, or perhaps a few, eigenvalues and vectors are required, and the matrix is not too large. The current algorithm requires O (N^3) processing time to extract a single eigenvector, with a typical statistical matrix or a reciprocal matrix. The time to extract all eigenvalues from a symmetric matrix will be O (N^4). The method described by Ortega (1967) will extract all eigenvalues in O (N^3) time. With a typical personal computer, however, our algorithm will extract all eigenvalues from an 8×8 matrix in a few seconds.

The algorithm may be exceedingly slow if two or more of the largest eigenvalues are very close together in size. Such matrices do not arise in least squares statistical work, nor in the notes for the application discussed below. The method converges quickly for matrices with positive elements.

Analysis

The method used is the well-known power method. It was employed widely for statistical work in the days when matrix operations were performed without computers (Kendall 1957). It is still recommended (Anton and Rorres 1991) as a practical algorithm for use when mathematical packages with standard eigenvalue facilities are unavailable or unsuitable.

Given the mathematical sophistication needed for dealing with eigenvalues, no discussion of the reasons why the algorithm works will be given. If you are interested in such reasons, you should consult the readable mathematical explanation given by Anton and Rorres (1991). There is an extensive test program, which is careful to test symmetric and nonsymmetric matrices, and those with complex eigenvalues. For the kind of application discussed below you should run into no trouble using this algorithm, provided that the calling program checks the value of Accuracy and takes appropriate action if the value is small.

You may question why the algorithm uses a random number generator to obtain the first approximation. It is often suggested that the sums of the rows or columns give a better initial approximation than a random vector. This approach has not been used because there is a risk that a zero vector will be produced, causing the algorithm to fail. When eigenvalues are widely spaced, the process converges only slightly more slowly by starting with a random vector.

The algorithm successfully extracts all the eigenvalues and eigenvectors from the ill-conditioned Hilbert matrix. It successfully reconstructs the Hilbert matrix by building it up from a zero matrix and the successive eigenvalues and eigenvectors obtained by Eigen~Find, using Eigen~Deflate as if it were Eigen~Insert. It accurately finds the single nonzero eigenvalue of a reciprocal matrix. It correctly determines the invalidity of an eigenvector extracted from a matrix with a complex largest eigenvalue. It does this by detecting oscillation rather than convergence of successive approximations to the eigenvector.

IMPLEMENTATION

Exported Names

Eigen~Find	Finds eigenvalue and vector of a square matrix (11.4.1)
Eigen~Deflate	Removes eigenvalue and vector from a symmetric matrix (11.4.2)

Imported Names

Random~Number	Computes a uniform random number using 32-bit arithmetic (8.1.1)

Similarity~Bits	Finds the number of bits in common in two numbers (2.3.1)
Similarity~Test	Tests the similarity of two numbers (2.3.2)
Nicknames	
N	Size of matrix
Root	Eigenvalue or characteristic root
V	Eigenvector
X	Matrix
Local Names	
New	New value of element of vector
P	New value of estimated eigenvector
Previous	Previous value of estimate for eigenvalue
Trace	Sum of absolute values of diagonal elements of matrix

11.4.1 Eigen~Find (receives X, N; supplies Root, V, Accuracy)

Pseudo Code

```
initialize vector V
loop
    calculate P by multiplying X by V and scaling it
    calculate Root from amount by which P is scaled
    estimate Accuracy of eigenvalue
end loop when estimated value of Root has reached steady state
```

Code

```
procedure Eigen~Find (X is matrix of real, N is integer, Root is real, V is array of
        real, Accuracy is integer)
    variable P is array 1 to N of real
    variables New, Previous, Trace are real
    let Trace = 0                                 Initialize first estimate of
    for i = 1 to N                                eigenvector
        let Trace = Trace + magnitude (X[i, i])
        call Random~Number (V[i])
    end for
    let Root = 0
    loop
        let Previous = Root
        let Root = 0
        for i = 1 to N                            Multiply matrix by estimate of
            let P[i] = 0                          eigenvector
            for j = 1 to N
                let P[i] = P[i] + (X[i, j] * V[j])
            end for
            let Root = Root + (P[i] * P[i])
        end for
        let Root = square~root (Root)
        let Accuracy = maxbits
```

```
        if Similarity~Test (Root, 0, Trace) = true then        Ensure exit if Root is
            let Root = 0                                       close to zero
            let Previous = 0
        else
            for i = 1 to N                                     Determine accuracy of eigenvector
                let New = P[i] / Root
                let Accuracy = minimum (Accuracy, Similarity~Bits (V[i], New,
                        Trace))
                let V[i] = New
            end for
        end if
    end loop when Similarity~Bits (Root, Previous, Trace) > maxbits – 3
end Eigen~Find
```

11.4.2 Eigen~Deflate (updates X; receives N, Root, V)

Pseudo Code

let $X = X - VV^T * \text{Root}$

Code

```
procedure Eigen~Deflate (X is matrix of real, N is integer, Root is real, V is array
        of real)
    for i = 1 to N
        for j = 1 to i
            check X[i, j] = X[j, i]
            let X[i, j] = X[i, j] – (V[i] * V[j] * Root)
            let X[j, i] = X[i, j]
        end for
    end for
end Eigen~Deflate
```

TEST PROGRAM

<u>Imported Names</u>

Random~Initialize	Initializes uniform random number generator (8.1.1)
Similarity~Test	Tests the similarity of two numbers (2.3.2)

<u>Local Names</u>

A	Accuracy
H	Hilbert matrix constructed from eigenvalues and eigenvectors
N	Size of matrix
R	Eigenvalue or root
V	Eigenvector
X	Matrix

Pseudo Code

build Hilbert matrix X
extract all eigenvalues and eigenvectors

build matrix H from extracted eigenvalues and eigenvectors
check H = X
build reciprocal matrix
extract first eigenvalue and eigenvector
check first eigenvalue = N and eigenvector elements are proportional
build matrix with complex eigenvalues
extract first eigenvalue and eigenvector
check accuracy of eigenvector is zero

Code

```
constant N = 8
variables X, H are matrices 1 to N, 1 to N of real
variable V is array 1 to N of real
variable R is real
variable A is integer
call Random~Initialize (maxinteger – 1)
for i = 1 to N                                       Build Hilbert matrix
    for j = 1 to N
        let X[i, j] = 1 / (i + j – 1)
        let H[i, j] = 0
    end for
end for
for k = 1 to N                                       Extract all eigenvalues of X and
    call Eigen~Find (X, N, R, V, A)                  reconstitute X in H
    call Eigen~Deflate (H, N, –R, V)
    call Eigen~Deflate (X, N, R, V)
end for
for i = 1 to N                                       Check that H is equal to the
    for j = 1 to N                                   original X
        check Similarity~Test (H[i, j], 1 / (i + j – 1), 1) = true
    end for
end for
for i = 1 to N
    for j = 1 to N                                   Build reciprocal matrix
        let X[i, j] = i / j
    end for
end for
call Eigen~Find (X, N, R, V, A)
check Similarity~Test (R, N, 1) = true               Check that first eigenvalue is N,
check A = maxbits                                    and accuracy is maximum
for j = 1 to N
    check Similarity~Test (V[1] / V[j], 1 / j, 1) = true    Compare eigenvector
end for                                                     against known values
for i = 1 to N
    for j = 1 to N                                   Build matrix with complex
        let X[i, j] = i – j                          eigenvalues
    end for
end for
```

call Eigen~Find (X, N, R, V, A) *check* R > 0 *and* A = 0	Check that eigenvalue accuracy is zero

NOTES—EVALUATION CRITERIA WEIGHTING

Assigning weights to evaluation criteria by a relatively objective method

The senior management of a public sector organization were asked to compare six criteria to be used for selecting the supplier of personal computers. The criteria were performance, reliability, supplier capability, maintenance arrangements, local content, and price. A pairwise comparison process produced the figures shown in Table 11.1.

Table 11.1

	Performance	*Reliability*	*Supplier*	*Maintenance*	*Local content*	*Price*
Performance		30:70	60:40	20:80	75:25	30:70
Reliability	70:30		70:30	60:40	75:25	50:50
Supplier	40:60	30:70		35:65	75:25	40:60
Maintenance	80:20	40:60	65:35		75:25	50:50
Local content	25:75	25:75	25:75	25:75		25:75
Price	70:30	50:50	60:40	50:50	75:25	

To take an example, the 30:70 comparison for Performance and Reliability means that the two criteria should be weighted 30 and 70 respectively with respect to each other. In other words, reliability is much more important than performance, specifically 70/30 times as important. In the Reliability row the figures 70:30 contain the same information concerning Performance, but the two component numbers are given in the reverse order. All figures above the main diagonal are reversed versions of the figures below the main diagonal.

The problem was to determine a single set of weights to be applied to the six criteria. The matrix was rewritten in the form shown in Table 11.2.

Table 11.2

	Performance	*Reliability*	*Supplier*	*Maintenance*	*Local content*	*Price*
Performance	1.0000	0.4286	1.5000	0.2500	3.0000	0.4286
Reliability	2.3333	1.0000	2.3333	1.5000	3.0000	1.0000
Supplier	0.6667	0.4286	1.0000	0.5385	3.0000	0.6667
Maintenance	4.0000	0.6667	1.8571	1.0000	3.0000	1.0000
Local content	0.3333	0.3333	0.3333	0.3333	1.0000	0.3333
Price	2.3333	1.0000	1.5000	1.0000	3.0000	1.0000

This matrix now is suitable for analysis using Eigen~Find (Saaty and Vargas 1982). Technically, it is called a reciprocal matrix, because an element X[I, J] = 1 / X[J, I]. The diagonal elements have been set equal to one, to indicate that any criterion compared with itself must have a ratio of one.

The matrix was processed by Eigen~Find, giving the eigenvalue 6.253 and the eigenvector 0.265, 0.561, 0.273, 0.538, 0.134, 0.482. The relative weights of the six criteria are in the relative proportions of the eigenvector elements. For convenience, the eigenvector elements were scaled by dividing them by the smallest value, giving the weights 1.98, 4.19, 2.04, 4.01, 1.00, and 3.60. Finally, the numbers were rounded off to the nearest integer, giving the approximate weights 2, 4, 2, 4, 1, and 4 for performance, reliability, supplier capability, maintenance arrangements, local content, and price respectively.

The pairwise comparisons may not, of course, be entirely consistent, and a measure of consistency is needed. It can be shown that the greater the inconsistency, the larger the first eigenvalue of the matrix of pairwise comparisons. This might suggest that dividing the number of criteria by the eigenvalue will produce a measure of the consistency. In the above example this consistency measure was calculated to be 6 / 6.253 = 96%. As this is an average across the whole matrix, it can mask an occasional large inconsistency.

The largest inconsistency in the matrix can be determined as follows. Calculate the elements of a matrix A, where A[I, J] = V[I] / V[J]. Each element A[I, J] is a kind of average pairwise comparison value that can be compared with the observed pairwise comparison value X[I, J]. Find the element that maximizes *magnitude* (*log* (A[I, J] / X[I, J])). In the above example, this element is in row 4 and column 1. The observed pairwise comparison was 25:75, but A[I, J] is effectively 34:66, a considerably larger difference than might be expected in the light of the 96% measure.

The comparison X[4, 1] is not necessarily "wrong" in itself. A better interpretation is that this element crystallizes inconsistency in the matrix as a whole. Usually, it is necessary to recompute all pairwise comparisons, with careful attention being paid to the meanings of the criteria. If the meanings are understood clearly, there should be little inconsistency in the pairwise comparisons.

12 Curve Fitting

The graphical capabilities of computers are being exploited more and more fully. As the old saying goes, "one picture is worth a thousand words". Some effort put into presenting computational results graphically pays dividends in user acceptance of programs.

One of the more difficult jobs to be done in generating graphical output is drawing a line through a set of points. The simplest type of curve involves connecting them up by straight lines. For example, daily newspapers print stock price variations over a few days as a picture in which the share price index at the end of each day is joined up by lines. This is a "sawtooth" representation. The simple algorithm for determining a sawtooth curve is mentioned in Section 12.2.

Engineers find that a sawtooth is not a useful way of representing many of the quantities they deal with. For example, an engineer might want to plot a curve showing the relationship between pressure and flow in a water pump. This is usually done by sampling various combinations of flow and pressure, then joining them up with a smooth curve. It would not make sense to plot the pump curve as a series of straight lines with sharp bends at the joins. Drawing a curve manually, an engineer or draftsperson would use a flexible ruler called a "spline" that can be bent smoothly to pass through all the points, and then draw a curved line along the spline. There is a mathematical equivalent called a natural spline, for which an algorithm is given in Section 12.2.

Statisticians find that neither sawtooths nor splines are suitable for many of their purposes. For example, in examining quarterly changes in the rate of inflation over the last ten years both of these ways of doing it have too much detail. A statistician wants a smooth curve that passes near to all of the points, but that does not necessarily pass through any of them. Sometimes a straight line showing an overall trend is all that is necessary. Sometimes a quadratic or cubic function is needed. The best algorithm for this purpose uses the method of least squares for finding a smoothed curve to fit the points. The algorithm is presented in Section 12.3.

On occasion, particularly in theoretical work, it is necessary to derive an exact algebraic specification of the curve being fitted. For example, suppose you had forgotten the formula to convert between Fahrenheit and Celsius. You can look up a table to find several corresponding temperatures, for example, 20°C = 68°F, 25°C = 77°F, 30°C = 86°F. What you want is the formula that connects the two temperature scales. You would like to end up with either F = 1.8 * C + 32 or the inverse, C = (F – 32) / 1.8. In Section 12.1 you will find an algorithm that computes exact coefficients for a polynomial through the supplied points. With the three points given in this example you expect a polynomial of the form $F = c * C^2 + b * C + a$. The algorithm outputs c = 0, b = 9/5, and a = 32.

Tradition has been followed in using the variables X and Y for the horizontal and vertical axes respectively. The curves are represented so that you specify an Xvalue and the algorithm determines a Yvalue. The Celsius to Fahrenheit formula has the form Yvalue = 1.8 * Xvalue + 32.

The concept of least squares is the basis for the algorithms in Sections 12.3 and 12.4. Rather than present the general theory, a specific example will be used for illustration. Suppose you wish to fit a straight line to the N points in arrays X and Y. The usual formulation for a straight line uses two "coefficients" that are numbers we will call A and B. Any Yvalue is determined from the formula Yvalue = B * Xvalue + A. The values of A and B are not known, and you wish to determine suitable values. Schematically, you can plot the points as shown in Figure 12.1 and see the kind of straight line you expect.

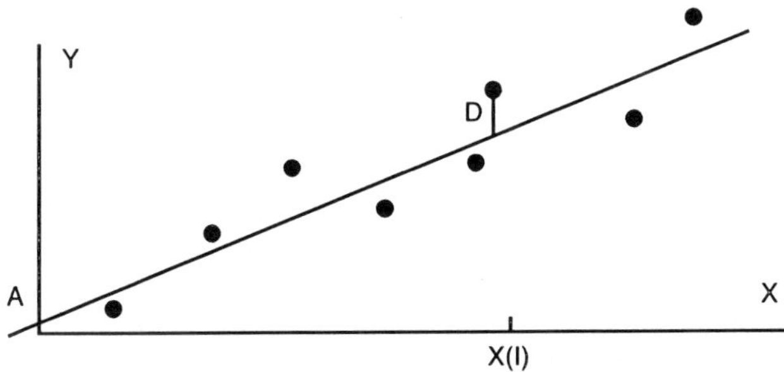

Figure 12.1

You want to choose values for A and B so that the straight line has the right slope and intersects the Y axis at the best place. When Xvalue is zero you can see from the formula that Yvalue = A, and so the value of A is the point on the Y axis at which the line intersects it. The value of B is the slope of the line. You need to focus on the vertical distance of D each point from the line. If you take any particular point, say X(I), the vertical distance is the difference between Y(I) and Yvalue computed from the formula. That is, D = B * X(I) + A – Y(I). Least squares involves choosing A and B so that the sum of the squares of all the D values is as small as possible. You could minimize other measures, such as the sum of the absolute values of D, or the maximum value of D, but the least squares criterion is tractable, well established, and gives a practical and usable result.

A shorthand way of describing sums and sums of squares makes the description easier to read. The statistician's Σ notation is used for this purpose. The Σ is read as "the sum over all data points of". For example, Σ X means the sum of all the X values and Σ XY means the sum of the X value for each data point multiplied by its corresponding Y value. You need to choose A and B so that ΣD^2 is as small as possible. Some elementary calculus is needed to differentiate the formula for ΣD^2 with respect to A and B. The derivatives must be equal to zero in order to obtain the minimum value of ΣD^2. The equations in which the derivatives are equated to zero are called the "normal" equations for some obscure reason. Without going through the differentiation process in detail you will find that two equations are produced:

$$B * \Sigma X + A * N = \Sigma Y$$
$$B * \Sigma X^2 + A * \Sigma X = \Sigma XY$$

Note the pattern of the Xs and Ys in these two equations. The second equation is similar to the first, with every term "multiplied" by X. This pattern is no coincidence. If you were to fit a quadratic equation $Yvalue = C * Xvalue^2 + B * Xvalue + A$ instead of a straight line, you would find that the normal equations have the same pattern:

$$C * \Sigma X^2 + B * \Sigma X + A * N = \Sigma Y$$
$$C * \Sigma X^3 + B * \Sigma X^2 + A * \Sigma X = \Sigma XY$$
$$C * \Sigma X^4 + B * \Sigma X^3 + A * \Sigma X^2 = \Sigma X^2Y$$

Solving the two equations for a straight line (using Gaussian elimination symbolically, Section 11.1), you arrive at the following formulas for calculating the least squares values of A and B. If you want to fit a straight line by least squares, you can use these formulas without resorting to the more advanced algorithms in Section 12.3. This result is referred to later in the chapter:

$$B = [\Sigma XY - \Sigma X * \Sigma Y / N] / [\Sigma X^2 - (\Sigma X)^2 / N]$$
$$A = \Sigma Y / N - B * \Sigma X / N$$

In Section 12.4 you will have an introduction to multiple linear regression. This is simply the least squares method outlined above, but fitting X_1 to separate variables X_2, X_3, X_4, and so on instead of Y to powers of one variable X. Other statistical quantities such as correlations, coefficients, means, and standard deviations may be determined easily from the basic regression model.

12.1 POLYNOMIAL

Fitting the Lagrange polynomial to a set of points

Example

To find the polynomial that connects Celsius and Fahrenheit temperatures, put somc Celsius temperatures in the array X and their corresponding Fahrenheit temperatures in array Y. The code:

variables X, Y, F *are arrays* 1 *to* 3 *of real*
let X[1] = 20; *let* Y[1] = 68
let X[2] = 25; *let* Y[2] = 77
let X[3] = 30; *let* Y[3] = 86
call Polynomial~Fit (1, 3, X, Y, F)

produces in the array elements F[1], F[2], and F[3] the polynomial coefficients 0, 1.8, and 32. The Fahrenheit temperature corresponding to 40°C is given by:

output Polynomial~Use (1, 3, 40, F)

Subprograms

12.1.1 Polynomial~Fit (receives Lower, Upper, X, Y; supplies F)
12.1.2 Polynomial~Use (receives Lower, Upper, Xvalue, F; *result real*)

Usage

Do not use this algorithm unless you know what you are doing. For general-purpose curve fitting, use another of the algorithms described in the introduction to this chapter. This algorithm has poor numerical stability unless the calculations are done without rounding. Loss of significance occurs particularly during subtraction if intermediate results are held as *real* numbers. The algorithm should be implemented using rational arithmetic, the subprograms for which are provided in Section 2.2. Replace the addition, subtraction, multiplication, and division of the elements of arrays X, Y, P, and F by calls to subprograms from Section 2.2. This will involve using two *integer* locations where one *real* location has been used for each element of each array. The algorithm has been presented without this modification to keep the code clean and simple.

Subprogram Polynomial~Fit is given the lower and upper bounds of the subscripts for the elements of the arrays X and Y in which the data points are stored. The lower and upper bounds are referenced by the nicknames Lower and Upper. There are N = Upper – Lower + 1 data points. The X values must be in a strictly increasing sequence. The computed coefficients for the polynomial are placed in the array with nickname F. The coefficient for the highest power of the X values is in F[Lower].

Polynomial~Use evaluates the polynomial for any given Xvalue, using the efficient Horner's rule. The end result is that it obtains Yvalue from the following formula:

$$\text{Yvalue} = \text{F[Lower]} * \text{Xvalue}^{N-1} + \text{F[Lower+1]} * \text{Xvalue}^{N-2} + \ldots + \text{F[Upper}-1] * \text{Xvalue} + \text{F[Upper]}$$

Analysis

The method used is based on the interpolation formula of Lagrange. This formula can be found in any elementary text on polynomial algebra. Despite some assertions to the contrary in the literature, the algorithm is not particularly difficult to implement, although one must obtain the right insight as to how to do it. The algorithm requires O (N^2) calculations to obtain the polynomial coefficients in the array F, and O (N) calculations to evaluate the polynomial at any given point. There are more efficient, but more complex, algorithms for computing the polynomial coefficients (Sedgewick 1988), although it is difficult to foresee applications requiring exact polynomials large enough to justify the use of such algorithms. When more than a few data points are supplied, one should almost certainly use the least squares algorithm in Section 12.3.

You do not need to use Polynomial~Fit at all if you are prepared to put up with O (N^2) performance for calculating Yvalue for every specified Xvalue. You can calculate a Yvalue from an Xvalue directly using the specified data points. The following code is a straightforward implementation of Lagrange's interpolation formula:

```
let Yvalue = 0
for i = Lower to Upper
    let Product = 1
    for j = Lower to Upper
        if j ≠ i then
            let Product = Product * ((Xvalue – X[j]) / (X[i] – X[j])
        end if
    end for
    let Yvalue = Yvalue + (Product * Y[i])
end for
```

If the calculation of Yvalue for a given Xvalue needs to be more efficient, you determine the polynomial coefficients in the array F for use by the Polynomial~Use subprogram. Trace through the Polynomial~Fit algorithm to see what it does. You will obtain a good understanding of the algorithm by working with just three data points, as per the example at the start of this section. For simplicity, assume that Lower = 1 and Upper = 3. In the first loop after the initialization of the arrays P and F the elements of P are set to components of what we call the "big" polynomial. The elements of P are just the collected terms of equal powers in the expansion of the polynomial (1 – X[1]) * (1 – X[2]) * (1 – X[3]).

P[0] = 1
P[1] = – X[1] – X[2] – X[3]
P[2] = X[1] * X[2] + X[1] * X[3] + X[2] * X[3]
P[3] = – X[1] * X[2] * X[3]

The remainder of the code is executed in a *for* loop, with the index *i* varying from 1 to 3. Consider the first iteration, in which the index *i* is equal to 1. Symbolically "divide" the first term (1 – X[1]) out of the big polynomial. You would expect to find the collected terms of equal powers of the expansion of the polynomial (1 – X[2]) * (1 – X[3]) in the elements of P, and indeed you do:

P[0] = 1
P[1] = – X[2] – X[3]
P[2] = X[2] * X[3]
P[3] = 0

Now obtain the value of what we call a multiplier. For this particular execution of the *for* loop you have a multiplier involving Y[1]. In the next two iterations you will use Y[2] and then Y[3]. The multiplier is equal to:

$$\text{Multiplier}_1 = Y[1] / ((X[1] - X[2]) * (X[1] - X[3]))$$

The small subscript refers to the iteration of the loop in which it is computed. The denominator contains the product of all terms X[1] – X[*j*], except of course X[1] – X[1]. The next loop accumulates components of the F array. The components of F are just the components of P multiplied by the multiplier. (But note that the subscripts of P take values one less than the values of the subscripts of F.) In this first iteration, for $i = 1$, you obtain:

$$F[1] = \text{Multiplier}_1$$
$$F[2] = -(X[2] + X[3]) * \text{Multiplier}_1$$
$$F[3] = X[2] * X[3] * \text{Multiplier}_1$$

The final part of the main loop restores the big polynomial to its original form. It is now ready to undertake the second and then the third parts of the calculation. The elements of F will then contain the sum of three terms, all similar in form to those above, but with the subscripts varying as discussed above. Thus you have two more multipliers:

$$\text{Multiplier}_2 = Y[2] / ((X[2] - X[1]) * (X[2] - X[3]))$$
$$\text{Multiplier}_3 = Y[3] / ((X[3] - X[1]) * (X[3] - X[2]))$$

and the final values of F are:

$$F[1] = \text{Multiplier}_1 + \text{Multiplier}_2 + \text{Multiplier}_3$$
$$F[2] = -(X[2] + X[3]) * \text{Multiplier}_1 - (X[1] + X[3]) * \text{Multiplier}_2 - (X[1] + X[2]) * \text{Multiplier}_3$$
$$F[3] = X[2] * X[3] * \text{Multiplier}_1 + X[1] * X[3] * \text{Multiplier}_2 + X[1] * X[2] * \text{Multiplier}_3$$

Polynomial~Use computes a Yvalue from an Xvalue using the formula:

$$\text{Yvalue} = F[1] * \text{Xvalue}^2 + F[2] * \text{Xvalue} + F[3]$$

You will know that the algorithm is correct if you get Yvalue = Y[1] when Xvalue = X[1], Yvalue = Y[2] when Xvalue = X[2], and Yvalue = Y[3] when Xvalue = X[3]. Each of F[1], F[2], and F[3] has three terms. Evaluate Yvalue for each of the three parts Yvalue_1, Yvalue_2, and Yvalue_3 and then obtain $\text{Yvalue} = \text{Yvalue}_1 + \text{Yvalue}_2 + \text{Yvalue}_3$.

First, compute the value of the first part Yvalue_1 for X[1]:

$$\text{Yvalue}_1 = \text{Multiplier}_1 * X[1]^2 - (X[2] + X[3]) * \text{Multiplier}_1 * X[1] + X[2] * X[3] * \text{Multiplier}_1$$

This expression simplifies easily to $\text{Multiplier}_1 * (X[1] - X[2]) * (X[1] - X[3])$, which on substituting the value of Multiplier_1 reduces to just Y[1]. By a similar calculation you find that Yvalue_2 and Yvalue_3 are both equal to zero. Therefore Yvalue is equal to Y[1] as required. You may easily demonstrate by similar calculations that Yvalue = Y[2] when Xvalue = X[2] and Yvalue = Y[3] when Xvalue = X[3].

This analysis shows that the polynomial passes through all the specified data points, using an example with just three data points. Although this does not prove conclusively that the method works, it gives some confidence in it. A polynomial algebra text should be consulted for further information.

IMPLEMENTATION

<u>Exported Names</u>

Polynomial~Fit	Computes Lagrange polynomial coefficients (12.1.1)
Polynomial~Use	Computes the Y value for a given X value (12.1.2)

<u>Nicknames</u>

F	Coefficients of the computed polynomial
Lower	Lower bound of the X and Y arrays
Upper	Upper bound of the X and Y arrays
X	Array of the X coordinates of the specified data points
Y	Array of the Y coordinates of the specified data points

<u>Local Names</u>

Multiplier	Multiplier of terms in Lagrange formula
P	Array of coefficients of the big polynomial
Sum	Progressive total computed by Horner's rule

12.1.1 Polynomial~Fit (receives Lower, Upper, X, Y; supplies F)

Pseudo Code

```
calculate coefficients of the big polynomial
for i = Lower to Upper
    divide term involving X[i] out of the big polynomial
    compute multiplier for i-th term
    accumulate components of output polynomial coefficients for i-th term
    multiply term involving X[i] back into the big polynomial
end for
```

Code

```
procedure Polynomial~Fit (Lower, Upper are integers, X, Y, F are arrays of real)
    variable P is array Lower–1 to Upper of real
    variable Multiplier is real
    let P[Lower–1] = 1                              Determine "big" polynomial
    for i = Lower to Upper                          containing all terms
        let P[i] = 0
        let F[i] = 0
    end for
    for i = Lower to Upper
        for decreasing j = i to Lower
            let P[j] = P[j] – (X[i] * P[j–1])
        end for
    end for                                         Divide current term out of big
    for i = Lower to Upper                          polynomial
        for j = Lower to Upper
            let P[j] = P[j] + (X[i] * P[j–1])
        end for
        let Multiplier = Y[i]                       Get multiplier
```

```
        for j = Lower to Upper
            if j ≠ i then
                let Multiplier = Multiplier / (X[i] – X[j])
            end if
        end for
        for j = Lower to Upper                  Accumulate components of F
            let F[j] = F[j] + (Multiplier * P[j–1])
        end for
        for decreasing j = Upper to Lower       Multiply by current term to
            let P[j] = P[j] – (X[i] * P[j–1])   restore big polynomial
        end for
    end for
end Polynomial~Fit
```

12.1.2 Polynomial~Use (receives Lower, Upper, Xvalue, F; *result real*)

Pseudo Code

```
initialize Sum of terms to zero
for i = Lower to Upper
    let Sum = Sum + lower order polynomial value * X[i] + next coefficient
end for
```

Code

```
function Polynomial~Use (Lower, Upper are integers, Xvalue is real, F is array of
        real) is real
    variable Sum is real
    let Sum = 0
    for i = Lower to Upper
        let Sum = (Sum * Xvalue) + F[i]
    end for
    result Sum
end Polynomial~Use
```

TEST PROGRAM

Imported Names

Similarity~Test	Tests the similarity of two numbers (2.3.2)

Local Names

F	Array of polynomial coefficients
L	Lower bound for arrays
U	Upper bound for arrays
X	Array of X coordinates
Y	Array of Y coordinates

Pseudo Code

```
set up data points obtained from curve y = exp (–x)
fit the polynomial to the data points
check that data points are on the fitted curve
```

Code

```
constants L = 1, U = 10
variables F, X, Y are arrays L to U of real
for i = L to U
    let X[i] = i
    let Y[i] = exp (–i)
end for
call Polynomial~Fit (L, U, X, Y, F)
for i = L to U
    check Similarity~Test (Polynomial~Use (L, U, i, F), Y[i], 1) = true
end for
```

12.2 CUBIC SPLINE

Fitting a smooth curve through a set of points

Example

Suppose you have 10 points with coordinates stored in locations 1 to 10 of the arrays X and Y. The following code prints the Y value on the curve corresponding to entered X values:

```
variables X, Y, P are arrays 1 to 10 of real
variable Xvalue is real
call Spline~Fit (1, 10, X, Y, P)
loop
    output "Enter X value"
    input Xvalue
    output "Y value is", Spline~Use (1, 10, X, Y, P, Xvalue)
end loop
```

Subprograms

12.2.1 Spline~Fit (receives Lower, Upper, X, Y; supplies P)
12.2.2 Spline~Use (receives Lower, Upper, X, Y, P, Xvalue; *result real*)

Usage

The points through which the curve is to pass must be stored as normal Cartesian coordinates in two arrays, which have the nicknames X and Y. The lowest and highest subscripts corresponding to the first and last points have the nicknames Lower and Upper respectively. The X values must be in strictly ascending sequence. A third array, with the nickname P, is used by Spline~Fit for the computed values of the curvature of the spline curve at the given points.

The function Spline~Use computes the value of Y for a given Xvalue, making use of the curvatures in the array P. More precisely, the function finds the two array points closest to the given point, and computes the Yvalue from the coordinates and the associated curvatures for those two points. In order to determine the closest points the function searches the X values using a specially tailored version of the binary search algorithm (7.4.3). The search process automatically deals with given X values that lie outside the extremes X[Lower] and X[Upper]. Outliers are forced to use the interval between the two points at the relevant end of the curve. This version of binary search should not be used as a general searching algorithm because it will not work for that purpose.

The test program fits a spline to a number of points on the graph of *exp* (–X). The function is smooth, decreasing rapidly in value from unity toward zero as X increases. The function asymptotically approaches the X axis. The spline curve fits the points very well, and so the test program checks that the accuracy of Yvalue for Xvalues halfway between specified points is accurate to at least five bits in each case. The test program also checks that the algorithm works correctly for an outlier.

Analysis

The algorithm fits a spline curve to N points, where N = Upper – Lower + 1. To take a specific example, think of seven points ranging from (X[1], Y[1]) to (X[7], Y[7]). In order to explain the process as simply as possible, first look at fitting straight lines (a linear spline as opposed to a cubic spline) to the points, so that you end up with something like the curve shown in Figure 12.2.

Figure 12.2

There is an unusual but useful way of representing a straight line. Zero in on the first straight line in the sequence of six above. Consider the formula:

Yvalue = T * Y[2] + (1 – T) * Y[1]

computed from various values of T. When T = 0, Yvalue = Y[1]. When T = 1, Yvalue = Y[2]. When T = 0.5, Yvalue = [Y[2] + Y[1]] / 2. In other words, as T varies from 0 to 1, Yvalue varies from Y[1] to Y[2] in a linear manner.

The value of T itself is defined as:

T = (Xvalue – X[1]) / (X[2] – X[1])

When Xvalue = X[1], T = 0. When Xvalue = X[2], T = 1. Thus, as Xvalue varies from X[1] to X[2], the value of T varies from 0 to 1 in a linear manner. The point of this explanation is that it provides a simple way to compute the Yvalue for a line segment given an Xvalue. First, get the value of T from the above formula and then use T to get the value of Yvalue from its formula. This approach can be applied to any of the line segments. You need to find the points on either side of a given Xvalue and then apply the process as illustrated here for the first and second points.

Now consider how to obtain a curving line joining up the points, such as the one shown in Figure 12.3.

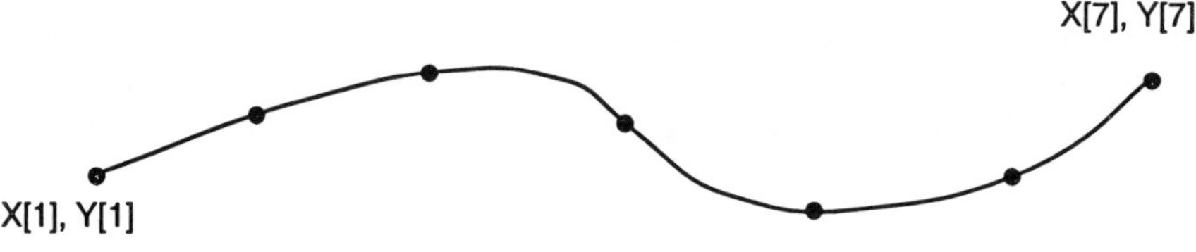

Figure 12.3

Again, you will use a separate curve in each segment between any two consecutive points, just as you used separate straight line segments above. The new formula uses T again, and is the same as for the straight line with the addition of a term we will call Yextra. The new term looks complicated at first sight, but we will explain it soon. The complete formula applied to the first curve between points 1 and 2 is given in two parts:

Yvalue = T * Y[2] + (1 – T) * Y[1] + Yextra
Yextra = T * (T – 1) * ((T + 1) * P[2] – (T – 2) * P[1]) * (X[2] – X[1]) *
(X[2] – X[1]) / 6

The formula for Yextra refers to the array P mentioned earlier. The Spline~Fit algorithm computes the values for array P, so that the computed Yvalues for all segments join up to produce a smooth curve. Just looking at the first two terms of the formula, you can see that the value of Yextra is zero when T = 0 or T = 1, regardless of the values of the elements of the array P. This ensures that Yvalue equals Y[1] and Y[2] when Xvalue = X[1] and X[2] respectively. In other words, the smooth curve is guaranteed to pass through all the points. So far so good.

The formula for Yextra involves T raised to the third power. The formula for T is linear in Xvalue. Therefore, Yextra in effect involves Xvalue raised to the third power. Hence the formula is a cubic equation, as would be expected for a "cubic" spline algorithm.

How does the algorithm ensure the curve is smooth? The key idea is to focus on the two curves on either side of each point (the first and last points are special cases). The algorithm makes sure that the slope of the left-hand curve is the same as the slope of the right-hand curve at each point. Then there is no sudden change of direction as occurs with the curve made up of straight line segments. Further, the curvature of both curves is equalized at each point, avoiding joins similar to the fixing of an umbrella handle to the shaft, where the curvature changes dramatically.

The algorithm has to determine the values for P[1] through P[7] so that these values can be plugged into the above formula for Yextra. All the other terms in the formula have known values. The values for P are determined by setting up seven simultaneous linear equations, and solving them by a specially tailored process of Gaussian elimination (see Section 11.1 for the general method). How can a mere seven equations ensure that the slopes and curvatures are all equal at the five interior points X[2] through X[6]? There would appear to be ten conditions (five slope equalities and five curvature equalities) to be taken into account.

Using elementary calculus, to differentiate Yvalue twice with respect to Xvalue, you can find that the slope Yslope and curvature Ycurve of the curve between points 1 and 2 are given by:

```
Yslope = (Y[2] – Y[1]) / (X[2] – X[1]) +
        (((3 * T * T) – 1) * P[2] – ((3 * T * T) – (6 * T) + 2) * P[1]) *
        (X[2] – X[1]) / 6
Ycurve = T * P[2] + (1 – T) * P[1]
```

The formula for Ycurve is beautifully simple, and identical in structure to the formula for Yvalue. When T = 0, Ycurve = P[1]. When T = 1, Ycurve = P[2]. Ycurve is the second derivative of Yvalue, and so is equal to the curvature of the curve. For any point X[I], the curvature of the curve at that point is P[I], and the curvature varies linearly as T moves through an interval.

Now look at the curves on either side of point X[2], say. The curve to the left involves points X[1] and X[2]. The curve on the right involves points X[2] and X[3]. The slope of the curve on the left at point X[2] is equal to the value of Ycurve = T * P[2] + (1 – T) * P[1] when T = 1, which reduces to Ycurve = P[2]. The slope of the curve on the right at point X[2] is equal to the value of Ycurve = T * P[3] + (1 – T) * P[2] when T = 0, which also reduces to Ycurve = P[2]. This vital finding shows that the curvatures of the two curves are automatically equal at point P[2], a fact that is entirely due to the choice of the formula for Yextra. Therefore, no equations need to be set up to equalize the curvatures of the curve segments.

It is *not* true that the slopes of the curves are automatically equal. Again choosing the point X[2], the value of Yslope for the curve on the left, involving X[1] and X[2] with T = 1, is easily seen to have a different formula from the value of Yslope for the curve on the right, involving X[2] and X[3] with T = 0. The two formulas are:

```
Yslope = (Y[2] – Y[1]) / (X[2] – X[1]) + (2 * P[2] + P[1]) * (X[2] – X[1]) / 6
Yslope = (Y[3] – Y[2]) / (X[3] – X[2]) – (P[3] + 2 * P[2]) * (X[3] – X[2]) / 6
```

You need to equate the above two formulas for Yslope to get one equation at the point X[2], involving three of the unknowns P[1], P[2], and P[3]. This equation is:

```
P[3] * (X[3] – X[2]) + 2 * P[2] * (X[3] – X[1]) + P[1] * (X[2] – X[1]) =
        (Y[3] – Y[2]) / (X[3] – X[2]) – (Y[2] – Y[1]) / (X[2] – X[1])
```

You can obtain four more similar equations at the points X[3], X[4], X[5], and X[6], the last of which involves the three unknowns P[5], P[6], and P[7]. This process has produced five of the required seven simultaneous equations.

You need two more equations in order to have enough information to compute unique values for the seven values in the array P. You can do this by assuming that the spline curve leaves the end points, before X[1] and after X[7], with zero curvature. This particular assumption distinguishes a "natural" spline from other types of spline. It requires setting P[Lower] = P[Upper] = 0.

If you are interested in dissecting the code of the algorithm you may wish to set up the simultaneous equations in symbolic form, and then apply Gaussian elimination symbolically. The equations form a tridiagonal system that is easily solved in this way. The code presented in the implementation of the algorithm will then be more readily understandable.

The algorithm is efficient, operating in time proportional to the number of points. The reason why the algorithm performs Gaussian elimination in O (N) running time rather than O (N^3) is that the matrix of coefficients has a particularly simple banded form. Such banded systems may be solved in linear time, as is the case for the natural cubic spline algorithm. The original implementation of the algorithm was published by Herriot (1973). The code follows the style of the procedure described by Sedgewick (1988).

IMPLEMENTATION

<u>Exported Names</u>

Spline~Fit	Determines cubic spline passing through specified points (12.2.1)
Spline~Use	Computes spline Y value corresponding to given X value (12.2.2)

<u>Nicknames</u>

Lower	Lowest subscript for arrays X, Y, and P
P	Array of computed second derivatives
Upper	Uppermost subscript for arrays X, Y, and P
X	Array of abscissa values for points
Xvalue	Value of abscissa for which value of ordinate for curve is required
Y	Array of ordinate values for points

<u>Local Names</u>

D	Array of first differences of adjacent X values
Df	Correction related to curvature of spline curve
Dx, Dy	Distance between X values (Y values) of adjacent points
I	Position in array P of second derivative applicable for Xvalue
L	Lower limit for binary search
S	Array of first differences of nonadjacent X values
T	Transformed value of Xvalue, to range 0 to 1
U	Upper limit for binary search
W	Array initially of first differences of slopes

12.2.1 Spline~Fit (receives Lower, Upper, X, Y; supplies P)

Pseudo Code

```
calculate off-diagonal coefficients D
calculate main diagonal coefficients S
calculate right-hand sides of equations W
perform forward substitution of Gaussian elimination
perform backward substitution giving results P
```

Code

```
procedure Spline~Fit (Lower, Upper are integers, X, Y, P are arrays of real)
    variables S, D, W are arrays Lower to Upper of real
    let D[Lower] = X[Lower+1] – X[Lower]
    let W[Lower+1] = (Y[Lower+1] – Y[Lower]) / D[Lower]
```

```
    for i = (Lower + 1) to (Upper – 1)              Calculate change in slope at
        let D[i] = X[i+1] – X[i]                    each point
        let S[i] = (X[i+1] – X[i–1]) * 2
        let W[i+1] = (Y[i+1] – Y[i]) / D[i]
        let W[i] = 6 * (W[i+1] – W[i])
    end for
    for i = (Lower + 1) to (Upper – 2)              Forward substitution for
        let W[i+1] = W[i+1] – (W[i] * D[i] / S[i])  Gaussian elimination
        let S[i+1] = S[i+1] – (D[i] * D[i] / S[i])
    end for
    let P[Lower] = 0
    let P[Upper] = 0
    for decreasing i = (Upper – 1) to (Lower + 1)   Backward substitution for
        let P[i] = (W[i] – (D[i] * P[i+1])) / S[i]  Gaussian elimination
    end for
end Spline~Fit
```

12.2.2 Spline~Use (receives Lower, Upper, X, Y, P, Xvalue; *result real*)

Pseudo Code

find points between which specified point falls
force out-of-range specified points to come within range
compute spline formula using points on either side of specified point

Code

```
function Spline~Use (Lower, Upper are integers, X, Y, P are arrays of real, Xvalue
        is real) is real
    variables I, L, U are integers
    variables Dx, Dy, Df, T are real
    let L = Lower                                   Binary search to find points
    let U = Upper                                   adjacent to Xvalue, forcing
    let I = (L + U) ÷ 2                             outliers to come into range
    loop until L + 1 ≥ U
        if Xvalue > X[I] then
            let L = I
        else
            let U = I
        end if
        let I = (L + U) ÷ 2
    end loop
    let Dx = X[I+1] – X[I]                          Compute spline formula using
    let Dy = Y[I+1] – Y[I]                          adjacent points
    let T = (Xvalue – X[I]) / Dx
    let Df = ((T + 1) * P[I+1]) – ((T – 2) * P[I])
    let Df = Df * T * (T – 1) / 6
    result Y[I] + (T * Dy) + (Dx * Dx * Df)
end Spline~Use
```

TEST PROGRAM

<u>Imported Names</u>

Similarity~Bits	Finds the number of bits in common in two numbers (2.3.1)

<u>Local Names</u>

L	Lowest subscript for arrays
P	Array of second derivatives
U	Uppermost subscript for arrays
X	Array of X values
Y	Array of Y values

Pseudo Code

```
initialize X values to successive integers
initialize Y values to values of exp (–X), for each X value
call Spline~Fit to determine the spline
for each interval between the points X, and one interval beyond the last X point
    let Xvalue = value halfway between successive X values
    compute the spline Yvalue corresponding to Xvalue
    check Yvalue approximately = exp (–Xvalue)
end for
```

Code

```
constants L = 1, U = 10
variables X, Y, P are arrays L to U of real
for i = L to U
    let X[i] = i
    let Y[i] = exp (–i)
end for
call Spline~Fit (L, U, X, Y, P)
for i = L to U
    check Similarity~Bits (Spline~Use (L, U, X, Y, P, i + 0.5), exp (–i – 0.5), 1) > 5
end for
```

12.3 SMOOTHED CURVE

Fitting a polynomial curve as closely as possible to a set of points

Example

Suppose you have 10 points with coordinates stored in locations 1 to 10 of the arrays X and Y. The following code prints the Y value on the least squares quadratic curve corresponding to entered X values:

```
variables X, Y are arrays 1 to 10 of real
variables SX, SY, V are arrays 0 to 2 of real
variables G, Xvalue are real
call Smoothed~Fit (1, 10, 2, X, Y, SX, SY, V, G)
```

```
loop
    output "Enter X value"
    input Xvalue
    output "Y value is", Smoothed~Use (2, Xvalue, SX, SY, V)
end loop
```

Subprograms

12.3.1 Smoothed~Fit (receives Lower, Upper, Order, X, Y; supplies SX, SY, V)
12.3.2 Smoothed~Use (receives Order, Xvalue, SX, SY, V; *result real*)

Usage

The points through which the curve is to pass must be stored as normal Cartesian coordinates in two arrays, which have the nicknames X and Y. The lowest and highest subscripts corresponding to the first and last points have the nicknames Lower and Upper respectively. The X values must be in strictly ascending sequence. The user must specify the value of Order, where Order = 0 if a horizontal line is required, Order = 1 for a straight line, Order = 2 for a quadratic, and so on. Three temporary arrays with nicknames SX, SY, and V are required, with dimensions from 0 to Order. These arrays contain values computed by Smoothed~Fit and used by Smoothed~Use.

The function Smoothed~Use computes the value of Y for a given Xvalue, making use of the values in SX, SY, and V. It is not necessary that Xvalue lie within the range of points X[Lower] through X[Upper].

The test program fits a smoothed curve to a number of points on the graph of *exp* (–X). The smoothed curve does not fit the points particularly well for small values of Order, but the accuracy improves for each higher value of Order used. The test program checks that the goodness of fit of the fitted curve increases uniformly. The measure of goodness of fit returned by the algorithm via the nickname Goodness is a number in the range 0 (no fit at all) to 1 (perfect fit through all data points). The curves in Figures 12.4 to 12.7 show how the approximation improves as Order is increased. The fitted curve of order 5 is virtually indistinguishable from the original, even though it was based on a sample of only 10 points. These curves were determined with data points at equally spaced intervals with X[*i*] = *i*, for *i* taking the values 0 through 9.

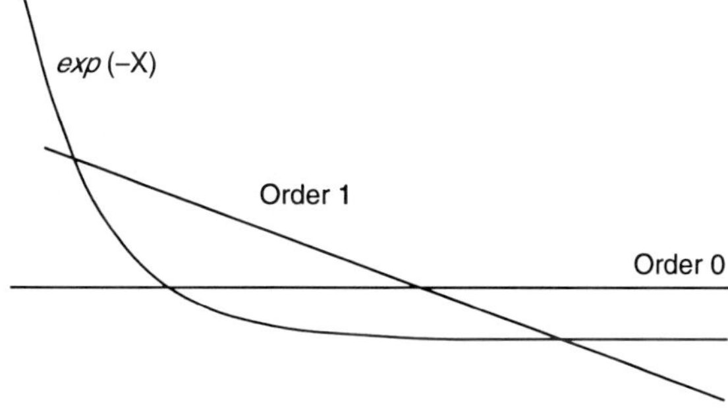

Figure 12.4

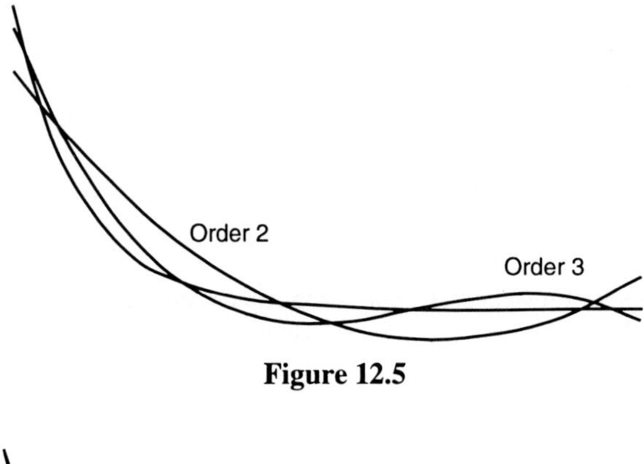

Figure 12.5

Figure 12.6

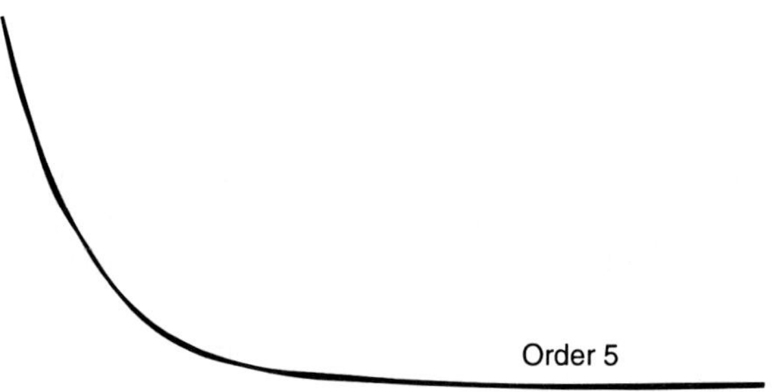

Figure 12.7

The test program computes the smoothed curve up to the maximum possible Order of the polynomial. The data points are at unequally spaced X intervals in the range 0–9. In practice, one would rarely compute curves of high orders, particularly for larger sets of data.

Analysis

The least squares smoothed curve algorithm relies on mathematical curiosities called "orthogonal polynomials". The technique makes it safe to fit curves of very high degree. Attempting to solve the normal equations without orthogonal polynomials can result in severe numerical problems. In fact, the normal equations for polynomials of high degree are as badly conditioned as the Hilbert matrix discussed in Chapter 11 (Forsythe 1957). The term "orthogonal" means "independent". The problem with the Hilbert matrix is that the rows and columns are very close to failing to be independent. For practical purposes, using numbers of finite length, the Hilbert matrix and normal equations of moderate to large order for polynomial fitting are singular. As the name implies, orthogonal polynomials transform the problem so that the algorithm works with robustly independent quantities rather than a Hilbert-type matrix.

To test the adequacy of the approach, we fitted a polynomial to 36 points for every order from 0 to 35, without difficulty. (The data consisted of changes in the quarterly Consumer Price Index in Australia from 1981 to 1990.) The orthogonal polynomials ensured that intermediate results kept within the numerical limits of the computer. This not only prevented overflow but also improved the accuracy of the final results.

A curve of maximum order, one less than the number of data points, is theoretically identical with the curve produced by the polynomial algorithm in Section 12.1. However, there are two very good reasons why the current algorithm should be used. Its efficiency is significantly higher, being proportional to the number of data points multiplied by the value of Order. In addition, its numerical stability is excellent, whereas that of the polynomial algorithm is poor unless the computations are done with rational arithmetic.

This is not the place in which to present the theory of orthogonal polynomials. If you are interested in the mathematical justification, you should consult the excellent, perhaps classical, paper by Forsythe (1957). This description is restricted to journeying through the first couple of iterations of the algorithm, to see that the results make sense.

The P and Q arrays contain the values of the orthogonal polynomials. You will not need to focus on the values in those arrays, but will be more interested in the values in the SX, SY, and V arrays. These are input by Smoothed~Use for calculating a Yvalue for a given Xvalue.

When Order = 0, you can find by desk checking the algorithm that Smoothed~Fit exits with V[0] = 0, SX[0] = Σ X / N, and SY[0] = Σ Y / N. In other words, SX[0] and SY[0] contain the means of the X and Y arrays respectively. Plugging these values into the calculations by Smoothed~Use you find that the value calculated for any Xvalue is just SX[0], or Σ Y / N. Thus, the curve that has been fitted for Order = 0 is just a horizontal straight line at Yvalue equal to the mean of the values in the array Y. Note that SX[0] was not used, although SY[0] was used.

When Order = 1, you have a little more calculation to do. Note that V[0], SX[0], and SY[0] have the same values as before. Indeed, this is true for all higher orders. The values of all array elements for any given Order are the same as those for Order+1 with the addition of new computed values for V[Order], SX[Order], and SY[Order]. You establish that V[1] = Σ (X − Σ X / N)^2 / N. Those with a background in statistics will recognize this formula as the "variance" of the X values. This is just the mean square of the deviations of the X values from their mean Σ X / N. The value of SY[1] turns out to be:

$$SY[1] = (\Sigma\,(X - \Sigma\,X / N) * Y) / \Sigma\,(X - \Sigma\,X / N)^2$$

With some juggling of the terms this turns out to be equivalent to:

$$SY[1] = \Sigma (XY - \Sigma X * \Sigma Y / N) / (\Sigma X^2 - (\Sigma X)^2 / N)$$

This is equal to the slope B of the straight line Yvalue = B * Xvalue + A, as identified in the introduction to least squares at the beginning of this chapter. Working through Smoothed~Use you find that Yvalue is computed by the formula:

$$Yvalue = SY[1] * Xvalue + \Sigma Y / N - SY[1] * \Sigma X / N$$

From the introduction you know that the constant term A is given by $A = \Sigma Y / N - B * \Sigma X / N$. Replacing SY[1] by B and other relevant terms by A you end up with:

$$Yvalue = B * Xvalue + A$$

which is the formula for a straight line as required. This has demonstrated that Smoothed~Fit and Smoothed~Use work correctly for Order = 0 and Order = 1. The demonstration process becomes unwieldy for larger values of Order, even for Order = 2. If further confirmation of the method is required, you will need to consult the literature.

Statistical mathematics has been avoided entirely in this implementation. It may be appropriate and useful to fit the "best" curve to a set of data by allowing the algorithm to choose the value of Order. The paper by Forsythe (1957) and the implementation by Makinson (1967) show how this is done.

IMPLEMENTATION

<u>Exported Names</u>

Smoothed~Fit	Determines smoothed curve passing near specified points (12.3.1)
Smoothed~Use	Computes Y value corresponding to given X value (12.3.2)

<u>Nicknames</u>

Goodness	Goodness of fit of the curve, between 0 and 1
Lower	Lowest subscript for arrays containing data points
Order	Order of polynomial to be fitted
SX	Sum of products involving X
SY	Sum of products involving X and Y
Upper	Highest subscript for arrays containing data points
V	Orthogonal polynomial coefficient
X	Array of X coordinates of data points
Xvalue	Value of X for a particular point
Y	Array of Y coordinates of data points

<u>Local Names</u>

Divisor	Main diagonal term from the matrix of normal equations
P	Array of orthogonal polynomial values
Previous	Previous value of Divisor
Pvalue	A particular orthogonal polynomial value
Q	Array of orthogonal polynomial values
Qvalue	A particular orthogonal polynomial value
Sum	Accumulated value of the polynomial
Total	Total sum of squares of Y values

12.3.1 Smoothed~Fit (receives Lower, Upper, Order, X, Y; supplies SX, SY, V)

Pseudo Code

```
initialize the orthogonal polynomials
compute total sum of squares of Y values for goodness of fit test
initialize
for j = 0 to Order
    compute contribution of j-th power of X to explaining Y using current
            orthogonal polynomial
    compute component of next orthogonal polynomial
    update goodness of fit
    complete computation of next orthogonal polynomial
end for
```

Code

```
procedure Smoothed~Fit (Lower, Upper, Order are integers, X, Y, SX, SY, V are
        arrays of real, Goodness is real)
    variables P, Q are arrays Lower to Upper of real
    variables Divisor, Previous, Total are real
    let Goodness = 0
    let Total = 0
    for i = Lower to Upper                          Initialize orthogonal
        let P[i] = 0                                polynomial values
        let Q[i] = 1
        let Total = Total + Y[i] * Y[i]
    end for
    let V[0] = 0
    let Divisor = Upper – Lower + 1
    for j = 0 to Order                              Iterate through the orders
        let SY[j] = 0                               required
        let SX[j] = 0
        for i = Lower to Upper                      Update sums of squares of X
            let SY[j] = SY[j] + (Y[i] * Q[i])       and Y
            let SX[j] = SX[j] + (X[i] * Q[i] * Q[i])
        end for
        let SY[j] = SY[j] / Divisor
        let SX[j] = SX[j] / Divisor
        let Goodness = Goodness + SY[j] * SY[j]     Calculate goodness of fit
                * Divisor
        if j < Order then
            let Previous = Divisor
            let Divisor = 0
            for i = Lower to Upper                  Calculate orthogonal
                call swap (P[i], Q[i])              polynomials for next order
                let Q[i] = ((X[i] – SX[j]) * P[i]) –
                        (V[j] * Q[i])
                let Divisor = Divisor + (Q[i] * Q[i])
            end for
```

```
            let V[j+1] = Divisor / Previous
        end if
    end for
    let Goodness = Goodness / Total
end Smoothed~Fit
```

12.3.2 Smoothed~Use (receives Order, Xvalue, SX, SY, V; *result real*)

Pseudo Code

```
initialize orthogonal polynomials
for i = 1 to Order
    update value of orthogonal polynomial
    accumulate contribution of current orthogonal component to Yvalue
end for
```

Code

```
function Smoothed~Use (Order is integer, Xvalue is real, SX, SY, V are arrays of
        real) is real
    variables Pvalue, Qvalue, Sum are real
    let Pvalue = 0.0
    let Qvalue = 1.0
    let Sum = SY[0]
    for j = 1 to Order
        call swap (Pvalue, Qvalue)
        let Qvalue = ((Xvalue – SX[j–1]) * Pvalue) – (V[j–1] * Qvalue)
        let Sum = Sum + (SY[j] * Qvalue)
    end for
    result Sum
end Smoothed~Use
```

TEST PROGRAM

Imported Names

Similarity~Test	Tests the similarity of two numbers (2.3.2)

Local Names

G	Goodness of fit
L	Lower bound of arrays
M	Maximum order
P	Previous value of G
SX	Sum of products involving X
SY	Sum of products involving X and Y
U	Upper bound of arrays
V	Orthogonal polynomial coefficient
X	Array of X coordinates of data points
Y	Array of Y coordinates of data points

Pseudo Code

```
set up X and Y arrays with points on curve Y = e^-X
for j = 0 to M
    fit curve of order j using Smoothed~Fit
    check that goodness of fit is better than for order j – 1
end for
check that curve of order M passes through all points almost exactly
```

Code

```
constants L = 1, U = 10, M = U – 1
variables X, Y are arrays L to U of real
variables SX, SY, V are arrays 0 to M of real
variable G, P is real
for i = L to U
    let X[i] = power (U – L, i / (U – L))
    let Y[i] = exp (–X[i])
end for
let P = 0
for j = 0 to M
    call Smoothed~Fit (L, U, j, X, Y, SX, SY, V, G)
    check G > P
    let P = G
end for
check Similarity~Test (G, 1, 1) = true
```

12.4 MULTIPLE LINEAR REGRESSION

Fitting a formula as closely as possible to a multidimensional set of points

Example

The amount of sugar obtained from a crop of sugar cane depends on rainfall and temperature. Suppose you hypothesize that there is a linear relationship of the form:

$$S = A + B \times R + C \times T$$

where S is the amount of sugar in tonnes per hectare, R is the rainfall for the season in mm, and T is the average daily temperature in degrees Celsius. Assume that the values of S, R, T for each of 50 sugar plantations are stored in three elements of each row of the matrix Data. Let SP be a matrix and U and X be arrays. The estimated amount of sugar obtained with a rainfall of X[2] = 2,000 mm and a temperature of X[3] = 28° is obtained as the value of X[1] by:

```
call Dispersion~Matrix (Data, 3, 50, SP, Mean)
call Regression~Stepwise (SP, U, 3, 0)
call Regression~Predict (SP, 3, Mean, U, X)
```

Subprograms

12.4.1 Dispersion~Matrix (receives Data, N, SampleSize; supplies S, Mean)
12.4.2 Regression~Stepwise (updates S, Used; receives N, Fraction)
12.4.3 Regression~Predict (receives S, N, Mean, Used; updates X)

Usage

The starting point for a regression analysis is the determination of a matrix of sums of squares and products nicknamed S. This is done by Dispersion~Matrix, which is given the raw data in the form of a matrix with nickname Data. The array Data has SampleSize rows, there being one row for each data point, and N columns, one for each variable. The dependent variable is assumed to be X_1. The other variables are the independent variables. Dispersion~Matrix calculates a matrix of "corrected" sums of squares and products S and an array Mean of the means of all variables.

The "stepwise" nature of the regression process operates as follows. Initially, the regression equation has no dependent variables in it. The least squares prediction for the dependent variable is equal to its mean. The algorithm finds the independent variable that makes the greatest contribution, that is, that explains as much of the variation in the dependent variable as possible. This variable is then "in" the equation. The algorithm then finds the independent variable that now makes the greatest contribution, and puts it in the equation. The process terminates when the amount of variation in the dependent variable yet to be explained becomes smaller than a predefined fraction of its original value, or when the algorithm runs out of independent variables.

As independent variables are put into the equation it may happen that previously entered variables become less valuable. For example, X_2 may be entered, and then X_4, X_6, and X_7. At this point you may find that you can remove X_2 without making much difference to the ability of the remaining variables X_4, X_6, and X_7 to predict the value of X_1. Indeed, the combination of X_4, X_6, and X_7 could perhaps do a much better job than X_2 alone. If this happens, X_2 is removed. Why was X_2 put in in the first place? The limitation of multiple linear regression is that it can only look one step ahead.

After calling Dispersion~Matrix it is necessary to call Regression~Stepwise to obtain the regression equation. The nickname Used is an array of *true-false* indicators, which tell you whether each variable is in or out of the equation. You must specify the value of the nickname Fraction, which tells Regression~Stepwise what remaining fraction of unexplained variable in the dependent variable you are prepared to accept.

In order to use the regression equation you may call Regression~Predict to calculate the value of X_1 given the values of X_2, X_3, ... If you need to know the values of the equation coefficients, simply examine the code for Regression~Predict to see how it calculates the value of X_1 from the other variables.

If you are experienced in statistical analysis you will want to use statistical tests in order to terminate the stepwise regression process. Mathematical statistics has been avoided to keep the presentation simple. All that is required is to calculate the value of Fraction required for a given level of significance from the relevant statistical tables, knowing the values of SampleSize and N.

If correlation coefficients are required, they may be obtained easily from the matrix S. The formula for correlation coefficients is C[I, J] = S[I, J] / *square~root* (S[I, I] * S[J, J]).

Similarly, variances and covariances may be obtained as V[I, J] = S[I, J] / (SampleSize – 1).

The test program tries to fit a polynomial to data derived from the equation Y = *exp* (–X). Clearly, this is a bad way to fit a polynomial, and in practice one would use the algorithm in Section 12.3 for that purpose.

The algorithms make use of only the lower triangle of the matrix S. The matrix of sums of squares and products is symmetric and so considerable redundant computation is avoided by working with only one half of the matrix. It is important to note that the Symmetric~Pivot algorithm has to be initialized. This is done with a call specifying a pivot row of zero. Normally, that call would be placed at the start of Regression~Stepwise. We have pulled it out into the test program. The reason is that we wanted to force variable X_N into the regression equation initially, so that we could be sure the removal algorithm would be tested. You should put the call to Symmetric~Pivot with a zero pivot row back into the code for Regression~Stepwise.

Analysis

Suppose, for example, you have three variables X_1, X_2, and X_3, and you wish to determine the regression coefficients A, B, and C that give the best least squares equation:

$$X_1 = A + B * X_2 + C * X_3$$

The normal equations are as follows, where K is equal to SampleSize:

$$\Sigma X_1 = A * K + B * \Sigma X_2 + C * \Sigma X_3$$
$$\Sigma X_1 X_2 = A * \Sigma X_2 + B * \Sigma X_2^2 + C * \Sigma X_2 X_3$$
$$\Sigma X_1 X_3 = A * \Sigma X_3 + B * \Sigma X_2 X_3 + C * \Sigma X_3^2$$

These equations can be reduced by solving for A, to produce equations that involve "corrected" sums of squares and products:

$$\Sigma X_1 X_2 - \Sigma X_1 \Sigma X_2 / K = B * (\Sigma X_2^2 - (\Sigma X_2)^2/K) + C * (\Sigma X_2 X_3 - \Sigma X_2 \Sigma X_3/K)$$
$$\Sigma X_1 X_3 - \Sigma X_1 \Sigma X_3 / K = B * (\Sigma X_2 X_3 - \Sigma X_2 \Sigma X_3/K) + C * (\Sigma X_3^2 - (\Sigma X_3)^2/K)$$

The corrected sum of squares for a variable measures its total variability about its mean. The corrected sum of products measures the total joint variability about two variables about their respective means, that is, their tendency to have simultaneously high or low values. Put the corrected sums of squares and products into the array S. For example, the corrected sum of products S[1, 2] = $\Sigma X_1 X_2 - \Sigma X_1 \Sigma X_2 / K$, and the corrected sum of squares S[2, 2] = $\Sigma X_2^2 - (\Sigma X_2)^2/K$. Now you have the simpler looking normal equations:

$$S[1, 2] = B * S[2, 2] + C * S[2, 3]$$
$$S[1, 3] = B * S[2, 3] + C * S[3, 3]$$

The aim in fitting the regression equation is to explain as much of the variability in the dependent variable X_1 as possible. The variability in X_1 about its mean is measured by its corrected sum of squares S[1, 1]. Therefore, it is useful to have the complete matrix of sums of squares and products available during the computations. The matrix is symmetric, with X[I, J] = X[J, I].

The insertion of a variable into the regression is accomplished by carrying out a pivotal transformation. You will need to be familiar with the discussion of this important algorithm in Section 11.2. The stepwise process is very reminiscent of the similar approach used in linear programming. The stepwise pivot selection process is discussed in Section 11.3. Multiple regression selects pivots based on the maximum reduction it can produce in S[1, 1].

The mathematics is too tedious to present fully here, but you may wish to demonstrate that the pivoting process quite conveniently leaves S[1, 1] containing the total amount of so far unexplained variation in X_1. All the algorithm has to do is to monitor the value of S[1, 1] at each iteration.

Largely, the method used is that described by Efroymson (1967), with simplifications. The algorithm removes any variables that make a contribution to S[1, 1] less than the contribution of the variable most recently inserted. Because of rounding errors there is an explicit test to prevent the variable just inserted from being inadvertently removed. Alternative removal strategies are available. Statistical mathematics has been avoided entirely. If you want to include appropriate statistical tests, you should consult the literature.

The calculation of corrected sums of squares and products can cause numerical problems, particularly with large values of the variables and small variances. It is not satisfactory to calculate total sums of squares and products and then to apply the correction at the end of the process. Dispersion~Matrix uses a recurrence relation in order to minimize such problems, generalizing a sum of squares formula from Chan and Lewis (1979) and West (1979).

In most practical uses of multiple linear regression the data points are given equal "weight". The theory of multiple regression is typically presented so as to permit data points to have different weights. If you want to weight the data points, the necessary modifications to the algorithms are very straightforward. Herraman (1968) may be consulted for the details.

The matrix of corrected sums of squares and products is symmetric. This property is exploited by calculating and transforming only the lower triangle of the matrix S. The special symmetric pivot algorithm is used. You should consult Section 11.2 to see how the space not used in the matrix S may be recovered by redefining S as an array instead of a matrix. Our approach is generally in accord with that proposed by Breaux (1968).

Broadly, the running time of the algorithm is proportional to the cube of the size of the problem. Dispersion~Matrix and Regression~Stepwise execute in O (N^2 * K) time. Regression~Predict requires O (N) execution time.

IMPLEMENTATION

<u>Exported Names</u>

Dispersion~Matrix	Develops matrix of corrected sums of squares and products (12.4.1)
Regression~Stepwise	Fits a linear relationship between X_1 and X_2, X_3, ... (12.4.2)
Regression~Predict	Computes X_1 from values of X_2, X_3, ... (12.4.3)

<u>Imported Names</u>

Symmetric~Pivot	Carries out a pivot step on a symmetric matrix (11.2.2)

<u>Nicknames</u>

Data	Matrix of data points
Fraction	Fraction of total sum of squares

Mean	Array of means
N	Number of variables
S	Matrix of sums of squares and products
SampleSize	Number of data points
Used	Indicators of variables in and out of the regression equation
X	Array of values of variables at one point

Local Names

Change	Amount by which S[1, 1] will be changed
Deviate	Amount by which element of matrix S will be changed
Limit	Fraction of sum of squares of X_1
MaxChange	Maximum value of Change
MinChange	Minimum value of Change

12.4.1 Dispersion~Matrix (receives Data, N, SampleSize; supplies S, Mean)

Pseudo Code

```
initialize Mean array and S matrix to zero
for k = 1 to SampleSize
    let Deviate = product of deviations of observation k on two variables from
            current means
    let S element = previous value of S element + (1 – (1 / k)) * Deviate
    let Mean element = previous value of Mean element + current deviation / k
end for
```

Code

```
procedure Dispersion~Matrix (Data is matrix of real, N, SampleSize are integers, S
        is matrix of real, Mean is array of real)
    variable Deviate is real
    for i = 1 to N                                  Initialize arrays
        let Mean[i] = 0
        for j = 1 to i
            let S[i, j] = 0
        end for
    end for
    for k = 1 to SampleSize
        for i = 1 to N                              Accumulate sums of squares and
            for j = 1 to i                          products
                let Deviate = (Data[k, i] – Mean[i]) * (Data[k, j] – Mean[j])
                let S[i, j] = S[i, j] + Deviate – (Deviate / k)
            end for
        end for
        for i = 1 to N                              Accumulate means
            let Deviate = Data[k, i] – Mean[i]
            let Mean[i] = Mean[i] + (Deviate / k)
        end for
    end for
end Dispersion~Matrix
```

12.4.2 Regression~Stepwise (updates S, Used; receives N, Fraction)

Pseudo Code

```
loop
    find variable not in equation that will reduce S[1, 1] the most when pivot
            performed
    pivot variable into the regression equation
    loop until all variables in equation contribute sufficiently to it
        find variable in equation that will increase S[1, 1] the least when pivot
                performed
        pivot variable out of the regression equation
    end loop
end loop when S[1, 1] reduced sufficiently, or no more variables left
```

Code

```
procedure Regression~Stepwise (S is matrix of real, N is integer, Used is array of
        true-false, Fraction is real)
    variables Change, Limit, MaxChange, MinChange are real
    variables Insert, Remove are integers
    let Limit = Fraction * S[1, 1]                      Accuracy required
    loop
        let MaxChange = 0
        let Insert = –1
        for i = 2 to N                                  Find variable that produces
            if Used[i] = false and S[i, i] > 0 then     largest change in S[1, 1]
                let Change = (S[i, 1] * S[i, 1]) / S[i, i]
                if Change > MaxChange then
                    let MaxChange = Change
                    let Insert = i
                end if
            end if
        end for
        call Symmetric~Pivot (S, N, Used, Insert)       Insert variable into equation
        loop
            let MinChange = MaxChange
            let Remove = –1
            for i = 2 to N                              Find variable that produces
                if Used[i] = true then                  smallest change in S[1, 1]
                    let Change = (S[i, 1] * S[i, 1]) / S[i, i]
                    if Change < MinChange and i ≠ Insert then
                        let MinChange = Change
                        let Remove = i
                    end if
                end if
            end for
            call Symmetric~Pivot (S, N, Used, Remove)   Remove variable from
        end loop when Remove ≤ 0                        equation
    end loop when S[1, 1] ≤ Limit or Insert ≤ 0
end Regression~Stepwise
```

12.4.3 Regression~Predict (receives S, N, Mean, Used; updates X)

Pseudo Code

```
initialize X[1] as mean of X_1
for j = 2 to N
    accumulate X[1] as sum of components S[j, 1] * deviation of X[j] from Mean[j]
end for
```

Code

```
procedure Regression~Predict (S is matrix of real, N is integer, Mean is array of
        real, Used is array of true-false, X is array of real)
    let X[1] = Mean[1]
    for j = 2 to N
        if Used[j] = true then
            let X[1] = X[1] + (S[j, 1] * (X[j] – Mean[j]))
        end if
    end for
end Regression~Predict
```

TEST PROGRAM

<u>Imported Names</u>

Similarity~Test	Tests the similarity of two numbers (2.3.2)
Symmetric~Pivot	Carries out a pivot step on a symmetric matrix (11.2.2)

<u>Local Names</u>

D	Data matrix
M	Number of data points
A	Array of averages
N	Number of variables
S	Matrix of sums of squares and products
T	Total sum of squares of residuals
X	Array of data points
U	Array of in/out indicators

Pseudo Code

```
set up "data" matrix of points on curve y = exp (–x)
calculate dispersion matrix
initialize regression with variable N in the equation
perform stepwise regression
calculate residual sum of squares of data points from regression line
check residual sum of squares is near zero
```

Code

```
constants M = 20, N = 20
variable D is array 1 to M, 1 to N of real
variable S is array 1 to N, 1 to N of real
```

```
variables A, X are arrays 1 to N of real
variable U is array 1 to N of true-false
variable T is real
for i = 1 to M                                          Initialize data matrix
    let D[i, 2] = i * 10 / M
    for j = 3 to N
        let D[i, j] = D[i, j–1] * D[i, 2]
    end for
    let D[i, 1] = exp (–D[i, 2])
end for
call Dispersion~Matrix (D, N, M, S, A)                  Fit equation to data points
call Symmetric~Pivot (S, N, U, 0)
call Symmetric~Pivot (S, N, U, N)
call Regression~Stepwise (S, U, N, 0)
let T = 0.0                                             Calculate residual sum of squares
for i = 1 to M
    for j = 2 to N
        let X[j] = D[i, j]
    end for
    call Regression~Predict (S, N, A, U, X)
    let T = T + ((X[1] – D[i, 1]) * (X[1] – D[i, 1]))
end for
check Similarity~Test (T, 0, 1) = true
```

NOTES—AFRICAN VIOLETS

Finding the best way to grow good specimens

In the lounge at home are twelve pot plants containing African violets. My wife has exhibited quite a talent for growing superb specimens of these plants. She appears to have discovered the right combination of three important variables: fertilizer, sunlight, and water. Evidence for this is the amount of unsolicited comment from our friends, and more significantly from our cleaning lady, who has considerable experience in growing these temperamental plants.

Recently, we decided to test the combinations of the variables scientifically. We wanted to validate my wife's judgment about the quantities of fertilizer, sunlight, and water needed to give optimum results. First, we defined an objective measure of "superb specimen". This required some discussion. We considered diameter of plant, total number of leaves, height, number of flowers, size of leaves, size of flowers, and length of time for which flowers were present. It became clear that what was most pleasurable was the number of flowers and the length of time for which they survived. In order to develop a single measure we decided to count the number of flowers on four successive occasions at two-week intervals, to give a total flower count.

My wife thought that fertilizing was important, so we settled on growing some plants with, and some without, fertilizer. She thought that a moderate amount of "morning sun" was needed. We decided to grow all the plants on coffee tables in front of the large floor-to-ceiling windows. Some plants would be close to the windows, where they would get the most sun. Some would be about two feet back, where they would receive about an hour less, and some more would be even further back to get less sun again. She thought that it was better to have the bottoms of the pots continually wet than to water the plants occasionally from the top. We decided to test both methods.

For brevity, we use the symbols F, D, and W for the three variables fertilizer, distance from window, and water respectively. We let F = 0 for no fertilizer, and F = 1 when fertilizer is used. Similarly, we let W = 0 for occasional watering, and W = 1 when the bottoms of the pots are kept continually moist. The distance from the window had three possible values, approximately 4, 6, and 8 feet. Twelve pots is a nice number to work with, because it gives a "balanced" experiment in which every possible combination of the three factors is used.

Now we want to see how we can obtain a predicting equation of the form:

Flowers = A[1] + (A[2] * F) + (A[3] * D) + (A[4] * W)

The four coefficients in the array A need to be chosen to give the best fit to the data we actually observed, that is, the numbers of flowers for the twelve pots. (See Table 12.1.)

Table 12.1

Flowers	*F*	*D*	*W*
96	0	4	0
109	1	4	0
121	0	6	0
126	1	6	0
110	0	8	0
120	1	8	0
109	0	4	1
124	1	4	1
128	0	6	1
137	1	6	1
123	0	8	1
126	1	8	1

Using Regression~Stepwise and Regression~Predict, the coefficients are determined and applied to give predicted numbers of flowers, assuming the linear equation specified above. The equation fitted to the data is calculated by Regression~Predict as follows:

Flowers = 119 + 9.2 * (F – 0.5) + 2.6 * (D – 6) + 10.8 * (W – 0.5)

Each of the variables F, D, and W has its mean value subtracted in this formula. We can simplify it to the form in which we originally specified it by collecting up all the constant terms:

Flowers = 93.7 + 9.2 * F + 2.6 * D + 10.8 * W

Rounding to the nearest integer, the actual and predicted numbers are as shown in Table 12.2.

The regression equation does not fit the data very well. The biggest difference between actual and observed number of flowers is 12, which is an error of about 10%. Nevertheless, the advantage of the regression equation is that random fluctuations are smoothed out, and the underlying patterns due to different levels of the three factors are more apparent. The errors could reflect either natural uncontrolled random variation or a defect in our model.

Table 12.2

Actual	*Predicted*
96	104
109	113
121	109
126	118
110	114
120	123
109	115
124	124
128	120
137	129
123	125
126	134

The raw observations indicate that the best result is the third last combination. The regression equation tells us that the last combination is the best. If we believe our model, which has the advantage of smoothing out random fluctuations, we will give the plants fertilizer, at a distance of eight feet from the windows, and keep water in the bottom of the pots. The experiment largely confirms my wife's intuition. The only point of contention is the amount of sunlight. The raw figures suggest that the amount of sunlight should be less than the optimum amount predicted by the regression equation. A more sophisticated analysis, which we won't describe here, reveals that the linear model is too restrictive and that the optimum distance is in fact closer to my wife's estimate. Whether or not the result is "statistically significant" is another question, one that we won't be able to pursue here.

There are techniques available that allow "balanced" experiments such as the one above to be analyzed with a great deal less computation. If you routinely need to carry out the analysis of large balanced experiments, it will be easier to use an algorithm that does not require the specification of all possible combinations of the values of the independent variables in the manner presented above. A convenient shorthand method of data presentation is available for such algorithms. The most straightforward of balanced experimental designs is the factorial design. Algorithms for the analysis of these are given by Howell (1969) and Oliver (1968).

13 Networks

The term "network" has a number of different, but related, meanings. A network may mean at one time a group of affiliated television stations, a set of interconnected electrical components, a number of people with similar interests who remain in contact with one another, and the communications infrastructure required to connect multiple computers and peripherals together. Algorithms for dealing with networks focus on the two aspects such networks have in common. There are typically people, points, nodes, or milestones that are connected by (or separated by) distances, lines, edges, or activities. The concept of a network is a very general one, which has many applications.

Technically, networks are examples of abstract entities called "graphs". Graph theory is a branch of mathematics that deals with the properties of graphs. Much of the textbook literature on graph algorithms is quite complex. Perhaps the reason for this is that graphs provide an avenue by which sophisticated programming techniques may be taught and learned. In practice, professional programmers wish to get a job done as simply as possible rather than learn techniques for their own sake. The pedagogic rather than applicative intent of the literature is evident in such comments as "cycle testing can be done ... with a much simpler strategy ... but ... [our algorithm] ... uses priority queues and union-find structures" (Sedgewick 1988, p. 461).

You will find three classic algorithms in this chapter that provide solutions to problems in graph theory. Each algorithm solves its particular problem in a straightforward manner. The algorithm presented in Section 13.2 deals with critical path scheduling. A typical application is in project management. One has a number of activities to perform, and has time estimates for each. Each activity in a project is typically constrained to be done before, or after, certain other activities. For example, in building a house one cannot put the roof on until the walls are up, which cannot occur until the foundations have been constructed.

The relationships among the activities in any project can be usefully represented as a "critical path" network (sometimes called a PERT network, for Program Evaluation and Review Technique). For example, suppose you have some free time to plan a vacation. You want to make the travel reservations as quickly as possible to take advantage of discounts that have just been advertised. On the back of an envelope you scribble out the critical path chart shown in Figure 13.1.

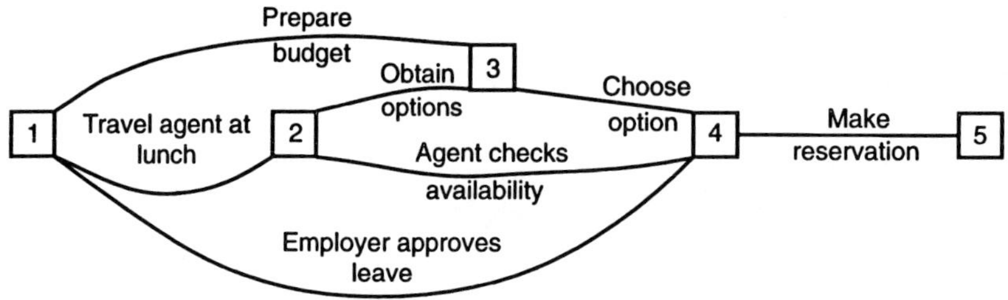

Figure 13.1

The chart indicates which tasks can be done in parallel, and which cannot. For example, you cannot make a choice from the travel options available until those options have been identified and you know how much you want to spend. The "nodes" numbered 1 to 5 represent points in time, or "events", or "milestones", where identifiable parts of the project have been completed. To see how quickly the entire job can be completed, you estimate the time taken for each task. (See Figure 13.2.)

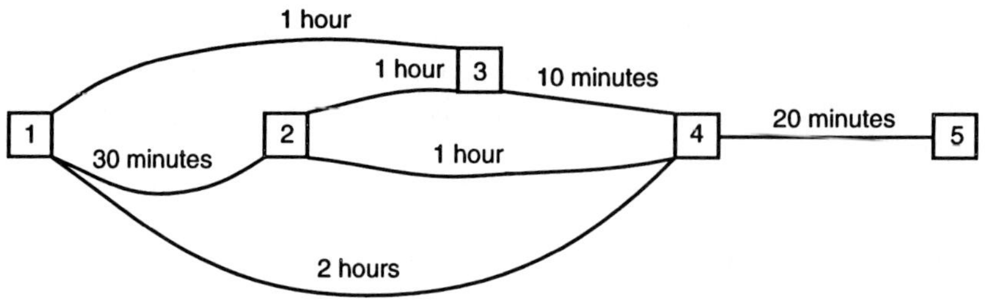

Figure 13.2

With a small network like this it does not take long to analyze it informally. You quickly realize that the project will require 2 hours and 20 minutes of elapsed time. The project cannot be speeded up by pressuring the travel agent. The time taken by your employer to approve your leave application is on the "critical path". To obtain your reservation faster you must seek a quicker response from your employer.

The critical path algorithm determines the activities on the critical path for a network of any size. The activities are input to the algorithm by naming their nodes and their times in the following manner:

1	2	30
1	3	60
1	4	120
2	3	60
2	4	60
3	4	10
4	5	20

The algorithm requires that the activities be sorted beforehand, just as they are here. Once a node has been listed as a beginning node of an activity, it does not appear further down the list as an end node for any other activity. Similarly, a node appearing as an end node in the list does not appear higher in the list as a beginning node. The list is said to be in topologically sorted sequence. There is an algorithm for topological sorting in Section 13.1. A file of activities must be topologically sorted before applying the critical path algorithm.

The critical path network has activities that imply a direction. Time moves forward and not backward. The technical term applied to such networks is "directed graph". The third algorithm deals with networks in which the edges are not directed. A good example is a network of computer terminals. How can you connect all terminals together by a bus that has the shortest possible length? It can be shown that the best set of connections forms a tree. The fact that the tree connects all terminals, or nodes, means that it "spans" them all. The best possible tree is called a "minimal spanning tree". The diagram in Figure 13.3 illustrates a minimal spanning tree for a small undirected graph.

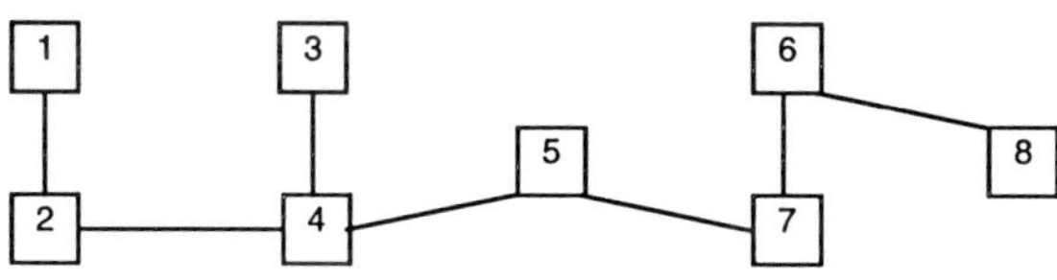

Figure 13.3

Section 13.3 contains an algorithm that finds the minimal spanning tree for such a network. The data file looks identical in form to the file prepared for the critical path algorithm. However, the direction of each connection is irrelevant when you are looking for a minimal spanning tree.

13.1 TOPOLOGICAL SORT

Sequencing the elements of a network

Example

If the "from" and "to" nodes of N activities are held in arrays F and T respectively, and the duration of each activity is held in corresponding locations of array D, the three arrays are sorted topologically by:

call Topological~Sort (F, T, D, N, M)

where M must be greater than the number of nodes in the network.

Subprograms

13.1.1 Topological~Sort (updates FromNode, ToNode, Duration; receives Nactivities, MaxNodes)

Usage

The arrays are sorted in place. The names of the nodes are assumed to be *text* strings that are held in the arrays that have nicknames FromNode and ToNode. The I-th activity is represented by its "from" and "to" nodes in FromNode[I] and ToNode[I], its duration being held in Duration[I]. The array subscripts are numbered from 1 to Nactivities. The nickname MaxNodes must contain an integer greater than the number of nodes in the network. Its value is used for allocating an array used for a hash table for the node names. Section 7.5 should be consulted for further information about the hashing method. The constant Factors, used by Hash~Search, must be defined as the product of the prime factors of MaxNodes.

Analysis

The algorithm is essentially that described by Knuth (1968), replacing his code for output of the network with an in-place sort. The network is converted into a linked list data structure. A linked list is attached to each node. Each list contains all activities that start from that node. Also for each node a count is obtained of the number of activities that terminate at that node.

The activities are renumbered in topological sequence as follows. The node counts are scanned repeatedly for those with predecessor counts of zero. All activities starting from that node are then examined and the end nodes for those activities are processed. The counts for the end nodes are decremented by one. This will send more counts to zero, and so the process is repeated. Activities are assigned a sequential number as they are processed, for later sorting. The arrays of activities and their "from" and "to" nodes are then permuted into order by the sequential number.

All parts of the algorithm operate in O (N) running time, where N is sometimes the number of activities and sometimes the number of nodes. This is not immediately apparent, because there are two double loops. The first merely processes all activities for every node, requiring Nactivities operations. The second, which permutes the activities, carries out at most Nactivities groups of exchanges.

IMPLEMENTATION

<u>Exported Names</u>

Topological~Sort   Sorts a directed graph topologically (13.1.1)

Imported Names

Hash~Initialize	Initializes the hash table (7.5.2)
Hash~Search	Finds a text string in a table (7.5.1)

Nicknames

Duration	Time for activity
FromNode	"From" node of an activity
MaxNodes	A number greater than the number of nodes
Nactivities	Number of activities
ToNode	"To" node of an activity

Local Names

J	Location of "from" node in hash table
K	Location of "to" node in hash table
Link	Counters of nodes, and then pointers to next node with zero count
N	Internal node number
Next	Pointers to activities from nodes, and then internal node numbers
NodeTable	Hash table of node names
Save	Temporary location for a node number
Successor	"To" node numbers
Top	Pointers to first "to" node in list of activities for each node
Zero	Pointer to next node with zero predecessor count

13.1.1 Topological~Sort (updates FromNode, ToNode, Duration; receives Nactivities, MaxNodes)

Pseudo Code

```
initialize node counters and pointers to activity lists
input activities and construct node table, lists of activities, and predecessor counts
link together all nodes with predecessor counts of zero
loop until list of nodes with predecessor counts of zero is empty
    get next node with predecessor count of zero
    loop through activities for node
        decrement predecessor count for "to" node of current activity
        if count is zero, add node to list of nodes with predecessor counts of zero
        attach sequential integer to activity
    end loop
end loop
sort activities based on sequential integer attached to activities
```

Code

```
procedure Topological~Sort (FromNode, ToNode are arrays of text, Duration is
        array of integers, Nactivities, MaxNodes are integers)
    variables Next, Successor are arrays 1 to Nactivities of integers
    variable Link is array 0 to MaxNodes of integers
    variable Top is array 1 to MaxNodes of integers
    variable NodeTable is array 1 to MaxNodes of text
    variables J, K, N, Save, Zero are integers
```

```
    for i = 1 to MaxNodes                                   Initialize node counters and
        let Link[i] = 0                                     activity list pointers
        let Top[i] = 0
    end for
    call Hash~Initialize (NodeTable, 1, MaxNodes)           Construct node name table
    for i = 1 to Nactivities
        call Hash~Search (NodeTable, 1, MaxNodes, FromNode[i], J)
        call Hash~Search (NodeTable, 1, MaxNodes, ToNode[i], K)
        let Link[K] = Link[K] + 1                           Predecessor count
        let Successor[i] = K
        let Next[i] = Top[J]                                Store activity in linked list
        let Top[J] = i
    end for
    let Zero = 0                                            Construct initial linked list of
    let Link[0] = 0                                         nodes with zero predecessor
    for i = 1 to MaxNodes                                   counts
        if Link[i] = 0 and Top[i] > 0 then
            let Link[Zero] = i
            let Zero = i
        end if
    end for
    let J = Link[0]                                         Take nodes one at a time from list
    let N = 0                                               of those with zero predecessor
    loop until J = 0                                        counts
        let K = Top[J]
        loop until K = 0
            let Link[Successor[K]] = Link[Successor[K]] – 1
            if Link[Successor[K]] = 0 then
                let Link[Zero] = Successor[K]               Append new node with zero
                let Zero = Successor[K]                     predecessor count to list
            end if
            let Save = Next[K]
            let N = N + 1                                   Sequentially number activity
            let Next[K] = N
            let K = Save
        end loop
        let J = Link[J]                                     Remove next node from list
    end loop
    for i = 1 to Nactivities                                Permute activities into required
        loop until Next[i] = i                              sequence
            call swap (FromNode[Next[i]], FromNode[i])
            call swap (ToNode[Next[i]], ToNode[i])
            call swap (Duration[Next[i]], Duration[i])
            call swap (Next[Next[i]], Next[i])
        end loop
    end for
end Topological~Sort
```

TEST PROGRAM

Local Names

D	Array of durations
Data	File number of data file
F	Array of "from" nodes
M	Maximum number of nodes
N	Number of activities
Results	File number of results file
T	Array of "to" nodes

Pseudo Code

```
read network from data file into arrays
call Topological~Sort
output arrays into results file
```

Code

```
constant M = 10
variables F, T are arrays 1 to M of text
variable D is array 1 to M of integers
variables Data, N, Results are integers
open Data file "Test Data"
open Results file "Results"
let N = 0
loop until end~of~file (Data)
    input from Data into F[i], T[i], D[i]
    let N = N + 1
end for
call Topological~Sort (F, T, D, N, M)
for i = 1 to N
    output into Results from F[i], T[i], D[i]
end for
```

Test Data

```
B  D  10
A  B  10
C  D  10
A  C  20
B  C   5
```

Results

```
A  C  20
A  B  10
B  C   5
B  D  10
C  D  10
```

13.2 CRITICAL PATH

Finding the longest path through a network

Example

If the "from" and "to" nodes of N activities are held in arrays F and T respectively, and the duration of each activity is held in corresponding locations of array D, the earliest start and latest finish times are produced in the arrays E and L by:

call Critical~Path (F, T, D, E, L, N, M)

where M must be greater than the number of nodes in the network.

Subprograms

13.2.1 Critical~Path (receives FromNode, ToNode, Duration; supplies Earliest, Latest; receives Nactivities, MaxNodes)

Usage

The names of the nodes are assumed to be *text* strings that are held in the arrays that have nicknames FromNode and ToNode. The I-th activity is represented by its "from" and "to" nodes in FromNode[I] and ToNode[I], its duration being held in Duration[I]. The array subscripts are numbered from 1 to Nactivities. The nickname MaxNodes must contain an integer greater than the number of nodes in the network. Its value is used for allocating an array used for a hash table for the node names. Section 7.5 should be consulted for further information about the hashing method. The constant Factors, used by Hash~Search, must be defined as the product of the prime factors of MaxNodes.

The arrays must be in topologically sorted sequence before calling Critical~Path. If the user cannot guarantee this, it is essential that Topological~Sort be called first, otherwise incorrect results will be obtained.

On return from Critical~Path the elements Earliest[I] of the array with nickname Earliest will contain the earliest time at which the I-th activity can start. The times are measured from the time of the earliest event (the first node in topological sequence), which is assumed to occur at time zero. Similarly, the elements of Latest will contain the latest time at which activities can finish. If the latest finish time minus the earliest start time is equal to the duration of the activity, the activity must be on the critical path. Any excess of latest finish time minus earliest start time over the duration of the activity is called "float". An activity with nonzero float does not have to start at the earliest start time, but may be delayed if required to as late as the latest finish time minus the duration.

Analysis

The algorithm is a simplification of that described by Leavenworth (1961). It operates in O (N) running time. More specifically, it requires one pass through the nodes and three passes through the activities.

The main calculations are carried out in two of the passes through the activities. The first of these passes examines the activities in increasing time sequence. The earliest start time for any given node is obtained by examining all activities terminating at that node. Because the activities are topologically sorted, the earliest start times for all predecessor nodes of the current node will be known. For the current node, the earliest start time is computed as the maximum of each predecessor start time plus activity duration. The latest finish times are computed in a similar manner by processing the activities in reverse sequence.

IMPLEMENTATION

Exported Names

Critical~Path	Finds the critical path, and start and finish times for a network (13.2.1)

Imported Names

Hash~Initialize	Initializes the hash table (7.5.2)
Hash~Search	Finds a text string in a table (7.5.1)

Nicknames

Duration	Time for activity
Earliest	Earliest start time for an activity
FromNode	"From" node of an activity
Latest	Latest finish time for an activity
MaxNodes	A number greater than the number of nodes
Nactivities	Number of activities
ToNode	"To" node of an activity

Local Names

Down	Latest finish time for node
F	Position of "from" node in hash table
T	Position of "to" node in hash table
NodeTable	Hash table of node names
Up	Earliest start time for node

13.2.1 Critical~Path (receives FromNode, ToNode, Duration; supplies Earliest, Latest; receives Nactivities, MaxNodes)

Pseudo Code

```
input activities, converting node names to position in hash table
initialize earliest start times for nodes to zero and latest finish times to infinity
for i = 1 to Nactivities
    if "from" node time + duration > "to" node time, save as maximum so far for "to"
            node
end for
for decreasing i = Nactivities to 1
    if "to" node time – duration < "from" node time, save as minimum so far for
            "from" node
end for
store node earliest start and latest finish times in arrays corresponding to activities
```

Code

```
procedure Critical~Path (FromNode, ToNode are arrays of text, Duration, Earliest,
        Latest are arrays of integers, Nactivities, MaxNodes are integers)
    variable NodeTable is array 1 to MaxNodes of text
    variables F, T are arrays 1 to Nactivities of integers
    variables Up, Down are arrays 1 to MaxNodes of integers
    call Hash~Initialize (NodeTable, 1, MaxNodes)
    for i = 1 to Nactivities
        call Hash~Search (NodeTable, 1, MaxNodes, FromNode[i], F[i])
        call Hash~Search (NodeTable, 1, MaxNodes, ToNode[i], T[i])
    end for
    for i = 1 to MaxNodes                          Initialize minimum and
        let Up[i] = 0                              maximum node times
        let Down[i] = maxinteger
    end for
    for i = 1 to Nactivities                       Compute earliest times
        let Up[T[i]] = maximum (Up[T[i]], Up[F[i]] + Duration[i])
    end for
    let Down[T[Nactivities]] = Up[T[Nactivities]]
    for decreasing i = Nactivities to 1            Compute latest times
        let Down[F[i]] = minimum (Down[F[i]], Down[T[i]] – Duration[i])
    end for
    for i = 1 to Nactivities                       Transfer node times to
        let Earliest[i] = Up[F[i]]                 activities
        let Latest[i] = Down[T[i]]
    end for
end Critical~Path
```

TEST PROGRAM

Local Names

D	Array of durations
E	Array of earliest start times
Data	File number of data file
F	Array of "from" nodes
L	Array of latest finish times
M	Maximum number of nodes
N	Number of activities
Results	File number of results file
T	Array of "to" nodes

Pseudo Code

```
read network from data file into arrays
call Critical~Path
output arrays into results file
```

Code

```
constant M = 10
variables F, T are arrays 1 to M of text
variables D, E, L are arrays 1 to M of integers
variables Data, N, Results are integers
open Data file "Test Data"
open Results file "Results"
let N = 0
loop until end~of~file (Data)
    input from Data into F[i], T[i], D[i]
    let N = N + 1
end for
call Critical~Path (F, T, D, E, L, N, M)
for i = 1 to N
    output into Results from F[i], T[i], D[i], E[i], L[i]
end for
```

Test Data

```
A  B  10
A  C  20
B  C   5
B  D  10
C  D  10
```

Results

```
A  B  10   0  15
A  C  20   0  20
B  C   5  10  20
B  D  10  10  30
C  D  10  20  30
```

13.3 SPANNING TREE

Finding the shortest tree that links every node in a network

Example

If the end nodes of N edges are held in arrays F and T respectively, and the distance for each edge is held in corresponding locations of array D, a spanning tree is computed by:

call Spanning~Tree (F, T, D, N, M)

where M must be greater than the number of nodes in the network.

Subprograms

13.3.1 Spanning~Tree (receives Node1, Node2; updates Distance; receives Nedges, MaxNodes)

Usage

The names of the nodes are assumed to be *text* strings that are held in the arrays that have nicknames Node1 and Node2. The I-th edge is represented by its beginning and ending nodes in Node1[I] and Node2[I], the distance between the two nodes being held in Distance[I]. The array subscripts are numbered from 1 to Nedges. The nickname MaxNodes must contain an integer greater than the number of nodes in the network. Its value is used for allocating an array used for a hash table for the node names. Section 7.5 should be consulted for further information about the hashing method. The constant Factors, used by Hash~Search, must be defined as the product of the prime factors of MaxNodes.

Spanning~Tree will always compute a spanning tree (or forest of spanning trees for disconnected networks). Spanning~Tree will only find a minimum spanning tree if the edges are in increasing sequence of edge distances. Sorting may be carried out by a sorting algorithm from Chapter 6.

The edges defining the tree are indicated by having their distances negated. If the edges are presorted into ascending sequence of edge distance, the tree will be a minimum spanning tree.

The test program uses a sample network given by Sedgewick (1988). The network has several minimum spanning trees (all with the same minimum total distance). Our algorithm produces a correct result that differs slightly from that supplied by Sedgewick.

Analysis

The algorithm is Kruskal's method described by Seppänen (1970), with the addition of a technique to improve its performance from O (N^2) to O (N). Kruskal's method proceeds by building a forest of trees from short edges, gradually merging them into a single tree. It starts by choosing the shortest edge. This is a "tree" involving two nodes. It then chooses the shortest remaining edge. Several cases can arise. If the beginning and end nodes of the new edge differ from the first two nodes, you have a second separate tree involving two nodes. If the new edge has one node in common with an existing tree, the edge is attached to the tree. If the new edge has one node in common with one tree and the other node in common with a second tree, the new edge is used to join the two trees together. If the new edge has both nodes in common with nodes in one existing tree, the edge is discarded because it would form a loop.

The process is aided by numbering each tree with an internal tree number as it is produced, that is, numbering with an identifying number all nodes spanned by a tree. The numbering is used when both the nodes of an edge are already in one or two trees. If the trees associated with the two nodes have the same tree number, the "two" trees are in fact parts of the same tree. If the trees have different tree numbers, they are different trees. The only complication arises when an edge is used to join up two trees, which of course have different tree numbers. It is necessary to renumber one of the trees, so that all its nodes have the same tree number as the nodes in the other tree.

The execution time would be O (N) except for the necessity to renumber trees on occasion. In order to make the tree numbering as efficient as possible the algorithm maintains a linked list of the nodes comprising each tree. The published algorithm requires us to visit every node instead of just the nodes in the tree being renumbered. With our modification the algorithm will operate as efficiently as an efficient sorting algorithm that arranges the edges into sequence.

IMPLEMENTATION

Exported Names

Spanning~Tree	Finds a spanning tree for a network (13.3.1)

Imported Names

Hash~Initialize	Initializes the hash table (7.5.2)
Hash~Search	Finds a text string in a table (7.5.1)

Nicknames

Distance	Distance for an edge
MaxNodes	A number greater than the number of nodes
Nedges	Number of edges
Node1	One node of an edge
Node2	Other node of an edge

Local Names

Count	Tree number
I, J	Hash table indexes for nodes
Link	Linked list of nodes in a tree
NodeTable	Hash table of node names
P	Previous node in linked list
T	First node in linked list
Top	First node in linked list for a tree
Tree	Array of tree numbers corresponding to nodes

13.3.1 Spanning~Tree (receives Node1, Node2; updates Distance; receives Nedges, MaxNodes)

Pseudo Code

```
initialize all nodes to be in no trees
loop until no edges left
    if neither node of edge is in a tree then
        assign new tree number to both nodes
    else-if exactly one node is in a tree then
        assign tree number from treed node to untreed node
    else-if nodes are in different trees then
        renumber nodes of one tree to the tree number of the other tree
    end if
end loop
```

Code

```
procedure Spanning~Tree (Node1, Node2 are arrays of text, Distance are arrays of
        integers, Nedges, MaxNodes are integers)
    variables Link, Top, Tree are arrays 1 to MaxNodes of integers
    variable NodeTable is array 1 to MaxNodes of text
```

```
    variables Count, I, J, P, T are integers
    for i = 1 to MaxNodes                                   Initialize trees to null
        let Tree[i] = 0
    end for
    let Count = 0
    call Hash~Initialize (NodeTable, 1, MaxNodes)
    for k = 1 to Nedges                                           Process edges
        call Hash~Search (NodeTable, 1, MaxNodes, Node1[k], I)
        call Hash~Search (NodeTable, 1, MaxNodes, Node2[k], J)
        let Distance[k] = –Distance[k]
        if Tree[I] = 0 then
            if Tree[J] = 0 then
                let Count = Count + 1                       New tree
                let Tree[I] = Count
                let Tree[J] = Count
                let Top[Count] = I
                let Link[I] = J
                let Link[J] = 0
            else
                let Tree[I] = Tree[J]                       Append node to existing
                let Link[I] = Top[Tree[J]]                  tree
                let Top[Tree[J]] = I
            end if
        else-if Tree[J] = 0 then
            let Tree[J] = Tree[I]                           Append node to existing
            let Link[J] = Top[Tree[I]]                      tree
            let Top[Tree[I]] = J
        else-if Tree[I] = Tree[J] then
            let Distance[k] = magnitude (Distance[k])       Discard edge
        else
            let T = Top[Tree[I]]
            let J = Top[Tree[J]]
            let Top[Tree[I]] = J
            loop until J = 0                                Renumber nodes of a tree
                let Tree[J] = Tree[I]
                let P = J
                let J = Link[J]
            end loop
            let Link[P] = T                                 Join trees together
        end if
    end for
end Spanning~Tree
```

TEST PROGRAM

<u>Local Names</u>

D	Array of distances
Data	File number of data file

F	Array of beginning nodes
M	Maximum number of nodes
N	Number of activities
Results	File number of results file
T	Array of ending nodes

Pseudo Code

```
read network from data file into arrays
call Spanning~Tree
output arrays into results file
```

Code

```
constant M = 100
variables S, F are arrays 1 to M of text
variable D is array 1 to M of integers
variables Data, N, Results are integers
open Data file "Test Data"
open Results file "Results"
let N = 0
loop until end~of~file (Data)
    input from Data into S[i], F[i], D[i]
    let N = N + 1
end for
call Spanning~Tree (S, F, D, N, M)
for i = 1 to N
    output into Results from S[i], F[i], D[i]
end for
```

Test Data

```
A  B  1
B  C  1
D  F  1
E  G  1
G  J  1
I  K  1
J  K  1
L  M  1
A  F  2
B  D  2
D  E  2
E  F  2
F  L  2
H  I  2
J  M  2
G  H  3
J  L  3
B  E  4
```

C	E	4
E	L	4
G	L	5
A	G	6

Results

A	B	–1
B	C	–1
D	F	–1
E	G	–1
G	J	–1
I	K	–1
J	K	–1
L	M	–1
A	F	–2
B	D	2
D	E	–2
E	F	2
F	L	–2
H	I	–2
J	M	2
G	H	3
J	L	3
B	E	4
C	E	4
E	L	4
G	L	5
A	G	6

References

Ahrens, J.H., and Dieter, U. (1988) Efficient table-free sampling methods for the exponential, Cauchy and normal distributions. *Communications of the ACM*, 31, pp. 1330–37.

Anton, H., and Rorres, C. (1991) *Elementary Linear Algebra*. 6th ed. New York: Wiley.

Arden, D.N. (1960) The solution of linear programming problems. See Ralston and Wilf (1960).

Baase, S. (1988) *Computer Algorithms: Introduction to Design and Analysis*. Reading, Mass.: Addison-Wesley.

Barrodale, I., and Stuart, G.F. (1981) Algorithm 576: A Fortran program for solving AX = B. *ACM Transactions on Mathematical Software*, 7, pp. 391–97.

Bentley, J.L. (1984) Programming pearls: Code tuning. *Communications of the ACM*, 27, pp. 91-96.

Bentley, J.L. (1985) Programming pearls: Thanks, heaps. *Communications of the ACM*, 28, p. 245.

Bentley, J.L. (1986) Programming pearls: Little languages. *Communications of the ACM*, 29, pp. 711–21.

Bentley, J.L. (1987) Programming pearls: A sample of brilliance. *Communications of the ACM*, 30, pp. 754–57.

Bentley, J.L., Sleator, D.D., Tarjan, R.E., and Wei, V.K. (1986) A locally adaptive data compression scheme. *Communications of the ACM*, 29, pp. 320–30.

Boothroyd, J. (1964) Algorithm 231: Matrix inversion. *Communications of the ACM*, 7, p. 347.

Breaux, H.J. (1968) A modification of Efroymson's technique for stepwise regression analysis. *Communications of the ACM*, 11, pp. 556–57.

Burr, J. (1980) Marginal totals for multidimensional arrays. *Australian Computer Journal*, 12, pp. 137–39.

Carta, D.G. (1990) Two fast implementations of the "minimal standard" random number generator. *Communications of the ACM*, 33, pp. 87–88.

Chan, T.F., and Lewis, J.G. (1979) Computing standard deviations: Accuracy. *Communications of the ACM*, 22, pp. 526–31.

Claussen, R. (1960) Algorithm 7: Euclidean algorithm. *Communications of the ACM*, 3, p. 240.

Dijkstra, E. (1976) *A Discipline of Programming*. Englewood Cliffs, N.J.: Prentice-Hall.

Duffet-Smith, P. (1990) *Astronomy with Your Personal Computer*. Cambridge: Cambridge University Press.

Dwyer, B. (1981) One more time: How to update a master file. *Communications of the ACM*, 24(1), pp. 3–8.

Efroymson, M.A. (1967) Multiple regression analysis. See Ralston and Wilf (1967).

Ehrlich, G. (1973) Loopless algorithms for generating permutations, combinations, and other combinatorial combinations. *Journal of the ACM*, 20, pp. 500–513.

Elias, P. (1987) Interval and recency rank encoding: Two on-line adaptive variable-length schemes. *IEEE Transactions on Information Theory*, IT-33, pp. 3–10.

Enbody, R.J., and Chu, H.C. (1988) Dynamic hashing schemes. *ACM Computing Surveys*, 20, pp. 85–113.

Er, M.C. (1987) An efficient implementation of permutation backtracking in lexicographic order. *Computer Journal*, 30, p. 282.

Fagin, R., Nievergelt, J., Pippenger, N., and Strong, H.R. (1979) Extendible hashing: A fast method for accessing dynamic files. *ACM Transactions on Database Systems*, 4, pp. 315–44.

Forsythe, G.E. (1957) Generation and use of orthogonal polynomials for data-fitting with a digital computer. *Journal of the Society for Industrial and Applied Mathematics*, 5(2), pp. 74–88.

Gentleman, J.F. (1975) Algorithm AS 88: Generation of all $^{N}C_{R}$ combinations by simulating nested Fortran DO loops. *Applied Statistics*, 24, pp. 374–76.

Goldberg, D. (1991) What every computer scientist should know about floating point arithmetic. *ACM Computing Surveys*, 23, pp. 5–48.

Gonnet, G.H., and Baeza-Yates, R. (1991) *Handbook of Algorithms and Data Structures*. Wokingham, England: Addison-Wesley.

Gorn, S. (1960) Algorithm 4: Bisection routine. *Communications of the ACM*, 3, p. 174.

Gower, J.C. (1962) The handling of multiway tables on computers. *Computer Journal*, 4, pp. 280–86.

Gower, J.C. (1968) Algorithm AS 1: Simulating multidimensional arrays in one dimension. *Applied Statistics*, 17, pp. 180–85.

Gumm, P. (1985) A new class of check-digit methods for arbitrary number systems. *IEEE Transactions on Information Theory*, IT-31, pp. 103–5.

Hall, P.A.V., and Dowling, G.R. (1980) Approximate string matching. *Computing Surveys*, 12, pp. 381–402.

Hamming, R.W. (1986) *Coding and Information Theory*. 2d ed. Englewood Cliffs, N.J.: Prentice-Hall.

Hatter, D.J. (1984) A generalized non-recursive binary tree traversal algorithm. *Computer Journal*, 27, pp. 178–79.

Heap, B.R. (1963) Permutations by interchanges. *Computer Journal*, 6, pp. 293–94.

Herraman, C. (1968) Algorithm AS 12: Sums of squares and products matrix. *Applied Statistics*, 17, pp. 289–92.

Herriot, J.G. (1973) Algorithm 472: Procedures for natural spline interpolation. *Communications of the ACM*, 16, pp. 763–68.

Hill, I.D. (1965) Algorithm 3: Easter. *Computer Bulletin*, 9, p. 18.

Hill, I.D. (1971) Algorithm AS 39: Arrays with a variable number of dimensions. *Applied Statistics*, 20, pp. 115–17.

Holt, R.C. (1990) *Turing Reference Manual*. Toronto: Computer Systems Research Institute, University of Toronto.

Howell, J.R. (1969) Algorithm 359: Factorial analysis of variance. *Communications of the ACM*, 12, p. 631.

Inglis, J. (1981) Updating a master file—yet one more time. *Communications of the ACM*, 24, p. 299.

Irving, R.W. (1984) Permutation backtracking in lexicographic order. *Computer Journal*, 27, pp. 373–75.

Ives, F.M. (1976) Algorithm 87: Permutation enumeration: Four new algorithms. *Communications of the ACM*, 19, pp. 68–72.

Kachitvichyanukul, V., and Schmeiser, B.W. (1988) Binomial random variate generation. *Communications of the ACM*, 31, pp. 216–22.

Kendall, M.G. (1957) *A Course in Multivariate Analysis*. London: Griffin.

Kendall, M.G., and Stuart, A. (1963) *The Advanced Theory of Statistics*. Vol. 1. London: Griffin.

Knuth, D.E. (1968) *The Art of Computer Programming*. Vol. 1, *Fundamental Algorithms*. Reading, Mass.: Addison-Wesley.

Knuth, D.E. (1969) *The Art of Computer Programming*. Vol. 2, *Seminumerical Algorithms*. Reading, Mass.: Addison-Wesley.

Knuth, D.E. (1973) *The Art of Computer Programming*. Vol. 3, *Sorting and Searching*. Reading, Mass.: Addison-Wesley.

Leavenworth, B. (1961) Algorithm 40: Critical path scheduling. *Communications of the ACM*, 4, p. 152.

Lelewer, D.A., and Hirschberg, D.S. (1987) Data compression. *ACM Computing Surveys*, 19, pp. 261–96.

Littlewood, B., and Strigini, L. (1992) The risks of software. *Scientific American*, November, pp. 39–43.

Liu, C.N., and Tang, D.T. (1973) Algorithm 452: Enumerating combinations of *m* out of *n* objects. *Communications of the ACM*, 16, p. 485.

Makinson, G.J. (1967) Algorithm 296: Generalized least squares fit by orthogonal polynomials. *Communications of the ACM*, 10, pp. 87–88.

Maurer, W.D., and Lewis, T.G. (1975) Hash table methods. *ACM Computing Surveys*, 7, pp. 5–19.

McKeeman, W. M. (1962) Algorithm 135: Crout with equilibration and iteration. *Communications of the ACM*, 5, pp. 553–55.

Moler, C. (1972) Algorithm 423: Linear equation solver. *Communications of the ACM*, 15, p. 274.

Motzkin, D. (1981) A stable quicksort. *Software—Practice and Experience*, 11, pp. 607–11.

Motzkin, D. (1983) Meansort. *Communications of the ACM*, 26, pp. 250–51.

O'Beirne, T.H. (1961) The date of Easter. *New Scientist*, 9, p. 828.

O'Flaherty, M., and MacKenzie, G. (1982) Algorithm AS 172: Direct simulation of nested Fortran DO-LOOPs. *Applied Statistics*, 31, pp. 71–74.

Oliver, I. (1967) Analysis of factorial experiments using generalized matrix operations. *Journal of the ACM*, 14, pp. 508–19.

Oliver, I. (1968) Algorithm 330: Factorial analysis of variance. *Communications of the ACM*, 11, pp. 431–32.

Ord-Smith, R.J. (1968) Algorithm 323: Generation of permutations in lexicographic order. *Communications of the ACM*, 11, p. 512.

Orden, A. (1960) Matrix inversion and related topics by direct methods. See Ralston and Wilf (1960).

Ortega, J. (1967) The Givens–Householder method for symmetric matrices. See Ralston and Wilf (1967).

Park, S.K., and Miller, K.W. (1988) Random number generators: Good ones are hard to find. *Communications of the ACM*, 31, pp. 1192-1201.

Pearson, P.K. (1990) Fast hashing of variable-length text strings. *Communications of the ACM*, 33, pp. 677–80.

Pike, M.C. (1979) Algorithm 5: RANCOMB. *Computer Journal*, 22, p. 88.

Ralston, A. and Wilf, H.S., eds. (1960) *Mathematical Methods for Digital Computers.* Vol. 1. New York: Wiley.

Ralston, A., and Wilf, H.S., eds. (1967) *Mathematical Methods for Digital Computers.* Vol. 2. New York: Wiley.

Ratcliff, J.W. and Metzener, D.E. (1988) Pattern matching: The Gestalt approach. *Dr Dobb's Journal*, July, pp. 46–51.

Reinehart, L. (1971) *The Dice Man*. London: Granada Publishing.

Rohl, J.S. (1978) Generating permutations by choosing. *Computer Journal*, 21, pp. 302–5.

Rutishauser, H. (1963) Algorithm 150: SYMINV2. *Communications of the ACM*, 6, p. 67.

Saaty, T.L., and Vargas, L.G. (1982) *The Logic of Priorities*. Boston: Kluwer-Nijhoff, pp. 15–41.

Sedgewick, R. (1977) Permutation generation methods. *ACM Computing Surveys*, 9, pp. 137–64.

Sedgewick, R. (1978) Implementing quicksort programs. *Communications of the ACM,* 21, pp. 847–57.

Sedgewick, R. (1988) *Algorithms*. 2d ed. Reading, Mass.: Addison-Wesley.

Seppänen, J.J. (1970) Algorithm 399: Spanning tree. *Communications of the ACM*, 13, p. 621.

Sheff, A.L. (1938) *Bookkeeping Made Easy*. New York: Barnes and Noble.

Siegel, S. (1956) *Nonparametric Statistics*. New York: McGraw-Hill.

Stewart, G.W. (1970) Algorithm 384: Eigenvalues and eigenvectors of a real symmetric matrix. *Communications of the ACM*, 13, pp. 369–71.

Stone, R.A. (1970) Algorithm 398: Tableless date conversion. *Communications of the ACM*, 13, pp. 621.

Sunday, D.M. (1990) A very fast substring search algorithm. *Communications of the ACM*, 33, pp. 132–42.

Tantzen, R.G. (1963) Algorithm 199: Conversions between calendar date and Julian day number. *Communications of the ACM*, 6, p. 444.

Wagner, N.R., and Putter, P.S. (1989) Error detecting decimal digits. *Communications of the ACM*, 32, pp. 106–10.

Weiss, M.A. (1991) Empirical study of the expected running time of Shellsort. *Computer Journal*, 34, pp. 88–91.

West, D.H.D. (1979) Updating mean and variance estimates: An improved method. *Communications of the ACM*, 22, pp. 532–35.

Wilkinson, J.H. (1967) The solution of ill-conditioned linear equations. See Ralston and Wilf (1967).

Xunrang, G., and Yuzhang, Z. (1990) A new heapsort algorithm and the analysis of its complexity. *Computer Journal*, 33, p. 281.

Index